The Theory and Practice
of Third World Solidarity

The Theory and Practice of Third World Solidarity

Darryl C. Thomas

PRAEGER

Westport, Connecticut
London

Library of Congress Cataloging-in-Publication Data

Thomas, Darryl C.
    The theory and practice of Third World solidarity / Darryl C.
Thomas.
        p.   cm.
    Includes bibliographical references and index.
    ISBN 0–275–92843–8 (alk. paper)
        1. Economic development.   2. International economic relations.
    3. International cooperation.   I. Title.
    HC59.7.T475   2001
    337′.09172′4—dc20   93–10900

British Library Cataloguing in Publication Data is available.

Library of Congress Catalog Card Number: 93–10900
ISBN: 0–275–92843–8

First published in 2001

Praeger Publishers, 88 Post Road West, Westport, CT 06881
An imprint of Greenwood Publishing Group, Inc.
www.praeger.com

Printed in the United States of America

The paper used in this book complies with the
Permanent Paper Standard issued by the National
Information Standards Organization (Z39.48–1984).

10 9 8 7 6 5 4 3 2 1

*To the memory of my grandparents Isaac and Iler Thomas
and my in-laws, Monroe L. and Rosetta Walton*

Table of Contents

Abbreviations   ix

Preface   xi

PART I: PAN-PIGMENTATIONALISM IN THE SOUTH: THIRD
    WORLD CHALLENGES TO GLOBAL APARTHEID   1

Chapter 1: Theories of International Relations, Racial Capitalism, and
    Global Apartheid   3

Chapter 2: Third World Challenges to Global Apartheid in the
    Post-Cold War Era   37

PART II: NONALIGNMENT: MODERATING EAST-WEST
    TENSIONS AND DEVELOPING THIRD WORLD
    DIPLOMATIC CONSCIOUSNESS   61

Chapter 3: Nonalignment and the Politics of a Third Force   63

Chapter 4: The Military and Strategic Dimensions of Nonalignment   85

PART III: THE POLITICS OF PAN-PROLETARIANISM: THIRD
    WORLD CHALLENGES TO THE INTERNATIONAL
    DIVISION OF LABOR   109

Chapter 5: The Politics of Pan-Proletarianism   111

Chapter 6: The Politics of Global Economic Restructuring
and the Demise of Third World Pan-Proletarianism, 1970–1990   137

PART IV: PAN-PROLETARIANISM PHASE II: RACE
CONSCIOUSNESS IN THE NORTH AND THE NEW ERA
OF GLOBAL APARTHEID   181

Chapter 7: The Political and Military Dimensions of Third World
Fragmentation   183

Chapter 8: Toward a New Era of Global Apartheid: The Development
of Race Consciousness in the North   241

Epilogue: Globalization, Democratization, and Transitions
in North-South Relations   281

Select Bibliography   295

Index   315

Abbreviations

ADC	Advanced Developing Countries
ANZUS	Australia, New Zealand, and the United States
ASEAN	Association of South East Asian Nations
CAP	Common Agricultural Policy
CENTO	Central Treaty Organization
CIEC	Conference on International Economic Cooperation
CMEA/Comecon	Council for Mutual Economic Assistance
CoCoM	Coordinating Committee on Multilateral Exports Control
ECLA	United Nations' Economic Commission for Latin America
ECOWAS	Economic Community of West African States
EEC	European Economic Community
G-7	Group of Seven
GATT	General Agreement on Tariffs and Trade
GCC	Gulf Cooperation Council
GDP	Gross Domestic Product
GNP	Gross National Product
IBRD	International Bank for Reconstruction and Development
ICBM	Intercontinental Ballistic Missiles
ILO	International Labor Organization
IME	Industrial Market Economies
IMF	International Monetary Fund
MIRV	Multiple Independently Targeted Reentry Vehicles
MOEC	Major Oil Exporting Countries
MPLA	Popular Movement for the Liberation of Angola
NAFTA	North American Free Trade Agreement
NATO	North Atlantic Treaty Organization
NEM	Non-Industrial Market Economies

NICs	Newly Industrializing Countries
NIEO	New International Economic Order
NME	Non-Market Economies
NOLDC	Non-oil Less Developing Countries
OAPEC	Organization of Arab Petroleum Producing Countries
OAS	Organization of American States
OAU	Organization of African Unity
OECD	Organization for Economic Cooperation and Development
OECS	Organization of East Caribbean States
OPEC	Organization of the Petroleum Exporting Countries
PLO	Palestine Liberation Organization
RENAMO	Mozambique National Resistance Organization
RoW	Rest of the World
SALT	Strategic Arms Limitation Talks
SAP	Structural Adjustment Programs
SEATO	Southeast Asian Treaty Organization
SLBM	Submarine-Launched Ballistic Missiles
UNCTAD	United Nations Conference on Trade and Development
UNESCO	United Nations Educational, Scientific & Cultural Organization
UNIDO	United Nations Industrial Development Organization

Preface

The purpose of this study is to examine four generations of developing solidarity among Third World states. First, Afro-Asianism emerged in the 1950s as the Third World response to the racial hierarchy in the world system. Second, nonalignment evolved as a reaction by Third World leaders to the Cold War conflict and the bipolar power structure in the world system. Third, the East-West conflict was replaced by the North-South conflict as the most salient issue confronting the collectivity of states known as the Third World during the 1970s. The quest for a new international economic order (NIEO) became the raison d'être for Third World solidarity from the 1970s to the 1980s. Fourth, the South-to-South dialogue developed in the 1980s as an important catalyst for community building in the South during an epoch of global restructuring. Collective self-reliance in the South had the possibilities of generating into sub-imperialism within the Third World as the semiperiphery or the newly industrializing countries sought to carve out their own niches in the changing international division of labor. The world system is entering a new era of global apartheid as race consciousness increases in the North and the white world closes rank after the Cold War. This may be one of the consequences of the Gulf War of 1991.

Third World solidarity evolved first and foremost as an issue of race, then progressed to a shared determination to avoid Cold War alliances, and is now predicated on a mutual interest in terminating poverty and inequality. Between the years 1955 and 2000, Third World solidarity has matured from pan-pigmentationalism (solidarity based on race and geography) to pan-proletarianism (solidarity based on economic disadvantages). Pan-pigmentationalism is entering a second phase with the development of race consciousness in the North.

This book seeks to examine Third World solidarity and fragmentation within a broader context of global restructuring. Periodically, the world system undergoes rhythmic cycles of restructuring that begets new hegemonic powers, international regimes, and new models of capital accumulation for regulating the interstate system and the world economy. At these junctures, the value systems and ideological underpinnings that support world structures, such as liberalism under Pax Britannica and neoliberalism under Pax Americana, undergo change. These cycles of systemic change have influenced the content and direction of Third World solidarity.

I also analyze the role of states in the intermediary position in the global hierarchy of wealth and poverty with special reference to the semiperipheral zones in the Third World. To what extent do they nurture Third World solidarity on the one hand, and extend exploitation on the other? To what extent do policies of those intermediary states influence the Third World policies of advanced capitalist states?

This inquiry is a chronological, historical, quantitative, and analytical account of the patterns of organization – including unity and disunity – in the Third World. It develops the theme that there have been important transformations in the structure of Third World unity, from Afro-Asianism in the 1950s to nonalignment in the 1960s, to the quest for a new international economic order in the 1970s, and more recently, the South-South dialogue as a source for community-building during this cycle of global restructuring. These changes in solidarity and fragmentation are influenced by cycles of systemic changes in the world system.

This book accepts the premise that Third World status involves more than a simple compilation of statistical indices on poverty and dependency. For example, Saudi Arabia, with no economic assets other than oil resources, cannot be classified as a metropolitan power. When the oil wells have dried up or an oil glut occurs on the market, the persisting dependency of the Third World status of Saudi Arabia and members of the Organization of Petroleum Exporting Countries (OPEC) will become apparent. Or take Cuba, which sought to enhance its security and to combat "Yankee Imperialism" by joining the former Soviet bloc. Membership in the Soviet bloc did not alter Cuba's subordinate status in the world system. In this inquiry, Third World status is conceptualized as a set of unequal power relationships between dependent peripheral, semiperipheral states and the advanced capitalist states, whether as colonies, as in the past, or as independent capitalist and socialist states today.

I also examine the Third World leaders' challenge to global apartheid from the sixteenth to the twentieth century. Global apartheid refers to Northern dominance of the political, economic, and cultural instruments of power in the world system during cycles of structural transformation. This study will analyze the degree to which racial capitalism evolved over time to become a permanent feature in the world system, and how, with the demise of slavery and colonialism, this system of racial inequality took on a life of its own. This book will examine the degree to which leaders in the North have been successful in developing more sophisticated regimes of global apartheid to combat the

South's rejection of their subordinate position in the world system. The collapse of the Soviet empire in 1989 has torn asunder the ideological and cultural barriers that separate the Northeast – the former Soviet Union, Eastern and Central Europe – and the Northwest – the United States, Western Europe, and Japan. As the global community enters the twenty-first century, the world system is becoming more polarized along racial and cultural lines across the North-South divide. The forces of globalization have unleashed a new wave of democratic capitalism that is reducing the role of the state in the economy and reinforcing the politics of differences. Increasingly, the politics of differences and identity is fostering the development of a new era of global apartheid as the new millennium begins.

This inquiry will examine the impact of the end of the Cold War on the strategic shift in the economic and military posture of the United States, Japan, and the European Economic Community away from the East-West geopolitical conflict. As geopolitics gives way to geo-economic conflict, the world system will be increasingly defined in North-South terms. The end of the Cold War dramatically symbolizes the advent of pluralism in many forms beyond the military-security arena. As the twentieth century draws to an end, the world system is moving toward a modern and more sophisticated form of global apartheid. At this juncture, American, German, and Japanese models of capital accumulation are vying for supremacy in this era of global restructuring. The outcome of this inter-capitalist rivalry will have serious ramifications for Third World solidarity and incorporation into the world economy in the twenty-first century. Agencies such as the Group of Seven (G-7), the International Monetary Fund (IMF), the World Bank, the General Agreement on Tariffs and Trade (GATT), the World Trade Organization (WTO), the Coordinating Committee on Multilateral Exports Control (CoCoM), and the United Nations Security Council have evolved over the last forty-five years into instruments of Northern dominance in North-South relations along both geopolitical and geo-economic lines. The Cold War era is being replaced by a new world order based on democratic capitalism and global apartheid. Globalization and fragmentation of the state has emerged, as new dynamic forces challenge the continuing priority given to Third World solidarity.

Since the emergence of the Third World as a dynamic force in world politics, this coalition of states has challenged the North's political, economic, and cultural hegemony. From the maroon societies in the Americas to the Haitian and Cuban revolutions, and the African revolt in South Africa, Third World leaders have created a variety of antisystemic movements in their quest to create a new world order.[1]

In the process of delineating the boundaries of this study, the advice of friends and colleagues has been invaluable. Special thanks is given to Ali A. Mazrui, Harold K. Jacobson, Joel Samoff, and Maxwell Owusu in this regard. Ali A. Mazrui and the late Terence Hopkins read earlier drafts and made very useful comments. Mazrui also encouraged me to refine the concept of global apartheid and to contextualize it within a historical and contemporary political milieu. Terence Hopkins drew my attention to the decline of the state in both the North and the South that was unfolding during this cycle of global restructuring. The late Archie Singham provided a remarkable example of scholarship and activism, and his work on nonalignment was an important foundation for my own work. Cedric Robinson also gave guidance through his scholarship and commitment to academic excellence and social responsibility. His work *Black Marxism: The Making of the Black Radical Tradition* was very important in the development and refinement of the concept of racial capitalism.

I received encouragement and intellectual stimulation on this project from my colleagues in the Institute of Global Cultural Studies, the Fernand Braudel Center, the Department of Africana Studies, and the Department of Political Science at Binghamton University. I received support for a research semester (Spring 1990) to complete most of the writing for this project from the former Dean of Arts and Sciences at Harpur College (Binghamton University), Sidonie Smith. In summer 1987, I received a Visiting Faculty Research Grant from the Center for Latin American Studies at the University of Chicago, which gave me an opportunity to use library resources and expand some of my ideas on Third World solidarity, especially with reference to Latin America and the Caribbean. Research assistance was provided by Judson L. Jeffries, Thomas Uthup, and Chakarin Komolsiri. A very special thanks to Nancy Flynn and Grace Houghton for their editorial assistance.

Special thanks also to my children for their support and patience. I am eternally grateful for the encouragement and support of my wife. She was an inspiration and provided both emotional and moral support for this project. I also send thanks to my extended family for putting up with my absence from family gatherings.

For the imperfections of this study, to quote Harry Truman, "The buck stops here!"

NOTE

1. By maroon societies, I am referring to those runaway slaves who had no intention of returning to slavery and sought refuge in palenques or quilombros communities established by Africans in the hills, forests, and other inaccessible areas in Florida, parts of Louisiana, Georgia, and the South Carolina sea islands. Africans escaping from slavery also joined forces with nearby Amerindian societies, such as the Seminole nation of Florida. For more information, consult Herbert Aptheker, *American Negro Slave Revolts* (New York: International Publishers, 1969); Richard Price, ed., *Maroon Societies: Rebel Slave Communities in the Americas* (Baltimore: Johns Hopkins, 1979); Michael Conniff and Thomas J. Davis, *Africans in the Americas: A History of the Black Diaspora* (New York: St. Martin's Press, 1994); Vincent B. Thompson, *The Making of the African Diaspora in the Americas 1441–1900* (New York: Longman, 1987); Hugo Prosper Leaming, *Hidden Americans: Maroons of Virginia and the Carolinas* (New York: Garland Press, 1993); and K. W. Porter, *The Black Seminoles: History of a Freedom-Seeking People* (Gainesville, FL: University of Florida Press, 1996).

Part I

Pan-Pigmentationalism in the South: Third World Challenges to Global Apartheid

Theories of International Relations, Racial Capitalism, and the Politics of Global Apartheid

S tudents of the Third World must struggle with the problems of definition, conceptualization, and identification of the actors comprising this collectivity of states. Changes in the conceptualization of the Third World correlates positively with modifications in the political and economic structures of the world system. During periods when the world system was identified with a tight bipolarity, students of the Third World focused their analytical lens on attempts by the superpowers to recruit these actors into their respective Cold War coalitions.[1] When the international system became characterized by a loose bipolarity or polycentrism, analysts focused on efforts aimed at coalition-building among Third World states on nonmilitary issues.[2]

Crisis in the capitalist economy can also trigger divergent approaches to classification schemes of the Third World. Scholars concentrating their efforts on the changing position of the peripheral and semiperipheral states in the international division of labor during periods of global restructuring have been forced to pay special attention to the fluctuation in Third World solidarity during the rise, consolidation, and decline of hegemonic powers.[3] Still others center their analysis on the extent to which the growth of manufacturing capability among Third World newly industrializing countries (NICs) symbolizes their graduation out of the periphery into the semiperiphery and another form of dependent development.[4]

This study operates on the assumption that the modern world system is undergoing a dramatic structural transformation in which the international regimes that govern the interstate system and the models of capital accumulation that regulate the world economy are being torn apart, thus ushering in a new modus operandi during this wave of global restructuring. This new era of global restructuring has become characterized by a growing incompatibility between the interstate system and the world economy. The result is a crisis that has created a divergent spatial dimension[5] to the international division of labor among core, peripheral, and semiperipheral states on the one hand and a period of intense competition among capitalist business enterprises on the other. Changes as fundamental as these have already begun to transform the political, economic, social, and cultural structures that have been in place since the end of the Second World War.

The world system has undergone similar cycles of structural changes that have reorganized capitalist business enterprises, the world economy, and the interstate system by means of global wars of hegemonic succession, long waves of colonization and decolonization, A (expansion) and B (contraction) phases of capitalist development, and organizational and technological innovations in capitalist business enterprises. During these eras of systemic change, the ideological assumptions and value systems that support models of capital accumulation and the international regimes that govern interstate relations have undergone major transformations.

Recent changes in the spatial dimension of the international division of labor between core, peripheral, and semiperipheral states made a number of the traditional elements of North-South relations null and void. Increasingly, nations beyond the core zones of the world economy are becoming much more than suppliers of commodities and raw materials for the industrial arena. Several nations in Asia,[6] Latin America,[7] and Southern Africa[8] are developing as important producers of manufactured goods. Starting in the mid-1960s, select Third World states became important investment outlets for multinational corporations. These pioneering developing states have launched competitive industrial policies that have fostered the development of domestic markets, competitive skilled labor forces, and export opportunities through investment by multinational corporations. Third World semiperipheral states provided the new niches and operational space for the competitive struggles among capitalist business enterprises in the 1970s and most of the 1990s. To dismiss the rise of Third World semiperipheral countries as mere subsidiary economies of core states is both ethnocentric and simplistic. Through their scholarship, serious students of the Third World have demonstrated that indigenous entrepreneurs in the South are becoming more innovative and assertive in their relations with foreign capital. Since the 1980s, Third World NICs and oil-producing countries have become very conservative on a number of North-South issues. While these actors are presently seeking membership in several Organization for Economic Cooperation and Development (OECD) alliances, they nevertheless remain aggressive and protective of their own local, regional, and global interests.

In recent years, many processes associated with global restructuring have contributed to increased bargaining power for select Third World states. As the world system approaches its spatial limits, the nature of Third World solidarity will need to undergo dramatic transformation. Third World solidarity and incorporation must be addressed within a broader context of global restructuring across space and time if we are to understand the changing nexus of unity and disunity among these actors. Issues of solidarity and incorporation must become a focal point of analysis rather than peripheral notations if we are to comprehend more fully the processes of systemic changes in the world system.

Side by side with the change in the international division of labor between the North and South, the Cold War has come to an end. The final blow came from within as the former Soviet empire disintegrated into eleven sovereign states. The Russians lost their powerful grip over East and Central European states that once comprised the Warsaw Pact. The world system is no longer characterized by bipolarity and has entered a "unipolar moment," at least in the military sphere, with the United States as the only superpower. In the global economic arena the world system is presently very fluid, with multiple centers of capitalism and divergent trajectories toward capital accumulation – America's rugged individualism and private entrepreneurship; Japan's partnership among the state, firms, and workers; and Germany's state monetary policies with a sprinkle of the welfare state – competing for supremacy.[9]

The end of the Cold War era has ushered in a new era of global apartheid with the convergence of interests between the Northeast – the former Soviet Union and the Warsaw Pact nations – and the Northwest – the United States, Western Europe, and Japan. In the aftermath of the Cold War, a new world order began in earnest under the leadership of former President George Bush and Mikhail Gorbachev's successor in the new Russian Republic, President Boris Yeltsin. This new world order required an acceleration in the cooperation between the Great Powers, including the former Soviet Union and its remnants, in order to manage regional conflict. This new collaboration between this diverse coalition of states provided the impetus for deploying the United Nations Security Council collective peace apparatus as an instrument for conflict resolution in outstanding conflicts or militarized disputes within and between states. Since 1989, there has been a growing convergence of interests between the Northeast and Northwest as "democratic capitalism" replaces the teachings of Marxist-Leninism through the principles of Adam Smith, thus nurturing free enterprise and entrepreneurship. As the new world order takes form, a new global rift is developing along North-South lines and is taking a decidedly racial characteristic. The emerging new world order has all the trappings of a new era of global apartheid.

This chapter will study the extent to which theories of international relations have adequately dealt with the international politics of the Third World and will examine theories and conceptual frameworks that are concerned with global power transitions, hegemonic power structures, and the impact of such changes on Third World development and incorporation. I will also analyze the role of race in world politics and the degree to which racial structures of power accompany changes in hegemonic power systems across space and time within the world system. Very few students of international relations have examined the impact of race on North-South relations, the international politics of the Third World, or world politics in general.[10]

THE REALIST PERSPECTIVE ON WORLD SYSTEM CHANGE

Since the end of the Second World War, the study of world politics has become dominated by the realist paradigm with emphasis on the competitive alliance system of the "Great Powers," national security in the nuclear age, balance of power, and the question of international peace in a tight, bipolar system.[11] The realist paradigm came under fire from a number of quarters, as global economic interdependence emerged as a key characteristic among the Great Powers during the 1970s. At this juncture, nonstate actors began to challenge the supremacy of the nation-state as the most important actors in world politics while multinational corporations, liberation movements, and transnational actors reached maturity, thus competing with states for influence in world politics. Scholars working within the dependency, world-system, complex-interdependence, and transnational-politics paradigms became concerned with the inability of the realist theoretical framework to explain or predict global wars of hegemonic succession, long waves of colonization and decolonization, and other dimensions of structural change in the world system. Likewise, these analysts became troubled over the absence of any examination of the role that both organizational and technological innovations in capitalist business enterprises have played in these rhythmic cycles of change in the world system.[12]

Scholars working within the complex interdependence and transnational-relations mode of analysis increasingly found the emphasis on the nation-state as the unit of analysis to be inadequate. From the beginning of the postwar era, nonstate actors became increasingly important factors in world politics. Beginning in the 1970s, a number of students of world politics began to examine the increased power and influence of nonstate actors on the world stage, for example, multinational corporations, international and regional organizations, and national liberation movements.[13]

The realist paradigm offers a number of premises that are consistent with the diversity of theoretical approaches in world politics ranging from Thucydides to Hans Morgenthau, and Thomas Schelling to J. David Singer. Many of these approaches defy direct comparison as a result of the assumptions of the world system and dependency-conceptual frameworks that do not address the same fundamental issues or analyze the same phenomena.[14] Scholars employing the world-system approach conceptualize the capitalist world economy as the starting point in their analysis. Their counterparts working within the dependency framework operate on the notion that external actors, from capitalist states to multinational corporations, disproportionately influence the decision-making processes within Third World states.

The realist paradigm works from the assumption that political power is the most important explanatory variable not only for world politics but for national politics as well. Those actors with the greatest concentration of military and/or political power determine the structure, major processes, and general evolution of the world community. The Great Powers occupy this role in the realist paradigm. According to this perspective, a hierarchy of actors defined by power exists in an anarchical international system. Dominant actors in the system play decisive roles in determining not only the organization and major rules and regulations but also the general growth and development of the world system as well. Hence, the action, reaction, and interaction of the Great Powers are fundamental to scholars employing the realist framework.[15]

Two fundamental characteristics that separate the realist paradigm from other theoretical frameworks is its emphasis on state sovereignty and the anarchical order. According to the realist paradigm, sovereignty means that the nation-state is the highest source of political authority. It is the state that regulates authoritative modes of behavior within its territorial boundaries, with the ultimate goal of creating and maintaining order. Sovereignty also signifies that the state is the final arbiter in the formulation of policies toward other states and nonstate actors, and the most important function of the states becomes the physical security of the population. This final goal becomes fortified by the principal goal of all states — the maintenance of territorial integrity against external invasion.[16]

Security dilemmas of the Great Powers are significantly different from those of their Third World counterparts. In recent years a proliferation of studies have emerged, drawing attention to the security dilemma facing developing countries. These studies emphasize the array of domestic factors that contribute to intrastate and interstate conflicts. Furthermore, these studies demonstrate that over time such conflicts tend to escalate into full-blown wars. Examples abound in such diverse places as Afghanistan, Angola, El Salvador, Chad, and the Sudan.[17] Instead of facing an anarchic international system, large numbers of African and Third World decision-makers face domestic anarchy as a result of the lack of social cohesion and state capacities to provide for basic needs such as food, shelter, economic well-being, political participation, and a routinized process of selecting leaders. This lack of state capacity to provide domestic order and tranquillity has also contributed to a serious question of internal security. Most African and Third World leaders face domestic sources of a "security dilemma" rather than an anarchic international system. In a nutshell, most African and Third World societies are not unitary actors.[18]

In accordance with the realist paradigm, security in human communities is assumed under five major sectors: military, political, economic, societal, and environmental. In general, military security concentrates societal efforts on the interplay of armed offensive and defense capabilities of states, and states' perceptions of the intentions of others. Security in the political sphere draws attention to the organizational stability of states, their systems of government, and ideologies that give them legitimacy. The economic dimensions of security focus on the accessibility to resources, finance, and markets necessary to support favorable levels of welfare and state power. Traditional patterns of language, culture, and religious and national identity and custom are the foci of societal security. The focal point of environmental security is the maintenance of the local habitat and the planetary biosphere as the essential support system for all human ventures. Barry Buzan has noted that these five interrelated security arenas do not operate in isolation from each other; all interact together in a strong web of linkages.[19]

The realist paradigm conceptualizes the world system of states as operating in a state of anarchy; thus states, by pursuing their individual national securities through such policies as arming, deterrence, and alliance, create and sustain an international environment of decreasing relative security for themselves and for the collectivity of states. The paradox revolving around the security dilemma hinges on the external-threat environment that states interact with, and as a result of their efforts, as unitary state actors, to meet those threats.[20] During the Cold War era, the security dilemma provided analysts with a critical angle for examining international security. However, when analysts turn their attention to contemporary Third World states, the security dilemma correlation and underlying rationalism do not hold up to investigation. Third World states face a disproportionate number of threats from within their societies, thus generating an "insecurity dilemma."

Third World "insecurity dilemmas" fall into four arenas: (1) a variety of communal groups fighting for their own security and hegemony over their competitors; (2) regimes in power usually lacking support from significant sectors of the population because the regime is perceived as representing the interests of a particular ethnic or social stratum, or an economic or military elite that has taken control of the reins of the state; (3) Third World states lacking the capacity to provide for basic needs and to maintain political order; and (4) regimes in which the real threat to the regime or leader is from within the state, and thus the distinction between threats to the leader and the state become blurred.[21]

Since a number of Third World leaders conceptualized domestic threats to their continuation in power as challenges to the state itself, this influenced decision-makers throughout the developing world facing similar insecurity dilemmas to adopt three strategies: (1) militarization, that is, developing and arming sizable military/police forces; (2) repression and state terror, that is, waging a battle against the alleged "enemy within;" and (3) diversionary tactics – identifying external enemies to distract attention from the situation at home.[22] Third World leaders employ these strategies to rationalize their purchases of conventional arms from the superpowers and their allies.[23] The realist theoretical framework does not address the insecurity dilemmas of Third World states. The question remains: will Third World insecurity dilemmas be addressed in the post-Cold War era?

The rise of the United States and the Soviet Union to superpower status reinforced the international security dilemma during most of the postwar period. The introduction of nuclear weapons undermined the domestic basis of national security, leading to the reliance on the superpowers and their alliance systems. The decolonization processes in Africa and Asia initially reinforced the superpowers' dominance in the security arena as these actors, the African and Asian states, became expected to join subsidiary alliances sponsored by the leaders of the East and West Cold War coalitions. However, a number of pioneering states, including Egypt, Ghana, India, Indonesia, and Yugoslavia (after Tito's withdrawal from the Warsaw Pact), became nonaligned. Starting in the 1970s, nonalignment became the preferred policy option for the majority of the Third World countries beyond the Latin American region. The 1947 Rio Pact tied most of Latin America to the American Cold War coalition, while the Cuban revolution and the increase in conflictual relations with the United States pushed Havana toward the Soviet camp. The inability of the superpowers to incorporate successfully the Third World into their sphere of influence set in motion forces that would eventually unravel the power and influence of both Cold War coalitions.

Starting with the introduction of détente as the modus operandi that governed superpower relations in the 1970s, the realist paradigm began to lose its explanatory power as economic factors surged to the top of the agenda in both regional and international institutions. Since the beginning of the postwar era, international economic issues had become relegated to the realm of "low politics." Scholars employing the realist theoretical framework were unprepared to deal with the increased rivalry among advanced capitalist states for markets, trade, and world products. This came on the heels of the epilogue of the Bretton Woods system and the decline of the United States dominance of the world economy and retreat from globalism that accompanied the American withdrawal from Vietnam and the ascent of Western Europe, Japan, OPEC, and Third World NICs as rival economic powers. As Western Europe and Japan recovered from the ravages of the Second World War, they began to demand a greater role in international economic decision-making. Third World semiperipheral states also called for changes in the international regimes governing the world economy. Both superpowers began experiencing challenges within their respective Cold War alliances. As a result, polycentrism became a systemic problem faced by both of these actors.

At the start of the 1970s, the world system began to move away from a tight, bipolar structure. Changes in military technology contributed to the reduction in value of forward bases not only for strategic reasons but also for supply of reconnaissance in large-scale conventional wars. Except those in Eastern Europe — where the Soviet Union continued to insist on a security belt composed of loyal allies — the cost of forward bases increased at an alarming rate. In other places, they became less credible while the price of protection continued to rise, for example, in Vietnam and Cambodia for the United States, and in Ethiopia and Somalia for the Soviet Union. This change in the political milieu generated more incentives for smaller states to strike a posture of independence with the hope for creating more opportunities for diplomatic maneuvering against both superpowers. In the 1970s, ideologies that made it imperative to mobilize the "good" people against the "bad" people on a global basis were pushed aside in favor of more pragmatic considerations.[24]

The growth of détente between the superpowers and interdependence among the advanced market economies of the North changed in the interstate system dramatically. As the Soviet threat declined, military and security issues lost their prominent position on the agenda of international institutions. The evolution toward interdependence hastened a crisis in the world economy, especially as it experienced the erection of trade barriers and the energy and monetary imbroglio of 1973-1974. The Arab-Israeli conflict introduced oil power as a new force in the international arena in the 1970s. The contour of powers in the world system became increasingly structured along economic dimensions.

Détente and economic interdependence were accompanied by a change in the number of significant actors on the world stage. This included a shift in the type and source of power employed by these actors as well as a dramatic modification in the values governing international institutions. The increased interdependence and economic diversity in the countries comprising the Third World combined with increased competition among advanced market economies of the North to weaken severely both the explanatory and predictive powers of the realist approach to world politics.

The paradigms of complex interdependence and transnational politics became the first alternatives to the realist theoretical framework. Over time they lost their analytical attractiveness. Both of these frameworks challenged the "state-centric" bias of realism and focused more attention on the host of nonstate actors that compete with and constrain the behavior of states. Scholarship guided by these two perspectives paid close attention to the rise of nonmilitary issues in regional and international institutions, the increased global reach of multinational corporations, the impact of liberation movements on the interstate system, and the Third World challenge to the international regimes of Pax Americana.[25]

However, the complex-interdependence and the transnational-politics paradigms failed to account for many significant factors. These included the continuing importance of military conflicts in the mid-1970s, the ability of some actors to cope with interdependence better than others, the persistence of poverty and dependence in the peripheral sector of the Third World, the movement toward industrialization in the semiperipheral sector of the Third World, and the increased economic plurality among the advanced market economies of the North. At the same time, analysts who employed these theoretical frameworks could not explain the rise, consolidation, decline, and re-assertion of Pax Americana. Neither of these theoretical frameworks could predict or explain the long waves of colonization and decolonization in the Third World, or the impact of technological and organizational innovations in capitalist business enterprises, historically and in the contemporary postwar era, on systemic change in the world system. Likewise, these frameworks fail to explain the changing role of Third World semiperipheral zones in the global division of labor. Analysts employing the interdependence and transnational-politics frameworks abandon their preoccupation with economic and military factors in order to pay attention to ideology and basic value systems that also undergird hegemonies.

Starting in the 1970s, many students of world politics began to question a number of Hobbesian notions about the anarchical international system that is in a "permanent state of war." These scholars departed from the state-centric perspective of classical realism and integrated the structuralism of world system analysis into their thinking. Scholars who continue to operate within this new theoretical and scholarly sphere are still grappling with the structural transformations that periodically occur in the world system and establish a new global political and economic order. Such crises erupt because of the growing incompatibility between the interstate system and the world economy. As new models of capital accumulation become conventional, intrafirm and interstate relations lose their validity, and states seeking new operational space in the world system engage in war in order to achieve their ends.[26]

NEOREALISM AND HEGEMONIC POWER AND STABILITY

Neorealism evolved over the last decade as a successor to classical realism. This theoretical framework provided answers to many of the puzzling questions over how international regimes developed to govern interstate relations. Neorealism also emerged as an answer to the queries about the evolution of models of capital accumulation that regulate the world economy. Analysts employing this conceptual framework argue that power cycles have become an integral part of the ascent, consolidation, and descent of hegemonies. Since the fifteenth century, these power cycles still remain an important component of the world system. Such power cycles are the "engines" that drive these periodic structural changes in the world system. According to neorealist scholars, global wars are the dynamic phases in which systemic reorganization takes place in the world system. Successive power cycles redefined the political and economic structures of the world system after the emergence of a new hegemon in the world community. Unlike world system analysts who conceptualize capitalism as the dynamic force behind systemic change, neorealists argue that each successive hegemon institutes new international regimes for both the interstate system and the world economy. Examples of these international regimes include the free trade system under Pax Britannica and the free movement of the factors of production under Pax Americana.

Neorealist analysts lack a consensus in their approach toward systemic change in the modern world system. Some theorists stress the unequal distribution of capabilities in the world system over the last 500 years that gives some actors global reach while limiting others to their own local or regional sphere of influence. Over time, the initial unipolarity gives way to multipolarity and rivalry. A new order emerges when a new world power evolves out of the global power struggle. This approach became the "long cycle of world leadership." World leadership includes those states who exercise leadership in either the political or economic sphere, while hegemony refers to global leadership in both spheres.[27]

Still others focus their analytical lens on a transition model that divides the world system between the dominant powers on the one hand and the ordinary powers on the other. The dominant powers usually possess a near monopoly over key military and economic capability. These actors exert influence over how the interstate system is organized and set the rules for global economic intercourse. As the initial competitive edge of the dominant power recedes in favor of the dissatisfied challenger, war erupts and a new international order emerges.[28] Robert Gilpin, another contributor to the neorealist theoretical framework, developed the hegemonic war and change model. For him, the distribution of relative power changes more quickly than the rules of the international system. This discrepancy between power distribution and status leads to disequilibrium. Former more powerful actors are no longer in a position to enforce the rules of the international system, while newly emerging powers lack international regimes to address their changing economic and military position in the world system. In the past this problem of status disequilibrium became resolved through global war, which restructures the hierarchy of the world system through a new distribution of political and economic power.[29]

Perhaps Paul Kennedy offers the best neorealist analysis of the relationship between economic change and military conflict in the world system since the start of the sixteenth century. Kennedy examines the rise of the West beginning around 1500; the initial Hapsburg dominance of the world system through Spain and Portugal; the nineteenth-century rise of Pax Britannica following wars of hegemonic succession in the years 1660 through 1763 and 1763 through 1815; the eventual rise of Pax Americana in the twentieth century; and, in the 1950s, the creation of a bipolar world as a result of the global hegemonic wars. According to Kennedy, imperial "overstretch" has become a major cause of Great Power demise since the sixteenth century. The history of the rise and eventual fall of the Great Power system confirms a significant correlation over time between producing and revenue-raising capacities on the one hand and military strength on the other.[30] By waging costly wars or overexerting themselves strategically, leading powers have squandered national wealth through military escapades rather than investing in revenue-generating activities. Kennedy also argues that Pax Americana is declining as a direct result of military overstretch, economic strain, and mismanagement.

Kennedy's book stirred a lively debate over the accuracy of the analysis which proclaims that American hegemony is on the decline. Joseph S. Nye has written a critical assessment of this theory in *Bound To Lead: The Changing Nature of American Power* (1990). Nye argues that empirical evidence does not support the decline of American power in either the economic or military arena. In fact, the counter evidence suggests that effects of the Second World War lasted for close to twenty-five years and that most of any alleged decline worked its way through the system by the mid-1970s and then stabilized.[31] Nye also questions Kennedy's thesis of imperial or military overstretch as well. He has marshaled an array of evidence that questions the extent to which the United States is overcommitted both militarily and strategically. Nye analyzed Communist, Allied, and United States domestic challenges to American power and found them lacking. Nye also questions the economic-deterministic language conveyed in the term as deployed by neorealist and world system scholars in analyzing systemic change.

Although neorealist scholars have come a long way in their quest to build a theoretical framework that offers greater explanatory and predictive power, scholarship in this school of world politics continues to revolve around "power politics." Analysts employing this theoretical framework still suffer from the Great Power bias. Since the Third World states have become peripheral to any power struggle that occurs in the global contest for hegemony or world leadership, these actors have also become marginal to the study of world politics. Historically, this zone became the arena of struggles against Northern hegemony, whether through the imperial policies of slavery, colonialism, neocolonialism, or dependency. Likewise, the demand for a new international economic order evolved as an attempt by Third World leaders to offer new international regimes and new models of capital accumulation to govern North-South relations. It is through such policies as slavery, colonialism, foreign aid regimes, and structural adjustment programs that the North forges new methods of incorporating the Third World into the changing international division of labor. Hence, Third World states provided operational space in the world system for the competitive struggles among advanced capitalist states and their multistate enterprises during periods of hegemonic decline.

While neorealist scholars may differ over the nature of systemic change in the world system, analysts who employ this approach to world politics continue to conceptualize Third World states as pawns on the chessboard of international relations. Since the fifteenth century, leaders in the Third World have challenged their divergent methods of incorporation into the world system from political, economic, cultural, and racial perspectives.

WORLD SYSTEM PERSPECTIVES ON HEGEMONY

The capitalist world economy's approach to systemic change in the world system starts from the fundamental assumption that the primary influence on the interstate system's structure is the cyclical alterations among a period of hegemony, the relative decline of hegemonies, and subsequent rivalry among core states for ascension to the position of hegemon.[32] Immanuel Wallerstein and his colleagues argue that there are long phases of economic prosperity and depression, and A and B phases of capitalist development that provide the impetus for the rise, consolidation, and decline of hegemonies and the reorganization of North-South relations across space and time.

Periods of economic expansion also involve political hegemony particularly when a single state succeeds others in commercial, financial, and production capacity and military strength. Following in the direction of Schumpeter,[33] Hopkins and Wallerstein contend that the hegemonic position in the world system revolves around the appearance of technological advantages that eventually wear down due to the diffusion of the original competitive edge and the appearance of new innovations in the production process. The introduction of new innovative technology spawns competition and rivalry among core states and, in some eras, encourages the expansion of colonial activity. Hopkins and Wallerstein identify four hegemonies in the world system: those of the Hapsburgs (1415–1559), the Netherlands (1620–50), Great Britain (1850–73), and the United States (1945–73).

Differences abound among theorists working within the capitalist world economy approach to systemic change. These differences evolve over the number of hegemonies across space and time, the forces behind these periodic cycles of change in the world system, and the role of technology in these processes. Christopher Chase-Dunn asserts that technology spreads not only to core powers, but also to select semiperipheral states. He draws attention to periods of rival imperialism and colonial expansion as the Great Powers act to claim potential areas for themselves during these cycles of intracore competitiveness and conflict. According to Chase-Dunn, three nations have achieved hegemony since the introduction of the capitalist mode of production: the United Province (the Dutch) in the sixteenth century, Great Britain in the nineteenth century, and the United States in the twentieth century. On the other hand, Albert Bergesen recognizes only two nations that achieved hegemony, the United Kingdom and the United States.[34]

In recent years the technological imperative has become an important factor in any analysis of systemic change in the world system. In his work on this subject, Giovanni Arrighi asserts that the process of "creative destruction" is the essence of capitalism and the motivating force of systemic change. The introduction of new technology and its accompanying innovations has the potential to transform the economic structures from within. It ceaselessly destroys the old and creates new modes of capitalist accumulation and development. According to this perspective, capitalist business enterprises that are on the cutting edge in terms of critical innovations will generate windfall profits, while those who lag will suffer significant losses. This process of creative destruction results in both disequilibrium and intense rivalry among such capitalist business enterprises. A consequence of these cycles of intracore competitiveness is that those firms that fail to innovate and change their labor, market, raw material, and capital goods networks will suffer significant losses. Through the creative destruction process intrafirm networks are torn asunder. This conceptualization corresponds to Hopkins and Wallerstein's A and B (or boom and bust) phases of capitalist accumulation and development. The boom and bust phases are also cycles of competitive struggles in the interenterprise system. Throughout the A phase, capitalist enterprises generally favor customary arrangements and networks that support relations that are cooperative and complementary. During the B phase, they enter struggles that bring to the fore-front competitive relations along with the arrival of innovative production technologies and revolutionary strategies for managing business enterprises.[35]

Arrighi presents a strong case for his belief that relations among capitalist enterprises are themselves anchored in world hegemonies, that is, the customary arrangements of the interstate system which insure the continuous and circular flow of economic life across state boundaries. These structures, much like routine arrangements of the interenterprise system, are subject to broadly cyclical patterns of construction and destruction. Nevertheless, such cycles of competition among capitalist business enterprises are important factors in these periodic cycles of change in the world system. Like Bergesen, Arrighi recognizes only two states that have successfully achieved global dominance in the world system, Great Britain and the United States. These two actors are responsible for introducing new international regimes and new models of capital accumulation, including strategies which revolutionize the management of business enterprises.

Theorists working within the world-system theoretical framework define change as occurring primarily in the core sector of the world economy. The introduction of new models of capital accumulation and the advent of new hegemonies contribute to new forms of Third World incorporation into the world system. Hence, these nations become conceptualized as pawns on the chessboard of the capitalist world system. Over time, Third World nations challenged their subservient roles in the capitalist world system, which have resulted from slavery, colonialism, dependency upon the Northwest, or their continuing positions as commodity producers in the global division of labor. These challenges contributed to the introduction of new models of capital accumulation and the rise of new power centers in the world system. Nonetheless, the world-system approach to systemic change lacks a critical analysis of the transnational social forces that serve to maintain the basic requirements of the global system of capitalism. Transnational forces also structure competition among advanced market economies of the North in a manner in which war between these actors will not erupt out of their intracore rivalry.[36] Likewise, world-system analyses fail to address the role of cultural forces in systemic change.

CULTURAL FORCES AND HEGEMONIC POWER AND STABILITY

Ali A. Mazrui recently turned his analytical lens to the transfer of power across space and time from the Semites to the Anglo-Saxons through the instrumentality of Pax Britannica and Pax Americana. In his provocative work, *Cultural Forces in World Politics,* Mazrui emphasizes the narrow cultural gap between the Northeast (the Soviet bloc) and the Northwest (the United States and the

Western allies). In addition, he examines the way in which the hidden power of culture and technology enlarges the power differential between the North and the South. Mazrui analyzes the cultural baggage that accompanied the rise of each hegemony along with the political, economic, and cultural consequences that such ascensions have had for countries in the Third World. His study examines the competing roles of race and gender in the development of hegemony. He also examines the impact of cultural and economic imperialism on the North-South conflict. He investigates how Anglo-Saxon hegemony encouraged the commercialization of racism and profit-seeking through the humiliation of Africa.[37] His analysis questions Kennedy's contention that Pax Americana is on the decline and that the world system is moving toward a Pax Nipponica under the leadership of Japan. Nevertheless, Mazrui does not anticipate the new era of global apartheid that confronts the Third World as the world system moves toward the twenty-first century.

Samuel P. Huntington has made a new addition to the cultural forces paradigm with his recent article emphasizing the clash of civilizations.[38] Conflict between nations in the post-Cold War era will converge along cultural lines where religion, history and ethnic differences may generate political violence. New battle lines are emerging in the Middle East, Central Asia, and the former Yugoslavia. Huntington asserts that people in most Third World nations desire both economic development and modernization. However, their longing for economic development and modernization does not necessarily lead to broad acceptance of Westernization. In the post-Cold War era, Huntington hypothesizes a world in which conflict will erupt between the Western and the non-Western societies, especially the worlds of Islam and Confucianism.

Huntington urges U.S. policy makers to forge new alliances with like-minded and culturally similar states, meaning the Northeast and Northwest. He urges these same policy makers to be willing to compromise with and confront these alien civilizations. Hence, the clashes of civilizations symbolically represent the new era of global apartheid in North-South relations. Huntington does not acknowledge the racial dimensions of his conflicting civilization thesis. Nor does Huntington place this discussion of the clash of civilizations into a broader theoretical paradigm. Huntington fails to address the North-South dimension of this emerging conflict.

CLASSICAL DEPENDENCY, DEPENDENT DEVELOPMENT, AND THE POLITICAL ECONOMY PERSPECTIVES OF SYSTEMIC CHANGE

Since the early 1970s, the semiperiphery has evolved as an important sector of world economy. The NICs from Latin America, southern Africa, and the Pacific rim are being hailed as confirmation of the conflicting approaches of the Western-oriented growth models and dependent development. Classical dependency – as originally defined by Andre Gunder Frank, Theotonio Dos Santos, and others — emphasizes stagnation and the continuing role of all Third World states as agrarian and commodity producers. In recent years, dependent development has become the theoretical rival of classical dependency with the ascent of the newly industrializing countries. Scholars who work within the classical dependent approach argue that the structure of the world system has severely constrained the development opportunities of Third World states. These theorists operate on four theoretical assumptions. First, the economies and societies of most Third World countries have become irreversibly affected by the fact that these nations originally became incorporated into the world economy as producers of raw materials and consumers of manufactured goods. Second, this international division of labor was maintained by the economic and political power of states in the North to serve their own ends. Third, this enforced incorporation into the world economy causes serious distortions of the domestic economies in the Third World, for example, domination by foreign multinational corporations. Fourth, these economic effects are carried over into the political and economic realm. Elite classes in the Third World form alliances with and become "bridgeheads" for states and corporations in the center and use their resultant power to monopolize societal resources. Dependency theory assumes that the structure of the world economy conditions economic growth, class relations, and political forms within the world's "sovereign" states.[39]

The study of political economy has gone beyond the limits of theoretical contentions between the developmentalist and dependency paradigms to integrate key elements of both approaches in a conceptualization of strong and dynamic states that successfully promote economic development. Cal Clark and Jonathan Lemco recognize several important functions for the developmentalist states in their promotion of industrialization: the mobilization of domestic resources, the guidance of the developing economy, and the control of external forces. Developmentalist states also channel activities of multinational corporations to aid rather than to exploit the indigenous economy, and create political coalitions that are critical to the support of economic and social transformation and the legitimation of policies and institutions. As a result of this thrust, a new body of scholarship has evolved, bringing the state itself back into the analysis of development and systemic change in the world system.[40]

Although the dependent-development and political-economy paradigms emphasize the importance of a strong state, scholars who employ these approaches have some measure of difficulty when they attempt to explain both the success and failure of the state to generate industrialization in various Third World states throughout time. What are the underlying factors in the world system that have contributed to the rise and initial success of many of the NICs? What factors explain and predict the success and failure of statist policies at divergent points in time? Why are some Third World NICs experiencing economic expansion while others are undergoing another round of underdevelopment? The answer to these questions can not be effectively addressed through the realist, neorealist, world system, dependency, or political economy approaches to systemic change. To paraphrase John G. Ruggie, there is equal danger in assuming that development and systemic change (for the purpose of our discussion) are solely the function of "the magic of the marketplace, the immutable international hierarchy, or the omnipotent state."[41]

NEO-GRAMSCIAN THEORY AND GLOBAL HEGEMONIES

In this study the central problem of analyzing Third World solidarity and fragmentation becomes inseparable from the ongoing theoretical debate concerning systemic change in the world system. Change in the nature of Third World solidarity also signifies the introduction of new international division of labor between the North and the South as these actors challenge the northern political, economic, and cultural hegemony. What does the neo-Gramscian theory of historical materialism have to offer to these puzzling questions? Does this theory provide greater flexibility along with stronger explanatory power with reference to the politics and international relations of the Third World?

Robert W. Cox developed the neo-Gramscian model of historical materialism. For analysts in this tradition, structural change in the capitalist world system requires a more flexible analytical approach than the structuralism of the world system and neorealist conceptual frameworks, allowing for the possibility of the analysis of transnational social forces, including the interplay between different interests in each individual state. For Cox, the key variables are interacting sets of social forces – ideas, institutions, and material capabilities – which affect the formation of transnational and national class factions of labor and capital, and the internationalized or transnationalized state.[42] These forces operate at three interrelated methodological levels: world orders, state-civil society complexes, and at the basic level of production. This conceptualization requires a different definition of the concept hegemony. Hence, hegemony occurs when there is a strong congruence among each of these social forces across each level.[43]

In *Production, Power and World Order*, Cox (1987) makes a strong case for the role of the changing hegemonic power structure in influencing state policy throughout the capitalist world system and defining the international division of labor along political and economic lines.[44] Third World incorporation into the world system required different frameworks during these cycles of global restructuring. He pays attention to the divergent logic influencing the Soviet Union's and the People's Republic of China's incorporation and adoption of a corporatist strategy as these actors abandoned the economic policies associated with socialism and as they work within the framework of ascending capitalism. Cox operates on the premise that such structures, as well as the political and economic processes of restructuring, are determined by the Great Powers. Accordingly, hegemony exists when a state's major institutions and forms of organization – economic, social, and political – as well as its key values become the model of emulation in other subordinate states. From this perspective, the pattern of emulation occurs in the Northwest and Northeast sectors of the world system rather than on the periphery and semiperiphery of the Third World. As such, hegemony becomes more intense and consistent in the core and laden with contradictions at the periphery and, to some extent, the semiperiphery.[45]

According to Cox, only two Great Powers have achieved complete and total hegemony: England in the early nineteenth century and the United States in the mid-twentieth century. Although the former Soviet Union, Japan, and, to a lesser extent, the newly industrializing countries from the Third World have offered valiant challenges to American power in recent years, these actors have failed to build a new historic bloc to replace American hegemony in the world system. These actors have not offered a valid alternative economic, financial and military model to the United States. Under American leadership, democratic capitalism has prevailed over Marxist-Leninism.

Cox also argues that hegemony, though firmly established at the center of the world system, wears thin at the peripheries.[46] This sector of the globe is more apt to challenge incorporation into the world system. The anticolonial struggles during the first and second wave of colonization and the Third World battles against classical dependency as associated with the demand for a new world order and a code of behavior governing transnational corporations are examples of these challenges. Anti-systemic movements, ranging from national liberation movements in Africa and Asia to revolutionary regimes from Castro's Cuba to Sandinista Nicaragua, have challenged the nature of their incorporation into the global division of labor as well as the dominant ideology of democratic capitalism that buttresses the existing world order.

Stephen Gill's *American Hegemony and the Trilateral Commission* (1990) represents another important contribution to the neo-Gramscian historical materialist perspective, demonstrating the extent to which the United States has reorganized its hegemonic system of power through the construction of new and more dynamic transnational networks. Gill also analyzes the extent to which American policy makers were successful in generating Northern solidarity through the Trilateral Commission networks. This study also questions analysts who argue that American hegemony is on the decline. With the end of the Cold War, the Trilateral Commission failed to maintain the sense of community and hegemony through a new cooperative international regime. International economic relations between Western Europe, Japan and the United States is dominated by competition and conflict.

Stephen Gill and his associates have revised their analysis concerning the decline of American hegemony and identified the fundamental turning points confronting the global community in the post-Cold War era. The collapse of the Soviet empire in 1989 and increased economic competition between the United States, Germany, and Japan has influenced Gill and his colleagues to revise their analysis. In *Gramsci, Historical Materialism and International Relations,* Gill and his colleagues offer their amendment to their analysis concerning American hegemony and global restructuring in the legitimacy of the world system. According to Gill, the emerging post-Cold War world order is currently undergoing a triple crisis, that is, a transformation encompassing three interlinked levels. First, the world system is undergoing an economic crisis that is restructuring global production, finances, and exchange, challenging customary economic and managerial arrangements and forms of economic organizations. Second, the world system is undergoing a political crisis in terms of institutional changes including changing forms of state, the internationalization, transnationalization or indeed globalization of the state, and what Robert C. Cox calls the emergence of the "post-Westphalian" inter-state system,[47] thus attesting to a change while neo-realists perceive a fundamental continuity. Third, a socio-cultural crisis refers to the way global restructuring at the political and economic levels also involves challenges to embedded sets of social structures, ideas, and practices, thus compelling and arresting the possibilities of change.[48] Hence, there are a range of global forces that are harmonizing the material, political, social, and cultural life of so many people in the world system, but which are simultaneously disintegrating previously establish forms of socio-economic and political organization. This dialectical process is unfolding in Eastern and Central Europe and parts of the Third World.

Alan W. Cafruny has built a neo-Gramscian approach to historical materialism that integrates international relations with the rise, consolidation, and decline of U.S. hegemony. Cafruny examines the voluminous secondary literature on Gramsci and identifies three categories or types of hegemony. These categories are ideal types, and are referred to as integral hegemony, declining hegemony, and minimal hegemony. Cafruny observes that these ideal types have not been employed by scholars of international political economy. Nevertheless, they are relevant for examining the changing U.S. role in the world economy.

Cafruny asserts that integral hegemony is the strongest and most consolidated form of power. It describes the evolution of a highly established leading state characterized by a well-developed sense of shared objectives and lack of overt antagonism among the various subordinate states. The leading state is capable of simultaneously satisfying its own economic goals and those of the system as a whole. Integral hegemony thus defines a particular type of power marked not only by strong intellectual leadership and the formation of consensus, but also by policies through which the ruling strata "really cause the whole community to advance, not merely satisfying its own existential requirements, but continuously increasing its cadres for the conquest of ever new spheres of economic and productive activity."[49]

Cafruny defines declining hegemony as a system in which contradictions between the interests of the leading state and subordinate groups have become more acrimonious. Accordingly, the disintegrative proclivities of the system are more pronounced. The leading state begins to experience difficulty pursuing both its own economic corporate interests and the long-range needs of the system as a whole, and the dispersal of costs becomes more asymmetric. The fairness of the system may become endangered by the hegemon's attempts to fulfill its own economic corporate interests. Nevertheless, the hegemon continues to lead the system, but opposing interests are more visible, underlying power relations are more transparent, and ideological consensus is more weak.[50]

In the Cafruny scheme, minimal hegemony is a regime under which the leading state does not wish to lead anybody, that is, there is no desire to persuade other states to share its interests and aspirations. Dominance becomes more important than exercising leadership per se. At this juncture, significant conflicts have evolved between the interests of the leading and subordinate states. Minimal hegemony is achieved through what Gramsci calls "passive revolution."[51] The leading state is no longer powerful enough to fashion policies capable of serving collective interests, but the subordinate states are too weak and disorganized to bring together a counterhegemonic bloc. The leading state maintains hegemony through co-optation of the leaders of rival blocs, leading to the formation of an even broader collective leadership. Nevertheless, minimal hegemony is characterized by instability and disintegration. However, coercion is not employed as a result of the co-optation of rival leading states.[52]

In examining U.S. hegemony, Cafruny has classified three phases of Pax Americana. Integral hegemony started in 1945 and lasted until the London gold crisis of 1960, which illuminated the fragility of the dollar and signaled the decline of U.S. power. Declining hegemony emerged in 1960, and lasted until 1971, when the U.S. decided to abandon the dollar-gold standard, confirming the growth in nationalistic and disintegrative tendencies that were becoming seductive for the United States as well as other countries. After 1971, the international political economy became a minimal hegemony.[53]

Although the Cafruny scheme does provide a framework for examining Pax Americana through the prism of time, he fails to address the Third World challenge to U.S. hegemony. Cafruny also fails to examine the emergence of global apartheid in North-South relations in the post-Cold War era.

Although the neo-Gramscian approach does much to elaborate the patterns of change in the world system and to delineate the structural and ideological prerequisites of hegemonic power structures across space and time, it fails to take into account the role of race and culture in generating the North-South hierarchy of wealth and poverty in the capitalist world system. With the introduction of the capitalist mode of production, a new economic and political order has evolved alongside a worldwide racial order that coincides with the global hierarchy of wealth and power. The racial nature of this order has been at times hidden behind such concepts as modernity, development, interdependence, integration, dependency, and more recently, globalization.

RACIAL CAPITALISM AND THE DEVELOPMENT OF GLOBAL APARTHEID

An obvious and vital conclusion that emerges from any study of the development of the capitalist world system is that capitalism does not and cannot mean the same thing to all nations and territories included in its system. At one end of the spectrum it can mean a higher standard of living, greater freedom, and a higher quality of life than humanity has ever known before for people or races of people; at the other extreme, it may mean grinding poverty, forced labor, racial humiliation, and the lash for the vast majority of humanity.[54] This system of inequality has become "racial capitalism."[55]

The origins of this racial order have been traced to the evolution of the capitalist world system and to the feudalistic structure in Europe. Under feudalism Europeans created an array of hierarchies based on language, ethnicity, religion, and culture. Racism was not simply a convention used to order the relations of European to non-European peoples but had its origins in the internal relations of European peoples. Hence, the development, institutionalization, and expansion of the capitalist world system followed an essentially racial dimension with the added support of the ideological structures, contrary to the theory of Marx and Engels. In other words, culture or the superstructure of ideology had a dialectical relationship to the development of capitalism. It sprang forth and shaped material reality. To paraphrase Ronald Takaki, "the phantoms" of the mind and the "sublimations of man's material life-process" constituted a shared set of ideas, images, values, and assumptions about human nature and society.[56] Racial ideology became predominant in terms of the way Europeans conceptualized the world around them. Culture and folklore also served an important economic function. They provided the ideology necessary for the legitimacy and development of the capitalist mode of production and the order of social relations in the world system. Over time, racialism as a material force permeated the structures of emergent capitalism, at first providing a mechanism for expansion. Later, it became an independent force.[57] The dehumanization that the Irish faced as a result of Ireland's colonization by England became a dress rehearsal for the racial subordination of Africans and other nonwhite people that was soon to follow.

Early on, the denial of the African and Third World past as well as denial of their contributions to the development of humanity became an integral part of the Western arsenal of divide and rule. This negation of African and the rest of the Third World's humanity took place as Europe was emerging from the shadow of Muslim domination and paternalism. The image of Africa underwent several distinctive planes of dehumanization structured by the emerging expressions of Western culture.[58] Starting in the seventeenth century Europeans and Africans met each other within the distorted context of the "peculiar institution" of slavery and the slave trade. They met not as diplomatic equals or political peers but rather, more often than not, as conqueror and captive, master and slave, white and black. As Paul G. Lauren (1988) has noted, such a warped, asymmetrical relationship naturally led to the European dominance and African subordination through slavery.[59] At this juncture, Europeans emphasized differences rather than similarities. Such degradation also worked to bind together the European population, creating a sense of community and solidarity. Over time, it became quite painless for Europeans to set the African population apart from themselves. They could describe Africans as "heathens" and "pagans" in religion, "bestial" and "brutish" in behavior, and "lewd" and "lustful" in sex, and thus their perfect fit for enslavement.[60] By the fifteenth century, the term *black* was linked with sin, damnation, death, despair, ugliness, and evil. Increasingly, a black skin became the badge of inferiority. A new racial order had begun.

Side by side with the creation of this new order, the Negro became a novel invention. In terms of Western historical consciousness, the term — whose origin could be found in the racial fabrications concealing the Slavs (the slaves), the Irish, and others — substantially eradicated the necessity of remembering the significance of Nubia for Egypt's development, of Egypt in the formation of Greek civilization, of Africa for imperial Rome, and, more pointedly, of Islam's influence on Europe's economic, political, and intellectual history. In practice, the Negro became a creature who existed beyond the boundaries of history and without a tradition or culture. In its place was the black slave, a consequence masqueraded as anthropology and history.[61] One result of this process was the de-Africanization of the black slaves. Much of the history of slave experience in the West amounted to the following command addressed to captives: "Forget you are Africans, remember you are Black!"[62]

Slavery was an integral part of the development of the world capitalist system. Black and other nonwhite labor provided the surplus capital that became essential to the expansion of this mode of production. Both black labor and slavery were organic to the historical development of capitalism. Although European Marxists have argued that slavery is yet another form of primitive capitalism and in effect antithetical to capitalism's very development, historical evidence does not support this assertion. For more than 300 years, slave labor has persisted beyond the origins of modern capitalism, complementing wage labor, peonage, serfdom, and other methods of labor coercion.

Over time a racial ideology emerged to justify the practice of discrimination based on race that continued to plague black and other nonwhite populations on a global scale, long after both slavery and the slave trade were abolished. The new racial order was fed by the expansionist and exploitative socioeconomic relations of capitalist imperialism. Racism became a permanent stimulus for the ordering of unequal relations of production and emerged as one of the justifications of these relations.[63] Racism became an integral part of the colonial expansion as Europe sought new markets and new laborers. In the words of Bernard M. Magubane, "Theoretically the blacks were part of the world proletariat, in the sense that they were an exploitative class of cheap laborers, but in practice they were not recognized by the world proletariat to any great extent."[64] They became the source of super profits at the same time they were the victims of physical oppression, social ostracism, economic exclusion, and personal hatred.[65] They were, according to W. E. B. Du Bois, an integral part of that dark and vast sea of human labor in China and India, the South Seas and all Africa; in the West Indies and Central America and in the United States — the great majority of mankind, on whose bent and broken backs rest today the founding stones of modern industry, [that] shares a common destiny; it is despised and rejected by race and color, paid a wage below the level of decent living; driven, beaten, prisoned, and enslaved in all but name; spawning the world's raw material and luxury — cotton, wool, coffee, tea, cocoa, palm oil, fibers, spices, rubber, silks, lumber, copper, gold, diamonds, leather — how shall we end this list and where? All these are gathered up at prices lowest of the low; manufactured, transformed and transported at fabulous gain; and the resultant wealth is distributed and displayed and made the basis of world power and universal dominion and armed arrogance in London and Paris, Berlin and Rome, New York and Rio de Janeiro.[66]

Du Bois conceptualized slavery and the slave trade as the pivotal founda- tion of the modern capitalist world system and redefined the "mere slaves" as "coerced workers" and the anchors of this economic system.[67] In his most influential work, *Black Reconstruction,* Du Bois elaborated on the continuing development of racial capitalism with the rise of the second wave of colonialism in Africa and Asia.[68] He argued that the colored people on a global scale perform the work and supply the mineral resources for Europe, making possible the wealth of the white world while being discriminated against on grounds of color.[69]

Du Bois began writing this book during the height of the Great Depres- sion, another period of fundamental global restructuring. The impact of the Depression on African Americans led Du Bois to review previous cycles of change.[70] He examined these cycles in the capitalist world economy, beginning with the era of the slave trade. He concluded that during each cycle of systemic change in the world system African Americans continued to constitute the most oppressed group in America.[71] Throughout the 1930s the economic situ- ation for African Americans worsened even more than that of whites. In the political arena, blacks were disenfranchised and lynching increased, with the Scottsboro case being the most representative of this trend. It was in this con- text that Du Bois criticized Marxists, particularly those associated with the Communist Party of the Soviet Union, for not recognizing the racial dimension of the class conflict within world system. According to Du Bois,

> This philosophy did not envisage a situation where instead of a horizontal division of classes, there was a vertical fissure, a complete separation of classes by race, cutting square across economic layers. Even if on one side of this color line, the darker masses were overwhelmingly workers, with but an embryonic capitalist class, nevertheless, the split between white and black workers was greater than that between white workers and capitalists; and this split depended not on simply economic exploitation but on racial folk-lore grounded on centuries of instinct, habit and thought and implemented by the conditioned reflex of visible color. This flat and incontrovertible fact, imported Russian Communism ignored, would not discuss.[72]

As a student of social movements, Du Bois became aware of how the Russian Revolution evolved into a dictatorship of the proletariat that became less democratic and less dependent on the deliberative action of the workers than was theorized by Marx and Engels.[73] For Du Bois, the working class in the Soviet Union was neither more skilled nor more intelligent as a result of the revolution.[74] The Communist Party directed the dictatorship of the proletariat from above. In 1938, Du Bois recognized the bankruptcy of the political ideology of democratic centralism, fascism, and the socialist economic policies as serious approaches to social change.[75] Democracy was on the defensive throughout Europe, where the forces of Russian communism and German and Italian fascism prevailed. These models of change replaced democracy with oligarchy and placed strict limits on the freedom of individuals. Marx's prophecy that the state would wither away has been invalidated by history.[76] Hence, Du Bois early recognized the limitation of democratic centralism as a bold and new alternative historic bloc to democratic capitalism.[77]

During the 1930s Du Bois elaborated further on the applications of Marxism to the race question in America in an article entitled, "Marxism and the Negro Question." In this work, Du Bois traced the evolution of Marxism and pondered its utility to the race question in America. Du Bois posed the following question:

> How does the philosophy of Karl Marx apply today to colored labor? First of all colored labor has no common ground with white labor. No soviet technocrats would do more than exploit colored labor in order to raise the status of whites. No revolt of white proletariat could be started if its object was to make black workers their economic, political, and social equals. It is for this reason that American socialism for fifty years has been dumb on the Negro problem, and the communists cannot even get a respectful hearing in America unless they began by expelling Negroes. We can only say, as it seems to me, that the Marxian philosophy is a true diagnosis of the situation in Europe in the middle of the 19th Century despite some of its logical difficulties. But it must be modified in the United States of America and especially so far as the Negro group is concerned. The Negro is exploited to a degree that means poverty, crime, delinquency, and indigence. And that exploitation comes not from black capitalistic class but from white capitalists and equally from the white proletariat. His only defense is such internal organization as will protect him from both parties, and such practical economic insight as will prevent inside the race group any large development of capitalistic exploitation.[78]

Starting in the fifteenth century, most of the Third World became part of the world capitalist system, and this incorporation had global consequences in the cultural, diplomatic, economic, political, and racial arenas. Wherever they went with imperialism, the Spanish, Portuguese, Dutch, French, and English encountered millions of nonwhite people who appeared very different from themselves. Although Europeans brought Third World nations a number of medical, technological, and educational benefits, they destroyed many indigenous peoples who appeared very different from themselves. Other non-Westerners began adapting to the white Western world in order to survive. As a result, international relations increasingly became interracial relations, the result of the disparity of power between the North and the South, and a response to intense and explicit racial ideologies. According to Paul G. Lauren, a few courageous individuals fought for the human rights of Third World people.[79] However, the majority supported, participated in, or benefited from colonization, slavery, immigration restrictions, imperialism, and the propagation of racial ideologies. These people enslaved blacks, excluded the yellow, dispossessed the red[80] and brown, and subjugated them all. These developments occurred not only in the periphery of the world system but also at the center of metropolitan Europe as well. The active participation of many of its greatest philosophers and thinkers, explorers and soldiers, scientists and scholars, political leaders, statesmen, and diplomats, businessmen and investors, clerics and even missionaries is testimony to this.[81] Past events have influenced the Third World response to Northern hegemony in the postwar era. Third World leaders challenged their lower status in the world system and sought to democratize the decision-making processes in the world system.

Gernot Kohler introduced the term global apartheid into the discourse in 1978. Kohler hypothesized that the world system had become identical to the apartheid system in the Republic of South Africa. According to Kohler, the similarity manifested itself in all major dimensions of analysis – political, economic, military, cultural, psychological, social, racial, and legal. This modern world system, which he sees as emerging in the fifteenth and sixteenth centuries, transcends national boundaries. It continues to cripple the economic circuits of Third World societies and generates artificial underdevelopment, affecting both the North and the South in various domains other than economic.[82]

Global apartheid is a structure of the world system that combines political economy and racial antagonism. It is one in which a minority of whites occupy the pole of affluence, while a majority composed of other races occupies the pole of poverty; social integration of the two groups became extremely difficult through barriers of complexion, economic position, political boundaries, and other factors; economic development of the two groups is interdependent; the affluent white minority possesses a disproportionately large share of the system's political, economic, and military power. Thus, like its South African counterpart, global apartheid is a structure of extreme inequality in cultural, racial, social, political, economic, military, and legal terms.

Kohler also argues that as long as the global apartheid system remains unchallenged from below, that is, by the people themselves, the self-interest of the upper stratum, as defined in narrow wealth and power terms, is tied to the perpetuation of the status quo. According to Kohler, once an effective challenge emerges from below, the costs of maintaining global apartheid will begin to rise. When the lower stratum of the system becomes self-assertive and permanently "unruly," the interests of the upper stratum are no longer served by its defense of the status quo.[83] In the past, Third World leaders challenged their nations' subordination through the anti-slavery revolts, anti-colonialism movements, and more recently through their demands for a new international economic order. At every stage of Third World incorporation, these states have waged a vigorous battle against their lower position in the global hierarchy of wealth and poverty during each stage of its incorporation into the capitalist world system, beginning as early as the sixteenth century, but has refrained from being "permanently unruly," as a result of the high cost associated with such behavior. This study will also draw attention to the collaboration and coordination that have evolved within the upper stratum across both space and time in order to maintain its position of power in the system. This is part of a fundamental crisis that has plagued the capitalist world system since its inception, in particular with its ongoing need to find new and novel ways to maintain the political, economic, and social power of the North over the South.

This study asks the following questions: To what extent has the Third World been successful in transforming the structures of global apartheid since the end of the Second World War? To what extent has the pan-pigmentation-alist dimension of Third World solidarity brought about changes in the global racial order? Have these changes been dramatic or mere tokens? To what extent has the North-South political and economic division undergone dramatic structural transformation with the deployment of the pan-pigmentation-alist or pan-proletarian dimensions of Third World solidarity?

Successful international challenge to the global racial order occurs in the wake of global wars of hegemonic succession, crises and revolutions. Upheavals and crises, particularly if accompanied by significant shifts in power, can provide the opportunity for reassessment and change. The French and Haitian revolutions are but two examples. Slavery in Spanish America ended only when the massive Spanish empire fell prey to the first wave of decolonization. The countries of El Salvador, Guatemala, Honduras, Nicaragua, and Costa Rica abolished slavery in 1824, but only after Spain had suffered armed invasion from the French army on land, humiliations from the British navy at sea, uprisings from revolutionaries at home, and military defeats during the wars of independence in Central America. In 1833 Britain emancipated slaves in its colonies only after a dramatic shift in domestic power that evolved as nothing short of a revolution. France ended slavery in its colonial possessions only after the revolution in 1848. Civil and foreign wars contributed to the abolition of slavery in Colombia, Argentina, Venezuela, and Peru throughout the decade of the 1850s. Likewise, in the United States slaves were emancipated by the Thirteenth Amendment of 1865 only after the Civil War inflicted what remains to this day the most devastating conflict in this nation's history. Cuba and Brazil retained slavery until additional wars and struggles forced them to abolish this peculiar institution in the late 1880s.[84]

The global wars over hegemonic succession contributed to the development in the postwar period of centrifugal forces that undermined the global racial order. In the post-1945 period, the second wave of decolonization and nationalism in the Third World challenged many tenets of global apartheid. A new world order emerged in which Third World leaders sought to rule their own societies.

The rise of the United States to the position of hegemon created a major contradiction in its domestic race relations. Those who are located at the periphery within hegemonies are also the least integrated with their domestic political system. American policy makers had to come to terms with their domestic Third World population, i.e., African Americans, Native Americans, Asian Americans, and Latinos, in order to modernize their racial dominance. Traditional race relations became increasingly inappropriate under the new order. The African American struggle against Jim Crowism provided a framework for the struggle against America's racial regime by the dispossessed – the nonwhite population.[85]

The civil rights struggle had its origins in the post-Reconstruction era as African Americans began to devise new strategies to challenge their subordination. Black nationalism and bourgeois reformism emerged as two approaches to this struggle. Booker T. Washington, Marcus Garvey, and W. E. B. Du Bois emerged as champions of these divergent strategies. In the postwar era Dr. Martin Luther King, Jr., and Malcolm X challenged America's racial order through bourgeois reformism and black nationalism and ushered in a new racial dispensation.

African Americans' conceptualization of democracy and freedom has historically been at odds with the practice of white America, especially with reference to their experience of disenfranchisement and systematic segregation, and as economic outcasts. Still, African Americans have held fast to their vision of a democratic social order. African Americans visualize a society with unfettered access to political, economic, and social rights, regardless of race, class, or gender. African Americans have referred to this vision as freedom. This vision of freedom has become a nightmare for African Americans dwelling in capitalist America. As a result, African Americans have had to search within and without for solace as they face the realities of capitalist America.[86]

African Americans have had to struggle over the question of their identity since the slavery period, when they were referred to by their oppressors primarily on the basis of their skin color – in Spanish Negro means black. To be "black" or, more commonly, a "nigger" in a social order based upon exploitation was to be a prisoner of one's skin color and the victim of the idea of immutable inferiority conveyed by an entire nation of people. From the arrival of the first African Americans during the colonial period to the post-Reagan period, white Americans continue to identify their national collective interests with those of European geopolitics, culture, philosophy, and values, and have perceived "blackness" through the destructive and false social construction of "race," – implying permanent inferiority and dominance for African Americans. From the first Reconstruction era (1860–1880) to the Second Reconstruction period (1954–1980), African slaves and their descendants in the United States have never accepted their oppressors' definition of their identity. These former slaves always looked backward, recalling their African roots, which became articulated through language, syntax, verb tenses, and idiomatic expressions. They forged within this system of oppression a deep sense of cultural and national identity as Americans of African descent.[87] This shift toward the term "African American" also brings attention to ties between the domestic struggle for freedom and the global battle against racial capitalism and global apartheid in the Third World.

The rise of the United States and the former Soviet Union to superpower status led to a bipolar-structured world system. In the aftermath of the Second World War, the two superpowers renewed their competition for power and their mutual struggle to create a world order based on the competing ideologies of democratic capitalism and Marxist-Leninism. The world system entered a cold war as this political, economic, and ideological battle between these two diametrically opposed systems waged wars for the soul of humanity. The emergence of this new era known as the Cold War prevented the world system from evolving into a global caste system with the North – including the East and West – at the top, and the South – the Third World – at the bottom. The anti-imperialism of Marxist-Leninism led the Soviet bloc to challenge capitalism and colonialism and to champion antiracialism. The Cold War divided the North along ideological lines and prevented polarization along the racial divide. The end of the Cold War era has launched a new era of global apartheid as the interests of the Northeast and Northwest converge and the former Soviet Union and the Warsaw Pact nations abandon the anti-imperialism of Marxist-Leninism.

Through an examination of Third World solidarity, we can analyze the divergent methods employed by these actors to change the set of unequal power relations between core, peripheral, and semiperipheral states in the world system. The theory and practice of Third World solidarity can be understood as the quest by elites in the periphery and semiperiphery to challenge the unequal power position between the North and the South from a political, economic, cultural, and racial perspective.

Racial capitalism as a model of systemic change in the world system operates from the neo-Gramscian conceptualization of civil society which includes a broader basis of political culture centered around identity and ideology. The traditional American belief with reference to possessive individualism, anticommunism, and Manifest Destiny became the driving force behind the emergence of not only the Pax Americana but additional strategies aimed at revitalizing American hegemony and structural dominance in the world economy since the 1970s. This way of thinking, which accompanied the American rise to globalism has had two ramifications for the global community. It has helped to provide a cultural context for the postwar era in the West, and its mainly liberal economic principles serve as organizing concepts for the debates between, and practices of, important political decision-makers from a range of countries. Thus, elements of legitimization and ideology interacted with a deeper epistemological level to create a global synergy of ideas beneficial to the outward extension or maintenance of American power. American policy makers have been successful in building a broad-based consensus of beliefs, values, and ideology to support its position as hegemon. Thus, most of the strategies, agendas, questions, and prescriptions to combat antisystemic alliance systems and states, ranging from the Russians and the Warsaw Pact of Nations to would-be Third World challengers from Vietnam to Iraq, have been American-centered since the end of the Second World War. The global political economy still operates primarily from a neoliberal (American) framework. Efforts by Third World leaders to dramatically redefine North-South relations have driven their divergent approaches to solidarity.

Third World solidarity first evolved as an issue of race, then progressed to a shared determination to avoid Cold War alliances, and is now based on a shared interest in terminating poverty and inequality. Between the mid-1950s and late 1990s Third World solidarity has matured from pan-pigmentationalism (solidarity based on race) to pan-proletarianism (solidarity based on economic disadvantages). As the twentieth century draws to an end, the polarization of race in the North may be ushering in a new era of global apartheid. Since the emergence of the Third World as an important force in the world system, this collectivity of states has been plagued by the twin pressures of individual state interest and solidarity. In spite of these contradictory tensions, a community of interest has managed to develop among Third World states.[88] Their quest to change the set of unequal power relations between the North and the South has been an important catalyst for such community-building.

NOTES

1. J. Bandyopadhyaya, "Non-Aligned Movement and International Relations" *India Quarterly* 33, no. 2 (1977): pp. 137–64; S. Bushan, *Non-Alignment: Legacy of Nehru* (New Delhi: Progressive People's Sector Publication, 1976); C. V. Crabb, Jr., *The Elephant and the Grass: A Study of Non-Alignment* (New York: Praeger, 1965).

2. A. A. Mazrui, "The New Interdependence," in *Beyond Dependency: The Developing World Speaks Out,* ed. G. Urb and V. Kallab (Washington, DC: Overseas Developing Council, 1975), pp. 38–56; A. A. Mazrui, "The Changing Focus Of Non-Alignment," *Alternatives* 3, no. 2 (December 1977); M. Handel, *Weak States in the International System* (London: Frank Cass, 1981).

3. A. Bergesen and R. Schoenberg, "Long Waves of Colonial Expansion and Contraction, 1415–1969," in *Studies of the Modern World System,* ed. A. Bergesen (New York: Academic Press, 1980), pp. 231–277; T. Hopkins and I. Wallerstein, eds., *Processes in the World System* (Beverly Hills, CA: Sage Publications, 1980).

4. D. G. Becker, et al., *Postimperialism: International Capitalism in the Late Twentieth Century* (Boulder, CO: Lynne Rienner, 1987); R. Munck, *Politics and Dependency in the Third World: The Latin American Perspective* (London: Zed Books, 1974); P. Evans, *Dependent*

Development: The Alliance of Multinationals, the State, and Local Capital (Princeton, NJ: Princeton University Press, 1979).

5. Divergent spatial dimension refers to the changing geographical location of the international division of labor. In the past, the Northwest has been the center of industrial production. Starting in the 1970s newly industrializing countries such as South Korea, Taiwan, Mexico, and Brazil emerged as key production centers in the changing global division of labor.

6. Taiwan, Hong Kong, South Korea, and Singapore.

7. Argentina, Brazil, and Mexico.

8. South Africa and Zimbabwe.

9. See Jeffrey E. Garten, *A Cold Peace: America, Japan, and Germany and the Struggle for Supremacy* (New York: Times Books, 1992).

10. See Ronald Segal, The Race War. (New York: Bantam Books, 1967); George Shepard, *The Study of Race in American Foreign Policy and International Relations* (Denver, CO:University of Denver Press, 1969); Paul G. Lauren, Jr., *Power and Prejudice: The Politics and Diplomacy of Racial Discrimination* (Boulder,CO: Westview Press, 1988) Ali A. Mazrui, *Cultural Forces in World Politics* (London: Heinemann., 1990).

11. A. Bergesen and R. Schoenberg, "Long Waves," pp. 231–77.

12. Ibid.

13. See R. O. Keohane and J. S. Nye, eds., *Transnational Relations in World Politics* (Cambridge, MA: Harvard University Press, 1972); R. Barnet and R. Mueller, ed., *Global Reach: The Power of Multinational Corporations* (New York: Simon and Schuster, 1974); S. Brown, *New Forces in World Politics* (Washington D. C.: Brookings Institute, 1974); R. O. Keohane and J. S Nye, eds., *Power and Interdependence: World Politics in Transition* (Boston: Little, Brown, 1977).

14. J. Levy, "War and the Great Powers" in *Contending Approaches to World Systems,* ed. W. R. Thompson, Jr. (Beverly Hills, CA: Sage Publications (1983), pp. 183–202.

15. Ibid., pp. 183–202.

16. Ibid., p. 186.

17. See Muhammed Ayoob, "Security in the Third World: The Worm About to Turn," *International Affairs* 60, no. 1 (1983): pp. 41–51; M. Ayoob, *Regional Security in the Third World* (London: Croom Helm, 1983); Edward E. Azar and Chung-in Moon, "Third World National Security: Toward A New Conceptual Framework," *International Interaction* 11, no. 2 (1984): pp. 103–35; Nicole Ball, *Security and Economy in the Third World* (Princeton: Princeton University, 1988); Barry Buzan, *People, States and Fear: The National Security Problem in International Relations* (Chapel Hill, NC: University of North Carolina Press, 1983); and *People, States and Fear: An Agenda for International Security Studies in Post-Cold War Era* (New York: Harvester Wheatsheaf, 1991); Alexander Johnston, "Weak States and National Security," *Review of International Studies* 17, no. 2 (1991): pp. 146–77; Edward Kolodziej and Robert A. Harkavy, *Security Problems in Developing Countries* (Lexington, MA: Lexington Books, 1982); and Caroline Thomas, *In Search of Security: The Third World in International Relations* (Boulder, CO: Lynne Rienner, 1987).

18. Brian L. Job, "The Insecurity Dilemma: National Regime and State Security in the Third World," in *The Insecurity Dilemma: National Security of Third World States,* ed. Brian L. Job (Boulder, CO: Lynne Rienner, 1992), p. 12.

19. Barry Buzan, *People, States, and Fear: An Agenda for International Security Studies in the Post-Cold War Era* (New York: Harvester Wheatsheaf, 1992), pp. 19–20.

20. Brian L. Job, ed., *The Insecurity Dilemma: National Security of Third World States* (Boulder, CO: Lynne Rienner Publishers, 1992), p. 17.

21. Joel Midgal, *Strong Societies and Weak States: State-Society Relations and State Capabilities in the Third World.*(Princeton: Princeton University Press, 1988).

22. Brian L. Job, "The Insecurity Dilemma: National Regime and State Security in the Third World," in *The Insecurity Dilemma: National Security of Third World States,* ed. Brian L. Job (Boulder CO: Lynne Rienner Publishers, 1991), pp. 17–18.

23. See Chapter 7 in this work; Darryl C. Thomas and Ali A. Mazrui, "Africa's Post-Cold War Demilitarisation: Domestic and Global Causes," *Journal of International Affairs* 46, no. 1 (1992): pp. 157–74.

24. S. Brown, *New Forces in World Politics,* p. 110.

25. C. F. Bergsten et al., "The Threat from the Third World," *Foreign Affairs* No. 11 (Summer 1973): pp. 102–124. R. N. Cooper, "Trade Policy in Foreign Policy" *Foreign Policy* No. 9 (Winter 1972–73): pp. 18–36. D. Blake and R. S. Walters, *The Politics of Global Economic Relations* (Englewood Cliffs, New Jersey: Prentice Hall, 1976). R. O. Keohane and J. S. Nye, *Power and Interdependence: World Politics in Transition* (Boston:Little, Brown, 1977).

26. Examples of this scholarship may be found in the following: Stephen Krasner, "Regimes and Limits of Realism: Regimes as Autonomous Variables," *International Organization* 36, no. 2 (1982): pp.497–510; *International Regimes* (Ithaca, NY: Cornell University Press, 1983); and *Structural Conflict: The Third World Against Global Liberalism* (Berkeley, CA: University of California Press, 1985). Kenneth N. Waltz, *The Theory of International Politics* (Reading, MA: Addison-Wesley, 1979); "Reflections on Theory of International Politics: A Response to My Critics," in *Neorealism and Its Critic ,* ed. Robert O. Keohane (New York: Columbia University Press, 1986), pp. 322–47. William R. Thompson, Jr., "Cycles, Capabilities, and War: An Ecumenical View," in *Contending Approaches to World System,* ed. William R. Thompson (Beverly Hills, CA: Sage Publications, 1983), pp. 141–164; "Succession Crises in the Global Political System: A Test of the Transition Model," in *Crises in the World System,* ed. Albert Bergesen (Beverly Hills, CA: Sage Publication, 1983); "Uneven Economic Growth, Systemic Challenges, and Global War," *International Studies Quarterly* 27 (September, 1983): pp. 341–55; and *Global War* (Columbia, SC: University of South Carolina Press, 1988). Robert Gilpin, *War and Change in World Politics* (Cambridge, MA: Cambridge University Press, 1981); and *Political Economy of International Relations* (Princeton, NJ: Princeton University Press, 1987). Robert W. Cox, "Social Forces, States, and World Order: Beyond International Relations Theory" *Millennium: Journal of International Studies* 10, no. 2 (1981): pp. 126–155; "Production and Hegemony: Toward A Political Economy of World Order," in *The Emerging International Economic Order,* ed. H. K. Jacobson and D. Sidjanski (Beverly Hills, CA: Sage Publications, 1982), pp. 37–58; "Gramsci, Hegemony and International Relations: An Essay in Method," *Millennium: Journal of International Studies* 12, no. 2 (1983): pp. 162–75; and *Production, Power, and World Order: Social Forces in the Making of History* (New York: Columbia University Press, 1987). Robert O. Keohane, *After Hegemony: Cooperation and Discord in the World Political Economy* (Princeton, NJ: Princeton University Press, 1984); "Theory of World Politics: Structural Realism and Beyond," in *Neorealism and Its Critics,* ed. Robert Keohane (New York: Columbia University Press, 1986); and *International Institutions and State Power: Essays in International Relations Theory* (Boulder, CO: Lynne Rienner Publishing, 1989). This list does not exhaust the quality or quantity of scholarship emerging from this new theoretical framework.

27. Analysts usually refer to the United Province (Dutch), Great Britain, and the United States as hegemonic powers.

28. A. F. K. Organski and J. Kugler, *The War Ledger* (Chicago: University of Chicago

Press, 1980).

29. R. Gilpin, *War and Change in World Politics* (New York: Cambridge University Press, 1981).

30. P. Kennedy, *The Rise and Fall of Great Powers: Economic Change and Military Conflict from 1500 to 2000* (New York: Random House, 1987).

31. J. S. Nye, *Bound To Lead: The Changing Nature of American Power* (New York: Basic Books, 1990), p. 7.

32. W. Goldfrank, *World System of Capitalism: Theory and Methodology* (Beverly Hills: Sage Publications, 1979); I. M. Wallerstein, *The Modern World System, I: Capitalist Agriculture and the Origins of the European World-Economy in the Sixteenth Century* (New York: Academic Press, 1974); "The Rise and Future Demise of the World Capitalist System: Concepts for Comparative Analysis," *Comparative Studies in Society and History* 16, no. 4 (1979): pp. 387–415; *The Capitalist World-Economy* (Cambridge: Cambridge University Press, 1979); *The Modern World System II: Mercantilism and the Consolidation of the European World-Economy, 1600–1750* (New York: Academic Press, 1980); *The Politics of the World-Economy* (Cambridge: Cambridge University Press, 1984); *The Modern World System III: The Second Era of Great Expansion of the Capitalist World-Economy, 1730–1840* (New York: Academic Press, 1988); "Three Instances of Hegemony in the History of the Capitalist-System," in *The Evolution of International Political Economy: A Reader,* ed. George T. Crane and A. Amawi (New York: Oxford University Press 1991); *Geopolitics and Geoculture* (New York: Cambridge University Press, 1991). T. K. Hopkins and I. Wallerstein with the Research Working Group on Cyclical Rhythms and Secular Trends, "Cyclical Rhythms and Secular Trends of the Capitalist World-Economy: Some Premises, Hypotheses and Questions," *Review* 2, no. 4 (1979): pp. 483–500. T. K. Hopkins and I. Wallerstein, *Process of the World System* (Beverly Hills, CA: Sage Publications, 1980); *World System Analysis* (Beverly Hills, CA: Sage Publications, 1982).

33. J. A. Schumpeter, *Business Cycles: A Theoretical and Historical Analysis of the Capitalist Process* (London: McGraw-Hill, 1939).

34. A. Bergesen, *Studies of the Modern World System.*

35. G. Arrighi, "Custom and Innovation: Long Waves and Stages of Capitalist Development," paper presented at the International Workshop, "Technological and Social Factors in Long Term Fluctuation," Certosa di Pontignamo, Siena (December 15–17, 1986).

36. S. Gill, *American Hegemony and the Trilateral Commission* (New York: Cambridge University Press, 1990).

37. A. A. Mazrui, *Cultural Forces in World Politics* (Portsmouth, NH: Heinemann, 1990), p. 52.

38. S. P. Huntington, "The Clash of Civilizations?" *Foreign Affairs* 72, no. 3 (1993): pp. 22–49.

39. B. Bornschier and C. Chase-Dunn, *Transnational Corporations and Underdevelopment* (New York: Praeger Publishers, 1985). F. Cardosa, and E. Faletto, *Dependency and Development in Latin America* (Berkeley, CA: University of California Press, 1979). A. G. Frank, *Capitalism and Underdevelopment in Latin America* (New York: Monthly Review Press, 1969). C. Clark and J. Lemco, *State and Development* (New York: E. J. Brill, 1988).

40. J. G. Ruggie, *The Antinomies of Interdependence: National Welfare and the International Division of Labor* (New York: Columbia University Press, 1983).

41. Ibid.

42. S. Gill, *American Hegemony and the Trilateral Commission,* p. 46.

43. R. W. Cox, "Social Forces, States, and World Orders: Beyond International Rela-

tions Theory," *Millennium: Journal of International Studies* 10, no. 2 (1981): pp. 126–155.

44. R. W. Cox, *Production and World Order: Social Forces in the Making of History* (New York: Columbia University Press, 1987), p. 261.

45. R. W. Cox, "Gramsci, Hegemony and International Relations: An Essay on Method," *Millennium: Journal of International Studies* 12, no. 2 (1983): p. 169.

46. Quoted in D. P. Rapkin, *World Leadership and Hegemony* (Boulder: Lynne Rienner, 1991), p. 4

47. See Robert C. Cox, "Structural Issues of Global Economic Governance: Implications for Europe," in *Gramsci, Historical Materialism and International Relations,* ed. Stephen Gill (Cambridge, U.K.: Cambridge University Press, 1993)

48. S. Gill, *Gramsci, Historical Materialism and International Relations,* p. 9.

49. A. W. Cafruny, "A Gramscian Concept of Declining Hegemony: Stages of U.S. Power and the Evolution of International Economic Relations," in *World Leadership and Hegemony,* ed. David P. Rapkin (Boulder, CO: Westview Press, 1990), p. 104.

50. Ibid., p.105.

51. J. Femia, *Gramsci's Political Thought: Hegemony, Consciousness, and the Revolutionary Process* (Oxford: Clarendon Press, 1981), p. 47.

52. A. W. Cafruny, "A Gramscian Concept," p. 106.

53. Ibid., pp. 106–107.

54. O. C. Cox, *Capitalism as a System* (New York: Monthly Review Press, 1964).

55. See C. Robinson, ed., *Black Marxism: The Making of the Black Radical Tradition* (London: Zed Books, 1990).

56. Ronald Takaki, *Iron Cages: Race and Culture in Nineteenth Century America* (New York: Oxford University Press, 1990).

57. Cedric Robinson, *Black Marxism,* p. 2.

58. Ibid., p. 4.

59. P. G. Lauren, *Power and Prejudice,* p. 8.

60. Ibid., p. 18.

61. C. Robinson, *Black Marxism,* p. 4.

62. A. A. Mazrui, *The Africans: A Triple Heritage* (Boston: Little, Brown and Company, 1986), p.110.

63. M. Marable, *Black American Politics: From Marches on Washington to Jesse Jackson* (London: Verso New Left Books, 1985), p. 5.

64. B. M. Mugabane, *Ties That Bind: African-American Consciousness of Africa* (Trenton, NJ: African World Press, 1987), p. 5.

65. Ibid.

66. W. E. B. Du Bois, *Black Reconstruction in America, 1860–1880* (New York: Athenium, 1975), pp. 15–16.

67. C. Robinson, *Black Marxism,* pp. 280–81.

68. W. E. B. Du Bois, *Black Reconstruction in America,* pp. 14–16.

69. Ibid., p. 15.

70. C. Robinson, *Black Marxism,* p. 277.

71. S. Stuckey, *Slave Culture: Nationalist Theory and the Foundations of Black America* (New York: Oxford University Press, 1987), p. 291.

72. W .E. B. Du Bois, *Dusk of Dawn* (New York: Shocken, 1940), p. 205.

73. S. Robinson, *Black Marxism,* p. 290.

74. W. E. B. Du Bois, "Judging Russia," in *The Seventh Son: The Thought and Writings of W. E. B. Du Bois,* ed. Julius Lester (New York: Random House, 1971), p. 270.

75. C. Robinson, *Black Marxism,* pp. 320–21.

76. W. E. B. Du Bois, "A Pageant in Seven Decades," Convocation, Atlanta University, in *W. E. B. Du Bois Speaks,* ed. P. Foner (New York: Pathfinder Press, 1970), pp. 65–66.

77. For an elaboration on the concept of historical blocs see R. W. Cox, *Production, Power, and World Order: Social Forces in the Making of History* (New York: Columbia University Press, 1987); O. C. Cox, *Capitalism As A System* (New York: Monthly Review Press, 1964); and W. E. B. Du Bois, *Black Reconstruction in America 1860–1880* (New York: Meridian Books, 1964), especially Chapters 1–2.

78. W. E. B. Du Bois, "Karl Marx and the Negro," in *The Thought and Writings of W E. B. Du Bois: The Seventh Son,* ed. Julius Lester, pp. 294–295.

79. P. G. Lauren, *Power and Prejudice,* p. 42.

80. Ibid., p. 43.

81. Ibid., pp. 42–43.

82. G. Kohler, *Global Apartheid,* World Models Project Working Paper No. 7, (1978), pp. 3–4.

83. G. Kohler, *Global Apartheid,* p. 3.

84. P. G. Lauren, *Power and Prejudice.*

85. By the struggle of America's racial regime we refer to the battle against segregation and second-class citizenship that most African Americans, Asian Americans, Latinos, and Native Americans endured prior to the Civil Rights Movement of the 1960s. We also are referring to their efforts to create a truly racial democracy in America.

86. M. Manning, *Race, Reform, and Rebellion: The Second Reconstruction in Black America, 1945–1990* (Jackson, MI: University of Mississippi Press, 1991), p. 229.

87. Ibid.

88. D. C. Thomas, "Evolving Patterns of Third World Solidarity." *Transafrica Forum* 4, no. 4 (Summer 1987): p. 75.

2

Third World Challenges to Global Apartheid in the Post-Cold War Era

Third World solidarity centered first on issues of race or color, geography, and culture as those who served as the "grave diggers of the capitalist world system"[1] sought to recapture their lost dignity and sovereignty. Racial sovereignty and regional cooperation among the new states of the Third World evolved over time as but one response among many to both imperialism and the inferior status that people and nations of color assumed upon their integration into the capitalist world system. In light of this, pan-pigmentationalism emerged as a major motivating force to build solidarity among the colonized peoples during the first and second waves of decolonization. Initially, the new states of Latin America sought to build a Pan-American confederation in order to protect their newly won sovereignty.[2] Early pioneers such as Jose de San Martin and Simon Bolivar were recipients of military and moral support from Haiti, the first black republic in the Western Hemisphere. The Haitians provided assistance on the condition that these "Latin revolutionaries" would end slavery as one of their first acts as sovereign nations. Hence, race, culture, geography, and challenges to the models of capital accumulation played a critical role in the early development of Third World solidarity. These lessons were not lost on the new Third World leaders during the second wave of decolonization.

At the end of the Second World War, the international community became divided into blocs and groups. Divisions typically formed along cultural, diplomatic, economic, ideological, military, racial, and religious lines. Superpowers established two conflicting Cold War coalitions.[3] Ideological and security issues were the driving forces behind the new postwar alliances. The North Atlantic Treaty Organization (NATO) alliance urged the world community to adopt capitalism as the most viable economic program and Western democracy as the most successful political model, while the Warsaw Pact preferred socialism as the most desirable economic program and communism as the most applicable political model. Both superpowers embarked on a global campaign to recruit the new states in Asia, Africa, and the Caribbean into their camps. The two superpowers dominated the emerging world order.

The growing antagonism between the United States and the Soviet Union during the postwar period had a profound effect on the world system. The Cold War restructured policies and goals of other states around the superpower rivalry. Security became a world issue. Since only the superpowers had the economic and military wherewithal to accumulate a nuclear arsenal, they became the guardians of security on a global scale.

At the same time, the European imperial order withered in Asia, Africa, and the Caribbean, leaving the Third World as an independent force. These new states began to organize their own blocs and groupings and to assert their cultural, diplomatic, economic, racial, religious, and security concerns. This development increased the diversity of political forces in the world economy, leading to profound effects on the entire international system.

Third World states have chosen sharply divergent strategies of economic development. Some of these actors – the Ivory Coast, Kenya, Brazil, and South Korea – have sought economic development within the framework of capitalism. Others have opted for indigenous brands of socialism: Chile under Salvador Allende, Cuba, Tanzania, Sri Lanka, and Ethiopia. Have these important differences also led some Third World states to pursue divergent approaches to solidarity? Has the strength of their similar environmental factors and the complexity of the issues led these actors, despite their different economic development strategies, to strive for similar goals in their pursuit of solidarity?

HISTORICAL DEVELOPMENT OF AFRO-ASIANISM

Starting at the end of the Second World War, the Southern Hemisphere began the transition from empire to nationhood. From the middle of the nineteenth century to the Second World War, most of the states in Africa, Asia, and the Caribbean, with the exception of Japan, Liberia, Ethiopia, and Haiti,[4] had been subjected to European colonial and semicolonial domination. To overthrow this domination, solidarity and cooperation among the people of these highly divergent regions were essential. In practice, they evolved slowly. The Bandung Conference in 1955 reinforced the Third World's cherished dream of Afro-Asian solidarity. For ten years, Afro-Asianism remained a dynamic force in the world system. Then, in 1965, cancellation of the Second Bandung Conference signaled the decline of Afro-Asianism as a major force in the world system.

Nevertheless, the origin of the idea of cooperative diplomacy between African and Asian leaders predates the Bandung conference. Asian and African nationalism contributed to the development of Afro-Asian sentiments while the First and Second World Wars were under way.[5] During these years, the Afro-

Asian states attempted to institutionalize such concepts as Pan-Africanism, Pan-Arabism, and Pan-Asianism. World War I and II were both examples of global conflicts over hegemony. These global militarized conflicts also contributed to the death of white supremacy among Asian and African people. They were critical in the rising consciousness of the colored people.[6]

NATIONALISM IN AFRICA AND ASIA

Although a thorough analysis of the rise of nationalism in Africa and Asia is outside the scope of this study, a brief review is important to an understanding of the historical development of Afro-Asianism. Initially, nationalist activities in both Africa and Asia were conducted primarily by small, well-educated elites who owed their existence to the colonial system. European colonialism had replaced traditional indigenous agriculture with a system that produced cash crops such as coffee, cotton, sisal, tea, and tobacco. Communal land became private under colonialism. A migration from rural to urban areas supported the emergence of new classes and integrated the colonies into the European imperial networks. New classes emerged: a rural bourgeoisie and an urban proletariat.[7] Colonial bureaucrats encouraged the development of a bourgeois stratum among the colonized as an answer to their labor needs in the colonial bureaucracy. This new stratum became an important component of the colonial bureaucratic apparatus.

Contact between the colonial bureaucrats and the African and Asian bourgeoisie was more pronounced. While the peasants in Africa and Asia had very infrequent interaction with colonial authorities, intellectuals and professionals that comprised these strata became socialized into the colonial language, culture, and method of control. Over time this new class grew to resent the authoritative structure of the colonial system because it got in the way of their upward mobility. The same political structure that attempted to assimilate them became their antagonist.

The lack of social mobility within the colonial structure contributed to the development of nationalism. Through their education in the colonial world and the metropolis, this same bourgeoisie internalized European egalitarian values. However, the colonial system proved to be a mockery of such values, since the indigenous populations in Africa and Asia had no rights that the Europeans recognized. In settler regimes – Algeria, Kenya, Namibia, and Zimbabwe – European populations retained a monopoly over power.

The first response to colonial authoritarianism was a demand for cultural autonomy. Educated Africans took refuge in their traditional values as an ideology of resistance. The development of *negritude* in French West Africa is an example of cultural nationalism. Blacks in French-speaking territories also found inspiration from two giants of Pan-Africanism, Du Bois and Garvey,[8] and began to express their newly found racial pride under the banner of negritude. The major proponents of negritude reached out to the black world, stressing their common African roots, unique cultural contributions, and historical achievements.[9] They encouraged their followers to recognize, in an objective fashion, these special accomplishments and feel subjectively the soul of their race.[10] In English-speaking Africa, the *African personality* evolved as an expression of the soul of the black race. Both of these tendencies represented an African rejection of the cultural imperialism of the North. Africans were reclaiming their humanity and redefining themselves within the context of their own cultural identity.

In Asia there were similar developments. In Vietnam as well as in China, Confucian scholars criticized their kings and emperors who had given in to foreign powers, and dreamed of restoring sovereigns worthy of "the mandate of heaven."[11] In Muslim countries, the Islamic community preached loyalty to traditional religion and way of life. In their quest for autonomy in the colonial situation, the African and Asian bourgeoisie spurned Western cultural practices. They began to emphasize their own indigenous history and culture. The precolonial African and Asian cultures were many and varied dynamic seedbeds of regional solidarity and diversity. Developing in different socioeconomic environments, subject to different historical experiences, the world of precolonial cultures was multidimensional. The colonized in Africa and Asia launched a challenge to the hegemonic cultural blanket of the colonizers by rejecting the Eurocentric conceptualization of their identity.[12] Cultural nationalism represented an attack on the colonial order, but it was not a sufficient strategy to overthrow the colonial order. However, these movements provided the ideological basis for Afro-Asian leaders to challenge Northern political and cultural hegemony in the postwar era.[13]

During the early stages of the anticolonial struggle, the period 1900 to 1945, there was very little interaction between Africa and Asia. Their mutual isolation was partly the result of a European imperialistic policy. Empire builders kept a careful watch on their colonies and did not encourage or provide avenues for interaction among the colonized. On the other hand, interaction between the colonizer and the colonized became the first priority among European policy makers. Leaders in the metropolitan arenas sought to integrate the colonial economy, making their colonies mere appendages to their domestic market. Policy makers in Europe kept a tight rein on the colonies, especially in the trade and commercial arena. Infrastructure for communication and transportation reinforced these imperial networks. Most railroads took goods to the coast; communication equipment generally accommodated the metropolitan linkages to the colonies rather than South-South interactions.

In the early years, nationalism in Asia and Africa was primarily an indigenous force. Nationalists, preoccupied with their own enemies (or even fighting the same enemies), were too busy trying to survive to devote any energy toward unity.[14] In light of this, African and Asian nationalists pursued divergent paths toward liberation and did not initiate collaborative activities outside their own nations.

EUROPEAN INFLUENCES

Despite attempts on the part of European countries to keep their colonies isolated, certain policies undermined this objective. A number of the children from the upper class and the rising middle class in Africa and Asia went to Europe and acquired higher education to ensure continued social mobility.[15] European policy makers expected these neophytes to become totally absorbed in Western culture and thus eclipse their own traditions. The by-product of such socialization would be an efficient cog in the colonial machinery. In Paris, London, and Brussels, however, Afro-Asian elites discovered an intellectual affinity with Europe's traditions of radical political thought. The theories of Karl Marx and Harold Laski shaped the political orientation of these African and Asian nationalists. In Paris, a predominating communist influence spread among young African, Asian, and West Indian students who were later to become national leaders. At one time or another, Ho Chi Minh, Felix Hou-phuet-Boigny, Aimé Cesaire, Franz Fanon, and C. L. R. James were all part of this group.[16] In London, Harold Laski tutored Jomo Kenyatta, Kwame Nkrumah, and Krishna Menon at the London School of Economics.[17]

The Russian Revolution also provided African and Asian nationalists with an ideological weapon against Western imperialism: the writings of V. I. Lenin. In his celebrated treatise, *Imperialism: The Highest Stage of Capitalism,* Lenin emphasized the underconsumption thesis originally posed by J. A. Hobson in *Imperialism: A Study,* and went a step further to characterize imperialism as a stage in capitalist development rather than one foreign policy option among many.[18] According to Lenin, this form of imperialism created new interactions among states in ways now referred to as North-South relations. In their quest for new spheres of economic influence, conflict among capitalist states increased, creating an era of rival imperialism. Lenin's work has been criticized in the West for its excessive dogma and economic determinism. Nevertheless, his analysis of capitalism provided Afro-Asian nationalists with an ideological weapon with which to wage their attack on Western imperialism. It was in the European theater that the seeds for increased Afro-Asian cooperation and collaboration were planted.

On February 27, 1927, the first meeting of the Congress of Oppressed Nationalists took place in Brussels. This proved to be a milestone in the evolution of Afro-Asian solidarity. African and Asian nationalists met at Brussels for the first time and laid the foundations for future communication. Approximately 200 delegates representing 134 organizations, as well as 300 visitors from India, China, Syria, Arabia (Palestine and Egypt), Korea, Indonesia, Indo-China, Annam, North and South Africa, North and South America, and almost every European state attended. Several Afro-Asian nationalists showed up at this gathering: Jawaharlal Nehru, Ho Chi Minh, Mohammed Hatta, Madame Sun Yat-sen and Leopold Senghor.[19]

The Congress of Oppressed Nationalists demonstrated the importance of cooperation and continuing interaction among African and Asian nationalists. It played a key role in acknowledging the fact that these nationalists were fighting the same enemy – imperialism – and reinforcing the importance of unity and solidarity.

This initial meeting of the congress produced forty resolutions, of which the most significant from an Asian perspective were the joint declarations by the Indian and Chinese delegations. These groups resolved to coordinate their struggles so that they could fight British imperialism on two fronts. Their manifesto ended with this statement: "The oppressed and enslaved nations, which represent the overwhelming majority of mankind, like the proletariat, can conquer the world, the world of the future. Oppressed Peoples and Oppressed Nations Unite!"[20]

ASIAN INFLUENCES

At the same time that anti-imperialism grew as a political force in Africa and Asia, sentiments in support of Pan-Africanism and Pan-Asianism surged as well. In Asia, Pan-Asianism gathered momentum, in part, from the Japanese victory over the Russians in 1905. As a result of this, elites in the rest of Asia became more self-confident in their struggle to eliminate foreign rule. Under Sun Yat-sen's leadership, a Pan-Asian front evolved out of the militant Black Dragon Secret Society,[21] which played a dynamic role in China's politics, especially with reference to Pan-Asianism.

Japanese nationalists, influenced by the militancy of the Black Dragon Secret Society, also developed Pan-Asian philosophies. In 1924, they began to seek ways to develop a similar association for a united Asia. The Association for a Greater Asia emerged two years later at the conference of Asian people held in Nagasaki in 1926. Delegations from several nations attended this conference, including India, China, and Korea. The Indian delegation was very strong.[22] New Delhi began to play an important role in Asian affairs before the end of colonial rule.

Indian nationalists also rallied around the cause of Pan-Asianism. Initially envisioned as an Asian Federation by Aga Khan in 1918, the concept became an important element in the Indian National Congress's ideology in the years that preceded the Nagasaki conference. In his presidential address of 1927, M. A. Ansari put forth the idea of an Asian Federation.[23] He conceptualized the Asian Federation as the only force that could check the forces of European imperialism and capitalism. In 1928, the Indian National Congress set up a working committee to establish contacts with other Asian countries – China, Japan, and Korea – as part of an effort to establish the first Pan-Asian Federation in India by 1930. At the same time, the congress began its own programs of mass action.[24]

The Japanese victory over Tsarist Russia provided a catalyst for Asian nationalism and created a favorable environment for Pan-Asianism. By the

1930s, a number of events had cast a shadow over Japanese Pan-Asianism. Starting in 1931, Japan began its long journey toward militarism and warfare. The Japanese launched an all-out attack on China, and eventually, the United States at Pearl Harbor. This decision to invest in an escalation of militarism led to the conquest and subsequent occupation of Southeast Asia during the Second World War. From 1931 onward, Japanese policy toward China became increasingly aggressive, developing into a full-scale war and, by 1938, the rape of Nanking.[25] As the Japanese policy of military aggression increased, other Asian nationalists increasingly questioned the Japanese conceptualization of Pan-Asianism, characterized by the expression "Asia for Asians."

Japanese military success undermined Western power in Asia. Their swift victories over the British in both Singapore and Burma, and over the Dutch in the Indies, and their defeat of the Americans in the Philippines had a lasting significance for the rest of Asia. Racial consciousness and Asian nationalism grew as a result of Japan's military ventures; at the same time, such triumphs demolished the myth of Western invincibility.

Even though these Japanese victories led to the creation of the Greater East Asian Co-Prosperity Sphere, some fundamental differences between the theory and practice of Pan-Asianism also emerged.[26] Japan's Pan-Asianism, anti-Westernism, and geopolitical strategy helped to unify its broad territory along ideological lines. The Japanese viewed the establishment of the East Asian Co-Prosperity Sphere as an act of liberation, freeing the colonial people of Asia and the Pacific from centuries of Western domination.[27] The East Asian Co-Prosperity Sphere gave the Japanese a framework within which they could institutionalize their ideas concerning Pan-Asianism and challenge Western hegemony in this zone of the world system.

Theoretically, Japan and all of the other Asian countries were equal and independent partners. Each territory had a constitution. These newly created governments then agreed to sign treaties with Japan under the shadow of Japanese military power in the region. Economically and strategically, the Greater East Asian Co-Prosperity Sphere became increasingly integrated. Each section would contribute to the general welfare of the whole and thus create an economically self-sufficient zone. The Japanese would supply the capital and technology (with the yen as the common currency), while the other Asian partners would develop agriculture and both heavy and light industries. In 1942, the Japanese established a ministry of East Asian affairs to administer this program. In many respects it was as if the Japanese sought to create their own North-South division of labor in East Asia.

In 1943, the Assembly of Greater East Asiatic Nations convened in Tokyo. The leaders of China, India, Thailand, Burma, and Manchukuo attended. At this conference they struck a positive chord for Asian nationalism by collectively challenging the Western allies' war objectives in Asia.[28]

Despite its many positive qualities, the East Asian Co-Prosperity Sphere experienced intraregional conflict. The Japanese were able to keep the coalition intact only by deploying military force. Japanese promises of freedom to Burma, Singapore, Korea, Formosa, and the other members of this coercive coalition remained empty until the war against Westerners intensified. Thus, the scheme soon lost its ideological and racial appeal to the other member countries throughout Southeast Asia and the Pacific. Asians found that a Japanese oppressor had replaced the colonial version. As the Second World War accelerated, and the conflict between the Japanese and the Western powers intensified, the tensions within the East Asian Co-Prosperity Sphere substantially increased. Japan fulfilled its promise of independence to various member countries. To do this, Japan employed intellectuals and nationalists from various member countries as indigenous collaborators in order to maintain its rule. People engaged in espionage activities and trained as soldiers to wage military campaigns against their enemies, stimulating a nationalist fervor. Although this military training was an asset for some nationalists in their postwar anticolonial struggles, during the duration of the war other Asian countries increasingly became subjected to the war needs of Japan. They provided the Japanese with food, vital raw materials, and labor for military projects, and other essential services. Burma and China started their own internal war with Tokyo in order to end colonial rule. These Asian nations sought to expel Japanese imperialism from their territories.

Although the Greater East Asian Co-Prosperity Sphere provided for the war needs of Japan, the scheme itself made a significant contribution to Asian nationalism and racial solidarity. Through Japanese occupation, the groundwork for the postwar anticolonial struggle throughout Asia emerged. It provided nationalists in Burma and other Asian nations the opportunity for self-rule and later independence.

PAN-AFRICAN INFLUENCES

Pan-Africanism became the challenge to end the struggle against global apartheid. Global apartheid means the worldwide domination of whites in the political, economic, military, and cultural arenas. By the turn of the century the capitalist division of labor was complete. Walter Rodney, observing the relationship between capitalism and racism, asserts, "It was a division which made capitalists dominant over workers and white people dominant over blacks." At this point, white people held a monopoly of power in every sphere of life.[29] Initial expressions of Pan-Africanism did not occur on African soil; instead the people of African descent in the Western Hemisphere – North America and the Caribbean – formulated this political philosophy.

The African slave trade that accompanied the introduction of the plantation system into the Western Hemisphere contributed to a mammoth dispersal of a large African population beyond the continent. Gradually cotton, sugar, and tobacco became major commodities produced by these coerced African laborers. Initially, cotton grew in the Leeward Islands and in North America.

Nevertheless, with the invention of the cotton gin in the United States, cotton graduated to the dubious dignity of "King." African slaves were brought to the Americas as an answer to the labor needs.[30]

Pan-Africanism evolved in the Western Hemisphere as Africans struggled for freedom from slavery and sought to maintain their humanity. In 1829 David Walker published a pamphlet called *Walker's Appeal to the Coloured Citizens of the World But in Particular and Very Expressly to Those in the United States of America*. Walker provided the rationale for the development of a Pan-African ideology in the United States. He called upon African Americans and Africans to break down the geographical barriers that separated them. He urged increased cooperation between Africa and the African Diaspora in their common battle against slavery and racism.[31] Paul Cuffe and Martin Delany also contributed to the development of a Pan-African tradition within the developing African-American community. Both of these African-American leaders were supporters of the back-to-Africa movement. Their position on returning African-Americans to the continent was different from the American Colonization Society scheme that sought to rid America of "uppity and recalcitrant slaves" who were unreconciled to slavery. They wanted to build a new society with an African value system. Cuffe and Delany became enraged over the colonial plunder that was descending on the continent in the name of civilization.

During the post-Reconstruction period, Edward Blyden and Alexander Crummell emerged as the two most prominent advocates of the back-to-Africa movement and continued the development of the black nationalist perspective of black liberation. They were advocates of the unique cultural heritage of African peoples. Blyden help forward research in African history and culture and propounded the idea that Africans were unique as a result of their spirituality and rejection of materialism. Crummell rejected all forms of racial separation and advocated a vigorous struggle by black people for political power. Crummell's ideology of racial solidarity and black pride had a profound impact on younger African American intellectuals of W. E. B. Du Bois's generation.[32]

People of African descent in the Diaspora began to connect their own struggle against racism and slavery within a larger context of the struggles of African peoples against colonialism. Bernard Magubane has observed that "the idea of Pan-Africanism arose as a manifestation of fraternal solidarity among Africans and people of African descent who had come under the yoke of European hegemony."[33] W. E. B. Du Bois and Marcus Garvey continued this tradition in the twentieth century.

Alexander Crummell was an important link in the expansion of the Pan-African ideology in the twentieth century. Traveling in England in the summer of 1897, Crummell met with Henry Sylvester Williams of Trinidad and T. J. Thompson of Sierra Leone, two law students who formed an African Association. Information about this organization was advertised in the black press in the United States.[34] After Crummell returned to the States, a call was issued to convene an international Pan-African conference, to be held in London in July

1900. Du Bois and several African American intellectuals made arrangements to attend.[35] The aims of the first Pan-African conference were (1) to act as a forum of protest against the aggression of white colonizers; (2) to appeal to the missionary and abolitionist tradition of the British people to protect Africans from the depredations of empire builders; (3) to bring people of African descent throughout the world into closer contact with each other and to establish more friendly relations between Caucasian and African races; and (4) to start a movement looking forward to securing for all African races living in civilized countries their full rights, and to promote their business rights.[36]

At this conference, Du Bois called on Britain to grant "the rights of responsible governments to the black colonies of Africa and the West Indies." For African Americans, Du Bois demanded the "right of franchise, and security of person and property." He called upon the Western world to support the national integrity of the sovereign states of Abyssinia, Liberia, and Haiti. Du Bois started his appeal with his famous prediction: "The problem of the twentieth century is the problem of the colour line."[37]

The end of Radical Reconstruction (1877) in the United States came at the same time that the second wave of colonization began in Africa and Asia. Third World political systems in these regions of the world lost their legitimacy in the eyes of the conquering Europeans as these people and states lost their sovereignty. At this juncture, the world system was going through another cycle of global restructuring as the rest of Europe and the United States adopted the industrialization model of capital accumulation introduced by the British. Scientific racism, paraded under the banner of Social Darwinism, provided the rationale for the developing North-South division. Du Bois's prediction concerning the color line captured the essence of an emerging global apartheid structure that accompanied the Third World's new incorporation into a changing capitalist world system as vast commodity zones.

In its initial stages, Pan-Africanism focused on the elimination of the collective humiliation faced by the black world as a result of the slave trade and colonization of the African continent by Westerners. From 1900 to 1945 this restoration of black dignity was a primary objective of the Pan-African movement and its ideology. Recognizing the global hegemonic structures and the implications for Africa, Du Bois's approach toward Pan-Africanism did not radically challenge the status quo. Although he supported African liberation, he preferred a gradualist approach to ending colonialism. Du Bois did not call for an immediate end to colonial rule, given the reality of European power.

Despite his stature and the importance of his ideas, Du Bois did not have a monopoly over the direction and content of the Pan-African movement, especially in the United States, where Marcus Garvey also made invaluable contributions to the movement. These two leaders competed for influence and provided alternative strategies for the movement.

Two highly different personalities, Du Bois and Garvey also represented two divergent theoretical positions with respect to Pan-Africanism. Du Bois made a name for himself as a scholar and university dean while Garvey came to prominence as a mass leader. Du Bois employed tact in his approach to black people's problems; Garvey's skills as an orator was a plus in mobilizing the black community into UNIA's Pan-African front.[38] His skills transformed black politics from an elite affair to a mass-based approach to politics..

Their strategies differed in fundamental ways. Du Bois wanted to enhance the dignity of blacks in Africa and the African Diaspora. He saw his concept of the "Talented Tenth" as a way of to do this. Initially, leadership would come from a group he labeled the Talented Tenth whose mission was to prove themselves equal to whites in intellectual acumen and culture. According to Du Bois,

> The Talented Tenth of the Negro Race must be made of leaders of thought and missionaries of the culture among their people. No others can do this work and the Negro colleges must train men for it. The Negro race, like all other races, is going to be saved by its exceptional men.[39]

Once educated, the talented tenth would first conduct research and scholarly studies of black people's situations in Africa and the African Diaspora, and work to disseminate that information. This would in theory lead to discussions of the global racial, political, and economic problems confronting Africans and people of African descent, using the Pan-African Congresses as a medium. Du Bois argued that increased cooperation between white rulers and Africans would speed black development. He appealed first to the colonizers and later to the League of Nations to bring the plight of blacks in Africa and the African Diaspora under serious consideration. This approach was very evident at the Second Pan-African Congress, which opened at the Grant Hotel in Paris on February 19, 1919. Du Bois drafted the principal report of the congress, which requested that the European and American powers turn over the former German colonies of Cameroon, Tanganyika, and Southwest Africa (Namibia) to an international organization. Delegates demanded that the Allies establish a code of international law to protect the rights of the indigenous population of Africa. They proposed a similar international code of behavior that corresponded to the international labor code.[40]

Du Bois sought to use moral persuasion as a method for black liberation and restoration of black dignity. In the end, his strategy was similar to the early phase of nationalism employed by the African and Asian bourgeoisie, one that relied upon an articulate elite and the development of traditional appeals and formal grievances.

Marcus Garvey arrived in New York on March 23, 1916, on a fundraising lecture tour for an industrial school to be built in Jamaica, and only intended to stay five months. At this time, he visited Tuskegee Institute to pay his respects to the dead hero, Booker T. Washington, toured thirty-eight states, and at the end of the year returned to New York City and set up a base in Harlem. At first, the black leadership establishment in Harlem rejected his bid to build a mass movement. He resigned his leadership post in the Jamaican branch of the Universal Negro Improvement Association (UNIA) and decided to stay in the United States and recruit more members. Within three weeks, Garvey claimed to have recruited over 2,000 new members, and by 1921 he claimed to have over 6 million members throughout the world.[41] As Cedric Robinson has noted, the dominant ideology of the UNIA was eclectic, incorporating key elements of Christianity, socialism, revolutionary nationalism, and racial solidarity. The UNIA continued to enlarge and expand the black nationalist tradition to the urban arena. Furthermore, this urban black movement was quite flexible with regard to its organizational structure.[42] The UNIA was more than a composite reflection of Marcus Garvey's personality.

Starting in 1919, Garvey started publishing a weekly newspaper, the *Negro World*. This journalistic enterprise emerged as the principal propaganda instrument of the Garvey movement. Copies of the *Negro World* were printed in English, French and Spanish. The newspaper focused primarily on the news and events concerning the global African community, with emphasis on culture, history, and racial news in Africa and the African Diaspora. The platform of the UNIA was an important item in every edition from 1919 to 1933. The UNIA sought to accomplish the following goals: (1) to champion Negro nationhood by the redemption of Africa; (2) to make the Negro race-conscious; (3) to breathe ideas of manhood and womanhood into every Negro; (4) to advocate self-determination; (5) to make the Negro world-conscious; (6) to print all the news that would be interesting and instructive to the Negro; (7) to instill racial self-help; and (8) to inspire racial love and self-respect.[43] Through the *Negro World,* the ideology of Pan-Africanism and black nationalism became widely circulated in Africa, the Caribbean, and the United States. The UNIA became the dominant mass-based movement for the new urban African Americans.

Garvey and the Harlem branch of UNIA organized the first international conference of the Negro people of the world in August 1920. Delegates representing twenty-five countries attended the proceedings in New York, although a number of the so-called foreign delegates actually resided in the United States, according to the Federal Bureau of Investigation (FBI).[44] The conference also featured parades with the participation of UNIA dignitaries, and the various auxiliary groups organized by the movement, including the Black Cross Nurses, the Black Flying Eagles, and the Universal African Motor Corps. The UNIA flag flew in bold relief on such occasions. The red represented the blood of Africans on the continent and in the African Diaspora, and the green represented the hopes for the African population. At these gatherings Garvey mobilized support for his vision of Pan-Africanism.

Garvey sought to use his annual international conventions in New York from 1920 onward as a Pan-African protest forum. According to Garvey, the problems of blacks in the Diaspora were analogous to those of Africans under colonialism.[45] Throughout his tenure in the United States, Garvey remained committed to the total liberation of Africa from colonial rule and the subsequent creation of a united, strong, and virile state.

Garvey also believed that there was no real hope for blacks in the Diaspora until African liberation from colonial rule became a reality. He viewed the African Diaspora community as the vanguard to continental liberation. As such, he advocated a policy of "selected colonization" of Africa by activists, technicians, and educators to aid in liberating and reconstructing the African continent. The UNIA sought to start its campaign of liberation and development in Liberia. Garvey desired to build a firm foundation for economic liberation based on cooperative black capitalism. It was his firm belief that collective self-reliance and solidarity among blacks necessitated worldwide economic organizations linking the African continent and the African Diaspora. Economic enterprises such as the Black Star Steamship Line and the Negro Factory Corporation reinforced this movement's commitment to entrepreneurial activities as well as to community and economic development.[46]

Through the UNIA, Garvey was able to bestow status on the black masses. He reinforced the collective status of men and women through such auxiliaries as the Black Cross Nurses, the Universal African Motor Corps, and the Juvenile and Black Flying Eagles. All of these institutions came equipped with officers and uniforms. Garvey sought to give the African Americans a sense of community within the context of black nationalism. Recent scholarship on the UNIA and Marcus Garvey confirms his black nationalist and Pan-Africanist orientation:

> The UNIA's official demands, set down in a Declaration of Rights of Negro Peoples of the World, included the right to vote, a fair share of political patronage, representation on juries and on the judge's bench, and full freedom of the press, speech, and assembly for all. The UNIA sought these basic freedoms primarily to create and strengthen a separate black world, while groups like the NAACP would use these freedoms primarily to create an integrated world.
>
> Socially, the UNIA was a huge social club and fraternal order. . . . For Garveyites, there was the fraternal camaraderie of all the black people of the world. UNIA parades, Saturday night parties, women's group luncheons, etc., had a significance far beyond that of providing social diversion. Their affairs were designed to build a pride and confidence in blackness.[47]

Garvey's ambitious movement required a great deal of capital. To finance his commercial ventures, he sold stock for his Black Star Line. In a long and contested trial for mail fraud, Garvey refused a lawyer and defended himself. As a result of defending himself and attempting to use the trial as a forum to promote the UNIA, he was convicted and sentenced to the federal prison in Atlanta. Garvey had also relied on help from friends or contacts in the government that might eventually intervene and rescue him; but no such help came forth until after he was in prison.

Establishing a community in Africa was a critical aspect of Garvey's and the UNIA's Pan-African ideology. This new African community was to be a laboratory for developing political, economic, cultural, and social structures for nation-building and liberation. This new political community would become the guardian of the interests of blacks in Africa and the African Diaspora. Garveyites envisioned that this new African nation, guided by a technocratic elite recruited throughout the black World, would become a protector of the human rights of all people of African descent. The principle of self-help would become the cornerstone of this new African society.[48] The UNIA failed to win a foothold in Africa, especially Liberia, and this also contributed to Garvey's decline. In 1927, following his release from federal prison, he was deported as an undesirable alien. Subsequently, Garvey's movement collapsed in the United States. He was unable to return the movement to its pre-1925 fame. He continued to wage a battle against colonialism in Jamaica and in England after his deportation. Garvey died in 1940 in London, a poverty-stricken and broken man.

W. E. B. Du Bois has placed the Garvey conception of Pan-Africanism into historical perspective.

> Moreover, shorn of its bombast and exaggeration, the main lines of the Garvey plan are perfectly feasible. What he is trying to say and do is this: American Negroes can, by accumulating and ministering their own capital, organize industry, join the black centers of the south Atlantic by commercial enterprise and in this way ultimately redeem Africa as a fit and free home for black men. This is true. It is *feasible*. It is, in a sense, practical; but it will take for its accomplishment long years of painstaking, self-sacrificing effort. It will call for every ounce of ability, knowledge, and experience and devotion in the whole Negro race. It is not the task of one man or one organization, but for coordinated effort on the part of millions. The plan is not original with Garvey but he has popularized it, made it a living, vocal ideal and swept thousands with him with intense belief in the possible accomplishment of the ideal.[49]

Garvey and his Universal Negro Improvement Association had a profound impact on the development of Pan-Africanism and of racial solidarity in Africa and the African Diaspora. His movement contributed to black consciousness in Africa and the African Diaspora in the 1920s. Garvey's ideas, though riddled with contradictions, laid the foundation for the postwar rise in African nationalism. The militant rhetoric of African liberation appeared a bit unrealistic in the military context of Western power. At this juncture, the African masses in Africa and the African Diaspora lacked a credible counterbalance. The colonists appeared to be in Africa to stay. However, Garvey's vision of a liberated Africa became the battle cry for postwar African nationalists such as Kwame Nkrumah of Ghana and Jomo Kenyatta of Kenya.

Du Bois maintained his dominance of the Pan-African movement from 1919 to 1927. During these years the majority of the participants came primarily from the African Diaspora. Increasingly, African students attending European schools, among them Jomo Kenyatta, Wallace Johnson, and Dr. Nnandi Azikwe, began to participate in these periodic Du Boisan Pan-African Congresses.[50]

The First World War marked a dramatic transition in the Pan-African movement, as Europe became the theatre of action on this front. From 1900 to 1927, the movement focused attention on the black problem on a global scale, and at the same time it worked to redeem the dignity of Africans and their descendants in the African Diaspora.

With the coming of the worldwide depression in the 1930s, Du Bois was unable to rally any support in the United States or abroad for the Pan-African movement. The depression led a number of African, African-American, and Caribbean intellectuals to question the Communist International's commitment to black liberation. In August 1933, George Padmore resigned from his various positions in the Communist Party, charging that the Comintern was preparing to abandon its anticolonial activities in order to reach a rapprochement with France and Britain against Nazi Germany.[51] Since Marxism was not serving the interests of black people in Africa and the African Diaspora, Padmore followed the steps of a number of black renegade intellectuals[52] in returning to the radical black tradition by participating in the struggle against global apartheid. After 1938, when Padmore, C. R. L. James, and other West Indian and African American intellectuals broke ranks with the Communist International, Britain became the focal point of the Pan-African movement.[53] Although Pax Britannica was waning as a military and economic force in the world system, Britain remained the citadel of the colonized world. Throughout the 1940s, Pan-Africanism turned inward and established as its top priority the liberation of Africa from colonialism. This change in emphasis had a profound impact on African nationalism as well as on the continuing evolution of Afro-Asianism.

During the 1940s, Africans moved to the front of the Pan-African movement. In 1944, self-help societies and political organizations changed their mission in order to accommodate the developing Pan-African agenda. These changes became necessary in order to form the Pan-African Federation under the leadership of the International African Service Bureau. George Padmore influenced the content and direction of the movement through his work, *Pan-Africanism or Communism*. Padmore was an ardent critic of communism and emphasized the need for Africans to take charge of their own liberation. He viewed the movement's changing direction with concern and urged the application of European liberal political theories. He believed that certain European political institutions, such as political parties, if successfully employed, could become the new weapons of African nationalists in their anticolonial struggle. Padmore provided the guiding light in the Pan-African movement's transition from an organization steeped in British and American abolitionist tradition to a more aggressive strategy aimed at the total liberation of the African continent.

Padmore's participation in the European liberal and radical political traditions had prepared him well for the task of building a militant anticolonial coalition within the context of Pan-Africanism.

This transition became more evident during the Sixth Pan-African Congress in Manchester, England, in October 1945. Two hundred or more delegates attended the Congress from both Africa and the African Diaspora.[54] For the first time since its inception, the Pan-African Congress offered a challenge to the colonial order in new and important ways. This particular session made a statement on African nationalism and racial sovereignty by declaring "Africa for Africans." Africans pledged to "fight in every way we can for freedom, democracy and social betterment," in the African Declaration to Colonial Powers.[55] This congress also marked the end of patient acceptance of the colonial status quo. New strategies ranged from recommendations for nonviolent direct action to violence and armed struggle. The congress called for unity among workers, farmers, and intellectuals in the anti-colonial struggle. Intellectuals and other members of the bourgeoisie heard the message that they could no longer wage such nationalist struggles alone and only on intellectual or cultural levels. They became convinced that success could be achieved only by enlisting the masses in the anticolonial struggle. These elites became more convinced that they needed to lift the veil that separated the struggle of the bourgeoisie from that of the masses and to mobilize the colonized into a genuine anticolonial struggle. Positive action in the form of strikes and boycotts provided novel ways to bring the colonial machinery to a halt.

On the whole, the Manchester Congress, with its emphasis on non-white identity as a bond of solidarity, made an invaluable contribution to the emergence of African nationalism and Afro-Asianism in the postwar era. In the words of George Padmore, African delegates left Manchester with the commitment to devote all their energies to the liberation of the continent. At this historic juncture, Pan-Africanism became a mechanism for the struggle of Africans and their descendants in the Diaspora to regain their dignity and strength, and a means to the liberation of the continent of Africa.

THE IMPACT OF WORLD WAR II

The advent of the Second World War brought about fundamental changes in the European colonial order. Imperial powers throughout Europe – Britain, France, Italy, and Belgium, to name a few – were exhausted, and their modern industrial infrastructures became ravaged by this global war for hegemony. War also unleashed pressures that undermined the power of imperial Europe over Africa and Asia. People in Africa and Asia began to perceive the weakness of their colonial masters as German armies occupied France, Belgium, and Holland, and Britain grew increasingly weaker. By destroying the myth of white invincibility, the introduction of African and Asian troops into the white man's war further undermined Europe's hegemony. When African soldiers saw white soldiers wounded and dying on the battlefields, color distinctions lost their legitimacy. After suffering side by side, Africans never regarded their white fellow soldiers in the same light. After spending four years hunting the "white enemy," the Africans would never again regard them as gods.[56] With the Second World War, the old magic of white invincibility began to wither away. The colonizer's spell wore off as the veil was lifted from the eyes of the colonized. This realization marked a crucial transition in relations between the North and South.

The Japanese victories over the British also worked to undermine this myth of white invincibility, ending the colonial order in Asia and at the same time unleashing strong forces of nationalism. The Japanese success stimulated a nationalist response in the rest of this region. As an aggressor Tokyo did help to make millions of Asians more nationalistic and race-conscious. Indeed, it was the Asian bayonets in the hands of the Japanese soldiers that routed the colonizers out of their comfortable enclaves of power and privilege all over the Far East. The British were flushed from the Raffle Bar in Singapore, Americans from the Army and Navy Club in Manila, and Dutchmen from their plantation homes in Java and Sumatra.[57]

Freedom, self-determination, equality, and other egalitarian ideals became internalized among the colonized in Africa and Asia. As a result of the Second World War, the various nationalist elites began to lose their monopoly over such values. The work of Zimbabwe nationalist, Rev. Nabaningi Sithole speaks to this shift:

> World War II taught the African most powerful ideas. During the war, the allied powers taught their subject people (millions of them!) that it was not right for Germany to dominate other nations. They taught their subject people to fight for freedom, rather than live and be subjugated by Hitler. The subject people learned their lesson well and responded magnificently, and they fought and endured great hardships and they died under the spell of freedom.[58]

Partially in response to changes brought about by the Second World War, a new politically aware segment of the African population became a part of the anticolonial struggle. New actors, including veterans, urban workers, and rural dwellers, became actively involved in the anticolonial battle for liberation. As a result, the anticolonial coalition throughout the African continent increased.

African veterans were a critical part of this politically relevant stratum. During their years of absence, they became increasingly alienated both from their traditional societies and from tribal authorities; in many cases family ties were broken. Dissatisfied with traditional values and mores, many ex-servicemen migrated to urban areas. Traditional rural-urban migration patterns underwent a dramatic change, exacerbating the problems associated with underemployment and unemployment in African colonial cities. They became an important component of social and political unrest in the period immediately following the war. This became apparent during the Accra riots of 1948.[59]

Starting in early 1948, the African population began boycotting European imported goods in Accra, Ghana. This boycott ended on February 11, 1948, when the colonial governor and the chambers of commerce agreed to lower prices on imported items. The African Ex-Servicemen's Union planned to present a petition to the governor setting forth their grievances on February 24, 1948, but postponed it until February 28, 1948. On the twenty-eighth, as they marched toward the governor's residence, they encountered a squad of police in their path. In the course of the dispute that followed, the superintendent of police, a white man, fired at the ring leaders, killing two of them and wounding four or five others. As news spread in the industrial districts of Accra, where for the first time in a month people were buying European goods, the people attacked the European shops and looted them. The police were unable to restore order for two days. The destruction of property by fire also accelerated, and at least fifteen people lost their lives and over a hundred suffered injuries in Accra alone. The outbreak spread to other areas of the colony.[60]

The national bourgeoisie expanded following the Second World War. Within the traditional elite sector of the colonized population, the notables and the few educated Africans of the older generation were increasingly replaced by younger leaders who came from the developing new middle class, which included small business owners, officials in the colonial bureaucracy, school teachers, and college and university professors. This new leadership clique brought with it new ideals and methods of organization. Trade unions, self-help organizations, and modern political parties developed. At demonstrations and rallies, where demands to the colonial authorities became the central focus, wartime loyalty and service by African troops was increasingly celebrated by the colonizers in order to arrest the drift toward nationalism. In Europe, African students agitated for the expansion of educational opportunities and Africanization of the colonial bureaucracy. Thus, changing times awakened the masses of the colonized to their condition.[61]

In Asia, the end of the Second World War also marked a critical transition in the colonial order. The war intensified Asian nationalism, resulting in a continental call for Asia for Asians. The European imperial order suffered a mortal blow with the independence of India and Mao Zedong's victory in the Chinese Civil War. These two events marked a turning point in Asia's decolonization. The Indian anticolonialist struggle led to similar movements throughout the British empire. India's success energized nations throughout Asia. The strong antiforeign content of Asian nationalism contributed to closer bonds between countries across Africa and Asia.

The Second World War also marked a crucial point in the development of Pan-Arabic sentiments. The Arab League started functioning as a full-fledged regional organization concerned with inter-Arab affairs on March 22, 1945, through the efforts of the Arab states. The primary purpose of the league was to strengthen ties among member states and coordinate their political programs in order to ensure genuine collaboration, while at the same time protecting their independence and sovereignty from both Soviet and Western domination.

Although political diversity was a defining characteristic of this collectivity of states, which ranged from monarchies and theocracies to military regimes and one-party states, the creation of the state of Israel has united them despite their political differences. To proponents of Pan-Arabism, the emergence in 1948 of a state dominated by citizens of European descent in the very heart of the Arab world symbolized a return to the colonial past. To others, the new Jewish state posed a serious challenge to the cause of Arab unity. To the Jewish inhabitants and their coreligionists abroad, the new state of Israel offered a haven from the persecution that they had encountered in Central and Eastern Europe, from the pogroms of the Russian tsars to the Holocaust of Hitler.[62] The Cairo Pact uniting the Arab League included as signatories Egypt, Iraq, Lebanon, Jordan, Saudi Arabia, Syria, and Yemen. From the very beginning, the Arab world and the state of Israel have been in a state of war.

Another result of the Second World War was the emergence of the Soviet Union and the United States as superpowers. Throughout the late 1940s and early 1950s, the increased competition between the superpowers brought the world to the brink of another global war. When the Moscow Conference of Foreign Ministers failed in spring 1947, the wartime entente between the Western powers and the Soviet Union collapsed. Propaganda was rampant. Capitalism opposed socialism, and democracy opposed totalitarianism. Subversion, guerrilla activities, border hostilities, and the ongoing threat of nuclear war created anxieties on both sides of the Iron Curtain.[63]

As it consolidated its position, each superpower competed for influence among the newly created states of Asia and Africa. As decolonization accelerated after the Second World War, each superpower sought to replace the old colonial masters in their former sphere of influence. Both superpowers offered trade, economic aid, and a security umbrella in order to assist these new actors in their quest to protect their newly acquired sovereignty. Many of these new states joined one or the other of the competing Cold War alliances established by the two superpowers; a few braved alternative, independent courses. Loathe to sell their sovereignty for security, these uncommitted states saw solidarity as a way to protect their newly acquired independence in a new age of entangling alliances.

AFRO-ASIANISM AND THE POLITICS OF PAN-PIGMENTATIONALISM IN THE 1950s AND 1960s

During the 1950s, Afro-Asianism emerged as the basis for Third World solidarity. Afro-Asianism emanated primarily from a sense of shared racial humiliation among nonwhites in Africa and Asia. This humiliation included the shared experienced of colonialism and Western domination despite the fact that some states in Africa and Asia escaped colonization by Europeans (Ethiopia and Liberia experienced nominal sovereignty by the European powers).[64] The struggle against racism and colonialism became the inner core of Afro-Asianism, thus reinforcing the desires for genuine autonomy from the Great Powers. Afro-Asianism marked an attack on the racial hierarchy of the world system. Kwame Nkrumah of Ghana and other leaders in the Third World demanded that the colonized should rule themselves. Racial sovereignty became an integral theme of Afro-Asianism. The expressions "Africa for Africans" and "Asia for Asians" were indicative of this call for racial sovereignty.

Afro-Asianism also represented a partial confirmation of W. E. B. Du Bois's assertion that "the problem of the twentieth century is the problem of the color line — the relations of the darker to the lighter races of men in Asia and Africa, in America and the islands of the sea."[65] It is the people of color, the grave diggers of capitalism, with their poverty, low standards of living and high mortality and morbidity rates, who constitute the majority of the developing world. Afro-Asianism also represents the consciousness of being the world's economic underdog, while being confronted daily by privileged white societies in the Northeast — the former Soviet Union and the Warsaw Pact nations in East and Central Europe — and the Northwest — the United States, Western Europe, and Japan. Hence, Afro-Asianism symbolizes the consciousness of being the "proletarian races of the world."

The Afro-Asian movement crystallized at the Bandung Conference in 1955. As a result of this conference of the "colored nations," the Third World emerged as a motive force in the world system. Many Third World leaders were unwilling to exchange old colonial masters for new ones by joining either superpower Cold War coalitions. Many Third World leaders had their own agenda — priority being placed on decolonization, economic development, and Afro-Asian representation in the decision-making arena of international organizations — and did not perceive the Cold War as the most critical international issue.

At first, the leadership of the Afro-Asian movement came primarily from the Asian sector of the alliance. At the Bandung Conference and throughout the 1950s there was modest representation and input from the African countries, partly because the majority of them were still under colonial rule. During this period Nehru and Sukarno laid claim to the leadership helm. As more African states became independent, the leadership locus of the movement shifted toward the Middle East and Africa. The Suez and Congo crises both contributed immensely to this change. From 1955 to 1965 the movement remained an important factor in the development of Third World solidarity.

Beginning in 1957 the Afro-Asian People's Solidarity Organization (AAPSO) became an important expression of Afro-Asian solidarity. AAPSO, with a strong anti-imperialist orientation, became an integral part of the strategy of the Soviet Union and the People's Republic of China to build a coalition

in the Third World. This new radical coalition included communist-front organizations, liberation movements, and nationalist organizations from the socialist bloc, as well as African and Asian countries as major participants. Most participants from Africa and Asia were nationalist in orientation. Cairo became the
site of the AAPSO Secretariat. The AAPSO conferences convened in Egypt,
Guinea, Tanzania, Ghana, and other Third World countries.

In the mid-1960s AAPSO began to decline as a result of the introduction
of the Sino-Soviet conflict into the movement. African participants began to
demand that AAPSO cease being a forum for the Sino-Soviet conflict at future
summits. After the Chinese, Indonesians, and Algerians failed to convene a second Bandung Conference, Afro-Asianism waned as a basis of Third World solidarity and non-alignment emerged as the organizing principle in the Southern
Hemisphere. The antiracial and anticolonial elements of Afro-Asianism became
important elements in the Non-Aligned movement.

Racial and geographical exclusivity had become an impediment to efforts
aimed at broadening the parameters of Third World solidarity. Afro-Asianism
had become an inadequate mechanism for dealing with the Cold War. A number
of Third World leaders from Africa and Asia who had participated in the Afro-
Asian movement held political allegiance to the Eastern or Western bloc. The
racial and geographical criteria made it difficult for Afro-Asian states to attend
or sponsor conferences with nation-states from Latin America and Europe
beyond the United Nations framework. Thus, Afro-Asianism became an
impediment to the development of Third World solidarity. The People's
Republic of China's usage of the "natural allies' thesis" as a bond between Beijing and the Afro-Asian states against the Soviet Union demonstrated some of
the inadequacies of race and geography as bonds for building Third World solidarity.

NOTES

1. Mamadou Dia, *The African Nations and World Solidarity* (London: Thames and Hudson, 1962), p.13.

2. The Latin precursors of Pan-Americanism were also fearful of the expansionism
emerging in the United States under such ideological premises as Manifest Destiny.

3. The North Atlantic Treaty Organization (NATO) with the U.S. leading Western
Europe, and the Warsaw Pact with the Soviet Union leading Eastern Europe. The
United States and the Soviet Union achieved superpower status, maintaining a balance
of power with a balance of terror.

4. W. Rodney, *How Europe Underdeveloped Africa* (Washington D. C.: Howard University Press, 1974).

5. See G. H. Jansen, *Afro-Asia and Non-Alignment* (London: Faber, 1966).

6. G. Chaliand, *Revolution in the Third World: Currents and Conflicts in Asia, Africa, and
Latin America* (New York: Penguin Press,1989), p.6.

7. I. Wallerstein, "The Colonial Era in Africa: Changes in Social Structure," in *Colonialism in Africa, 1870-1960,* ed. L. Gann and P. Duigan (Cambridge: Cambridge University Press, 1970).

8. Du Bois and Garvey were two giants in the development of Pan-Africanism as an ideology of anticolonial resistance among people of African descent throughout the world. They were opposed to racism as a form of oppression against people of color. Du Bois adopted a gradualist approach and sought to work with the Great Powers. He also relied on his Pan-African Congresses and the leadership of African, Caribbean, and African American elites rather than on the masses. Garvey used his annual Pan-African Conferences, sponsored by the Universal Negro Improvement Association. He mobilized mass support for liberating Africa and called for the liberation of Africa, although he lacked the military means to accomplish this task. Nevertheless, he captured the imagination of the African Diaspora and of the masses in Africa in support of African liberation.

9. Jean Price-Mars, Aimé Cesaire, and Leopold Senghor were major proponents of negritude.

10. P. G. Lauren, *Power and Prejudice: The Politics and Diplomacy of Racial Discrimination* (Boulder, CO.: Westview Press, 1988), p. 109.

11. G. Chaliand, *Revolution in the Third World*.

12. S. Goonatilake, *Crippled Minds: An Exploration into Colonial Culture* (New Delhi: Vikas Publishing House, 1982), p. 43.

13. D. Kimche, *The Afro-Asian Movement: Ideology and Foreign Policy of the Third World* (Jerusalem: Israel University Press, 1973), p. 2.

14. G. H. Jansen, *Afro-Asia and Non-Alignment* (London: Faber and Faber, 1966) p. 20.

15. Ibid.

16. D. Kimche, *The Afro-Asian Movement,* p. 3.

17. Ibid.

18. K. T. Fann and D. C. Hodges, *Readings in U. S. Imperialism* (Boston: Porter and Sargent, 1971), pp. 33–38.

19. G. H. Jansen, *Afro-Asia and Non-Alignment,* p. 29; Kimche, *The Afro-Asian Movement,* p. 4.

20. G. H. Jansen, Ibid., p. 30.

21. The Black Dragon Secret Society was an alliance among several Chinese nationalist organizations.

22. D. Kimche, *The Afro-Asian Movement,* p. 7.

23. Ibid., p. 7.

24. D. N. Sharma, *The Afro-Asian Group in the United Nations* (Allahabad, India: Chaitanya Publishing House, 1962), p. 15.

25. Paul Kennedy, *The Rise and Fall of the Great Powers: Economic Change and Military Conflict from 1500 to 2000* (New York: Random House, 1989), pp. 300–302.

26. The Asian countries that participated in this Japanese venture included Burma, Thailand, Malaya, and Indo-China on the Asian continent, the component parts of the Dutch East Indies, the Philippines, and islands in the South and Central Pacific. In addition, the section of China under the Nanking government was also included.

27. A. Iriye, *The Cold War in Asia: A Historical Introduction* (Englewood Cliffs, NJ: Prentice-Hall, 1974), p. 60.

28. G. H. Jansen, *Afro-Asia and Non-Alignment,* p. 34.

29. W. Rodney. *Groundings With My Brothers* (London: Bogle L'Ouverture Publications, 1970), p. 17.

30. Under the Spanish and Portuguese, millions of Africans were brought to the Americas: minimum figures of imported slaves included 3.6 million in Brazil, 702,000 in Cuba, 200,000 in Mexico, 200,000 in Colombia, 121,000 in Venezuela, and 95,000

in Peru. Before the demise of the transatlantic slave trade and the abolition of slavery itself, millions more Africans were transported: over 600,000 to the United States, 365,000 to Martinique, 364,000 to tiny Barbados, 290,000 to Guadeloupe, over 500,000 to the Guyanas, and 77,000 to Puerto Rico. See Manning Marable, *African and Caribbean Politics: From Kwame Nkrumah to Maurice Bishop* (London: Verso Press, 1987).

31. See Bernard Magubane, *Ties That Bind: African-American Consciousness of Africa* (Trenton, NJ: Africa World Press, 1987) p. 139; and Sterling Stuckey, *Slave Culture: Nationalist Theory and the Foundation of Black America* (New York: Oxford University Press, 1987) pp. 134–135.

32. Manning Marable, *W. E. B. Du Bois: Black Radical Democrat* (Boston: Twayne, 1986), pp. 32–33.

33. B. Magubane, *Ties That Bind,* pp. 139–140.

34. M. Marable, *W. E. B. Du Bois,* p. 39.

35. The African-American delegation was represented by Bishop Alexander Walters, a Washington D.C. educator; Anna Cooper; Anna H. Jones of Missouri; and Du Bois. From Liberia came F. R. S. Johnson, the country's former attorney general; from Ethiopia, Benito Sylvain, assistant to Emperor Menelik II. See ibid., p. 39.

36. V. B. Thompson, *Africa and Unity: The Evolution of Pan-Africanism* (London:Longman, 1969), pp. 24–25.

37. M. Marable, *W. E. B. Du Bois,* pp. 39–40.

38. V. B. Thompson, *Africa and Unity,* p. 24.

39. W. E. B. Du Bois, "The Talented Tenth," in *The Seventh Son: The Thought and Writings of W. E. B. Du Bois,* Vol. 1, ed. Julius Lester (New York: Random House, 1971), pp. 388–403.

40. M. Marable, *W. E. B. Du Bois,* p. 102.

41. John White, *Black Leadership in America: From B. T. Washington to Jesse Jackson* (New York: Longman, 1990) Second Edition, p. 83.

42. C. Robinson, *Black Marxism: The Making of the Black Radical Tradition* (London: Zed Press, 1991), p. 296.

43. John White, *Black Leadership in America,* p. 84.

44. Ibid., p. 87.

45. E. U. Essien-Udom, "Marcus Garvey and His Movement," in Eric Foner, ed., *America's Black Past: A Reader in Afro-American History* (New York City, New York: Harper and Row, 1970), p. 170.

46. Ibid., p. 360.

47. C. Robinson, *Black Marxism,* p. 298

48. Ibid., p. 29

49. Julius Lester, *The Seventh Son,* p. 180.

50. These leaders emerged as important contributors of the anti-colonial struggles in the postwar period.

51. M. Marable, *African and Caribbean Politics,* p. 44

52. C. Robinson, *Black Marxism,* p. 257.

53. C. Legum, *Pan-Africanism: A Short Political Guide* (New York: Praeger, 1965).

54. The Manchester Congress marked the entrance of the African nationalist elite into decision-making roles in the Pan-African movement. Leaders who would play roles in the future anticolonial struggle were the following: from the Gold Coast (Ghana), the late Kwame Nkrumah, Dr. J. C. de Graft Johnson, J.Annam, E. A. Ayikuma, Edwin J. DePlan, the late Dr. Kurankyi Taylor, and Joe Appiah; from Nigeria, Magnus William and Chief S. L.Akintole; from Kenya, the late Jomo Kenyatta; from Sierra Leone, Wal-

lace Johnson; from Togo, Dr. Raphael Armattoe and Otto Makonnen, who was director of the African Affairs Center in Accra; from South Africa, Peter Abraham and Marko Hlubi, representing the African National Congress.

55. The Pan-African Congress, Manchester 1945, in *Pan-Africanism,* ed. Robert Christman and Nathan Hare (Indianapolis: The Bobbs-Merrill Co., 1974), pp. 303–306.

56. N. Sithole, *African Nationalism* (New York: Oxford University Press, 1968), p. 62

57. L. A. Rose, *Roots of a Tragedy: The United States and the Struggle for Asia, 1945–1953* (Westport, Connecticut: Greenwood Press, 1976).

58. N. Sithole, *African Nationalism,* pp. 47–48.

59. T. Smith, *The End of Empire: Decolonization After World War II* (Lexington, MA: D. C. Heath and Company, 1975).

60. C. L. R. James, *Nkrumah and the Ghana Revolution* (Lawrence Hill and Company, 1977), pp. 42–43.

61. I. L. Markovitz, *Power and Class in Africa* (Englewood Cliffs, NJ: Prentice-Hall, 1977), p. 188.

62. W. L. Keylor, *The Twentieth Century World: An International History* (New York: Oxford University Press, 1984), p. 311.

63. Q. Wright, "The Study of War," *International Encyclopedia of Social Sciences,* Vol. 16 (New York: MacMillan, 1968).

64. G. Chaliand, *Revolution in the Third World,* p. 4.

65. M. Marable, *W. E. B. Du Bois,* pp. 39–40.

Part II

Nonalignment: Moderating East-West Tensions and Developing Third World Diplomatic Consciousness

3

Nonalignment and the Politics of a Third Force

The vast majority of states that emerged from Africa and Asia did not participate in the decision-making processes that structured the postwar world system in which they were born. Leaders from the Third World argued that the Eurocentric international system was ineffective in dealing with the issues that confronted them. These issues ranged from economic development, colonialism, and racism in Southern Africa to the changing economic and political structures that govern North-South relations. North-South relations undergo dramatic structural transformation during the rise, consolidation, and demise of hegemonies. The postwar era was no exception to this rule. The nonaligned movement represented the Third World challenge to the Eurocentric and bipolar structure of the interstate system during the consolidation of Pax Americana.

During the second wave of decolonization and the consolidation of Pax Americana (1945–1975), new states from Africa and Asia faced problems affirming their "sovereign equality" in an era in which the prerequisites of power had undergone dramatic change with the advent of the superpowers and the introduction of nuclear weaponry. The United States and before it, Great Britain, provided a framework for the incorporation of these actors into the global political system. This became institutionalized through the United Nations, while multinational enterprises, foreign aid, and Cold War subsidiary alliances provided a mechanism for integrating Afro-Asian states into the world economy. With the decline of colonialism, Africa and Asia were ripe for the coming invasion of multinational corporations from the United States. Latin America and the Caribbean region had served as a laboratory for the nurturing and maturing of American multinational enterprise during the consolidation and ultimate decline of Pax Britannica.

The term "Third World" implies both a third force in world politics and symbolizes a challenge to the bipolar structure that dominated international politics in the three and a half decades that followed the Second World War. At first, the term became useful as a rhetorical response to the bipolar-structured world system. The bipolar model of the world system assumed that all nations would participate in Cold War coalitions that evolved at the end of the Second World War, partially in response to the power vacuum left by the decline of the Great Powers and the rise of the two superpowers, the United States and the Soviet Union. The only alternative to alignment was neutrality legally recognized by both the United States and the Soviet Union. Switzerland was a classic example of this option. For most of the emerging nations neutrality (isolationism) was not a positive alternative to alignment.

Many Third World leaders from Africa and Asia sought an alternative to the legal neutrality practiced by Switzerland. In the 1950s the Afro-Asian movement provided an alternative to traditional nonparticipation in world affairs as found in traditional diplomacy. Many participants in the Afro-Asian movement were also members of Cold War coalitions. However, a few pioneering states were nonaligned with reference to the Cold War. Most states from the Third World shared similar attitudes on such issues as colonialism, racism, and economic development regardless of their alignment status. As the Afro-Asian movement began to decline in significance, nonalignment evolved as a new basis for Third World solidarity. Nonalignment provided an alternative to alignment and legal neutrality while offering a new basis for protecting the newly acquired sovereignty of Third World states. Nonalignment also evolved as a Third World response to the Eurocentric bias that pervaded the postwar era.

PHASE I: THE COLD WAR

The bipolar system that emerged after the Second World War reduced the flexibility within the international system. The foreign policy objectives of most states became increasingly polarized as they renewed their prewar competition and conflict. Ideology and security became the dominant issues of world interaction.

According to Morton A. Kaplan, the rise of powerful deviant actors, inadequate countermeasures by such nondeviant actors as Britain and France, and the growth of supranational organizations such as the communist bloc with its internationally organized political parties sounded the death knell of the balance of power in the prewar interstate system. As the competition between the two superpowers accelerated, the world community entered a state of war.

Alexis de Tocqueville anticipated the rise of the United States and the Soviet Union to the position of dominant world powers and the development of a bipolar interstate system as early as the 1830s. He asserted that Americans and Russians, although "their starting point is different and their courses are not the same," seemed "marked out by the will of heaven to sway the destinies of half the globe."[1] However, de Tocqueville failed to anticipate the introduction of nuclear weapons and the manner in which they would alter the nature of warfare. Nuclear weapons dramatically restructured military power and transformed the meaning of national security. The atomic explosions at Nagasaki and Hiroshima demonstrated the new power capable of destroying nations and their citizenry. The nuclear arsenal built by the superpowers trivialized the traditional military instruments for national security. With their nuclear weapons, the superpowers became the new guardians of international security. Concern for national security and fear of their increased vulnerability led many nations, either voluntarily or involuntarily, to seek refuge within the two Cold War coalitions.

At the end of the Second World War the wartime alliance between the Soviet Union and the United States began to crumble. The competitive and conflictual interaction that characterized the relationship between the capitalist Western powers and the anticapitalist Soviet Union before the war re-emerged. The Soviet Union emerged as the only credible antisystemic power in the postwar era that had the potential military power to mount a serious challenge to the consolidation of Pax Americana.

Although ideology played an important role in the Cold War, the tensions that emerged between the Soviet Union and the United States are partially the result of competing conceptions of how to construct the postwar world order. The wartime allies' lack of consensus on the political character of postwar Europe dramatically intensified competition and conflict between the superpowers. The Soviet Union was able to achieve dominance over seven Eastern European countries – Albania, Bulgaria, Hungary, Poland, East Germany, Yugoslavia, and Rumania – whose absorption into its sphere of influence became a policy objective during the last years of the war. Joseph Stalin committed the Soviets neither to withdraw nor to introduce the political and economic institutions of the West to Eastern Europe. As a result, Soviet power extended over half of the European continent. Communist expansion became a threat not only to the postwar world order but also to the cultural norms that dominated this new order. Winston Churchill put into words what the Anglo-Saxon bourgeoisie feared.[2] In a speech delivered at Fulton, Missouri, Churchill called on the English-speaking world to unite against Soviet communism. Churchill made the argument that if democracy was to survive, foreign policy in the West had to be dominated by the containment of communism. The British, exhausted and still recovering from the global war of hegemonic succession, also called on the United States to fill the military and political void in Europe left by London as the new order was unfolding.

The containment philosophy became a basis for the U.S. response to Soviet expansion. In 1947 the United States took two specific steps to counter USSR's challenge. Through the Truman Doctrine, the United States took over from Britain the responsibility for protecting Greece and Turkey from communism. On March 2, 1947, President Harry Truman made a dramatic appearance before a joint session of Congress to request funding for a new foreign policy initiative revolving around containment. He spoke of the growing conflict between the antagonistic social systems of capitalism and socialism. Truman requested $400 million to help Greece resist communist-led attacks against the government and to bolster Turkey against Soviet pressures.[3] The Truman Doctrine went far beyond aid to Greece and Turkey and declared universal war on communist expansionism. Advocates of the containment policy assumed that the Soviet Union would expand outwardly by any means possible and that Moscow's probes required counter force. The militarization of containment, so deeply deplored by its spiritual father, George Kennan, testifies to the priority that the competitive aspects of world affairs received throughout this period.[4]

In June 1947, in a commencement address at Harvard University, General George Marshall proposed the outline of a vast European Recovery Program. The objective of the Marshall Plan was ultimately to restore Europe's economies through aid from the United States. Initially, the Marshall Plan was offered to both Eastern and Western Europe and lacked any overt anti-Communist overtones. However, the Soviet Union rejected the Marshall Plan for Eastern Europe, and as a result the Plan adopted a more anticommunist orientation. The Soviet Union responded by creating its own counterpart to the Marshall Plan. Beginning in 1949, Bulgaria, Czechoslovakia, Hungary, Rumania, and the Soviet Union formed the Council for Mutual Assistance (Comecon, or CMEA) as an economic response to the U.S. initiative. The countries of Eastern Europe began to adopt long-range development plans based on the Soviet model and to direct more of their trade toward the Soviet Union.

At this juncture, the Soviet Union and the United States had reached a stalemate over the Cold War issues as each side blamed the other for the deterioration in their relations. The superpowers became locked into a competitive and conflictual interaction that governed their relations from 1947 to 1989. The tense nature of superpower interaction had consequences for the world system. National security became a paramount concern in the interaction between nations. Security became increasingly dependent on membership in either coalition as the Cold War became the dominant issue on the international agenda. Europe divided into rival blocs led by the two superpowers.

The United States institutionalized its containment policy in a series of Cold War coalitions in Europe, Asia, and the Middle East. The Soviet Union established its own Cold War alliance in Eastern and Central Europe as a response to the Kremlin perception of capitalist encirclement. As the new postwar world order unfolded, the United States and Soviet Union came forth as the two centers of global power, and the world system assumed a bipolar character.

The economic and political arenas were not the only spheres in which the East-West conflict abounded. The increased tension over the status of Berlin also played an important role in accelerating the military dimension of the Cold

War. In 1949 the Soviets rebuilt the armies of Eastern Europe, modernizing their weapon systems and command structures according to Moscow's needs. The Soviet blockade of Berlin, which began in early 1948, marked the first open challenge by the Soviets to America's military resolve.[5] The Berlin Crisis demonstrated U.S. determination to implement its containment policies militarily. The Berlin Crisis was also critical in the formation of the North Atlantic Treaty Organization (NATO). Although the two superpowers disagreed on a range of issue areas, they found themselves taking a similar position on the creation of the state of Israel. All hope of Great Power unanimity and consensus within the United Nations Security Council evaporated with the onset of the Cold War.

Both superpowers engaged in an active campaign to recruit other states into their coalitions. Although some states joined out of "national interest" or for military assistance against a regional or traditional enemy, ideology and security became important bases for membership in these rival Cold War coalitions. The United States and the Soviet Union competed in Europe and later in Asia and Africa for new clients and allies. In Germany, East and West were separated, leaving Berlin a small island in a communist sea, while in China the communists won a conclusive victory over the Kuomintang, and Chiang Kai-shek's forces had to evacuate, mostly to Formosa. In Korea, the Russian-dominated North faced the American-occupied South. In Greece, Turkey, and Iran, communist pressures failed to achieve their objectives.[6] The only overt loss of an ally suffered by either side during this period was Yugoslavia's defection from the communist camp.

The early phase of the East-West struggle highlights the difficulty of sorting out causes. Ideology was fundamental to this conflict. It was equally clear that the Cold War also grew out of the meeting between Russian and American power in the heart of Europe. Both superpowers sought to fill a power vacuum in a weakened Europe at the close of the Second War. John Stoessinger has made a strong case for the futility of trying to delineate the prime causes of the struggle, because each move by one superpower led to a countermove by the other. What is important is that the East-West conflict had frozen Europe by 1949. There was virtually no maneuverability left as power confronted concerted counterpower. Thus, it was no accident that the center of the East-West struggle during the next decade shifted from Europe. The rise of the People's Republic of China as an independent power center in the communist world helped direct world attention toward East Asia.[7]

Another development that separates this postwar era from others was the affirmation of the superpower's dominance in the world system. The Suez and Hungarian crises reinforced the supremacy of the United States and the Soviet Union over their allies. The orbiting of Sputnik in autumn 1957 and the Soviet Union's apparent lead in the arms race led to heated debate within the U.S. foreign policy community over alleged Soviet superiority in space-age warfare. During this period each alliance system became more hierarchical for a num-

ber of political and strategic reasons. Nikita Krushchev's first priority after the
Hungarian Revolution was to stamp out revisionism. He used the fortieth
anniversary of the Soviet Union to wring from the ruling Communist parties a
declaration that referred to the "invincible camp of Socialist countries headed
by the Soviet Union."[8] At this juncture, the Chinese did not publicly disagree
with the Soviets or question Soviet hegemony.

The Suez Crisis greatly diminished the prestige and influence of Britain
and France not only in the Third World but also with their European and
Commonwealth allies. The rapidity of decolonization had undermined their
power and influence in the world system. European power became increasingly
diminished. With the arrival of tactical nuclear weapons in the European theater, the United States consolidated its position as political and strategic decision maker in NATO,[9] thus defining the strategies and conflicts for the alliance
that policy makers considered essential for their survival.

As the 1950s came to an end, both superpowers increased their power and
influence in their Cold War coalitions. At this juncture, they focused their
attention on the Third World. Given the general economic status and the political fluidity of the new states of Asia and Africa, it was assumed that the leaders of the Third World had no alternative but to align with the Eastern or Western bloc. Both superpowers saw the new states as pawns on the chessboard of
the East-West struggle, lacking a foreign policy agendas of their own. Policy
makers in Moscow and Washington conceptualized the interstate system as
being in a state of war in which all nations great and small had to choose sides.
Thus, the Cold War and the bipolar structure that emerged after the Second
World War played a vital role in the historical development of Third World
states. At this time, we will focus our analysis on the role of the nonaligned
movement in strengthening the bonds of Third World solidarity as a dynamic
force in world politics.

THE COLD WAR EXTENDS INTO ASIA

In 1950, the Korean Crisis threatened to change the Cold War into
another world war. The Korean Crisis also expanded the East-West conflict
into the Asian continent. The new states of Asia and Africa became important
targets of superpower rivalry and the East-West conflict. Recruitment in Asia
and Africa also led to divisions among new states into aligned and unaligned.
Thus, the Korean conflict was important not only in drawing attention to the
militarization of the U.S. containment policy, but also in introducing the Cold
War in bold relief to the new states of the Third World.

The Korean War began as a United Nations operation designed to repel a
North Korean invasion south of the 38th parallel. By January 1951, the Korean
conflict escalated into a major Sino-American confrontation fought mostly on
Asian soil.

Many of the new states of Asia and Africa made a neutralist response to the conflict, refusing to take sides with either adversary or to take a position supporting either ideology. The neutralists, led at times by India, sought to use the United Nations Security Council and the General Assembly as forums to resolve the conflict. India, which in later years became an important member of the nonaligned movement, played a pivotal role in the efforts of the neutralist states to demilitarize the Korean conflict.

A major result of the Korean crisis was an intensification of superpower recruitment activities in the Third World. The Cold War became globalized rather than geographically specific. In 1974, Seyom Brown observed that the United States and the Soviet Union viewed the Third World through doctrinal lenses during the height of the Cold War,[10] perceiving it as a vast power vacuum in which each superpower employed its own imperial designs. The majority of these nations were politically and economically underdeveloped and required substantial economic aid in order to avoid collapse. Because only the United States and the Soviet Union emerged from the Second World War with resources essential for supporting their global interests, they began expecting every new state to choose one of them as its benefactor.[11]

At the time of the Korean Crisis, the East-West conflict had run its territorial distance in Europe. In Asia, Japan was securely in the Western camp, while the People's Republic of China was in the Eastern camp. If either side was to gain in the global balance of power, it would be through the powerless but geopolitically significant Third World.

AMERICA'S COLD WAR MANEUVERS IN ASIA

Beginning with Japan in 1951, the United States established a policy of peace-aid reconciliation. The Americans signed the United States-Japanese Security Treaty, arousing the fear of several states in the region concerning Japanese rearmament. In response to this perceived threat and, more important, as part of the American containment policy, the United States entered into the Philippines-American Defense Pact in August 1951. In September 1951, Australia, New Zealand, and the United States became signatories to the ANZUS Treaty. These security pacts committed the United States to guarantee the member states against any attacks, whether from a resurgent Japan, a belligerent Indonesia, or an expansionist People's Republic of China.

In order to shore up an inherently weak Geneva Settlement of the Indo-China crisis, the Southeast Asia Treaty Organization (SEATO) became America's answer to suspected communist activities in this volatile Third World region. Many neutral states such as India considered SEATO a subsidiary to NATO, targeted primarily at the People's Republic of China. The United States signed a bilateral treaty with South Korea in 1953, and a multilateral accord with SEATO that included Thailand and Pakistan in 1954. A protocol to this treaty involved the United States even more deeply by unilaterally extending SEATO's mandate to South Vietnam, Laos, and Cambodia. Pakistan joined SEATO primarily as a result of conflict over the Kashmir question. The creation of the SEATO security pact divided Asia into neutral, Western, and Eastern camps.

In a continuation of the militarization of its containment policy, the United States extended its alliance system into the Middle East to fill a power vacuum left by the British and French. A framework for a collective security pact became established in 1954, with Pakistan playing a pivotal role.

At this time delicate negotiations were taking place among Turkey, Iraq, Iran, Pakistan, and Britain regarding the creation of an alliance system with U.S. support. The Baghdad Pact was the result of this tactful negotiation. The United States agreed to provide military assistance to member states. Such neutrals in the region as Egypt and Syria became unhappy with the extension of the American Cold War coalition into the region and were wary of Western intentions. The timing of the pact guaranteed Arab nationalist opposition to this development.[12] Egypt and its Arab neighbors saw Iraq's decision to participate in the Baghdad Pact as a knife in the back of Arab solidarity. The Arab League established a military wing as a response to this development. Iraq became isolated from the Arab world for participating in this American-led security pact. This posture was very similar to the position taken by Arab states toward Egypt as a result of the Camp David peace accords between Cairo and Tel Aviv. After a regicide in Iraq a more neutralist government came to power. The Baghdad Pact became the Central Treaty Organization (CENTO).

Thus, the United States extended its containment policy outside the European theater by establishing military and security pacts in Asia and the Middle East. The Third World became an important ideological and strategic battleground for superpower rivalry following the military stalemate in Europe. Although a number of states began to adopt a neutral posture toward the Cold War, Dullesian analysis allowed only two positions: support for the United States or for the Soviet Union.[13]

THE SOVIET UNION'S COLD WAR MANEUVERS IN ASIA

The Soviet Union had responded to U.S. militarization of containment by establishing its own comprehensive multilateral security pact in Eastern Europe. Beginning in 1955, the Soviet Union signed the Warsaw Pact Treaty Organization with the existing communist regimes in Europe except for Yugoslavia. The signatories of this treaty included Albania, Bulgaria, Czechoslovakia, East Germany, Hungary, Poland, Rumania, and the Soviet Union.

The Soviet Union also launched a new ideological and diplomatic offensive toward the Third World in 1954. On the Soviet front, a major result of the Korean War was a closer working relationship among the Soviet Union, the People's Republic of China, North Korea, and North Vietnam. Before 1954, Western powers were the principal dispensers of economic aid to new countries in Africa and Asia. In 1954 the Soviet Union initiated its own economic aid program to new states in the Third World. This development added a new dimension to the Cold War/superpower rivalry in the dispensation of foreign aid. In January 1954, Afghanistan became the first noncommunist regime to receive a Soviet loan in the sum of $3.5 million. In the first year, the total aid from the Soviet Union and other communist countries to noncommunist countries was $10.6 million. Soviet aid to the Third World rose from $305 million in 1955, to $1 billion in 1956, and hovering around $2 million in 1957.[14] The United States, however, greatly exceeded the Soviets' efforts, giving greater priority to Israel, Libya, South Korea, Laos, and Formosa, while the Soviets targeted foreign aid to Syria, Yugoslavia, Afghanistan, India, Egypt, Cambodia, Ceylon, Indonesia, and Nepal. The Soviet diplomatic and ideological offensives sought to counter the new American containment offensive embodied in such NATO-type subsidiary alliances as SEATO, CENTO, and ANZUS.

Moscow began its new offensive with a number of advantages over its American counterpart: the novelty of the Soviet aid program; the prevailing Afro-Asian anti-imperialist image of the USSR; the apparent absence of political or military strings; the procedural advantage of totalitarian governments in operating aid programs; and the fact that the East bloc aid was growing at a faster annual rate than Western aid. In assisting these countries the Soviet Union was moving with the tide of events. As in Egypt and Syria, Soviet contacts with Indonesia increased rapidly, for assistance from the Soviet bloc became a valuable asset to the nationalist leaders in the new states of Asia and Africa, especially with reference to their domestic and international politics. When the pro-western Iraqi regime of Nar-Es-Said lost power in July 1958, the USSR immediately welcomed its successor led by General Kassemi. The Soviet Union was also successful in making diplomatic overtures to the Sudan in 1956 (to change in 1959) and to Guinea in 1960.[15]

Another important aspect of the new Soviet offensive toward the Third World was ideological. At the Twentieth Party Congress in 1956, First Secretary Nikita Khrushchev asserted that peaceful coexistence was "the general line" and "a fundamental principle of Soviet foreign policy," not merely a tactical move.[16] This meant, he added, that competition between the capitalist and the socialist systems had begun in the economic sphere. The Soviet Union had a definite role for the emerging nations of Asia and Africa to play in the Cold War. The Soviets hoped to increase the zone of peace, or the Soviet sphere of influence, around the world to combat "capitalist penetration," their definition of U.S. containment policy. According to Roger Kanet, the Soviet evaluation of the Third World failed for three reasons: (1) its emphasis on the importance of the anticolonial movement for international affairs; (2) its optimism over developments in the Third World and the impending collapse of capitalism; and (3) its lack of detailed information or ideological formulations on domestic developments in the Third World.[17]

The Soviet initial optimism that the new states of Asia and Africa would join their zone of peace was proven wrong as contact and interaction with neutralists in the Third World increased. With the exception of Cuba, no developing country had embarked on a socialist path toward development or aligned itself fully with the Soviet Union in international affairs. The failure of this hope led Soviet policy makers to reformulate their approach toward neutralism. Soviet theoreticians began to speak of two sides to neutralism, the positive side, which they sought to exploit, and the negative side, which they opposed. The Soviets discovered that the Third World had an agenda of its own.

NONALIGNMENT AND THE POLITICS OF A THIRD FORCE

The Afro-Asian states comprised the weakest actors in the global community, especially with reference to the economic, political, and military components of power. With the exception of Latin America, the new states of the Third World had a common past, common attitudes toward their former colonial rulers, and a common set of problems in the 1950s. They shared the same intellectual baggage: nationalism, anticolonialism, and a propensity toward nonalignment. Similar experience of Western domination, poverty, and nonwhiteness served as a bond for Third World solidarity. Starting with the Bandung Conference, these states challenged the existing international economic, political, racial and cultural order. As the first conference sponsored by the "colored nations," Bandung came to symbolize the Third World's transition from diplomatic dependency on the West to increased independence and self-assertion in world affairs.

The division of the Afro-Asian delegates into pro-Western, pro-Eastern, and neutral camps, however, colored the debate on a number of issues. The issue of collective security and military pacts led to acrimonious debates that threatened to disrupt the conference. Nehru epitomized the position of most nonaligned delegates on this issue when he asserted that India would not sacrifice its dignity to either Cold War coalition:

> I belong to neither bloc and I propose to belong to neither whatever happens in the world. I am afraid of nobody. I suffer from no fear complex. My country suffers from no fear complex.[18]

Many delegates responded to Nehru's call for nonalignment by proposing that India lead a "third bloc" composed of the colored nations of Africa and Asia. Nehru declined the offer, however, and no other delegate arose to assume the leadership role. Unlike their contemporaries in OPEC and the NICs, these delegates lacked the prerequisites of power that could lead the Third World in their quest for increased independence and self-assertion. Sir John Kotelawla, the prime minister of Ceylon (Sri Lanka), outlined the political, economic, and military weakness of Afro-Asian states vis-à-vis the West, "We by contrast come to the conference weak and relatively unarmed. We have no thermonuclear bombs in our pockets, no weapons of chemical or bacteriological warfare up our sleeves, no plans for armament, factories or blueprints for more deadly methods of genocide in our briefcases. These were the sins of the mighty, the arsenal of others."[19] The Afro-Asian states' lack of military power to counterbalance the influence of superpowers undermined the development of a third force in the world system.

Although a number of delegates sought to precipitate a nonaligned posture among the Bandung conferees, Cold War divisions eclipsed desires for nonalignment. The Bandung Conference was, however, an important milestone in the evolution of nonalignment as a basis for Third World solidarity. In spite of the diversity of perspectives, Cold War divisions, and regional disputes, the Bandung Conference fostered communications and interaction among Afro-Asian states. Hence, a community of interest evolved that became anticolonial, antiracialist, and antibloc in character. Bandung provided Afro-Asian states a framework for enhancing solidarity and cooperation. In so doing, it ushered in a new era of international relations.

Throughout the 1950s, the terms neutralism and nonalignment were employed by diplomats and scholars alike to describe the Cold War policies of a large number of Third World states. Yet, by drawing attention to the bipolarization of the world system into antithetical, ideological camps, these states created an alternative to traditional anti-alliance postures such as neutrality, neutralization, and isolation.[20] Neutrality refers to a state's impartial nonparticipation in disputes of other states. Neutrality of a state may provide voluntary safeguards only insofar as other nations respect this international code of behavior, or if belligerent nations forcibly maintain sanctions. *The International Relations Dictionary* states that the rights of neutral states recognized by belligerents include (1) freedom from territorial violation; (2) acceptance of the fact of neutralist impartiality; and (3) freedom from interference with commerce except to the degree sanctioned by international law.[21]

By Cold War standards, neutrality meant nonparticipation in international affairs. One of the principal hypotheses of the Cold War was that all nations, small and large, European and non-European, were expected to participate in international affairs by choosing sides in the East-West conflict. This assumption lost its validity as an increasing number of new African and Asian states chose not to join either Cold War coalition. Nevertheless, delegates from these states actively participated in decisions of the United Nations General Assembly and the Security Council. Former President Modita Keita of Mali expressed the perspective of a number of Afro-Asian leaders when he asserted, "We shall study all existing views and we shall express ourselves in support of those providing for the most objective settlement."[22] Afro-Asian leaders did not conceptualize their role in international politics as pawns whose position on the East-West conflict and other issues followed the policy orientation of the superpowers. Nonalignment evolved in the 1950s as an affirmation of the sovereign right of Third World states to make independent decisions on issues confronting the international community rather than observing strict ideological criteria.

Afro-Asian leaders adopted nonalignment for a number of reasons. First, these leaders sought recognition and dignity for their societies. Leaders in the Third World desired to overcome the humiliation experienced during the colonial period. Western domination left a mark of oppression that did not disappear with the advent of sovereignty. The late Kwame Nkrumah, former President of Ghana, observed in 1963, "The European relegated us to a position of inferiors in every aspect of our daily life. Many of our people came to accept the view that we are an inferior people."[23] The Afro-Asian movement had emphasized the recovery of their lost dignity by Afro-Asian states as an important basis for solidarity. Nonparticipation in Cold War alliances reinforced these efforts.

Second, nonalignment was attractive to Afro-Asian states as a result of the anticolonial and antiracial platform of the movement. During the 1960s newly independent states from Africa sought to eliminate the last remnants of white minority rule in Southern Africa. India led the fight against racism and apartheid in the early years of the United Nations. The struggle against racism and the reimposition of colonial rule became important components of the movement.

Afro-Asian states desired to protect their sovereignty from encroachment from any power. These newly emergent states did not want to become pawns of either superpower coalition. Hence, it was in their national interest to pursue nonalignment and expend their energies on more pressing issues such as colonialism, economic development, and eliminating racism and the remaining relics of global apartheid.

The notion of a buffer zone between capitalism and socialism was first articulated in Asia. It was no accident that first in Colombo, then Bandung, and finally in Belgrade, the leading proponents of nonalignment insisted on safeguarding their newly won sovereignty. Leaders in the Third World were fearful of socialism and opposed to the overwhelming influence of American capitalism. These leaders (Nehru, Sukarno, Nasser, and Nkrumah) were essentially *petit bourgeois*. They sought domestically and internationally to find a middle passage between capitalism and socialism.[24]

By 1961, the major tenets of nonalignment had crystallized. Nonparticipation in either military or political alliances with major powers had become a requirement for membership and the basis for solidarity. With the evolution of the nonaligned movement, leaders in the Third World sought to create a distinct diplomatic role for these states in world politics. At the first Belgrade Conference of the Non-aligned, they asserted their desire to play an active role in conflict resolution. Delegates gathered at Belgrade adopted nonalignment as the name of their movement and asserted that nonalignment did not necessarily imply neutrality.

THE THEORETICAL CREED OF THE NONALIGNED MOVEMENT

In 1961, the ideological and theoretical basis for the nonaligned movement became institutionalized at Belgrade by twenty-five countries with a shared interest in developing an alternative path in the world system to alignment and entangling alliances. These actors sought to create flexible and nonhierarchical structures in their bid to design a new constellation of nonaligned states born into a bipolar-structured interstate system. Their shared interest became the guiding creed for the nonaligned movement. Archie W. Singham and Helen Hune have identified five key elements of the nonaligned ideological and theoretical creed: (1) peace and disarmament, especially the reduction of tension between major powers; (2) independence, including the right to self-determination of all colonial peoples and the right of equality between all races; (3) economic equality, with emphasis on restructuring the existing international economic order, particularly with respect to the growing and persistent inequality between the Northern and Southern Hemispheres; (4) cultural equality, with emphasis on restructuring the global information and communication order, and opposing cultural imperialism and the Northern monopoly of information systems; and (5) universalism and multilateralism, through strong support for the United Nations system – whose principles support nonalignment – as the appropriate forum to deal with all global issues. Hence, the nonaligned movement has resisted efforts within its own ranks to create alternative structures that might compete with the United Nations.[25]

The nonaligned movement did not pursue efforts to codify these ideological and theoretical principles until the Sixth Summit in Havana in 1979. The development of the nonaligned credo has come from a variety of sources, ranging from the leaders and governments of the nonaligned countries to those who pioneered this alternative path to world politics, such as Tito, Nehru, Nasser, Sukarno, Nkrumah, and Ahmed Ben Bella, and many others. Nehru focused most of his attention on the right of self-determination and the capacity of newly independent states to protect their sovereignty, especially in a world system characterized by a bipolar power structure. Tito emphasized international peace and sought a reduction in tensions between the superpowers in order to avoid a nuclear confrontation. Nasser sought to reduce the influence of foreign powers in the Middle East and to provide diplomatic and military support for the dispossessed Palestinians. Surkarno was a militant anticolonialist and a radical nationalist. He promoted the idea that newly emerging states should be free to choose their own social, economic, and political relations, including the right to form links with communist states such as the People's Republic of China. Nkrumah concentrated his efforts on the struggle against global apartheid and decolonization on the African continent and sought to end white minority regimes in Southern Africa.[26] Since the creation of the nonaligned movement, Third World leaders from Ben Bella and Houari Boumedienne of

Algeria to Fidel Castro of Cuba and Julius Nyerere of Tanzania have made significant contributions to the content and direction of this Southern institution, through their emphases on national liberation and the need for economic liberation. At this juncture we will elaborate more fully on the creed of the nonaligned movement.

THE COLD WAR AND PEACE

The newly emerging nations from Asia, Africa, and the Caribbean rejected alliances and military pacts with the Great Powers. These neophytes sought to promote peace because they believed that only through international peace could their aspirations and needs be fulfilled. There is substantial evidence to support claims that the nonaligned countries have contributed to world peace by sending peacekeeping troops to Africa and the Middle East. These states have also contributed financially to such efforts by the United Nations.[27] The movement has developed a three-year cycle in which to survey the global situation to identify crisis areas that could escalate into conflict between the major powers and hence result in a nuclear war and threaten global annihilation. The nonaligned movement has examined disarmament and peace theoretically and has distinguished between various types of conflicts within the global community: (1) conflict between major nuclear powers; (2) wars of self-determination and liberation; (3) internal civil wars resulting from political secessionist movements; and (4) armed conflict between nonaligned member states that could lead to a conflict between the major powers.

The movement has made a distinction between just and unjust wars. It has consistently argued that wars of self-determination and liberation are justifiable, requiring support from the international community. The nonaligned movement justifies the deployment of punitive sanctions as diplomatic instruments to deter or resolve such conflicts. The movement has also argued that war was often the only method by which Third World people could resist continued colonial subjugation. This focus on the right to wage armed struggle differentiates the nonaligned movement from other pacifist or neutralist organizations. The nonaligned movement has supported national self-determination and liberation movements globally, notably in Algeria, Vietnam, and the former Portuguese colonies in Africa and Southern Africa. It has consistently supported the rights of the Palestinian people, including their right to a homeland, and of the peoples of Southern Africa to oppose apartheid white minority regimes in the region, with armed struggle if necessary. Likewise, the movement has supported antisystemic movements in the Caribbean and Central America. Hence, the nonaligned movement has supported efforts by leaders in the Caribbean and Central America to oppose indigenous ruling classes who have made alliances (economic and diplomatic) that reinforce classical dependency and patron-client relations with the United States, thus compromising the economic, cultural, and political sovereignty of these nations.[28] Thus, the nonaligned movement was very supportive of the revolutions in Grenada and Nicaragua.

The nonaligned movement has sought to use its organization as a forum to reduce and manage conflict among Third World states before these battles escalate into confrontations in which the Great Powers may become involved. Examples of inter-Third World or nonaligned conflicts are those in Vietnam and Kampuchea, Uganda and Tanzania, Iraq and Iran, and the Second Persian and Arabian Gulf War of 1990 and 1991, which finally escalated into a war between Iraq and the U.S.-led coalition that included Saudi Arabia, Syria, Turkey, Egypt, Kuwait, Britain, France, the USSR, and Italy. The Iraq-Iran conflict also led to a delay of the 1983 nonaligned summit. Since 1979, the movement has sought to create a variety of mechanisms, ranging from the Good Office format to the Chair of the organization, to reconcile conflict between nonaligned and Third World states. However, to date, such efforts have not been very successful.

ANTICOLONIALISM AND THE BATTLE AGAINST GLOBAL APARTHEID

As I have emphasized earlier, the right to self-determination of colonial peoples and the right of equality between all races predates the formation of the nonaligned movement. What brought these newly emerging states from Asia and Africa together was obviously the second wave of decolonization that occurred as a result of the global war of hegemonic succession that we traditionally refer to as the Second World War. These anticolonial movements represented the resentment of Third World people against the policies of the colonial powers. The road toward freedom and liberation remained hard, especially for those nations and people still pursuing statehood. Newly independent Third World states became champions of anticolonialism and provided political refuge to exiled nationalists struggling against colonial rule. Thus, after India, Ghana, and Egypt[29] achieved independence, anticolonialism became an important component in their foreign policy as these actors also provided a political sanctuary for a variety of liberation movements as part of their contribution to the anticolonial cause. Anticolonialism became a major theme on the three continents of Asia, Africa, and Latin America. The nonaligned movement also became an important forum for the colonized to present their case for sovereignty and independence before the international community. Before Algeria, Vietnam, Angola, Zimbabwe, and Namibia acquired their independence, for example, it recognized their national liberation movements, accepted their provisional governments as members, and welcomed their leaders as heads of state. The movement provided legitimacy to new states as they entered world politics.

The nonaligned movement has provided support for two major struggles for self-determination and liberation in the postwar era. The movement has provided legitimacy to the anticolonial movement on the African continent. Independence was achieved through non-violent means by most of the African states north of the Zambezi River, with the exceptions of Algeria and Kenya (the Mau Mau movement in the 1950s contributed to the British decision to transform this colonial territory from a settler colony). The Portuguese colonies, Zimbabwe and Namibia, also achieved independence as a result of armed struggle. South Africa supported these recalcitrant colonial states and white settler populations in their efforts to maintain these racist regimes through a policy of "destructive engagement" against the front-line states and the liberated territories in the region.

South Africa's apartheid policies were universally condemned starting in 1948. The nonaligned movement joined forces with the international anti-apartheid coalition to isolate this racist regime from the international community and to attack Northern economic, cultural, diplomatic, and military support for Pretoria. These efforts bore fruit with the release of Nelson Mandela on February 11, 1990, and of other African National Congress and Pan-African Congress political prisoners, and with the attempt to dismantle the remaining mechanism of "petty apartheid." However, "grand apartheid" continues to dominate the political landscape in South Africa. The road toward a multiracial democracy suffered a number of setbacks with the increase in black-on-black violence supported by segments of South Africa's security forces and the rise of white vigilante violence.

Starting in 1975, the nonaligned movement has argued that there is a correlation between the experiences of the black population of Southern Africa and the disenfranchisement of the people of Palestine. They drew parallels between the situation in Palestine and that in South Africa where two settler states have adopted policies that have resulted in the domination, exploitation, and segregation of the indigenous population. In their declarations and activities in the United Nations, nonaligned countries have attempted to bring the rights of the Palestinians and the African majority in Southern Africa to the attention of the global community. Since 1975, the nonaligned countries have argued that Zionism is a form of racism. They have faced hostility from the North in the form of withdrawal of financial support to international institutions that have attempted to isolate the state of Israel or prevent its delegates from participating in these global forums. Examples of Third World-dominated international institutions pursuing such policies range from the International Labor Organization (ILO) to the United Nations Educational Scientific and Cultural Organization (UNESCO). In recent years, a number of nonaligned states have retreated from their hostility toward Israel and have renewed diplomatic relations. Likewise, a number of these actors have moved toward a mutual recognition of the rights of the Israelis and of the Palestinian right to a separate state. In addition, former President Jimmy Carter was successful in his bid to reduce the tensions between Egypt and Israel through the Camp David Accords.[30]

The Persian Gulf War of 1990–91 turned the spotlight once again toward the Middle East. U.S. policy makers pursued a strong policy in delinking the conflict with Iraq over Kuwait from the Palestinian issue and other sources of conflict between the Arabs and the Israelis.

ECONOMIC DECOLONIZATION AND THE DEMAND FOR A NEW ORDER

Problems associated with dependency and underdevelopment have been important agenda items at nonaligned summits since 1961. New states from Africa and Asia found themselves in the same boat with Latin American and Caribbean counterparts who had achieved independence during the first wave of decolonization and consolidation of Pax Britannica. The new nations in Latin America and the Caribbean were born into a world system in which the models of capital accumulation that structured the world economy and the international regimes that govern interstate relations were established by the new hegemon and, to some extent, the Great Powers. These actors also defined the parameters by which new emerging states were reincorporated back into the capitalist world economy, thus maintaining their dependent status. Latin and Caribbean states sought to challenge their economic, political, and cultural subordination and to protect their sovereignty through Pan-Americanism from 1826 to 1889.

Leaders from this sector of the Third World also sought to codify domestic, regional, and international law to give these actors sovereign rights over their natural resources and to nationalize such resources if they deemed that to be their national interest. Latin international jurists also sought to settle the score with foreign investors at a price that they felt was fair. Such diplomatic activities placed these actors on a collision course with the Great Powers. After 1889, Pan-Americanism increasingly became a diplomatic tool for U.S. hegemony in this vital zone of the world system. Nevertheless, efforts by Haitian, Mexican, and Argentine diplomats to challenge the North-South political, economic, and cultural divide found fertile ground in the postwar era as these actors sought to assert their perspectives in international affairs.

Most of the nonaligned member states became convinced that the international economic, financial, and trading regimes operated to their comparative disadvantage. These actors argued that the international regimes governing the world economy contributed to their underdevelopment. The international regimes associated with Pax Americana failed to address the economic concerns of developing nations through a Marshall Plan for the Third World. Most of the African, Asian, and Caribbean states that became politically independent during the postwar period lacked economic liberation to give substance to their newly acquired status as sovereign states. Under the leadership of the nonaligned movement, economic decolonization became as potent a force in the 1970s as political decolonization had been in the 1960s.

The nonaligned movement was successful in forging a dynamic alliance among its members — whose ideological predispositions spanned the horizon from bourgeois conservative authoritarian dictatorships, to socialists and social democrats, to Marxist-Leninists — to challenge the North-South divide. It was at Algiers in 1973 that the nonaligned movement called for structural changes in the global economy and the establishment of a new international economic order. Their basic demands can be summarized as follows: (1) the establishment of producer associations by producer nations following the model set by the Organization of Petroleum Exporting Countries; (2) creation of new commodity agreements to assure just prices; (3) indexation; (4) sovereignty over natural resources; (5) transfer of technology; (6) greater control over the two major types of private international organizations — transnational corporations and transnational banks. The nonaligned movement played a pivotal role in the North-South conflict. These actors made this conflict the most salient issue confronting the Third World in the postwar era.

CULTURAL EQUALITY AND THE QUEST FOR A NEW WORLD INFORMATION ORDER

The nonaligned movement became concerned with the unequal cultural exchange that accompanied their incorporation into the capitalist world economy during the first and second waves of colonization and that still pervades the postwar world order. The imperial powers of the North denied that people and nations of the South had any culture worth preserving and that these actors had made any significant contribution to the development of the human family. The North also rationalized their conquest of the South on cultural grounds and argued that colonial conquest was an integral part of the "white man's burden" to bring the blessings of civilization to the natives. Anticolonialism also took on a cultural dimension during the first and second waves of decolonization in the Third World. Since the end of the Second World War, Third World leaders have discovered that the North maintains a monopoly on how the South is conceptualized by the international community. The North exercises this control over both the content and the technology of communication. Hence, the nonaligned movement has emerged as an important champion of a new world information and communication order. The movement has focused attention on the ability of new communications systems that are predominantly Western owned and controlled to penetrate any nation-state and undermine traditional values.

Starting in the 1970s the nonaligned movement made the liberation of Third World mass communication systems an important item on their agenda. As part of their efforts to decolonize the news, the movement formed a nonaligned news pool and has begun the task of linking radio communications. As with the new international economic order, nonaligned states have begun to develop a strategy of increasing horizontal linkages among themselves instead of relying on the old vertical linkages with the Northern capitals for information. However, the introduction of new communication and computer technologies, ranging from fiber optics, fax machines, the modem, faster and more powerful personal computers and scanning devices by the North, has reinforced rather than delinked informational ties between the North and South. The global economic crisis and the adjustment problem faced by many nations in the South have made it more difficult for them to acquire the new technologies. The challenge to erect a new world information order has not diminished as a result of these technological changes.

THE NONALIGNED MOVEMENT AND THE UNITED NATIONS

The nonaligned movement affirmed the importance of the United Nations as the most essential international institution for new states in the postwar era through its participation in and expansion of its role as a global forum for conflict resolution in the cultural, economic, and political sphere. Given their peripheral status in the world system and their concern for the possible outbreak of nuclear war, it is natural that nonaligned states should support the United Nations. During the height of the Cold War, the superpowers, protected by their nuclear shield, relied less on the United Nations than did the members of the nonaligned movement. Third World states aligned with the East or West received assurances from both superpowers against aggression and became reluctant to turn to the United Nations. However, nonaligned states had only themselves upon which to rely for protection and therefore found the United Nations more appealing. The United Nations emerged as an important institution for protecting the sovereignty and independence of the new states in Africa, Asia, and the Caribbean.

With the advent of a large number of new states from Africa, Asia, and the Caribbean, the character of the United Nations underwent a significant change. Third World states constituted the vast majority of this international institution. The nonaligned movement has influenced the direction taken by the United Nations with its vigorous attack on a number of global issues since 1965. It has made profound physical and ideological changes in this international institution, bringing a non-Western and non-Eastern perspective on global issues.

Initially, the United Nations was conceptualized by a number of Third World leaders as a Western Club guided by Western parliamentary practices and procedures, and led, for the most part, by staff members and diplomats from the North. Despite Soviet obstructionism, the United Nations did what the Western world wanted it to do,[31] functioning as a "white man's club," as the Northwest − the United States, Western Europe, and Japan − set the agenda and financed its operation. The nonaligned movement played a critical role in transforming this institution into a forum that could help protect the sovereignty of new states. The U. N. emerged as a forum in which a small state without much status or prestige could greatly enhance its influence by joining with other states in adopting a common policy objective. There are three areas in which the United Nations has been important to the nonaligned movement. First, it has provided international recognition for newly independent states that have joined it, without regard to their status, power, or wealth. Second, it has put new states on an equal footing with all other members of the General Assembly, giving them the opportunity to debate and vote on many international issues, some of which are not of immediate concern to them. This also gives them an opportunity to make their voices heard and to earn respect for their points of view. Third, it has provided the nonaligned movement with a platform from which to exert significant influence on issues such as decolonization, economic development, disarmament, and East-West and North-South relations.[32]

The United Nations Security Council has remained a private club for the Great Powers, operating as a citadel of power from which victors of the Second World War preserve the status quo in the world system. It has become a predominantly Western-dominated institution where Russia and the commonwealth of independent states operate on the periphery. In 1963, after much debate, the Security Council expanded from eleven to fifteen members (five permanent and ten elected) to reflect the increased membership of the U.N. Membership in the Security Council grew to include the interests of Africa, Asia, the Caribbean, and a changing Latin America (the Latin nations were increasingly becoming part of the Third World alliance in the United Nations system).[33]

Since the end of the Second World War, all major conflicts in the world system have occurred in the Third World, primarily in Southeast Asia, Western Asia, Southern Africa, Central America, and currently in the Middle East and the former Yugoslavia. The nonaligned movement has also intensified its efforts to secure representation for its members in the Security Council, and has waged a valiant battle to change its voting and decision-making processes. It has also sought similar changes in other relevant international bodies such as the International Monetary Fund and the World Bank. The nonaligned movement became committed to restructuring the power equations in international institutions to reflect its numerical majority. The North, however, led by the United States, has refused to abandon its veto power. In spite of these problems, the United Nations has emerged as an important force in the nonaligned movement's attack on the unequal distribution of economic, political, and cultural power in the world system.

Since 1961 the nonaligned movement has attempted to steer a different, independent course in world affairs. While Switzerland has even refused to participate in such international institutions as the United Nations, the nonaligned movement has been very active in world affairs, leaving its stamp on international affairs. Finally, nonalignment has represented its ideological identity in an era of competing capitalist and socialist moralities.

NOTES

1. W. LaFeber, *The American Age: United States Foreign Policy at Home and Abroad Since 1759* (New York: W. W. Norton, 1989), p. 152.

2. A. W. Singham, *The Non-Aligned in World Politics* (Westport, CT: Lawrence Hill and Company, 1977), p. viii.

3. L. Halle, *The Cold War as History* (London, Chatto and Windus, 1967), p. 120.

4. S. Hoffmann, *Primacy or World Order: American Foreign Policy Since the Cold War* (New York: McGraw-Hill, 1978), p. 7.

5. C. L. Robertson, *International Politics Since World War II: A Short History* (New York: John Wiley and Sons, Inc., 1975), p. 79.

6. P. Lyon, *Neutralism* (Leicester: Leicester University Press, 1963).

7. J. Stoessinger, *The Might of Nations: World Politics in Our Times* (New York: Random House, 1979), p. 51.

8. A. Buchan, *The End of the Postwar Era: A New Balance of World Power* (London:Weidenfield, 1974), pp. 20–21.

9. Ibid., p. 23.

10. S. Brown, *New Forces in World Politics* (Washington D. C. : Brookings Institute, 1974).

11. Ibid., p. 62.

12. P. Lyon, *Neutralism,* p. 51.

13. John Foster Dulles was President Dwight Eisenhower's Secretary of State. He was a key member of the defense and foreign policy task force that was responsible for refashioning U.S. foreign policy. He favored the following options:

1. containment: a continuation of the basic structure of policy as exercised during the Truman years.

2. a policy of Global deterrence in which American commitments actually would be extended and Communist transgressions met with severe punishment.

3. liberation: political, psychological, economic, and even paramilitary warfare designed to penetrate the communist empire, "roll it back," and liberate captive peoples.

Dulles did not believe that American response to Communist aggression should be limited to a conventional response à la Korea. If American interests were global and indistinguishable, and the threat to those interests was monolithic and undifferentiated Soviet Communist aggression, then the United States and the free world then felt free to direct its response directly against the Soviets (or any other communist aggressor such as China). Having solved the problem of military and defensive strategy, the free world could undertake what had long been delayed – a "political offensive": liberation. John Foster Dulles proposed a policy of boldness and political offensive with a shift in deterrence to include the technology of air and sea power.

14. Lyon, op. cit., p. 46.

15. C. Stevens, *The Soviet Union and Black Africa* (New York: Holmes and Meier, Publishers, 1976), pp. 9–10.

16. R. Kanet, *The Soviet Union and Developing Countries* (Baltimore: John Hopkins University Press, 1974).

17. Ibid.

18. G. H. Jansen, *Afro-Asia and Non-Alignment* (London: Faber and Faber, 1966), p. 209.

19. F. Ajami, "The Fate of the Non-Aligned," *Foreign Affairs* 59, no. 2 (1981/82): p. 367.

20. N. Choucri, "The Perceptual Base of Non-Alignment," *Journal of Conflict Resolution* 13, (1969): p. 124.

21. J. C. Plano and R. Olton, *International Relations Dictionary,* 3rd ed. (Santa Barbara, CA: ABC-CLIO, 1982), p. 262.

22. C. L. Legum, *Pan-Africanism: A Short Political Guide* (New York: F. A. Praeger, 1965), p. 56.

23. K. Nkrumah, *Africa Must Unite* (London: Heinemann, 1963), p. 32.

24. A. W. Singham, *The Non-Aligned in World Politics.*

25. A. W. Singham and H. Hune, *Non-Alignment in an Age of Alignment* (London: Zed Press, 1986), pp. 14–15.

26. Ibid., p. 14.

27. A. Lassassi, *Non-Alignment and Algerian Foreign Policy* (Brookfield, Vt.: Aveberry Publishers, 1988), pp. 30–31.

28. A. W. Singham and H. Hune, *Non-Alignment in an Age of Alignment,* pp. 16–17.

29. Egypt had a military coup in 1952 which overthrew the monarchy and diminished the influence of the British in Cairo.

30. A. W. Singham and H. Hune, *Non-Alignment in an Age of Alignment,* p. 21.

31. Ibid., p. 28.

32. A. Lassassi, *Non-Alignment and Algerian Foreign Policy,* p. 41.

33. A. W. Singham and H. Hune, *Non-Alignment in an Age of Alignment,* p. 29.

4

The Military and Strategic Dimensions of Nonalignment

S tarting in the early 1970s, relations among the United States, the Soviet Union, and the People's Republic of China underwent fundamental changes. The apparent thaws in the Cold War symbolized the dynamic change at hand in the interstate system. The East-West conflict was losing its dominant position on the agenda of the international community as the primary determinant of state-to-state interaction.

As Cold War coalitions weakened, ideological bonds that held them together loosened as well. Multipolarity and interdependence in the industrialized North and continued dependence in one form or another in the South – that is, Third World states – replaced the rigid bipolarity that had characterized the world system since the beginning of the postwar era. In the beginning, the Cold War between the United States and the Soviet Union included the monolithic Eastern and Western blocs as the primary adversaries. After the Sino-Soviet conflict escalated into a full-blown socialist discord, polycentrism and independence became defining characteristics in both Cold War coalitions. The Sino-Soviet conflict injected an independent and assertive People's Republic of China within the communist bloc. NATO encountered similar problems as France under Charles de Gaulle charted an independent strategy and behaved with new freedom of action.

Western Europe and Japan began to exercise more independence, especially in the economic arena. Both Japan and Western Europe had recovered sufficiently from the Second World War to compete effectively with the United States for world markets. The Western alliance no longer automatically followed American leadership on security issues, and no longer viewed the Soviet Union or the People's Republic of China as ultimate threats to international peace.

The Sino-Soviet conflict escalated from being a minor policy irritant to a full-scale rift between these two communist giants. The Soviet Union replaced the United States as China's number one enemy. The Chinese intensified their own "cold war" with the Soviet Union throughout the 1970s. Among Eastern European states, traditional leadership lost legitimacy. Revisionism dominated the political equation in Czechoslovakia, and to some extent in Rumania. In 1968 the Soviet Union used its military force to crush revisionist experiments in Prague. Throughout the 1970s, Soviet hegemony was disputed in Eastern Europe. Détente did not result in stability in either Cold War coalition.

The transition in the nature of superpower interaction introduced a degree of flexibility into the international community. Security issues became less important in international institutions. Nonmilitary issues began to assume more importance in the bargaining among members of the Cold War coalitions. Developmental crises in the Third World played a pivotal role in mobilizing conservative, moderate, and radical African, Asian, Caribbean, and Latin American states into coordinating their demand for a new international economic order. In the decade of the 1970s, the "oil weapon" gave new confidence to the Third World in its interaction with the industrially developed North.

The recently independent nations making up the nonaligned movement began to spend less energy on such issues as the Cold War and more on such issues as the economic disparity between the developing countries of the Southern Hemisphere and the industrially developed countries of the Northern Hemisphere. Starting in the 1970s the North-South conflict replaced the Cold War as the motivating force behind the movement. The nonaligned movement began to change its orientation toward challenging the global economic status quo.

By the late 1960s, decolonization had so advanced that the more visible and explicit political regimes of domination had virtually disappeared, with a few exceptions in Southern Africa. Freedom became less restricted by politics. However, many leaders of the new states in Africa, Asia, and the Caribbean found that the global economic system constrained their nations' freedom. The existing international economic order, they believed, intruded on the sovereignty and development of their societies. Leaders in Africa, Asia, the Caribbean, Latin America, and the Middle East began to envision a broader solidarity based on shared economic concerns.

The nonaligned movement changed substantially, accommodating a broader diversity of ideological stances than had been necessary at its inception in 1961, when the movement became an "exclusive club." The militant cadre of leaders in those early days had defined their movement and based their membership on nonparticipation in Cold War coalitions. Alliances, even relations with either Cold War coalition, had become conceptualized as a serious breach of nonalignment. The broader movement of the 1970s included the Latin American states.

Since the Cuban missile crisis in 1962, U.S.-Soviet relations had been in flux. That crisis marked a watershed in superpower relations. U.S. and Soviet nuclear forces faced one another in a battle over a Third World nation in which a nuclear war became more than a military exercise or a simulation game. The narrow escape from nuclear war left a deep impression on the leadership of both countries. Slowly, the frozen hostility of the Cold War thawed and gave way to a less abrasive relationship characterized by greater realism and a more businesslike approach. Ideology and polemics were replaced by more objective assessments of each other's character, intent, and power. An environment of hostile interaction gave way to an attitude conducive to productive negotiations.[1]

The Cuban missile crisis also sealed the U.S. leadership position in NATO in the 1960s. The manner in which President John F. Kennedy handled the crisis, his successful use of the right level of force, and his sensitivity to the relationship between the crises in the Caribbean and in Europe enhanced American prestige in the alliance. Since Cuba's proximity to the United States became a critical issue in this conflict, American allies felt that Washington's response was in the best interest of the Western alliance. Nevertheless, the Cuban missile confrontation led to the Atmospheric Test Ban Treaty of 1963 to which the United States, the Soviet Union and Great Britain were signatories. Another aftermath of the Cuban missile confrontation was the installation of a hotline between Moscow and Washington. This conflict clarified what had been implicit since the Geneva Conference of 1955, namely that the two superpowers had a relationship with each other, whether of conflict or cooperation, that they did not have with their own coalition partners. The Soviets' posture on the Cuban missile crisis intensified the growing conflict between Moscow and Beijing. The People's Republic of China began to question the Soviets' position on doctrinaire issues such as the "inevitability" of war between socialist and capitalist powers; they supported wars of national liberation and openly challenged Soviet leadership in the Third World. The Sino-Soviet conflict emerged as a major issue in the Soviets' coalition.

In the postcrisis atmosphere, Khrushchev agreed to a partial test ban treaty and seemed eager to reduce the tensions that defined U.S.-Soviet relations. Without informing the "old Russian hands" at the State Department, Kennedy drafted an extraordinary speech, which he delivered on June 10, 1963, at American University in Washington, D. C. Soviet citizens found it electrifying. For months many Soviet citizens carried clippings of it in their wallets. It was the first speech by an American president in more than a decade and a half to note that the people of the Soviet Union were human beings and to pay tribute to their bravery and suffering in the Second World War.[2] This speech marked the first attempt to exorcise the devil theory that had determined official attitudes and public opinion toward the Soviet Union. President Kennedy's speech became a forerunner to the Nixon-Kissinger policies of détente.

With the end of the Soviet threat to Berlin, the surmounting of the Cuban missile crisis, and the beginnings of a serious Soviet-American dialogue over arms control, the chilliest years of the Cold War came to an end. Discussions began in Western academic circles and foreign offices about a return to a more normal Great Power relationship, motivated more by rational calculations than by ideology or mutual fear. Discussion ensued on a natural evolution to a polycentric world as the economic strength of first Europe and then Japan advanced, and more and more powers acquired the technology to manufacture nuclear weapons.[3]

POLYCENTRISM IN THE EASTERN AND WESTERN BLOCS

The Soviet Sphere

The road to détente was not an easy one for either superpower. Particularly rough were the relations with their Cold War coalitions. Having suffered a major diplomatic reverse over Cuba, the Soviet Union became engaged in a major ideological and leadership battle with its largest ally, China. The Soviets hoped to improve their position by expanding their influence in certain key areas of the Third World (Egypt, Syria, and India) and by sowing dissension in Western Europe and the United States. China and the United States had become adversaries in a war (the Korean conflict) a decade earlier. During this period the United States became engaged in a major conflict in South Vietnam. The People's Republic of China supported the North Vietnamese in their quest to liberate South Vietnam from the West. If the United States had offered an olive branch, it is doubtful that the Chinese response would have been positive.

The People's Republic of China began to plot its own diplomatic course. The frustrations of China's external policy, growing Soviet support for China's Asian rival, India, declining Chinese influence in Indonesia after 1965, Chinese failure to rally the Third World in a Second Bandung Conference, coupled with fears of American intervention in Southeast Asia, contributed to conflicts in Beijing that led to the Cultural Revolution in 1966. However, the conviction that the Soviet Union was becoming bourgeois in its ideology and imperialist in its interests was more important. The Cultural Revolution, with its xenophobia, its withdrawal of ambassadors from overseas posts, and its virtual closure of the Ministry of External Affairs, made China from 1966 to 1969 a power with whom it was difficult to cultivate relations.[4]

The evolution of détente as an integral part of the Soviets' grand strategy created problems in Eastern Europe as well. As détente unfolded as more than an expedient tactic, as the cultivation of normal state-to-state relations with members of the opposing ideological bloc eclipsed postures of militant hostility, and as a sequence of arms limitation agreements underlined the common overarching interest of the Soviet Union and the United States in reducing the likelihood of general war, it became increasingly difficult for the Kremlin to sustain the Marxist argument of two implacably contradictory social systems. If the communist bloc no longer conceptualized world politics as the anticipation of the impending class war, then the need to acquire a completely bona fide socialist commonwealth faded, as did the need to mobilize the camp in a rigidly hierarchical system.[5]

During the 1960s Premier Nikita Khrushchev sought to rejuvenate the moribund CMEA as an instrument for the promotion of intra-Comecon trade. Greater policy coordination, standardization of industrial products, emphasis on long-term trade agreements, establishment of an international bank for socialist countries, and increased specialization and division of labor among Comecon countries became targets for expansion in trade. The result of this policy posture was disappointing because of the persistence of the previous bias toward economic self-sufficiency, scarcity of goods, and the poor quality of the goods available.[6] By the mid-1960s it had become clear that the East could not bridge the technology gap and achieve intensive growth rapidly without foreign technology. The East would need to turn to the West in order to develop its vast natural resources, produce cars and trucks, improve agriculture, and even develop a tourist industry.

Trade between Eastern and Western Europe played an important role in undermining Soviet leadership in the Warsaw Pact. Commerce with the developing noncommunist world, much of it bilateral between individual Eastern European and Western countries, began to play a more important role in many of the economies of the Warsaw Pact.

East European trade with the West, including the United States, expanded rapidly in the 1970s. Eastern European debt rose from $13 billion to $55 billion between 1974 and 1978. The political implications of this debt, owed primarily to Western banks, emerged as a critical policy issue in the Soviet bloc in the 1970s. Throughout this decade, Eastern European countries became more dependent on the capitalist countries of the West, as trade, technological, and financial relations increased. Furthermore, Western countries gained some influence over Eastern European nations' domestic policies. In 1979, Poland allowed Western banks to monitor its economic policies as a prerequisite for a new loan. The banks made it clear to the Polish leadership that if they were to meet their payments on the $15 billion they owed the West, they would have to adopt a policy of austerity. The Polish austerity policy was partially responsible for the emergence of Solidarity, the anti-Communist Polish labor union that became a policy nightmare for the Soviets.

Economic interaction between Eastern and Western Europe also led some members of the socialist commonwealth to postulate economic programs that diverged from the Soviet model. The doctrine of "many roads to socialism" became the ideology for domestic and foreign policy in such states as Czechoslovakia, Hungary, and Yugoslavia (the latter was now once again accepted as a member of the socialist community despite its continuing international posture of nonalignment).[7] The Communist Party of the Soviet Union had always feared the rise of nationalism, revisionism, and reformism within Eastern Europe.

Since the beginning of the postwar era, the Soviets had held a militarized buffer around Eastern Europe. The primary reason put forward by the USSR for maintaining a militarized buffer area on its western flank was German revanchism during the Second World War. This argument became less salient in the early 1970s with the negotiation of the Bonn-Soviet, Bonn-Warsaw, and Bonn-Prague treaties renouncing the use of force and pledging to respect the existing status quo, the Berlin agreement, and the normalization of relations between the East and West German states. To the extent that détente and increased East-West communications replaced deterrence as a basis for security in Europe, the geopolitical rationale for maintaining major deployments of Soviet troops in Eastern Europe and a tight, Kremlin-controlled military alliance system became further weakened. In spite of the treaties with Bonn, the Soviet Union continued to maintain a tight military rein on Eastern Europe throughout the 1970s.

Starting in the late 1960s the Kremlin's nightmare concerning nationalism, revisionism, and reformist tendencies became a reality. In 1968 the Dubček government in Czechoslovakia became a spokesman for anti-Soviet national-ism and reformism and was forced out of power by the Soviets. Rumanian dis-sidents expressed their differences with the Soviets in such arenas as interna-tional Communist Party congresses, military planning committees of the War-saw Pact, the Council for Mutual Economic Assistance (Comecon), and vari-ous all-European forums, whereas in the nonproliferation treaty negotiations, Rumania delegates openly attacked Soviet-sponsored proposals as "profoundly discriminatory" against non nuclear countries.[8] After the tragedy of 1956, Hungarian policy makers engaged in a variety of domestic experiments that were impeccably in deference to Soviet views on interbloc diplomatic relations. The reforms found in Budapest's New Economic Mechanism (NEM) only intensified Hungarian needs for Western machinery and technology and made Hungary progressively more eager to become a full participant in the world economy. During the 1970s Budapest policy makers applied for membership in the General Agreement on Tariffs and Trade (GATT) which, to some degree, reduced Moscow's influence over Hungary's political economy.

After the end of World War II the Russians feared the disruptive impact that the rise of self-determination and nationalism in Poland might have on Eastern Europe. The communist lid on Polish nationalism threatened to blow up in Soviets' face; this nearly happened in 1956 at the time of the Hungarian revolution, when Wladyslaw Gromulko successfully faced down the threat of Soviet military intervention. In 1956 Premier Khrushchev made his peace with Polish nationalism by granting Gromulko more autonomous control over his internal affairs than allowed to any other member of the Warsaw Pact.

In 1979 the Polish regime enacted a number of austere economic policies to combat debt problems with Western banks. These policies resulted in a number of labor strikes throughout Poland with demands not only for higher wages but also for an independent trade union beyond the control of the Com-munist Party. Throughout 1979--1980, Solidarity became a dynamic political force in Polish society. The Soviet Union threatened to intervene militarily if Polish authorities could not bring Solidarity under control and restore Poland to a "socialist path." Solidarity increased its demands and began to ask for participation in the political process, decision-making apparatus with reference to economic development, and even selection of politburo members in which the union supported, rather than the Communist Party candidates. In December 1980, when it became apparent that the Solidarity experiment had gone too far, the Polish army intervened, establishing martial law and arresting the leadership of Solidarity. Although the Polish army action preempted Soviet military intervention, the result was a limitation on the Solidarity experiment and restoration of Soviet hegemony.

In some respects, polycentrism in the Soviet bloc was not new. Periodic assertions of Eastern European independence, despite the shadow of the Red Army, marked the behavior of the East Germans, the Poles, and the Hungarians during the 1950s. However, the Sino-Soviet split and the crisis in Poland combined with economic growth, resurgent nationalism, and a declining sense of outside military threat to produce more visible and perhaps more permanent fissures. Between 1962 to 1973 cracks emerged in the Western alliance that threatened to diminish efforts at community building. Eastern Europe underwent another wave of revisionism, nationalism, and democratization in the late 1980s from which the Soviet empire did not recover.

The American Sphere

During the height of the Cold War era, economic interactions among industrially developed nations reinforced the military and ideological foundations of the U.S.-led coalition. The predominance of security issues was evident through the early 1960s when Charles de Gaulle attempted to form the Bonn-Paris axis of economic, technological, and military collaboration. At this juncture, Bonn was unwilling to support measures that might lead the Americans to reduce their military deployments in Germany. Disagreements between the United States and its Atlantic allies over such issues as payments, trade, and monetary matters became increasingly subordinated to the need to resolve the issues of NATO defense operation. Differences between the Americans and Europeans continued over strategies for standing firm against Soviet attack in Western Europe and the question of sharing or centralizing control of strategic nuclear weapons. By the early 1970s, serious cracks appeared in the U.S.-led coalition as Western European fears over Soviet and Chinese expansion began to decline. New changes emerged in the Western alliance as nonmilitary issues became more salient than security ones and became subject to political bargaining among members of the coalition. Reductions in external security concerns provided the opportunity for nonmilitary issues to rise, both relatively and absolutely, to a level where they frequently challenged the institutions and those of the anticommunist security community itself.[9]

The heightened salience of nonmilitary issues was attributed to the growing capabilities of America's own alliance partners, to the point that the United States suffered a decline in its ability to impose its own chosen solutions to nonmilitary questions. In 1947 the United States accounted for half of the world's total gross national product; this declined to 34 percent in 1960 and 24 percent in 1975. In 1973 the combined output of the European Economic Community (EEC) and Japan was more than $90 billion greater than America's output. Only twenty years earlier it had been less than three-quarters of America's output.

Starting in the 1970s the United States no longer could function as the global economic hegemon. Increasingly, U.S. policy makers encountered challenges to their decision-making role in international trade, finance, and the world economy from Western Europe and Japan. Western allies became dissatisfied with their decision-making role on international economic issues.

The growing economic strength of Western Europe and Japan relative to the United States and the resultant lessening of their dependency upon the United States increased the ability of each to steer an independent course. Militarily, this position has not materialized. The dispersion of economic wealth and productivity will continue to make it difficult to resolve major international economic issues by the assertion of the U.S. position and the concurrence of three or four other powers.[10]

Debates over size, composition, and deployment of forces by various NATO members became less important than the distribution of economic burdens of alliance membership. Prior to the 1970s, when the United States insisted that the economically thriving NATO countries contribute more to their own defense and purchase military equipment in the United States to offset the balance-of-payment costs of keeping U.S. forces in Europe, it was easier to compel agreement on the basis of the security issue. Starting in the 1970s the question of military burden-sharing became identified with monetary and trade issues or projects for cooperation in the energy field, and the United States had to bargain against a coalition composed of the European Economic Community within NATO.[11]

Within the Western alliance, for example, Greece's disengagement from NATO following the Turkish invasion of Cyprus in 1974 demonstrated the primacy of issues other than interalliance solidarity in the face of an external threat. The coup in Portugal and the near-electoral victory of the Communist Party in Italy were other domestic concerns potentially disruptive of the Western alliance. Again, the rise in the importance of nonmilitary issues corresponded with these specific events.

Similarly, Japan's position for bargaining with the United States on both economic and security matters became fortified by the Cold War alignment in Asia, signaled by President Richard Nixon's visit to China in February 1972. During the 1960s, Japan's gross national product and her external trade had more than quadrupled, to the extent that Tokyo had become the world's third strongest economic power. America's détente with China liberated Japan somewhat from the highly structured Japanese-American security relationship, which the United States was in the habit of using in bilateral negotiations with Japan. Japanese intransigence in the trade and monetary arena began to undercut America's usage of the security issue as a pressure point in bilateral negotiations. At this juncture the Japanese were free to pursue their own bilateral relations with mainland China, the USSR, and the Third World. Policy makers in Tokyo could pursue the trading nation policy orientation[12] while the U.S. continued providing security for this region. By the time of the Middle East war of 1973, Japan felt free to make its own economic deals with Arab oil producers against the wishes of the United States.[13]

The American-led coalition was experiencing some degree of fragmentation when the energy crisis emerged as a major issue in the international community in 1973. During the Middle East Crisis of 1973, Arab countries used the oil weapon to pressure European and Japanese governments to support their cause against Israel. Both the Europeans and the Japanese resented Henry Kissinger's suggestion that America's coalition partners were looking out for their own narrow interests while the United States worked to preserve world order. Starting in 1974 divisions within the Western alliance had become so volatile that America's offer to pool current and future energy resources for NATO was seen as a strategy to revive American hegemony.[14]

The polycentric fragmentation of NATO and the Warsaw Pact was manifestation of the evolving structural characteristics of the world system at large. Rapid technological innovation in major weapon systems of the superpowers became the principal catalyst of change in the polarity structure of the international system. In particular, the advent of technologically sophisticated intercontinental ballistic missiles (ICBM) decreased the need for forward base areas for the purpose of striking at the heart of the adversary's territory, thereby diminishing the need for a cohesive alliance system composed of reliable members. In addition, the deterioration of alliance groupings was accelerated by the shrinking gap between Soviet and American military capabilities as the balance of power became less of a "balance of terror." European members of NATO began to question whether the United States would indeed trade Washington, DC, or New York City for Paris, Bonn, or London.

Fragmentation within the Soviet and American Cold War coalitions accelerated the movement toward détente. The changing balance of military capability between the two superpowers also contributed to the development of détente.

DÉTENTE TAKES FORM IN EUROPE

The first concrete result of the movement toward détente was the partial nuclear test ban treaty concluded in Moscow in 1963. During the remainder of the decade, despite the rapid escalation of the Vietnam War, Soviet-American relations gradually changed. Agreements were made to prevent the proliferation of nuclear weapons and protect outer space and the ocean floor from the atomic arms race.[15]

Beginning in 1969, framers of American foreign policy openly began expressing a new policy posture toward the Soviet Union. President Richard Nixon declared that "an era of negotiation" would begin, and the Soviet leadership, with a wary eye on China, decided to cooperate with its great capitalist adversary. The process of gradual détente that followed contributed to a relaxation in the Cold War and the beginning of a new era of "adversary partnership" in the 1970s. This change in superpower interaction had broad ramifications for the international community. Throughout the 1970s, nonmilitary issues temporarily replaced security issues as the dominant concern of the international community as détente continued to unfold on the continent of Europe.

During the 1960s, détente began to develop in Europe as a serious policy posture in the Cold War. After assuming power, the Brezhnev-Kosygin leadership team continued Khrushchev's "opening to the West," with its attention toward France. The Soviet media had long castigated French colonialism in Southeast Asia and North Africa, and when Charles de Gaulle returned to power in 1958, Moscow attacked him for seeking to establish a military dictatorship and for refusing to grant independence to Algeria. De Gaulle did not permit the Soviet interest in penetrating the Third World to interfere with his European policy.

The Soviet leadership saw France as the odd member out of NATO and expressed satisfaction with the Gaullist preference for a Europe of cooperating but nationalistic and independent sovereignties, which conflicted boldly with the "Atlantic Alliance" formulation of American and British decision makers. De Gaulle's distinctive blend of unsentimental realism and striking purposefulness (for example, his veto in January 1963 of the British application for membership in the Common Market) intrigued Moscow, so much so that it was deterred from pressing for closer bilateral relations with the U.S. by his *force de frappé* (independent nuclear force), his refusal to sign the nuclear test ban treaty or discuss arms control, his tenacious opposition to Soviet pressure during the Berlin and Cuban crises, and his cultivation of a special relationship with Bonn.[16]

In 1965 Soviet Foreign Minister Andrei Gromyko visited de Gaulle. At this time Charles de Gaulle desired a different role for France in the international system and sought to challenge American leadership in NATO, withdrawing from NATO and demanding that all U.S. troops leave French territory. In June 1966 he traveled to Moscow, where Brezhnev broached the idea of a European security conference. The Moscow declaration on June 30, 1966, announced the plan of the two governments "to continue regular consultations." For the Soviets, détente with France meant a welcome increase in tensions within the Western alliance.

Moscow continued its efforts to strengthen that relationship with France, but after the Soviet invasion of Czechoslovakia, a certain disenchantment and constraint emerged in Paris. Georges Pompidou and Giscard Valery d'Estaing continued Paris's high-level visits, however, and Soviet leaders regularly returned them.

France was not the only European country to expedite the process of détente. The Federal Republic of Germany (FRG) was another important Western country toward which Soviet diplomacy became targeted. From 1955 onward, the Soviet Union sought Western acceptance of the territorial status quo in Europe, recognition of the division of Germany and the legitimacy of the German Democratic Republic (GDR), a weakening of ties between West Berlin and Bonn, and a minimal level of rearmament by the Federal Republic of Germany.

During the years of the so-called "grand coalition" (1966–1969), when Willy Brandt was foreign minister, Ostpolitik and détente became a respectable issue for discussion for the first time as the result of the French withdrawal from NATO; this moved had called into question the whole Western anti-Soviet strategy. The price was still too high for West Germany to strike a separate treaty concerning these issues with the Soviets. The division of Germany between the East and the West complicated the negotiation process. The Russian desire to weaken the ties between Bonn and Washington was too high a price for Soviet-West German entente in the early 1960s.

In the fall of 1969, the Social Democrats won a clear majority, and Willy Brandt became the new German chancellor. In less than a year Ostpolitik, embodied in a Soviet-German treaty and a Polish-German treaty, became a reality. The border between East and West Germany and the Oder-Niesse Line dividing East Germany and Poland received legal recognition and legitimacy. Brandt declared in a speech in Moscow in 1970 that Russia is a critical part of the history of Europe, not only as an adversary and threat but also as a partner from a historical, political, cultural, and economic perspective.

The treaty between the Soviet Union and West Germany stipulated that the two parties (a) "undertake to respect without restriction the territorial integrity of all states in Europe within their present frontiers; (b) declare that they have no territorial claims against anybody nor will [they] assert such claims in the future; (c) regard today and shall in the future regard the frontiers of all states in Europe as irrevocable such as they are on the date of signature of the present Treaty, including the Oder-Niesse line." For Moscow, the treaty was a major step on the road to Western recognition of Soviet hegemony in Central and Eastern Europe. It also accelerated the acquisition of advanced technology and extensive credit from West Germany, an objective that was increasingly important for Moscow.[17]

The growing rapprochement between the Soviet Union and Western Europe accelerated the process of questioning many of the major ideological, territorial, and political foundations of the Cold War on the European continent. It also accelerated the gradual process of détente that was evolving between the two superpowers. Détente between the superpowers also led to relaxation of tensions between the United States and the People's Republic of China.

DÉTENTE BETWEEN THE U.S., THE USSR, AND THE PEOPLE'S REPUBLIC OF CHINA

The process of gradual détente that began on the heels of the Cuban missile crisis took on new momentum in the early 1970s. The Nixon-Kissinger policy of détente was an attempt to create a stable international system through a greater degree of cooperation between the United States and the Soviet Union. Earlier attempts at easing East-West tensions had not been the cornerstone of American foreign policy. Furthermore, such efforts as Eisenhower's Spirit of Geneva speech, Kennedy's Non-Proliferation Treaty of 1963, and Johnson's doctrine of building bridges in the mid-1960s had encountered continuing hostility from the Soviet Union. When Nixon took office and when Henry Kissinger became his chief foreign policy advisor, the easing of U.S.-Soviet tensions became a major objective of American foreign policy and the cornerstone of the U.S. global strategy. Furthermore, the Soviets became committed to improving superpower relations.[18]

Détente became the defining characteristic of U.S.-Soviet relations in the 1970s. Nevertheless, competitions between the superpowers remained as the possibility of nuclear holocaust made cooperation imperative. The adversary relationship continued between the superpowers as policy makers in Washington and Moscow sought to establish an environment in which they could regulate and restrain their differences. Détente contributed to the development of a conducive environment for achieving this goal.

Beginning in March 1970, the United States and the Soviet Union began talks on the status of Berlin. While little visible progress emerged during 1970, the talks signaled a shift in policy toward recognizing the status quo in Europe as a requirement for further consultations in this critical area of conflict. In 1970 two rounds of Strategic Arms Limitation Talks (SALT) convened in Vienna and Helsinki, emphasizing the interest of the two superpowers in negotiating bilateral agreements on weapon controls.

Negotiations on both the Berlin issue and SALT continued in 1971. The first phase of quadripartite negotiations on Berlin was completed, leading to subsequent negotiations between East and West Germany.[19] SALT talks resumed in March 1971 despite escalation of fighting in Vietnam. These discussions were concluded in December 1971. The escalation of fighting in Southeast Asia did not negate further interest in SALT I. The Soviet interest in détente became enshrined and legitimated by the Twenty-Fourth Communist Party Congress in March 1971, and by Secretary Brezhnev's call for a relaxation in world tensions and improved relations between the United States and the Soviet Union in April 1971. In May a new era of cooperation between the two superpowers emerged when Soviet officials made it known that they wanted to negotiate a trade agreement with the United States.

Between the start of the serious back-channel negotiations and the signing of the agreement, Kissinger made a trip to China that accelerated the détente process. At this juncture, Sino-Soviet relations reached their lowest ebb. The Soviet defense posture along the Sino-Soviet border created conditions that enhanced the prospects for United States-Chinese détente. In March 1969 fighting broke out on Damansky Island (Chanpao Island) in the Ussuri River, which flows between Manchuria and the Mari Republic in the Soviet Far East. The following summer, further clashes occurred in the Amur River and on the boundary of Sinkiang province. Negotiations to resolve the three centuries of border disputes that had sparked the fighting came to a standstill.[20] The Soviets began a campaign that raised the specter of a preemptive strike on the Chinese nuclear force. This event persuaded the Chinese to turn more quickly toward the United States.

On March 15, 1979, the United States lifted the final restrictions on travel by American nationals to China, and three months later ended the last embargoes on the export of nonstrategic goods. In April the Chinese invited the American and British ping-pong teams to visit Beijing. Zhou Enlai used that occasion as an opportunity to speak of "a new stage in the relations between the Chinese and American peoples."[21] This crucial occurrence contributed to one of the most dramatic moves in current diplomatic history, with the arrival in Beijing of Henry Kissinger, the President's chief advisor on national security affairs, who had traveled through Europe and Pakistan, leaving a trail of different cover stories behind him in various capitals. On the same day the Chinese declared that the President had accepted Zhou Enlai's invitation to visit Beijing by May 1972.[22]

The Sino-American rapprochement had ramifications in the political and military spheres. The Nixon administration had not made a practice of consulting with allies on Asian questions for some time, with the exception of its association with France during the Vietnam peace negotiations and its use of British and Canadian diplomatic channels in relations with China. President Nixon's decision to enter normal diplomatic relations with China emerged without detailed discussions with such Pacific allies as Japan, New Zealand, and Australia.

By 1971 it had become evident that the Soviet Union had another rationale for accelerating détente. The Sino-American rapprochement made Soviet-American détente a necessity as a counterweight to China's expanding role. Domestically, shortages in vital sectors of the Soviet economy had made rapid trade expansion with the United States most advantageous. American policy makers established guidelines for economic intercourse between Washington and Moscow, including the sale of 3 million tons of feed grain. This transaction allowed Moscow to cover the shortfall resulting from a poor harvest.

Nevertheless, there remained a number of items that acted as barriers to trade between the two superpowers. From the Soviet Union's perspective, these barriers included the absence of most-favored-nation status, the lack of export credits, and the extensive list of strategic goods blocked for sale to communist countries. The question of Soviet Jewry and the outstanding Second World War lend-lease debt served as negative factors. Nevertheless, limited trade continued when contracts permitted the sale of $65 million of American mining equipment in exchange for the purchase of $60 million of nonferrous metals from the Soviet Union.

The process of détente between the United States and the Soviet Union reached its climax in 1972, when more cooperative agreements were consummated between the superpowers than at any time since diplomatic relations began in 1933. The United States and the Soviet Union were able to reach agreements in a number of arenas including the protection of the environment, science and medicine, and outer space. They agreed on a treaty on the limitation of antiballistic missile systems, a strategic arms limitation treaty on offensive weapon systems, and a set of basic principles governing behavior between the two nations. On June 3, 1972, the United States, Britain, and France signed the final protocol of the Berlin Agreement, and treaty ramification instruments between West Germany and the Soviet Union were exchanged in Berlin. These agreements cleared the way for the initial preparations for the Conference on Security and Cooperation in Europe. On July 8, the United States and the Soviet Union signed an agreement allowing the Soviets to purchase $750 million of American grain between August 1, 1972, and July 20, 1975, with credit offered through the Commodity Credit Corporation. In August American policy makers acknowledged that Soviet grain purchases could far exceed the $750 million foreseen in the previous agreement. At this juncture, the Occidental Petroleum Company began negotiating an agreement with the Soviet Union for the sale of fertilizer chemicals valued at $3 billion.[23]

In October 1972, negotiations on the lend-lease base issue concluded with the Soviet agreement to pay $722 million over twenty-nine years to settle their outstanding Second World War debt. In November 1972, Phase II of the SALT talks dealing with further limits on strategic offensive arms began in Geneva.

The gradual process of Sino-American rapprochement began to take concrete form in 1972. On August 2, 1972, Secretary of State William Rogers expressed support for China's entrance into the United Nations, provided it did not prejudice the status of Taiwan. On October 25, 1972, while Kissinger was paying a second visit to Beijing, the General Assembly voted by a large majority to accord the Chinese seat in the United Nations to the Beijing government. The delegation from Taiwan then withdrew. In November the representative from Beijing took his seat in both the Security Council and the General Assembly.[24]

Détente continued to expand in 1973, although a number of issues threatened rapprochement between the superpowers, among them, the Middle East, the Soviet role in Asia, and the fate of Soviet Jews. Premier Brezhnev warned that American-Soviet relations hinged on peace in Vietnam. At this juncture both superpowers entertained certain aspects of linkage as a mechanism to improve relations. Representative Wilbur Mills, the chairman of the House Ways and Means Committee, threw his weight behind the forces opposing further liberalization unless Moscow rescinded its exit fees and allowed Jews to emigrate freely. In March more than 70 senators and 260 representatives supported legislation that would withhold most-favored-nation status. In April President Nixon asked if he could grant trade concessions to the Soviet Union without linking them to changes in Soviet emigration policy. In Moscow, Premier Brezhnev, in his May Day speech, stressed the need for a further relaxation of tensions with the United States.

The second Nixon-Brezhnev summit convened in Washington in June 1973, at which a number of agreements between Washington and Moscow were signed, covering transportation, agricultural development, oceanography, and cultural and scientific exchange. These accords also focused on procedures for taxing nationals who resided in the other country, creating a Soviet-American Chamber of Commerce, the allocation of office space for trade missions, and increased air service between the two countries.[25]

The United States and the Soviet Union made progress on arms control during this period of rapprochement, consummating an accord on the avoidance of nuclear conflict. Both sides agreed to refrain from the use of force or the threat of force, concluding that consultations and negotiation should be the preferred method of conflict resolution. This accord also urged both superpowers to seek the participation of interested third parties to resolve such conflicts. The June 1973 conference did not resolve the question of strategic arms or provide the Soviets with the most-favored-nation status in the field of trade. Nevertheless, the détente conferences in 1972 and 1973 granted the Soviet Union at least the symbolic status of an equal superpower.

The Nixon administration's concept of SALT became grounded in the view that a strategic arms control agreement with the Soviets might slow down the growing momentum of their strategic force expansion and perhaps establish more predictable and stable relations between the two superpowers. Secretary of State Kissinger's negotiating strategy toward the Soviets focused on offering limited antiballistic missile (ABM) deployment. In exchange, Moscow would freeze their strategic expansion during the life of the agreement. This accord lasted for five years. By the time the agreement was consummated in 1972, the Soviets had achieved higher force levels than the United States in both ICBMs and submarine-launched ballistic missiles (SLBMs). However, the superior quality of American strategic forces and the very large number of long-range bombers in the American arsenal provided assurances to U.S. nuclear strategists with reference to the quantitative advantages of the Soviet Union. The American advantage with respect to multiple independently targetable reentry vehicles (MIRVs) was crucial in this accounting, since the ability of the United States to place high-accuracy multiple warheads on missiles despite the greater number of Soviets missiles allowed under the agreement made up for the quantitative disadvantage through more accurate missiles. Washington's nuclear strategists decided against adopting the Soviet policy preference for greater throw weight and hence, greater destructive power, over precision. Moscow sought to compensate for their lack of technological wherewithal through larger and more destructive missiles. U.S. policy makers concentrated their efforts on smaller missiles by exploiting American technological advances in accuracy, warhead design, and propulsion systems.[26] Nevertheless, the Nixon administration was able to guarantee that the Soviets would not assemble any more strategic weapons than they had been planning to deploy in 1972.

At this juncture, the United States did not sacrifice any of its programs directed at offensive force expansion in order to achieve the goals of this treaty. The Soviets, for their part, retained the option to develop MIRVs in the future and achieved formal recognition by the United States that they had indeed reached a degree of parity with the United States.[27] As a strategy of peace, détente established an environment of cooperation and restraint in which competitors could adjust and check their differences and ultimately move from competition to collaboration. The policy of relaxing tensions with the Soviets and moving toward permanent accommodation and cooperation relied on the theory of "linkage": the development of economic, political, and strategic ties between these nations, mutually rewarding to both, would bind the two in a common fate, thereby removing the incentives for conflict and war. The linkage theory rested on the premise that the Soviet Union was no longer militarily inferior to the United States.

The 1970s had ushered in a strategic challenge to Cold War liberalism in the United States. Increasingly, world communism lost its distinction as the enemy because there was no such thing as a monolithic communist bloc. Communists in Russia and China were seeking détente with America and fighting their own Cold War with one another. The most pressing threat to U.S. security became its dependence on foreign oil. Declining U.S. hegemony in the world economy and environmental and international financial crises had little to do with the Cold War. Moreover, Henry Kissinger's *Realpolitik* had disturbed the ideological neatness of traditional Cold War rhetoric. The evil of the communist system made it impossible to have normal relations with the dictatorships of the Soviet Union and China. Nevertheless, Nixon and Kissinger reached out to China when that whole society was being consumed by the cruelty of the Cultural Revolution, and the Nixon administration encouraged trade with Moscow even as it turned a deaf ear toward the dissidents, refuseniks, and other victims of Brezhnev's repressive policies.[28]

In spite of increased cooperation, Soviets and Americans never held compatible ideas about why détente happened or what it proposed to bring. The relationship that Kissinger articulated for the United States was a web of interrelationships that would tie the superpowers together, maximizing cooperation between them while discouraging uncontrolled competition. The effect of this new approach toward a traditional America dilemma became how to "contain" the Soviet Union.[29] Rhetoric aside, relations between the United States and the Soviet Union remained very competitive.

From the Soviet perspective, the beginning of détente became irrefutable proof that the "correlation of forces" in the world had shifted to the Soviet advantage. Hence, the Soviet's viewpoint of détente provided not just the appearance of superpower equality, but the reality of a bipolar structured world order. The idea that the United States and the Soviet Union could eventually share responsibility for managing the global community of nations, perhaps even divide it up between them, appealed enormously to Soviet leaders. Originally, détente looked in Moscow like a first step toward just such an arrangement.[30]

The divergence in perceptions concerning the meaning of this cooperative process led eventually to the demise of détente by 1980. Initially, the bloom of détente did not entirely fade even under the strains imposed by events like the Yom Kippur War of 1973 and the deployment of Cuban troops to enforce Soviet support of the Movement for the Popular Liberation of Angola (MPLA) in Angola in 1975. However, the ultimate collapse of Soviet-American détente occurred because of the fundamental contradictions and expectations for their new relationship. Unless the two could have found ways to resolve those contradictions as the relationship developed, the demise of this Soviet-American détente was probably inevitable. Soviet intervention into Afghanistan marked the end of détente. It also led to a return to a Cold War posture by the United States.

Nevertheless, détente played an important role in the development of superpower relations and led to the emergence of less hostile international environment in the 1970s.

DÉTENTE AND THE YOM KIPPUR WAR

In October 1973, détente underwent its first major test with the outbreak of war in the Middle East. Tensions between the superpowers ran high. In this zone of the world system, the Soviets were responsible for disruptions in international order while at the same time Washington tried to minimize Moscow's influence. The education of the Soviet Union in the limitations of influence accorded by the United States was forceful and frequently undertaken without consultation with or consent of America's allies, the Congress, and in one instance, the Joint Chiefs of Staff.[31] American forces were placed on alert and the U.S. threatened to intervene with troops against the objections of the Joint Chiefs of Staff. Although American policy makers supported détente and some sense of a condominium of power between the two superpowers, Secretary of State Henry Kissinger sought to dictate the terms and the strategic arena for cooperation and shared conflict resolution between Washington and Moscow.

The Middle East was considered an arena of vital interest for the United States and was outside of any zone of collaboration between the two superpowers. Moreover, American policy makers initiated a series of diplomatic and military activity designed specifically to convince Moscow of the futility of supporting antisystemic action in this vital arena, as well as the frivolity of the Soviet Union's seeking a strategic role in conflict resolution in the Middle East.

In September 1970 American military power was deployed in an effort to force the Russians to withdraw their support from the Syrians when they moved tanks into Jordan to help the Palestinians against King Hussein. American troops were mobilized to intervene in this ensuing conflict. American policy makers sought no Congressional advice and proceeded despite the objections of the Joint Chiefs of Staff, who opposed intervention on both political and military grounds. No allies gave American-based C-130's landing rights on their way to the Middle East. The Russians received the severest warning of "the gravest consequences" if the Syrian tanks did not desist. Secretary of State Henry Kissinger held the Soviets responsible for the action of their clients, the Syrians.[32]

Then a fourth Arab-Israeli war broke out in October 1973 during Yom Kippur. The Egyptians launched a tank-led attack across the Suez Canal into Sinai. At the same time the Syrians attacked Israel from the north. Many Israeli tanks and airplanes were ruined by Russian-made missiles, which were skillfully employed. Fighting ended on October 22, before the Israelis could complete their counterattack, though they had managed to cross to the west side of the canal and take the city of Suez. They violated the cease-fire to finish surrounding an Egyptian corps in Sinai, cutting off its water supply. President Sadat asked for joint U.S.-Russian military intervention to enforce the cease-fire.[33] Brezhnev proposed to President Nixon that both superpowers intervene in order to enforce the cease-fire. At this juncture the United States called a military alert based on possible Soviet troop movements. The tension declined when the Soviet Union informed the United States that it would not insist on sending its own troops to police the cease-fire, and both superpowers agreed on the creation of a United Nations Emergency Force. While both sides paid tribute to the role of détente in facilitating the resolution of this conflict, the October Yom Kippur War raised serious questions in many quarters concerning the durability of the new Soviet-American relations.

During the Yom Kippur War, Egypt and Syria not only attacked Israel but also imposed an export embargo on oil sales to the United States, the Netherlands, and Denmark until such time as these countries withdrew their support from Israel. When Americans sought to supply Israel, Britain warned that U.S. aircraft could no longer land in Ireland, and Germany forbade the loading of U.S. ammunitions onto United States ships at Bremerhaven. Europe thus grounded American NATO supplies and troops. Italy's foreign minister Aldo Moro demanded that Israel withdraw from all occupied territory.[34]

Additional pressures came from Saudi Arabia and Kuwait to embargo any nation passing its oil to the United States. This threatened to immobilize the American Seventh Fleet. This lack of support by American allies in Europe, combined with efforts by Third World states in the Middle East and Southeast Asia, compromised Washington's ability to carry out its military commitments elsewhere in the world. Nations supporting the United States and Israel became targets of an economic boycott by the Organization of Arab Oil-Exporting Countries (OAPEC).

On October 16, OAPEC unilaterally increased the price of its crude oil to $5.12 a barrel. Other oil producers followed with comparable price increases. On December 23, OPEC unilaterally raised the price of Persian Gulf oil to $11.65, to take effect January 1, 1974.[35] This action intensified conflict within the Western alliance. An international energy crisis ensued as power to set price shifted to the producers. OPEC became the first Third World producer cartel to inflict economic harm on the industrialized countries, and thus became an important new force in world politics throughout the 1970s. The world energy crisis created a new factor in East-West relations. In the 1970s oil became a potentially destabilizing international force.

In the meantime, Kissinger not only succeeded in bringing about a cease-fire and disengagement of Arab and Israeli forces, but through shuttle diplomacy between Arab capitals and Israel in 1973, and again in 1974, firmly established the United States as the only mediator acceptable to the major parties to the Middle Eastern conflict. The Syrians remained dependent on the Soviets for military assistance but continued to work with Kissinger in developing the cease-fire and disengagement agreements of June 1974. Egypt, which since the 1950s had borne the brunt of four wars with Israel, became an active and supportive participant in Kissinger's "shuttle diplomacy."[36] In the interim, however, there was no further recourse to military means in the 1970s. The United States became firmly positioned as intermediary between Egypt, the largest of the Arab states, and Israel; and perhaps more important from the perspective of the Soviet-American relationship, the United States seized the diplomatic initiative and consigned the Soviets to the sidelines.[37]

The Soviets subsequently became a significant supporter of antisystemic forces in Africa when the opportunity presented itself in Southern Africa during the latter part of the Ford administration. The Nixon administration conceptualized the white minority regimes in Angola, Mozambique, Guinea-Bissau, Rhodesia, Namibia, and South Africa as permanent fixtures on the global landscape. By 1974 a military coup in Portugal had led to the emergence of a Marxist-Leninist regime in Mozambique, and civil war raged among contending liberation movements in Angola. By 1975 a Soviet- and Cuban-backed Marxist-Leninist regime defeated a U.S.- and South African-backed liberation movement in the Angolan conflict. The Ford administration attempted to extend U.S. assistance to Jonas Savimbi and the Union for the Total Liberation of Angola (UNITA), but was blocked by overwhelming congressional votes against any further assistance to pro-Western Angolan insurgents. By 1980 a

Marxist-oriented regime emerged in what was Rhodesia/Zimbabwe and thereafter became Zimbabwe. Throughout the 1970s American policy makers warned the Soviets that their adventurous activities in the Third World endangered the continuation of détente.

DÉTENTE AND THE WORLD SYSTEM IN THE 1970s

Soviet-American détente successfully survived the threats to this new relationship posed by the Yom Kippur War of 1973. This crisis demonstrated the importance of détente in preventing a nuclear holocaust and how essential it was for both superpowers to avoid participation in local conflicts that might escalate into major confrontations. Soviet-American détente also signaled that important changes were taking place in the world system. These changes included the shape of the international power configuration, the nature of significant actors, and the rules under which the interstate system operated.

Prior to the 1970s, power in the world system, as conceptualized by analysts, laymen, and politicians alike, has emphasized the military capability of nation-states. Political scientists have spent an enormous amount of time attempting to define and measure power relations. The key question puzzling many analysts has been why some nations are able to influence the behavior of others in the interstate system and what sources of power lead to this measure of influence. Hans Morganthau's *Politics Among Nations* has a long checklist of variables that increase or decrease power in the world system. They include geography (isolation, defensible frontiers), natural resources (food, raw materials), industrial capacity, military preparedness, population, national character, national morale, the quality of diplomacy, and the quality of government.[38] Other analysts have included material power, military power, motivational power, achievement, and potential.[39]

Traditionally, military power has been the most essential factor in determining power in the international hierarchy. During the period of industrial expansion, it was the superior military capability of the Europeans, backed by sophisticated technology, that led to conquest of Asia, Africa, and Latin America. Military power is dependent upon a nation's level of technological development, industrial infrastructure, quality and quantity of population, access to natural resources, and geographical location. High-technology countries have traditionally dominated the world system.

The new military technology has transformed nuclear weapons from the exclusive sphere of the superpowers to that of a nuclear oligarchy. In the contemporary interstate system, at least six countries, the United States, the Soviet Union, Great Britain, France, China, and India, possess nuclear arsenals, and several smaller countries (South Africa and Israel) either now possess these weapons of mass destruction or have the technology to develop them. Iraq and Pakistan have made great efforts to join the "nuclear club." The superpowers' arms race, revolving around nuclear weapons and the association of these weapons of mass destruction with political power, has propelled Third World states to build their own nuclear arsenals.

Starting in the 1970s, the world system began to move away from a strict bipolar system. Changes in military technology have reduced the value of forward bases not only for strategic missions but also for supply and reconnaissance in large-scale conventional war. The breakup of the Soviet empire in 1989 has led to emergence of new nuclear powers in Eastern and Central Europe, as well as in the Commonwealth of Independent States. Russian and Ukrainian policy makers are fighting over the fate of the Black Sea naval base and nuclear weaponry. The quest for nuclear power has become intoxicating for regional Third World powers as a direct result of the second Gulf War. Superpower protections became less credible and lost value when Russia refused to offer Baghdad its nuclear shield, thus abdicating its global role as protector of antisystemic Third World states. The world system entered a unipolar moment when the U.S. emerged as the only superpower in the military sphere. These changes in the global political milieu generate high incentives for regional Third World powers to strike a posture of independence and for some to acquire their own nuclear arsenal as a deterrence against military aggression and intervention from the North. Iraq's military defeat in the Gulf War persuaded these actors to purchase high-tech conventional weaponry that might increase the cost to the North of employing military instruments for conflict resolution. Ideologies that made it imperative to defend on a global basis the "good" people against the "bad" have lost legitimacy to more pragmatic considerations.[40]

The interstate system was primarily bipolycentric[41] rather than multipolar in the 1970s because the two superpowers were still the most powerful actors. Smaller states were taking a more assertive and independent posture in the Cold War period. These events contributed to changes in the global power matrix. Military power was no longer the major variable in international relations. Smaller states increasingly created coalitions with one another or with nonaligned countries, and even with members of the Cold War coalition when nonmilitary matters were at issue. Environmental constraints, higher prices for fuel and nonfuel minerals, capital shortages, slower increases in labor productivity, and a host of other factors made the traditional guns-and-butter approach to warfare impossible. The economics of warfare placed unmanageable demands on contemporary industrial powers. The dynamics of bargaining with the superpowers gave many countries big incentives to place nonmilitary issues at the top of the international agenda. In this way the demise of the Cold War coalition, once begun, set in motion other forces that tended to accelerate the pace and force of erosion.

NOTES

1. J. Stoessinger, *The Might of Nations: World Politics in Our Times* (New York: Random House, 1979).

2. R. J. Barnet, *The Giants: Russia and America* (New York: Simon and Schuster, 1977).

3. A. Buchan, *The End of the Postwar Era: A New Balance of World Power* (London: Weidenfield, 1974), p. 25.

4. Ibid.

5. S. Brown, *New Forces in World Politics* (Washington D. C.: Brookings Institute, 1974).

6. C. Kegley and E. R. Wittkopf, *American Foreign Policy: Patterns and Process* (New York: St. Martin's Press, 1981), pp. 208–209; J. E. Spero, *The Politics of International Relations* (New York: St. Martin's Press, 1981), pp. 299–300.

7. S. Brown, *New Forces in World Politics,* p. 25.

8. S. Brown, *The Faces of Power* (New York: Columbia University Press, 1974), p. 571.

9. R. N. Cooper, "Trade Policy in Foreign Policy," *Foreign Policy* 5 (Winter 1972–73): pp. 18–36.

10. C. Kegley and E. R. Wittkopf, *American Foreign Policy,* p. 107.

11. S. Brown, *New Forces in World Politics,* p. 32.

12. R. Rosecrance, *The Rise of the Trading State* (New York: Basic Books, 1986).

13. S. S. Harrison, "Nixon Journey Spurs Japan to Recast Policy." *Washington Post,* 2 March 1971; D. Oberdofer, "The Japan-China Pact: Gains for Both, Risks for the US," *Washington Post,* 30 September 1972.

14. C. Kegley and E. R. Wittkopf, *American Foreign Policy,* p. 36.

15. J. Stoessinger, *The Might of Nations,* p. 60.

16. A. W. Rubinstein, *Yugoslavia and the Non-Aligned World* (Princeton, NJ: Princeton University Press, 1970), p. 102.

17. Ibid., p. 99.

18. J. E. Spero, *The Politics of International Relations,* p. 261.

19. J. Stoessinger, *The Might of Nations.*

20. R. Barnet, *The Giants,* p. 37.

21. J. Spanier, *Games Nations Play: Analyzing International Politics* (New York: Holt, Rhinehart and Winston, 1981), pp. 42–43.

22. A. Buchan, *The End of the Postwar Era,* p. 45.

23. J. Stoessinger, *The Might of Nations,* p. 63.

24. A. Buchan, *The End of the Postwar Era,* p. 45.

25. J. Stoessinger, *The Might of Nations,* p. 64.

26. See Henry Bretton, *International Relations in the Nuclear Age: One World, Difficult to Manage* (Albany, NY: State University of New York Press, 1986), p. 354; James Fallows, *National Defense* (New York: Random House, 1982).

27. J. A. Nathan and J. K. Oliver, *United States Foreign Policy and World Order* (Boston: Little, Brown and Company, 1985), p. 353.

28. R. Barnet, *The Rockets' Red Glare: When America Goes to War/The President and the People* (New York: Simon and Schuster, 1990), p. 358.

29. R. G. Kaiser, "US-Soviet Relations: Good-bye Détente," *Foreign Affairs* 59, no. 3 (1981): p. 501.

30. Ibid.

31. J. A. Nathan and J. K. Oliver, *United States Foreign Policy and World Order,* p. 357.

32. Ibid., p. 358.

33. R. H. Ferrell, *American Diplomacy in the Twentieth Century* (New York: W. W. Norton

and Company, 1988), p. 377.

34. M. Hudson, *Global Fracture: The New International Economic Order* (New York: Harper and Row, 1977), p. 65.

35. J. Spero, *The Politics of International Politics,* p. 226.

36. Kissinger's so-called step-by-step approach of dealing with immediate military problems and avoiding the deeper and more controversial issue of the establishment of a Palestinian state ultimately bogged down.

37. J. A. Nathan and J. K. Oliver, *United State Foreign Policy and World Order,* p. 359.

38. H. Morgenthau, *Politics Among Nations* (New York: Alfred Knopf, 1979), p. 34.

39. D. Pirages, *The New Context of International Relations: Global Ecopolitics* (North Scituate, MA: Duxbury Press, 1978).

40. S. Brown, *New Forces in World Politics,* p. 110.

41. The concept "bipolycentric" refers to a bipolar system with respect to nuclear power and the Cold War and multiple poles of power in the nonmilitary arenas.

Part III

The Politics of Pan-Proletarianism:
Third World Challenges to the
International Division of Labor

5

The Politics of Pan-Proletarianism

S tarting in the 1950s and the 1960s Third World leaders followed the example of Kwame Nkrumah and sought first the political kingdom. Anti-colonialism, antiracialism, and the protection of their newly acquired sovereignty consumed their efforts with reference to generating solidarity. However, during the 1970s these leaders turned their attention to the economic kingdom in quest of full sovereignty of every state over its natural resources and economic activities. Nationalization policies and the subsequent creation of producer cartels were the preferred mode of operation as Third World leaders launched their attack on the most fundamental instrument of private and foreign capital under Pax Americana – the multinational corporations. Third World leaders challenged their subordinate position in the global division of labor through nationalization policies.[1] Nationalization became integral to the quest for permanent sovereignty over natural resources and economic activities in the Third World. This crusade for permanent sovereignty through nationalization and cartelization became very clear in the wave of nationalization in natural resource industries that swept the Third World in the late 1960s and early 1970s.[2] The U.S.-sponsored coup d'état in Chile (1973) accelerated this trend throughout the Third World among moderate, conservative, and radical states alike. The nonaligned movement played a pivotal role in the transition from political to economic decolonization in the 1970s, and concentrated its efforts on solving the global economic problems that continued to plague the South after decolonization.

Pan-proletarianism developed in the 1970s and 1980s as a Third World response to the continuation of *global apartheid* in the economic arena. Global apartheid refers to the continuation of white-minority dominance of the political, social, legal, cultural, and economic decision-making apparatus within the world system. Gernot Kohler observed in the late 1970s that about two-thirds of the world's population is nonwhite. In the world system, being "white" and belonging to the upper stratum tend to go together, although there are poor whites and rich nonwhites. Kohler also produced data that demonstrated the continuation of economic stratification along racial as well as North-South lines. The rich countries occupied the top-dog position while the poor remained at the bottom in terms of per capita gross national product. Approximately two-thirds of humankind live at the bottom of the socioeconomic pyramid of the world; this group constituted the vast majority of the Third World. The one-third of humankind that lives in the middle and top positions in the socioeconomic pyramid define the international regimes that govern interstate relations and the world economy. The Northwest (the First World) and the Northeast (the Second World) occupy the top and middle positions. These countries are predominantly white, with the exception of Japan. They represent the top-dogs of the world community. Income inequality is also problematic. Twenty percent of the world's population receives 71% of the world's income.[3] Table 5.1 provides evidence to support this assertion.

Table 5.1

World GNP, in Constant 1975 Dollars (Percentage of Total)

1950 (total $2 trillion)		*1980 (total $8 trillion)*	
N. America	36.6	N. America	25.6
W. Europe	28.6	W. Europe	25.9
Japan	3.0	Japan	8.0
Rest of World	32.1	Rest of World	40.5

Source: Stephen Gill, *American Hegemony and the Trilateral Commission*, p. 65.

In terms of life expectancy, members of the predominantly white societies of the Northwest live longer than members of the poor, predominantly nonwhite societies of the Third World. Similarly, most of the world's weapons of mass destruction are possessed by white societies of the "North" – the United States, Russia, France, and Great Britain. In recent years these states have collaborated in an effort to restrict the exportation of nuclear weapons to the South. Nevertheless, these same actors have exported conventional arms to the Third World and have accelerated the conflict between militarization and development. Table 5.2 illustrates the disparity of military power between the North and South. The pivotal instrument of power resides in the Northern tier of the world system.

The pan-proletarian dimension of Third World solidarity sought to challenge the continuing legacy of global apartheid by changing the decision-making processes in international institutions. Starting in the 1970s, the Third World mounted a serious effort to alter the decision-making apparatus with reference to international economic concerns. The quest for a new international economic order by the Third World mobilized its efforts to restructure the North-South global division of labor. What follows is an analysis of the pan-proletarian dimension of Third World solidarity.

Table 5.2

World Military Expenditures, 1975–84(selected years)
In billion of dollars at 1980 Prices and Exchange rates.

	1975	1981	1982	1983	1984	World share (%)
IMEs	257,534	290,278	307,827	324,230	348,697	53.7
NMEs	171,972	185,448	189,757	191,671	196,133	30.2
MOECs	33,352	45,143	48,598	44,598	44,988	6.9
RoW	43,452	54,238	61,862	60,018	57,419	8.8
World	507,480	576,860	609,900	622,800	649,070	100.0

Sources: R. Luckham, "Disarmament and Development," *IDS Bulletin* 16 (October 1985), p. 3; and S. Gill, *American Hegemony and the Trilateral Commission,* 1990, p. 79.
Notes: Industrial market economies—IMEs; Non-market economies—NMEs; Major oil exporting countries—MOECs; Rest of World—RoW.

The advent of complex interdependence between the United States, Western Europe and Japan and the introduction of détente in superpower relations contributed to the development of a "trade-unionist" strategy among Third World states as these actors challenged their assigned roles in the international division of labor. The end of the postwar boom provided the political milieu for Third World states to openly question the basic tenets of North-South relations.

During the 1970s the world system entered another round of global restructuring in which some of the models of capital accumulation regulating the world economy and the international regimes governing the interstate system lost their legitimacy. This crisis eventually contributed to the development of a new international division of labor between the North and South. The world system entered a period of intense competition among capitalist business enterprises. Fundamental changes were under way throughout the 1970s, transforming political, economic, social, and cultural norms as we had known them since the end of the postwar period. Since the early 1970s the world economy has been in a downswing, bringing to an end the greatest economic boom in the history of the capitalist world system.

Although the spatial dimension of the international division of labor was undergoing dramatic change throughout most of the 1970s, the locus of decision-making remained in the Northern tier of the world system. The term *international division of labor* masks the reality of the power of transnational corporations.

These Northern economic enterprises decide what is to be produced, the site of production, and what regions or zones of the world economy will emerge as the most dynamic growth areas. Decisions concerning the geographical location of transnational corporations involve an analysis of many factors, including local and regional conflicts, the skill-level of the labor force, and the bargaining power of the host nation. Locational decisions are also the product of the competitive pressures among capitalist business enterprises in advanced capitalist states.

Growing economic competition among the advanced capitalist states helped to dethrone the dollar as the world reserve currency and undermined the dominant position of the United States in the world economy. Globalization of production accompanied the worldwide economic crisis of the 1970s and 1980s. Spatial change in the location of production sites brought industrial production into the semiperipheral sectors of the Third World. (Specifics of the rise of the newly industrializing countries in the Third World are dealt with in Chapter 6). Traditional macroeconomic policy instruments normally deployed by national governments during periodic business cycles lost their vitality and effectiveness in the 1970s. This global economic crisis compelled transnational corporations to seek new forms of economic collaboration with the Third World because transnational corporations were on a collision course with the Third World. As multinational corporations penetrated Third World states and gained control over the commanding heights of many developing countries' economies, North-South conflicts began to loom large in global politics.

The rise of the United States to the position of hegemonic power in the postwar era was partially the result of the transition from a colony and a peripheral state to a semiperipheral state. After the Civil War the United States made the change from a perimeter core to superpower.[4] This change in economic and political status was due to organizational and technological innovations by American business enterprises and the deployment and projection of American military power. American firms began experimenting with new organizational frameworks in the 1880s. The transition from the family and partner-oriented business enterprise to the multinational, multicomponent, multidivisional corporation represented an economic, managerial, and organizational innovation by American firms. The expansion of a continental market revolutionized transportation and communication networks. These innovations spawned further developments in the size and vertical structure of capitalist business enterprises.

Starting in the 1970s, business enterprises from Western Europe and Japan began absorbing the innovative economic, managerial, research and technological developmental features of American-based multinational corporations and ceased fighting this formidable economic institution through political integration, building a sense of community, and economic nationalism. These actors began to compete with the United States for markets and new investment outlets throughout the world economy.

The growth of interdependence among advanced capitalist states became an important force in the era of détente between the superpowers. The expansion of the industrial world and the accompanying development of an international trade system have integrated every sector into the capitalist world system. Capitalism has become a worldwide system intertwining countries in Africa, Asia, the Middle East, the Caribbean, and Latin America in a web of economic interaction with North America, Western Europe, and Japan. Soviet bloc participation in the capitalist world system remained very modest until the

1970s. Interdependence is a term that became very popular in the 1970s for describing the change in the economic relations between the United States and its Western allies. Put most simply, interdependence describes a situation in which two actors become mutually dependent. In the case of nation-states, it means that national populations become closely linked through international transactions. Interdependence usually leads to mutually beneficial outcomes, although changing distributions of benefits over time may make the outcome more favorable for one actor than another.[5] However, many analysts employ the terms *dependence* and *underdevelopment* to describe the role of the Third World in the capitalist world economy.[6]

The spread of industrialization and the accompanying development in the interstate system has integrated most sectors of the globe into a system in which the fortunes of all actors became connected. On the most basic physical level, all of humankind shares one environment. What one nation does to the planet earth has consequences for the rest of the family of nations. No longer can any advanced capitalist state "exit" from the capitalist world economy. Economic conditions in the United States have an impact on Western Europe and Japan, and vice versa.

In the 1970s the United States continued its role as the custodians of strategic security of the Western alliance and *primus inter pares* at the level of trade and monetary relationships. During this period the Western industrial powers grew increasingly dependent on imported raw materials, most particularly oil. The need to coordinate policies emerged as an important issue for Western solidarity.[7] Agreeing on a common policy toward OPEC was a very difficult task for the United States, Japan, and Western Europe.

During the Cold War, concerns about a communist military threat helped stimulate Americans to make short-run economic sacrifices (that is, to exercise leadership) to develop and preserve the liberal postwar economic regimes that contributed to European and Japanese recovery. Many of the major advances in international economic relations came during the long period of maximum Cold War tensions from 1947 (the Truman Doctrine) to 1963 (the Test Ban Treaty). In these years, the International Monetary Fund (IMF), the World Bank (IBRD), the General Agreement on Tariffs and Trade (GATT), and the Organization for Economic Cooperation and Development (OECD) began to function; currency convertibility finally materialized and major tariff cuts were implemented; and the Common Market emerged.[8] United States security leadership was prized by its allies, and the American perception of high threat from the Soviets encouraged U.S. policy makers to grant economic concessions to the Europeans and the Japanese.

DIVISIONS WITHIN THE CAPITALIST WESTERN CAMP

By the 1970s, however, the Bretton Woods system began crumbling and the management of the international economy was gravely threatened. Important changes in each of the three political bases of the Bretton Woods system undermined political management. Power structures lost legitimacy, leadership was weakened, and the consensus on a liberal, limited system dissolved.[9]

The advent of détente in superpower relations and the sharp reduction in perceived Soviet threats prior to the 1980s helped to reduce the ability of the United States to translate its military leadership of the alliance into economic leadership without resorting to overt and highly resented linkages. In the 1970s American allies became less willing to act as junior partners once they perceived that the external threat had diminished.[10]

In the 1960s Europe experienced a period of great economic growth and dynamism in international trade. First six, and then nine European nations united to form the European Economic Community, an economic bloc competing with the U.S. economy, and a potential political force. Japan's economic growth was even more spectacular. In the 1960s Japan became a major world economic power and joined the ranks of advanced capitalist countries. At the same time the United States, still the world's dominant economy, faced important problems. On the international front a weakened dollar and a declining balance of trade undermined American economic power vis-à-vis Western Europe and Japan. These actors launched their initial challenge to American leadership in the international economic arena in the 1970s. These actors posed the first threat to the American conception and leadership of the postwar liberal world economy.

THE DOLLAR PROBLEM

For twenty-five years international monetary relations under American leadership were stable, providing a basis for international trade, economic growth, and political harmony among the developed market economies. By American choice — the Bretton Woods agreement of 1944 — the dollar gradually replaced the gold standard, which over time became a pure dollar standard as the supply of gold proved inadequate to the enormous expansion of world trade, and the position of the pound sterling as an alternative reserve currency largely disappeared throughout the 1960s.

After 1964 the outflow of dollars began to accelerate, partly because of Lyndon Johnson's unwillingness to finance the cost of the Vietnam war by increasing taxation, which created domestic inflation that put American prices out of line with those of its major trading partners. In addition, American corporations found more lucrative investment opportunities beyond the United States. During the mid-1960s Washington had modest deficits of $1.9–3.8 billion; but by 1971, the deficit soared to $10.6 billion.[11] The alarming level of the U.S. deficit raised concerns about the power and vigor of the American economy. Reliance on the dollar collapsed as the above events threatened to unleash international monetary chaos.

The Nixon administration initiated a number of policy reforms that relieved the United States of its obligation to convert dollars to gold. First,

Washington insisted that its primary economic partners enjoying payment surpluses should assume a major portion of the burdens of minor modification required to restore the United States to payment equilibrium, in return for past American actions on their behalf.[12] The United States insisted that the Japanese yen and German mark be revalued upward to assist the American trade imbalance; this action would have the same effect as a dollar devaluation. Second, side by side with the currency realignment, the Nixon administration imposed an across-the-board 10 percent surcharge on all imports. Third, the United States repudiated its pledge of twenty-five years to exchange gold for dollars. Finally, the Nixon administration called for intensive global bargaining on trade and monetary issues, hoping to restore stability and to strengthen the U.S. payments and trade position.[13] These unilateral actions by the Nixon administration in August 1971 marked the end of the Bretton Woods system.

Throughout the fall of 1971, the Western world negotiated the status of the international monetary system. In December 1971 an agreement was reached calling upon the signatories to preserve a minimum level of international monetary cooperation. This accord became known as the Smithsonian Agreement. The price of gold became very fluid. The dollar began to decline in relation to gold. There was a realignment of other exchange rates, and provisions for some increased flexibility in exchange rates. After the Smithsonian meeting, currencies would float moving upward and downward around 2.25 percent of parity, twice the range of the Bretton Woods agreement. The Smithsonian accord provided a breathing space as the signatories debated the future of international monetary and economic reform.

In June 1972 Great Britain and Ireland were the first Western European countries to depart from the Bretton Woods system. They began allowing their currencies to float and to rely more on the vagaries of the market. A new currency crisis developed in January and February 1973. By March 1973 all major world currencies had withdrawn support from fixed exchange rates and were floating. The market became the primary manager of currencies, with minor assistance from central bankers who intervened minimally in exchange markets on a somewhat cooperative basis in order to prevent extreme fluctuations.[14]

INFLATION AND STAGFLATION

Starting in the 1970s inflationary growth plagued most industrial market economies. The system of fixed exchange rates collapsed and the float emerged. Double-digit inflation erupted. Inflation in the United States resulted largely from economic mismanagement. In the late 1960s, the vast dollar outflow created by inflation led to an overvalued dollar and the policy of benign neglect transformed U.S. inflation into global inflation. The boom of the 1970s created commodity shortages that reinforced the inflationary processes already in existence. Liberals and conservatives disagreed over the cure for inflation.

Surprisingly, they reached consensus on the causal factors behind this inflationary spiral in the 1970s. Liberals and conservatives alike blamed President
Johnson's policy errors on the Vietnam War and President Nixon's obsessive
effort to obtain a huge plurality in the 1972 election through massive deficit
spending as the sources responsible for this crisis. American expenditure
abroad exported much of the inflationary spiral to the global marketplace.[15]

The worldwide inflation of the 1970s was different from that of the 1960s
in that an accompanying rise in unemployment increases the severity of this
economic turning point. A new word was coined to replace the term *stagflation:*
slumpflation. In the United States a certain amount of unemployment and inflation had risen together in the years following the 1957–58 recession, but in the
1970s a sharp increase in unemployment and prices had become a global phenomenon.

The crisis associated with inflation exacerbated the problem of international management in an increasingly interdependent world. Global inflation
further demonstrated that in an interdependent system, management depends
on the coordination of economic policies previously considered to be strictly
national prerogatives.[16]

U.S. monetary policy moved toward competitive depreciation between
1971 and 1978. During this period, the dollar continued to decline, dropping
by more than one-third against the yen and deutsche mark. U.S. exports
increased in proportion to world trade, and the balance of trade was in Washington's favor, especially with reference to the European Economic Community. Increases in United States exports were partially tied to growth in oil
prices. Over time the inflationary results of the depreciation undermined confidence in the dollar and the Europeans proposed replacing the dollar regime
with an Eurocurrency.[17] Between 1979 and 1985, U.S. policy makers pursued
a policy of national and global fiscal regime, precipitated by Federal Reserve
Board Chairman Paul Volker's decision to restrict the money supply in the late
1970s. Although this fiscal policy was successful in shoring up the dollar, it had
a disastrous effect on the U.S. and world economic activity, resulting in high
interest rates, large inflows of capital to the United States, and consequent large
trade deficits. By some calculations the dollar soared in value by as much as 50
percent or more, in terms of the foreign currency (Japanese yen, French francs,
German marks) for which it could be exchanged.[18] Through the Plaza (1985)
and Louvre (1987) agreements an orderly reduction in the value of the dollar
was achieved, which fell even lower following the stock market crash in October 1987. Monetarists lost their influence in the Reagan administration during
the middle 1980s. Despite the substantial depreciation of the dollar against the
yen, the United States continued to run a huge trade deficit with Japan.[19]
Increasingly, U.S. policy makers came face to face with a serious problem of
industrial competitiveness that exacerbated its trade relations with the European Economic Community and Japan.

PROBLEMS IN THE TRADING ARENA

Starting in the 1970s, a number of industrialized countries began to enact neomercantilist trade policies in order to protect domestic producers from foreign competition. Neomercantilism is a trade policy designed primarily to protect national producers and maintain domestic employment to the detriment of competitive foreign producers and laborers. This policy instrument created tensions within the Western alliance. The inflationary spiral that confronted all advanced capitalist states in the 1970s increased interest in using trade policy to protect domestic producers from price rises.[20]

Japan's share of the world's export market almost doubled during the 1960s, rising from 3.2 percent to 6.2 percent. Starting in 1970, Japanese exports began to expand at a rate of 20 percent per year. At this juncture, Japan was able to generate a trade surplus and to protect domestic production by maintaining an undervalued yen. A large variety of import barriers and foreign investment restrictions operated to make it extremely difficult for American and European firms to penetrate the expanding Japanese market. These economic measures became a source of resentment in the United States, because America had contributed to the Japanese economic recovery.

In Western Europe the EEC adopted similar neomercantilist policies that are reflected in a variety of trade agreements restricting imports in sensitive industries such as textiles, automobiles, electronics, as well as steel. U.S. policy makers assert that the Common Agricultural Policy (CAP) is the ultimate example of mercantilism. Since its introduction in the 1960s, CAP has provided protection to inefficient European farmers, thus stimulating high-cost domestic agricultural production within the Common Market by placing variable duties on agricultural imports. In the absence of production controls, this policy generated agricultural surpluses in Europe with prices too high to compete in the world agriculture markets as a result of continuing inefficiency in the production process. However, the revenue derived from agricultural imports' duties subsidized EEC agricultural exports to world markets. Without these subsidies, Europeans were otherwise unable to penetrate these markets. American trade officials and farmers bitterly oppose CAP because far more efficient U.S. agricultural producers are being denied their full export potential not only in Europe, but also in Third World markets captured by subsidized EEC exports. Since the 1970s, CAP has emerged as a major conflictual issue between the EEC and the United States.[21]

Although the United States was a major proponent of free trade, it adopted neomercantilist policies as well. When foreign imports of steel and textiles began to offer a serious challenge to domestic producers in the 1960s, the American response was to reduce the competition faced by inefficient domestic producers by applying vigorous pressures on other countries and their more efficient domestic producers to impose "voluntary" export controls on the sale of these products in the American market. The United States insisted that these policies were in response to the mercantilist policies of Europe and Japan, in particular to CAP, which resulted in a decline in American agricultural exports to the EEC; to Europe's barrier to Japanese exports, which made the United States bear the burden of the rapidly expanding export sector in Japan; to the EEC's creation of regional preferential trading arrangements that discriminated in favor of trade with numerous Mediterranean and African states; and to Japanese barriers to American imports and investments.[22]

The emergence of interdependence gave rise to debates about whether the United States had entered into a cycle of hegemonic decline reminiscent of the destiny of world powers in previous historical periods. Paul Kennedy, in *The Rise and Fall of Great Powers,* drew parallels with the cases of Spain after the seventeenth century and Great Britain in the early and mid-twentieth century. Kennedy conceptualizes U.S. global positions in the financial, monetary, and trade arenas as examples of imperial overstretch, in which excess commitments contribute to a decline in national power.[23] Robert Gilpin also focused his analytical lens on the historical experiences of Athens, Rome, Holland, Britain, and the United States. Gilpin asserts that hegemonic decline is a more complex process involving the interaction of several factors. In analyzing cycles of hegemonic decline, Gilpin emphasizes the external burden of leadership, internal tendencies toward rising domestic consumption, and the global diffusion of technology. According to Gilpin, these factors work in concert to fracture the base of hegemonies.[24] Robert Keohane contends that while cooperation may be advanced by hegemony, the existence of a single world leader is neither an essential nor sufficient circumstance for world order. He argues that cooperation can take place in the absence of hegemony. Shared interests, expectations, and practice, as well as the momentum created by international regimes, can make up for the lack of hegemony.[25] Cooperation in the advanced capitalist economies of the Northwest was critical in managing the mechanism of alliance throughout the 1970s and the 1980s.

Alan W. Cafruny has developed a neo-Gramscian approach to historical materialism and international relations on the question of the decline of U.S. hegemony. Cafruny has examined the voluminous secondary literature on Gramsci and identified three categories or instances of hegemony. These categories may be considered ideal types and are referred to as integral hegemony, declining hegemony, and minimal hegemony.[26] Cafruny has observed that these three categories of hegemony have not been employed by scholars of international political economy. For Cafruny, this schema is especially relevant in examining the changing role of the U.S. in the world economy.

In examining U.S. hegemony, Cafruny divides Pax Americana into three distinct time periods. Integral hegemony started in 1945 and lasted until the London gold crisis of 1960. This crisis illuminated the fragility of the dollar and signaled the decline of U.S. power. Declining hegemony emerged in 1960, lasting until 1971 when the U.S. decided to abandon the dollar-gold standard. These actions verified economic growth and nationalistic tendencies were becoming more significant to the United States; the U.S. began to pursue its own economic interests rather than looking out for the interests of the western alliance. After 1971, the international political economy became a minimal hegemony.[27] Cafruny's scheme does provide a useful framework for examining Pax Americana through time. However, he fails to address Third World challenges to U.S. hegemony through pan-proletarianism. His analysis is more concerned with international economic relations among advanced market economies. Nevertheless, he does capture the degree to which the United States was successful in defining the rules of the world economy after 1971.

Starting in 1971, international economic relations has reflected the growing importance of continuity and cooperation in the Northwest, especially with reference to North-South relations. Relations among the advanced market economies did not deteriorate to levels comparable to the 1930s. The United States was successful in exercising hegemony, albeit minimally, by exerting pressure in the bargaining or negotiation process, or through domestic macroeconomic policies. Advanced market economies were successful in generating cooperative agreements on interest rates, exchange market intervention, and international debt, and returned the system to temporary equilibrium without resolving the underlying problems.[28] These formal instances of international cooperation obscure the sharp discontinuities in the system.

New challenges to the power of the advanced capitalist states, the internal weakening of leadership, and the collapse of the liberal consensus undermined U.S. political management of the world economy. Chaos and crisis emerged when an effective international monetary regime ceased to function smoothly in an era of complex interdependence. The international monetary regime was in disarray. Individual states began to erect new barriers to trade. A handful of oil producers forced the powerful advanced capitalist states to submit to their demands, and the Third World called for a new international economic order and threatened to wreak havoc on the world economy if it was not established.

In the 1970s, détente between the superpowers and growing interdependence in the economic realm among Western allies led to changes in the world system. The Soviet threat declined as a major issue, and security-related issues increasingly became secondary to nonmilitary issues. The growth of interdependence led to a number of international economic crises ranging from the erection of trade barriers to monetary quagmires and the energy crisis of 1973–74. The energy crisis introduced oil power as a new economic force in the international system. The contours of power in the world system began to converge along economic dimensions. These changes had serious ramifications for Third World solidarity in the 1970s.

The coming of détente among the superpowers and China, and the necessity of economic interdependence in the world economy raised serious questions about the viability of the nonaligned movement in the 1970s. At this juncture we will examine the changing nexus of Third World solidarity in the 1970s with reference to the nonaligned movement in the era of détente. The following questions will be examined: How do the weak, Third World countries gain leverage in "the world of the strong?" How do they exert pressure on the stronger advanced capitalist states to get their share of power in the world system? What kinds of coalitions or alliances did the Third World countries build in order to press their case for systemic change? What were the multiple coalitions and issue areas that forged Third World solidarity in the 1970s?

THE POLITICS OF PAN-PROLETARIANISM

The acquisition of nuclear weaponry has decreased the superpowers' desire to intervene conventionally against peripheral and semiperipheral Third World states when there is a chance of confronting another nuclear power and therefore of risking escalation. The Cuban missile crisis of 1962 and the Middle East War of 1973 brought this important principle to the attention of both superpowers. Likewise, such intervention may also lead to long and expensive political and military investments from which the superpowers find it difficult to disengage themselves — witness the United States in Vietnam and the Soviets in Afghanistan. When the superpowers have intervened beyond their recognized sphere of influence they have cautiously avoided the possibility of confronting another nuclear power.

If a tight bipolar nuclear system provided increased freedom of action to weak states who opted for nonalignment, a loose bipolycentric system[29] in the 1970s granted some nonaligned states even more flexibility and freedom. This is the result of the escalation principle, that is, local wars can escalate into major conflicts involving nuclear powers. Since the superpowers continued their competition, albeit under the rubric of détente, the possibility of escalation was still great. Nonaligned actors had more freedom of action during the era of détente and complex interdependence. The fear of major nuclear confrontations between the two superpowers limited their ability to take advantage of their military superiority over weak Third World states.[30] As Stanley Hoffmann observed, "Small states are weak but not meek."[31] Thus, Third World states became more willing to pursue goals beyond survival and security. While the superpowers continued to concentrate their efforts on the requirements of security and survival, they became prisoners to their own nuclear weapons.

Starting in the 1970s, security and survival issues lost their luster among some Third World states, especially with reference to the nonaligned movement. At this juncture, the roles of the two types of states almost became reversed: "the strong do what they must (and can only do a little more), the weak do a little better than they must."[32] Third World leaders intensified their efforts to set the international agenda in the 1970s.

As noted above, the decline in security concerns allowed many nations to pursue other issues. The problems of economic development became an important concern of Third World solidarity movements. In the 1970s the Group of 77 and the nonaligned movement collaborated in organizing an effective Third World coalition on international economic issues as their interests began to converge. This transition was partially the result of the growing trade unionism among Third World states, who increasingly saw themselves as proletarian nations bargaining for better wages (prices for their commodities) from the advanced capitalist states. During this period, pan-proletarianism (the demand for economic justice) became the basis for Third World solidarity. Third World leaders from Africa, Asia, Central and South America, the Middle East, and the Caribbean began to raise fundamental questions concerning the international regimes that govern the world economy and structure the international division of labor between the North and the South. The nonaligned movement became an important catalyst in forging a Third World coalition around the demands for a new international economic order. Beginning with the Dar es Salaam Preparatory Conference in 1970, and the Lusaka Conference in the same year, continuing with Georgetown in 1972 and the Algiers summit in 1973, the nonaligned movement demonstrated a marked transition away from the Cold War.[33] At the Algerian summit in 1973, this transition toward pan-proletarianism reached its climax. After the Colombo meeting in 1976, pan-proletarianism began to decline as a basis for solidarity.

By 1970, leadership of the nonaligned movement began to shift away from India, Indonesia, Egypt, and to some extent, Yugoslavia. The oil-producing states began to take over the leadership of the movement.[34] This shift in leadership coincided with the changing orientation of the movement. These states had economic resources at their disposal. They did not depend totally on the persuasiveness of their arguments as a mechanism for mobilization.

Algeria played a pivotal role in a number of Third World-oriented international and regional institutions, including the nonaligned movement, the Group of 77, the Organization of African Unity (OAU), and the Arab League. In 1974 Algerians called for a special session of the United Nations to deal with international economic issues. This event had a profound impact on the nonaligned movement and forcibly demonstrated the change in focus and orientation. The demand for a new international economic order, articulated by the Third World at the Sixth Special Session of the United Nations General Assembly, was an important step in the development of pan-proletarianism among Third World states.

Several other international and regional institutions contributed to coordination and consensus building among Third World states: the United Nations Economic Commission for Latin America, the Association of Southeast Asian Nations (ASEAN), and the United Nations Conference on Trade and Development (UNCTAD). In the 1970s the arena of interest between the nonaligned movement and the Group of 77 substantially converged on the economic disparity between the industrialized North and the developing South as the fundamental crisis confronting the international community.

During the 1973 Middle East War, OAPEC nations instituted an oil embargo against Western countries that "blindly" supported the Israelis. On

October 17, 1973, OAPEC[35] employed an oil embargo on the United States (and all locations transshipping oil to or processing oil for the United States or the U.S. military overseas), the Netherlands, Portugal, and South Africa. By 1974 the Organization of Petroleum Exporting Countries (OPEC) had increased the price of oil and introduced oil power as a new force in the world system. No longer could the oil-producing areas be treated as a mere cog in the machine of the international economic order created by the advanced capitalist states and the major multinational corporations. This episode marks the first time that any group of commodity producers in the Third World had taken their own destinies in hand so decisively. Leaders throughout the Third World were able to identify a major weakness in the Western arsenal as a result of OPEC action.

THIRD WORLD STRATEGIES IN THE 1970s

Since the emergence of the Third World in international affairs, leaders from this zone of the world have employed a variety of strategies in order to leave their stamp on the international system. These strategies have included (1) creating universal organizations such as the nonaligned movement and the Group of 77; (2) establishing regional organizations such as the OAU, the OAS, and the Arab League; and (3) creating resource organizations such as OPEC. In the 1970s Third World leaders utilized several of these strategies to press their demands for a new international economic order. Universal coalitions such as the nonaligned movement and the Group of 77 were important in the 1970s because they became central forums for Third World solidarity and changed their strategies significantly in the period of détente and complex interdependence. These universal coalitions also became important forums for launching the North-South conflict as the most salient issue area confronting the international community.

FOURTH CONFERENCE OF THE NONALIGNED COUNTRIES

The Algerians initiated a diplomatic campaign to turn out a large gathering at the Fourth Conference of the Non-Aligned Countries, held September 5–9, 1973, in Algiers. Between July and August 1973 the Algerians waged a vigorous campaign to convince their Third World comrades of the importance of this conference. As a result, seventy-five states had representatives at Algiers as compared to fifty-three at Lusaka in 1970. Even more significant was the fact that fifty-four states were represented by their chief of state or head of government – over twice the number that had attended the previous summit. Virtually every Third World figure of international reputation was present in Algiers, making it the diplomatic equal of the Bandung Conference in 1955.[36]

The earlier Bandung Conference had played an important role in asserting the importance of Third World issues and signaled the growing importance of nonwhite nations in the international community, and the rise of the Third World as an important motive force in the world system. Two decades later, the Algerian Conference signaled an important change as the nonaligned movement began to focus on the common denominators of poverty and underdevelopment. After the Algerian summit, Third World solidarity was based on the community of color, poverty, and underdevelopment, or what we refer to as pan-proletarianism. Pan-proletarianism emphasized economic justice and the demand for a new international economic order.

The Algerian summit provided a forum for Third World leaders to assess critically the impact of détente on international politics of the Third World and to chart an independent path by emphasizing the North-South conflict as the most salient issue confronting this collectivity of states. In the Political Declaration, leaders in the Third World asserted,

> As long as colonial wars, apartheid, imperialist aggression, alien domination, foreign occupation, power politics, economic exploitation and plunder prevail, peace will be limited in principle and scope. In a world where side by side with a minority of rich countries there exist a majority of poor countries, it would be dangerous to accentuate this division by restricting peace to the prosperous areas of the world while the rest of mankind remained condemned to insecurity and the law of the strongest. Peace is indivisible; it can not be reduced to a mere shifting of confrontation from one area to another nor should it condone the continued existence of tension in some areas while endeavoring to eliminate it elsewhere. Détente would remain precarious if it did not take into consideration the interests of all countries.[37]

Algeria was one of the first Third World states to argue that détente had not led to peace and prosperity. The breakdown of the bipolar structure was a positive opportunity for the Third World if it could organize itself into one of the power centers in a changing world system. Boumedienne presented Algeria's conception of the nonaligned movement as a "pole of attraction" around which the Third World should coalesce for resolute action. The key to such a coalition, Algeria argued, lay in establishing a permanent institution.[38]

The militant states gathered at Algiers called for the creation of a permanent secretariat. Although this proposal lacked support, the conference decided to change the name of the Preparatory Committee to the Non-Aligned Coordinating Bureau in order to give the movement a sense of permanence. The Algiers Summit of the Non-Aligned Countries incorporated the essence of the economic ideas of the Third World into its Political Declaration: not only war, but also poverty and deterioration of economic conditions were major threats to international peace. Third World states gathered at Algiers asserted that for genuine peace to become a reality the very nature of the international economic system required change. Third World leaders recognized that improving the situation of developing countries was not only a technical matter but also a political matter requiring bold changes in the international environment, whose mechanisms and structures are important determinants of the developmental process. The objective at Algiers became to change the international environment in such a way as to make it more responsive to the needs of Third World states. Through Algerian leadership, changes in the international economic system became a major priority of the nonaligned movement.

The interests of the Group of 77 and the nonaligned movement began to converge around international economic concerns. This convergence of interests began to take form in 1967 and reached a turning point in Algiers in 1973. At this juncture, the Group of 77 and the nonaligned movement became concerned with the international economic needs of developing nations and abandoned the East-West conflict as the most salient issue confronting them. The nonaligned movement emerged from Algiers as a major catalyst for replacing the East-West conflict with the North-South conflict as the most important issue confronting the international community.

From 1973 to 1976, the Algerians held the chairmanship of the Non-Aligned Coordinating Bureau, and used that platform to maximum advantage to promote Third World issues. Their political standing became fortified by their position as the intermediary between the African states concerned with the liberation of Southern Africa on the one hand and the oil-producing Arab states concerned with Israel on the other. Their mediating skills became highly developed. For three important years, leaders in Algeria restructured the perspectives and enlarged the aspirations and activities of the Third World.[39]

In Algiers, the Arabs gained African support for their anti-Israel position in exchange for Arab oil producers' support against white minority regimes and for financial and material aid for liberation movements. Cuba challenged the United States over Puerto Rico's right to self-determination from quarters not necessarily supportive of the radical camp within the nonaligned movement. These votes were cast in exchange for support by radical states like Cuba on such issues as assured access to seaports for landlocked nations or price stability on commodities. The delegates gathered at Algiers gave their support to the Provisional Revolutionary Government of Vietnam as well.

Thus, the issues of Vietnam and the Middle East, which had become so divisive in the late 1960s, became major policy concerns for the nonaligned in the early 1970s. The radical/conservative split evolved over how to respond to U.S. involvement in Vietnam, while the Arab/non-Arab split was over relations with Israel and the Palestinians. Over time a consensus developed as the majority of Third World leaders reconciled their position to the minority supporting the Provisional Revolutionary Government of Vietnam and the Palestinian Liberation Organization. Initially, only a minority had been hostile to the U.S. and Israel. These issues became key components of Third World ideology in the 1970s. Third World ideology emphasized this international coalition's opposition to power politics and the struggle against colonialism.

At the fourth summit of the nonaligned movement, the change in orientation from military and security concerns was complete. The nonaligned movement emerged from this conference as a major force in the quest to establish a new international economic order. At the same time, the movement acquired the organizational substance and operational framework to place Third World concerns at the top of the international agenda. The advent of the Yom Kippur War of 1973 ushered in oil power as a dynamic force in world politics. The Arab and Muslim countries began to play a more active role in the movement. OPEC and OAPEC became important actors in the Third World.

In 1974 the Algerians called for a special session of the United Nations to deal with international economic issues. This event had a profound impact on the nonaligned movement and forcibly demonstrated the change in focus and orientation. The demand for a new international economic order (NIEO), articulated by the Third World at the Sixth Special Session of the United Nations General Assembly, was an important step in the development of pan-proletarianism among Third World states.

The Sixth Special Session, which took place from April 19 to May 2, 1974, was the first special session of the United Nations General Assembly convened at the initiative of the Third World, and the first one that did not focus on security-oriented issues. It also marked the first time that a session of the General Assembly focused attention exclusively on the problems of development.[40] On May 1, the session adopted a Declaration and Programme of Action on the establishment of a new international economic order:

> We the members of the United Nations . . . solemnly proclaim our united determination to work urgently for the *establishment of a new international economic order* based on equity, sovereignty, equality, interdependence, common interest and cooperation among all states irrespective of their economic and social systems, which shall correct inequalities and redress existing injustices, make it possible to eliminate the widening gap between developed and developing countries and ensure steadily accelerating economic and social development and peace and justice for present and future generations.[41]

This declaration emphasized the right of every state to full, permanent sovereignty and "effective control" over its natural resources and, as a logical extension, over "their exploitation, using means suitable to its own situation, including nationalization or transfer of ownership to its nationals." The declaration reaffirmed the national right of sovereignty over natural resources expounded by the Third World at the Algiers Summit in 1973.

Furthermore, the Programme of Action outlined the policy implications of the principles set forth in the declaration. The Sixth Special Session dealt with many issues that the Group of 77 and the nonaligned movement had advocated to no avail. These issues ranged from proposals for new codes to regulate transnational corporations to Third World debt renegotiation. The NIEO resolutions gave greater saliency to these long unsatisfied Third World grievances.

The joint keynote address by Boumedienne and Henry Kissinger demonstrated the conflict of interest between the North and South on international economic issues. Boumedienne asserted that Third World states considered the existing economic order to be as unjust and outmoded as the colonial order. In this system a minority of industrial powers controls the levers of the world economy and determines the distribution of world resources as a function of its own hierarchical needs.[42] The action taken by OPEC, even though it hurt fellow Third World states (especially the developing countries without oil resources and the periphery), was an important step toward the South's regaining control over certain of these levers of power. The Third World was asserting its right to play an important role in international economic decision-making.

Secretary Kissinger saw nothing fundamentally wrong with the existing international economic, financial, and trading regimes governing the postwar world economy. He emphasized instead Third World attitudes. According to Kissinger, the problem was not a global cleavage between the North and South, but rather the adoption of a "politics of pressure and threats." Kissinger ignored the agenda item in the proposed resolutions and was very critical of producer associations and commodity agreements.

The gap between Boumedienne's and Kissinger's conception was as wide as the gap between the North and South. They represented divergent approaches to the North-South economic conflict. Each demanded a fundamental revision of the other's position. For Boumedienne, structural change was essential for North-South cooperation. For Kissinger, it was political modification by the Third World that was needed.

Resolutions of the Sixth Special Session, which together formed the substance of NIEO, were enacted by consensus voting. Most of the major states in the North, however, found them inadequate or so repugnant that nearly all had read numerous and substantial reservations into the record. The Great Powers from the European Economic Community (EEC), the United States, and Japan expressed their reservations concerning the permanent sovereignty of every state over its natural resources and economic activities, and even the right of nationalization without any reference to a corresponding duty of compensation. U.S. Ambassador John Scali called the declaration a significant political document but maintained that it did not represent unanimity of opinion in the United Nations General Assembly.[43]

The Charter of Economic Rights and Duties of States was enshrined into international discourse on December 12, 1974. The United Nations General Assembly adopted this new international code after a vote of 120 in favor, 6 opposed including the United States, and 10 abstentions. The question of nationalization and compensation was a primary concern of the United States. The Charter's section on nationalization became the target for negative votes. The General Assembly rejected a proposal put forth by developed countries that a provision be added requiring nationalizing states to pay "just compensation in light of all relevant circumstances." These delegates urged Third World states to "fulfill in good faith their international obligations." Proponents of this proposal lost by a vote of 71 to 20, with 18 abstentions. Third World delegates defeated another proposal by Western powers stating that an undertaking to import foreign capital should be observed in good faith.[44] This proposal lost by a vote of 87 to 19, with 1 abstention.

The passage of the NIEO did not establish a new order. However, these resolutions did give rhetorical force to the long-standing Third World claim of the right to development. The severity of the North-South cleavage became certified in these resolutions, making it difficult to ignore development and poverty as international issues. Third World leaders emerged from the Sixth Special Session with a strong sense of unity.

Since 1974 Third World demands for a new international economic order have been fairly consistent. In the trade arena major demands have included (1) various forms of international commodity agreements; (2) a common fund that would provide a financial umbrella for these commodity agreements; (3) nonreciprocal reduction in developed countries of barriers to Third World countries' export of processed raw materials and semi-manufactured and manufactured goods; (4) expanded generalized trade preferences for the Third World to better enable them to compete with industrial countries in the markets of the North; and (5) better financed domestic adjustment assistance programs in the North which, by easing the transitional pains accompanying the restructuring of Northern economies, would facilitate imports of Southern manufactured goods. Third World leaders sought some form of price indexation between primary and industrial goods.

The essential task for Third World leaders after the Sixth and later the Seventh Special Session became the translation of their demands for a new international economic order into reality. This process involved multilateral discussions in a variety of forums ranging from the United Nations General Assembly, UNCTAD, the United Nations Industrial Development Organization (UNIDO), and the Conference on International Economic Cooperation (CIEC) in Paris, France, to the Cancun Summit in Mexico in 1981.

THE NORTH-SOUTH STALEMATE AND THE DIALOGUE OF THE DEAF

From 1977 to 1980 the proponents and opponents of the NIEO were at an impasse. The North, led by the United States, refused to alter the locus of decision-making on international economic issues from GATT, IMF, and the World Bank. The Third World stood by its demand to relocate the decision-making apparatus to UNCTAD, and the General Assembly, where the principle of "one man, one vote" would prevail.

Third World leaders' failure to establish a new order accelerated the tensions among states. Increasingly, the newly industrializing countries from Latin America, the East Asian Pacific rim and Southern Africa[45] and a number of states in OPEC[46] took advantage of economic opportunities within the existing order. These states comprised the semiperipheral sector of the capitalist world system. Their economic performance outpaced the peripheral sector of the Third World. A number of these states adopted an outward-looking policy as well as increased integration of their economies into the world economy. By 1977 increased Third World diversity in economic, political, and ideological spheres led to conflict over the means for achieving a new order.

Several factors contributed to fragmentation among these actors: the gap between OPEC and non-oil least-developed countries (NOLDCs) and the recurring conflict over oil prices; the emergence of newly industrializing countries into the ranks of the LDCs (their success led to a different posture on North-South issues and attempts by the North to both coopt and separate them from the Third World coalition); the relative success of OPEC and NICs, or "advanced developing countries" (ADCs), as they were called by the Carter administration, in comparison with the least developed Third World states in Africa, Asia, and Central and South America (NICs and OPEC represent the rise of the semiperiphery as major actors in the capitalist world system).

Although Third World leaders have sought to maintain a solid united front on the NIEO, differences in economic performance, ideology, and military posture toward the superpowers began to take their toll and undermine the panproletarian dimension of Third World solidarity. Third World states opting for increased integration into the global political economy postulated different strategies on the North-South stalemate than those opting for self-reliance and disengagement. Leaders throughout the Third World began to put their individual state interests over broader concerns of the Third World.

During the 1970s the Carter administration gave lip service to the Third World demand for a new order. Both Secretary of State Cyrus Vance and the U.S. Ambassador to the United Nations, Andrew Young, gave lukewarm support to the NIEO. At this juncture, American policy makers sought to recruit select OPEC members and the newly industrializing countries in Latin America and East Asia into economic and military partnership with the Northwest. These same policy makers began to focus on the "basic need" approach as the best formula to solve Third World economic problems, emphasizing equity, the reduction of poverty, agrarian reform, rural development, and a "bicycle culture." Hence, the problems facing the Third World states remained internal, requiring therefore a new internal economic order rather than a new international economic order. OPEC and the NICs were used as concrete examples by the Northwest to argue that Third World states could develop and graduate from their peripheral status. The success of these actors confirmed the viability of the capitalist world system to policy makers in the Northwest.

With the advent of the Reagan administration, the Cold War once again became the raison d'être of American foreign policy. The Reagan administration rejected the notion that the East-West conflict was manageable through détente. The bipolar approach to world politics relegated the importance of local, regional, and a number of global issues such as the North-South conflict to the back burner. Conflicts and victories, issues and interests were evaluated in relation to the overarching Soviet-American rivalry.[47]

The Reagan administration launched a new offensive toward the Third World in the 1980s. This new foreign policy sought to counter Soviet influence in the Third World and arrest the drift toward antisystemic activities in the Southern Hemisphere. The primary goal of this offensive was the restructuring of the global division of labor in ways that would allow Northern states and firms to establish social and political control over global labor in strategic peripheral and semiperipheral states.

American policy makers introduced "Reaganomics" as the answer to the Third World demand for a new world order. At the Cancun Summit of 1982, President Ronald Reagan called upon Third World leaders to rely on the "invisible hand of the market" in their efforts to develop, modernize, and industrialize their societies. President Reagan also restated the traditional American position that the locus of decision making on international economic issues would remain in Northwestern-dominated international institutions such as GATT, the IMF, the World Bank, and OECD. As a precondition for U.S. participation in this summit, the Americans insisted on Cuba's exclusion. Mexico complied with the American request. This was a major setback for the nonaligned movement, since Castro was chairman of the movement in 1981. Cancun marked another chapter in the North-South stalemate.

The Reagan and Bush administrations continued their attacks on anti-market and statist policies of Third World states in multilateral agencies and international institutions by refusing to provide loans or foreign aid to states that had expropriated property of transnational corporations or limited the access of these economic actors to their markets. Debt rescheduling became a lever that allowed advanced capitalist states of the Northwest to penetrate the markets and growing sectors of the newly industrializing countries. Structural adjustment programs (SAPs) evolved into Northern levers over economic decision making in socialist and capitalist states in the Third World with strong state involvement in the economy. SAPs also fostered entrepreneurial activities, reliance on market forces, and return of ownership and operation of state corporations in the developing world to the private sector in the 1980s. The worldwide economic crisis that engulfed the world economy in the 1980s gave policy makers in the North an opportunity to reassert their guidance of the capitalist world system through the Group of Seven. American policy makers under President Reagan's leadership fostered increased cooperation in the Northwest through the annual meetings of the Group of Seven[48] which focused attention on global economic issues that are important to the United States, Western Europe, and Japan.[49] Through the Group of Seven's annual summits, the Northwest was able to reassert its collective hegemony over international economic decision making and dramatically reduce the power and influence of the Group of 77, UNCTAD, and the nonaligned movement on such issue-areas. During the 1970s and 1980s the United States withdrew its moral and financial support from international organizations dominated by Third World interests, such as the International Labor Organization (ILO), United Nations Educational, Scientific, and Cultural Organization (UNESCO), and the International Court of Justice.

In stark contrast to the Nixon, Ford, and Carter administrations' policies of retreat (from Vietnam and active military adventures in the Third World), ambivalence, and uncertainty, the Reagan and Bush foreign policy teams instead acted assertively to make the Third World safe for Northern capital. The Reagan and Bush administrations were also more willing than their predecessors to challenge the Soviets and their Third World allies militarily, thus taking the Soviet-American rivalry into this zone of the world system. Conflicts among and within Third World states intensified as both superpowers demonstrated their willingness to export arms to Third World combatants involved in ethnic and communal conflicts, civil wars, and inter-state battles.

After 1971 the cardinal convictions supporting the Northwest's approach to the world economy were gradually undermined. Once again, the United States provided the intellectual authority for changing the ideology and values that supported the new approach toward the world economy during this period of global restructuring. These new ideas have gradually penetrated other states of the Northwest, inducing modifications in these societies. The ascendant philosophy of the 1980s − neoliberalism − clearly articulates significant modifications in U.S. domestic and global agenda. Neoliberalism represents an aggressive offensive on the legitimacy of state intervention into market relations, especially with reference to the major tenets of the NIEO. In domestic politics this new philosophy has led to a relaxation of state regulatory and redistributive policies. In the world system, neoliberalism has provided the rationale for Northern policies emphasizing market forces and export-led growth.[50] The rise of neoliberalism has also contributed to cracks in the Third World coalition as they struggle to create a new international economic order.

Although Third World leaders sought to maintain their diplomatic unity on the NIEO issues, the unfolding economic crisis of the 1980s and the intensification of conflicts in the Third World began to take their toll as the Southern Hemisphere became the primary battleground for the Second Cold War. With the advent of militarized disputes between and within Third World states, Third World insecurity dilemmas took priority over such issues as the North-South conflict.

NOTES

1. T. H. Moran, "Multinational Corporations and Developing Countries: An Analytical Overview," in *Multinational Corporations: The Political Economy of Foreign Direct Investment*, ed. T. H. Moran (Lexington, MA: Lexington Books, 1985) pp. 6–7.

2. M. Schaffer, "Capturing the Mineral Multinationals: Advantage or Disadvan-

tage?" in *Multinational Corporations: The Political Economy of Foreign Direct Investment,* ed. T. H. Moran (Lexington, MA: Lexington Books, 1985) p. 27.

3. G. Kohler, *Global Apartheid, World Order Models Project Working Paper No.7* (New York: Institute for World Order, 1978).

4. Perimeter core is a state whose economic, military and political power places it a notch ahead of the semiperiphery but out of the decision-making loop of the other core powers. Italy and Spain have been in this position since the end of the Second World War.

5. D. Pirages, *The New Context for International Relations: Global Ecopolitics* (North Scituate, MA: Duxbury Press, 1978), p.38.

6. A. G. Frank, *Capitalism and Underdevelopment in Latin America* (New York: Monthly Review Press, 1969).

7. A. Buchan, *The End of the Postwar Era: A New Balance of World Power* (London: Wiedenfield, 1974), p. 71.

8. R. O. Keohane, and J. S. Nye, eds, *Power and Interdependence: World Politics in Transition* (Boston: Little, Brown and Company, 1977), p. 47.

9. J. E. Spero, *The Politics of International Economic Relations* (New York: St. Martin's Press, 1979), p. 25.

10. R. O. Keohane and J. S. Nye, eds., *Power and Interdependence,* p. 47.

11. D. H. Blake and R. S. Walters, *The Politics of Global Economic Relations* (Englewood Cliffs, NJ: Prentice-Hall, 1987), p. 76.

12. These actions included postwar U.S. aid to Europe and Japan, as well as massive defense expenditures incurred by the United States, assumed to enhance the security of its principle allies. In addition, the U.S. had maintained the value of its currency since the Second World War, thereby contributing to the stability of the international monetary order.

13. D. H. Blake and R. S. Walters, *The Politics of Global Economic Relations,* p. 71.

14. J. E. Spero, *The Politics of International Economic Relations,* p. 59.

15. A. G. Frank, *Crisis in the World Economy* (New York: Holmes and Meier, 1981), p. 51.

16. J. E. Spero, *The Politics of International Economic Relations,* p. 53.

17. A. W. Cafruny, "A Gramscian Concept of Declining Hegemony: Stages of U.S. Power and Evolution of International Economic Relations," in *World Leadership and Hegemony,* ed. David P. Rapkin (Boulder, CO: Lynne Rienner Publishers, 1990), p. 112.

18. R. J. Lieber, *No Common Power: Understanding International Relations* (New York: HarperCollins Publishers, 1991), p. 337.

19. A. W. Cafruny, "A Gramscian Concept," p. 112.

20. D. H. Blake and R. S. Walters, *The Politics of Global Economic Relations,* p. 21.

21. Ibid., p. 19.

22. Ibid., p. 20.

23. P. Kennedy, *The Rise and Fall of Great Powers: Economic Change and Military Conflict from 1500 to 2000* (New York: Random House, 1987).

24. R. Gilpin, *War and Change in World Politics* (New York: Cambridge University Press, 1981).

25. R. O. Keohane, *After Hegemony: Cooperation and Discord in the World Political Economy* (Princeton: Princeton University Press, 1984).

26. For a fuller examination of this schema see A. W. Cafruny, "A Gramscian Concept," pp. 97–118.

27. Ibid., pp. 106–107.

28. Ibid., pp. 113–114.

29. In the military arena the world system was characterized as bipolar with the U.S. and Russia as the two dominant nuclear powers. In the global economic arena the world system was characterized as polycentric with the decline of U.S. power and the rise of Japan, Western Europe, OPEC, and the newly industrializing countries of the Third World.

30. Until the 1980s the Great Powers and their superpower allies were unwilling to take advantage of their military superiority. The Falklands crisis opened the floodgates for U.S. intervention into Grenada, Panama, a couple of dogfights with Libya, and covert action in Nicaragua. The Gulf crisis of 1990 put the Third World on notice that the restraint of the past would be curtailed as long as Russian acquiescence continued.

31. S. Hoffmann, *Gulliver's Troubles: On Setting American Foreign Policy* (New York: McGraw-Hill, 1978), p. 58.

32. Ibid., p. 39.

33. For a more detailed analysis of the transition toward pan-proletarianism between the third and fourth nonaligned conference you may review the following: A. W. Singham and Helen Hune, "The First, Second and Third Summit: The Formative Years," in A. W. Singham and Helen Hune, *Non-Alignment in an Age of Alignment* (London: Zed Books, Ltd., 1986), pp. 79–118; and Darryl C. Thomas, Chapter 6, "The Economic Aspects of Non-Alignment," in Darryl C. Thomas, "Theory and Practice of Third World Solidarity: From Afro-Asianism, Non-Alignment to the Quest for a New International Economic Order, 1955–1980" (Ph.D Dissertation, the University of Michigan, 1987), pp. 263–223.

34. Algeria, Nigeria, Venezuela, Iraq, and Saudi Arabia, to name but a few.

35. Saudi Arabia, Kuwait, Iraq, Libya, Algeria, Egypt, Abu Dhabi, Bahrain, and Qatar comprised the OAPEC.

36. R. A. Mortimer, *The Third World Coalition in International Politics* (New York: Praeger Publishers, 1980), p. 39.

37. O. Jankowitsch and J. P. Sauvant, *The Third World Without Superpowers: The Collected Documents of the Non-Aligned Countries,* Vols. 1–4 (New York: Oceana Publications, 1978), p. 139.

38. R. A. Mortimer, *The Third World Coalition in International Politics*, p. 40.

39. W. H. Wriggins and G. Adler-Karlsson, *Reducing Global Inequities* (New York: McGraw-Hill, 1978), p. 68.

40. J. Singh, *A New International Economic Order: Toward A Fair Redistribution of World Resources* (New York: Praeger Publishers, 1978).

41. A. G. Moss and H. N. M. Winton, *A New International Economic Order: Selected Documents, 1945–1975,* vol. 1–2, (New York: Unitar, 1976).

42. R. A. Mortimer, *The Third World Coalition in International Politics*, p. 54.

43. J. Singh, *A New International Economic Order;* R. A. Mortimer, *The Third World Coalition in International Politics.*

44. P. Sigmund, *Multinational Corporations in Latin America: The Politics of Nationalization* (Madison: University of Wisconsin Press, 1981), p. 5.

45. Brazil, Mexico, South Korea, Taiwan, Singapore, Malaysia, South Africa and Zimbabwe, to name but a few.

46. Saudi Arabia, Abu Dhabi, United Arab Emirates, and Libya, to name but a few.

47. S. J. Katsikus, *The Arc of Socialist Revolutions: Angola to Afghanistan* (New York: Schenkman Publishing Co., Inc., 1982).

48. The Group of Seven includes the United States, Britain, France, Italy, Canada, Germany, and Japan.

49. See Henry R. Nau, *The Myth of America's Decline: Leading the World Economy into the 1990s* (New York: Oxford University Press, 1990).

50. A. W. Cafruny, "A Gramscian Concept," p. 114.

6

The Politics of Global Economic Restructuring and the Demise of Third World Pan-Proletarianism, 1970–1990

Starting in the 1970s the newly industrializing countries joined forces with the resource-rich and with poor states of the Third World to demand a new international economic order. Both the newly industrializing countries (NICs) and OPEC became vocal antagonists in the Third World's quest to implement their vision of a new order on the basis of the "one man one vote" mechanism. This voting procedure became fundamental in the decision-making apparatus of the United Nations General Assembly, the United Nations Conference on Trade and Development (UNCTAD), the International Labor Organization (ILO), and the United Nations Industrial Development Organization (UNIDO). Third World leaders sought this change in order to counter the Northern monopoly of power over international economic issues. These actors exercised control through the decision-making processes in such key international institutions as the International Monetary Fund (IMF), the World Bank, and the General Agreement on Tariffs and Trade (GATT). Third World states sought to take control of the decision-making processes on international economic issues away from the IMF, the World Bank, and GATT and give it to Southern-dominated international institutions such as UNCTAD, UNIDO, ILO, and the United Nations General Assembly.

Increasingly, leaders in the Third World conceptualized their societies as "proletarian nations" bargaining for a better wage, that is, prices for their commodities and manufactured goods, from the advanced capitalist countries of the Northwest. During this period, pan-proletarianism – solidarity based on economic justice and an international class consciousness – became the basis for Third World unity. Beginning in the early postwar period a Third World perspective developed on the economic gap between the Northern and Southern hemispheres. During the 1970s Third World solidarity evolved around the North-South conflict. Leaders throughout the Third World began to make demands for a new international economic order to correct the injustices of the Bretton Woods system, having come to the conclusion that the "invisible hand" of the world economy was operating to their comparative disadvantage.

This chapter will examine the changing role of the Third World's rich and poor states in the North-South conflict from the 1970s to the 1990s. This inquiry will pay special attention to the changing fortunes of the rich and poor commodity producers and how their increased participation in the capitalist world economy has contributed to their marginalization. The NICs will be examined with an emphasis on their role in the changing global division of labor. Along with these changes, this chapter will also analyze the demise of the Third World coalition against the North. It will also examine the extent to which the changing international divisions of labor that accompanied the global economic restructuring processes contributed to the growth of political and economic diversity within the Third World, thus challenging the "logic for collective action" especially with reference to Third World leaders' adoption of trade unionism or pan-proletarianism as a strategy for solidarity.

This chapter begins with a theoretical discussion of the application of David Truman's and Mancur Olson's theories of group dynamics and other related theoretical frameworks that seek to explain Third World coalition-building in the world system. Next, it compares and contrasts the economic performance of divergent Third World regions during the global economic crises of the 1970s and 1980s and the extent to which the South developed a more diversified interest toward the new world order, and therefore became more divided. It will compare the economic performance of African and Latin American peripheral states with that of the newly industrializing countries, i.e., semiperipheral states in East Asia and Latin America. This inquiry also focuses on semiperipheral states in Southern Africa and Europe, and demonstrates that states from Southern Europe began changing their traditional agricultural and commodity production roles in the world economy. These actors experienced spurts of growth and stagnation very similar to those undergone by the semi-peripheral sector of the Third World. Next, it examines the degree to which the U.S. and its Northern allies have been successful in dividing NICs and OPEC from the rest of the Third World coalition, co-opting them and thus compromising the pan-proletarian dimension of solidarity. Finally, it demonstrates how policies by key states in the Northwest and international financial institutions have made it almost impossible for other Third World regions to replicate the policies of East and Southeast Asia.

COMPETING THEORIES OF COLLECTIVE ACTION

David Truman, in *The Governmental Process: Political Interest and Public Opinion,* outlines three major assumptions that govern the formation of interest groups: (1) when groups share a common interest, they will organize and become politically active; (2) potential interest groups are always present to act as a countervailing pressure against dominant interest groups; and (3) the size of an interest group does not make a difference in terms of its ability to organize around specific issues.[1] In the world system, cooperation, alliances, and coalitions among states are functions of their divergent interests and needs. However, the size, composition, and interests of such organizations in the world system may result from certain prerequisites. Truman postulates that the interests of potential groups are usually widespread, loosely articulated, and not organized in any cohesive fashion. For Truman, these weak groups have potential power to threaten the political system through aggressive organized counteraction that may undermine the public good of all groups if the interests of subgroups are not taken into account.[2] Truman assumes that most interest groups in a political system are close to parity with reference to the resources that they can bring to bear to further their interest. This pluralist perspective does not take into account the inequality that exists between actors or how the size differences of coalitions may influence their success.

Mancur Olson believes that collective action by interest groups happens as a result of certain specific conditions. The point of departure for his analysis is that collective behavior typically exists to further the common interest of groups of actors.[3] This common interest is organized around the provision of "public" or "collective" goods for the members of the group.[4] Furthermore, Olson argues that not all members of the group have an interest in paying the cost of providing the collective good. Olson's theory of collective action functions on the supposition that there are actors willing to pay the cost for others in the alliance to earn the public good. Olson asserts,

> The necessary condition for optimal provision of a collective good, through voluntary and independent action of the members of a group, can . . . be stated very simply. The marginal cost of additional units of the collective good must be shared in exactly the same proportion as the additional benefits. Only if this is done will each member find that his own marginal costs and benefits are equal at the same time that the total marginal cost equals the total or aggregate marginal benefit.[5]

Olson argues that it is important to take into account the size of the interest group or coalition, challenging one of the fundamental assumptions of David Truman. Olson argues that relatively small groups or coalitions can better achieve the collective goods for their members. These groups are more successful in identifying those actors who are willing to pay the cost of providing for the collective good. In smaller coalitions one member may be willing to pay all of the costs involved in achieving the collective good if this actor believes that the benefits will exceed the initial outlay or cost. In contrast, Olson states, large groups have a far more difficult time achieving the collective good based on voluntarism. Large coalitions lack incentives for any actor to pay the costs of collective action. Actors in large coalitions gain whether or not they pay; and no actor can make a "noticeable contribution." The difference in the size of coalitions is critical to our understanding of how interest groups succeed in achieving their goals. Olson argues that

> distinction between the privileged and intermediate interest group, on the one hand, and the latent group, on the other, also damages the pluralistic view that any outrageous demands of one pressure group will be counterbalanced by the demands of other pressure groups so that the outcome will be reasonably just and satisfactory. Since relatively small groups will frequently be able voluntarily to organize and act in support of their common interests, and since large groups normally will not be able to do so, the outcome of the political struggle among the various groups in society will not be symmetrical.[6]

Truman's and Olson's analysis of the dynamics of interest group politics are also applicable to coalition-building among like-minded states in the world system. Olson stresses the size of such coalitions and the extent to which some actors benefit without paying a cost and thus exercising the free-rider option.

The rational actor or public choice theoretical framework seeks to analyze political processes and the interaction between the economy and the political system by employing the tools of modern neoclassical analysis. This theoretical framework provides an explicit positive approach to the working of international institutions and to the behavior of governments, parties, voters, interest groups, and public bureaucracies. From a normative perspective, public choice analysts seek to ascertain the most desirable and effective political institutions. Changes in actors' preferences, actions, and reactions are thus driven by their knowledge of the options available to them. Analysts employing the public choice framework assume that actors are knowledgeable concerning these relationships. Hence, actors' preferences remain consistent. Scholars employing the public choice theoretical framework also emphasize empirical testing of propositions as an important exercise in theory building.[7]

Students of international organizations apply public choice analysis emphasizing the costs and benefits of joining such institutions, their decision-making apparatus, and internal bureaucracy, as well as an examination of the bargaining and political milieu of such institutions. Most of the research in this arena has stressed the advantage of small regional and international institutions in providing public or collective goods to national government. Very few such studies have paid attention to efforts by Third World nations to implement their international economic policies through international and regional organizations. The logic of Third World collective actions in international and regional organizations has received scant attention by students of alliances.

Most of the literature that has addressed participation by the Third World in international and regional organizations has concentrated on global bargaining and regime analysis. Robert Rothstein provides an overview of the attempt by Third World states to use negotiation and bargaining to dramatically change North-South relations through the instrumentality of the quest for a new international economic order (NIEO). His analysis focuses on how international regimes may impose constraints on the behavior of Third World nations in the world economy and the extent to which these regimes have mobilized in international institutions such as UNCTAD in order to alter the rules of the game. Rothstein argues that the Third World states were success-ful in the 1970s in organizing a morally compelling case for a new world order that addressed North-South global economic and political inequality, but that they failed to persuade leaders in the Northeast and Northwest of the need for such a dramatic change. In the years since the publication of his study,[8] the Third World coalition has become fragmented in world politics as a result of the worldwide economic crisis, the debt crisis, and the escalation of militarized conflicts in this zone of the world system.

Stephen Krasner's work does not address the constraints that international regimes impose on Third World nations. His analysis is very supportive of the realist school of thought and integrates regime analysis with neorealism. From Krasner's perspective, international regimes function in the interest of hege-monic powers. In order to maintain legitimacy, hegemonic powers tend to allow international institutions that enforce international regimes some degree of autonomy in their operations. Regime autonomy gives some actors, espe-cially Third World states, an opportunity to restructure international regimes along lines suited to their interests. The political weakness and economic vul-nerability of Third World states push these actors to bond together, seeking to use their majority of numbers in international institutions to alter the rules of the international economic game. Krasner postulates that regimes are a form of "meta-power," that is, these actors attempt to define how power will be exer-cised in specific international arenas where global bargaining cannot ensue between the North and South. Furthermore, Krasner argues that Third World leaders formulated the NIEO primarily as a mechanism of control, rather than as a corrective measure to end global inequality between the North and South that would undermine the "liberal international regime."[9] Elites in the Third World would benefit from the NIEO rather than the poor, whom it was pri-marily designed to help.

Krasner has failed to analyze the degree to which the North has employed its power in such international institutions as GATT, the Group of Seven, the IMF, and the World Bank to maintain its control over the Third World. Through these institutions the North maintains its control over global eco-nomic decision making. Krasner does not evaluate the extent to which the United States and other advanced capitalist states have withdrawn financial resources from such international institutions as the ILO and UNESCO. The alleged meta-power of the Third World has been ineffective against the North's power of the purse.

Although the world system theory does not deal with the creation of inter-est groups per se, this theoretical framework has much to offer in analyzing the conflict of interest that exists between states based on their position in the hierarchy of wealth and poverty in the world system. At this juncture, I will outline the *world system perspective* on competing coalitions in the *world system* with reference to the world economy.

One of the central theoretical claims of world system analysis is that nation-states perennially battle among themselves to move up the global ladder of wealth and poverty and that the outcome of these enduring struggles depends on their location in the world system rather than their membership in a coalition or the overall size of such collective entities. A nation's location in the global hierarchy of wealth and poverty influences the outcome of these battles for primacy. In addition, world system theory asserts that the hierarchy of wealth consists of three discrete layers or clusters. States in the higher clusters routinely appropriate a disproportionate share of the benefits of the international division of labor and, in this sense, constitute the core of the capitalist world system. States in the lower cluster reap benefits that, at best, cover their long-term cost of participation in the global hierarchy of wealth and poverty, and constitute the periphery of the capitalist world system. States located in the intermediate cluster appropriate benefits in excess of the long-term cost of participating in the global division of labor but short of what is necessary to keep up with normal criteria of wealth in core states.[10] This intermediate cluster makes up the semiperiphery.

The world system theory also focuses on the inequality among states by paying attention to their relative position as well as the cost these actors pay to participate in the different clusters of the capitalist world system. The structural position as well as the divergent cost of participation for core, peripheral, and semiperipheral states necessitates divergent interests even among the less developed countries, which become divided along economic lines. Mancur Olson does not deal with the structural position of divergent coalitions or groups vis-à-vis the world system or the differences in cost that they pay to participate in that system.

This chapter operates on the assumption that the modern world system is undergoing a dramatic structural transformation in which the international regimes that govern the interstate system and the models of capital accumulation that regulate the world economy are being torn apart. During this new wave of global restructuring new international regimes are evolving for the interstate system and the world economy. This new era of global restructuring has contributed to a growing incompatibility between the interstate system and the world economy. The result is a crisis that has created a divergent spatial dimension to the international division of labor between core, peripheral and semiperipheral states on the one hand and a period of intense competition among capitalist business enterprises on the other. Changes as fundamental as these have already begun to transform the political, economic, social and cultural structures that have been in place since the end of the Second World War.

The world system has undergone similar cycles of structural change that have reorganized capitalist business enterprises, the world economy, and the interstate system by means of global wars of hegemonic succession, long waves of colonization and decolonization, A (expansion) and B (contraction) phases of capitalist development, and organizational and technological innovations in capitalist business enterprises. During these eras of systemic change, the ideological assumptions and value systems that supported models of capital accumulation and the international regimes that governed interstate relations were transformed.

During the two decades following the Second World War, the capitalist world economy experienced the greatest boom in its history. This boom reached its climax at the close of the 1960s. The world economy encountered decline in growth and intense structural change. These changes resulted in heightened political instability as the ideological underpinnings of the liberal world order fell apart.[11] The international regimes that govern the interstate system and the models of capital accumulation that regulate the world economy are being transformed, ushering in a new era in North-South relations as we approach the twenty-first century. The world system has undergone similar transformations in the past, introducing new hegemonic powers and dramatically remaking the international division of labor. These cyclical changes in the world system were propelled by the political, economic, social, and cultural innovations in the state and the economy. Neither North nor South, East nor West escaped from these changes.

This study operates from the premise that pan-proletarianism was a driving force behind solidarity and the tendency of Third World states in the peripheral and semiperipheral sectors of the world system to act as a "diplomatic unit" on North-South issues during the 1970s and 1980s. The focus on pan-proletarianism among Third World leaders drew attention to their perceptions of the global economic inequalities within the world system and their commitment to securing economic justice for the people and nations of the Southern Hemisphere. This perspective also acknowledges the political and economic diversity within the Southern Hemisphere and how these differences in the long run created cracks in the Third World's united front as the global economic crises of the 1980s forced a focus of their energies on their own individual nation's economic and financial problems. As this economic downturn in the world economy intensified during the 1980s, states throughout the Third World adopted unilateral rather than multilateral policies and in the end relied on the World Bank and the IMF to provide relief for their economic woes.

PAN-PROLETARIANALIST DIMENSION OF THIRD WORLD SOLIDARITY

Starting in the late 1970s, collective self-reliance emerged as an important component of the pan-proletarian approach to Third World solidarity. Collective self-reliance became a weapon to combat Northern efforts to divide critical elements of the Third World coalition on the North-South conflict. South-to-South economic cooperation emerged as a new stimulus among Third World states to reverse the vertical links between the North and South.

During the late 1970s, President Julius Nyerere of Tanzania became a major proponent of collective self-reliance as an important strategy to overcome Third World fragmentation, co-optation, and the North-South stalemate. According to Nyerere, Third World diversity in the economic and political arena and differences in natural resources need not lead to the development of separate camps within the South. He urged Third World leaders to avoid falling prey to the old imperialist policy of divide and rule. Nyerere called upon the semiperipheral states of the Third World to spurn offers of special treatment or representation in Northern-dominated international institutions such as GATT, the IMF, and the World Bank. He warned Third World leaders that the cold winds of Western recession were blowing in their direction, generating strong temptation to look inward as individual nations rather than continue supporting the collective grievances of the Third World.[12] Third World fragmentation increased the likelihood that this collectivity of states would become an ineffective coalition within the world system. Nyerere urged Third World leaders to maintain a united front on North-South issues.

> Ours is a kind of Trade Union of the Poor. Sometimes, perhaps, we negotiate about different aspects of our demands for a New International Economic Order and settle for the best compromise we can receive at the time, sometimes, however, we may be forced to call a strike in order to show that certain things are no longer acceptable.[13]

Nevertheless, Nyerere did recognize that a trade union's strength is in proportion to its solidarity. When deciding to strike, a trade union must recognize the political realities of its constituency and its adversaries alike. In the 1980s, the Group of 77 comprised approximately 129 states whose diversity in the political and economic arenas had increased substantially since 1964. Trade unionism at the domestic level was quite different than at the global level, especially when it involved nation-states.

In the 1980s the Third World coalition lacked a strike fund. Asking countries such as Chile and Zambia to stop exporting copper, or Kenya and Colombia to cease exporting coffee to advanced capitalist economies, for example, would be asking leaders in these nation-states to commit economic suicide. Their governments naturally would not agree to pursue such policies. The advanced capitalist economies were very familiar with the economic vulnerabilities in the Third World and devised appropriate policies to accomplish their goals of maintaining control over international economic decision making and resisting the change to a "one man one vote" regime.

The global economic crisis of the 1980s emerged at the same time that Third World leaders were calling for collective self-reliance. The crisis forced these actors to abandon their preferred strategy of collective action as the IMF and the World Bank began to dictate economic and fiscal policies throughout the Third World. Most Third World states experienced economic stagnation and marginalization between the 1970s and the 1990s as they increased their participation in the world economy. The African continent suffered the worst economic downturn of any Third World region in the 1970s and 1980s. This negative economic spiral continued throughout the 1990s with notable exceptions in Mauritius, South Africa, and Ghana. The fate of peripheral states in this zone of the world economy forced these actors to turn to the IMF and the World Bank for redemption and to abandon their call for a new order. The debt crisis forced a number of semiperipheral states throughout the world system to abandon their expansion into more competitive niches in the world economy and to devote their efforts to rescheduling their international financial obligations. The East Asian advanced developing states were the only actors that continued their economic pace; they moved into more lucrative technological markets in spite of the crisis. At this juncture we will examine the impact of the global economic crisis on the African continent and the ramifications for the North-South conflict and Third World coalition or trade unionist politics.

AFRICA AND THE GLOBAL ECONOMIC CRISIS

Over the two last decade, the African continent has lagged behind other regions with reference to economic development and industrialization. The vast majority of Africans have become impoverished and their countries' economies have become burdened by debt. Twenty-eight African countries, located in sub-Saharan Africa, rank among the world's forty-two poorest. According to the World Bank, during the 1980s, six more African states slipped into the low-income category. Sub-Saharan debt climbed to nearly U.S. $250 billion, roughly equal to the region's total product (regional GNP), and three and one-half times its export earnings. At the same time, debt service obligations equaled almost half the region's foreign exchange earnings, although actual payments averaged just over a quarter of its 1985–88 exports. The African continent has become a net exporter of capital to the International Monetary Fund (IMF), transmitting nearly U.S. $1 billion in 1986 and 1987.[14]

Economic growth in sub-Saharan Africa hovered around 1.5 percent by the 1990s. The region's 530 million people have a combined GNP of less than $150 billion, nearly the same as that of Belgium and its 10 million inhabitants. Food production had fallen 20 percent lower than it was in 1970, when its population was half its current size. Life expectancy is around 51 years, and half of the world's refugees are Africans, fleeing drought or civil wars or both.[15] The 1980s have been disastrous by any reasonable standard. Only nine out of thirty countries registered any per capita gross domestic product (GDP) increases in the 1980s.

Even in the 1970s most sub-Saharan African states experienced sluggish economic growth. However, this era of slow growth resulted from the oil crises of 1973–74 and 1979, which put enormous pressure on African import capacities; the subsequent worldwide inflation, which compounded rising import costs; the sharp recession and stagflation in the industrialized Northern tier of the world system, which reduced demand and sometimes prices for African exports; and a rise in Western protectionism. At the same time a number of domestic or African-oriented causes also contributed to economic slowdown. Domestic factors included major, multi-year droughts in West and East Africa. Most African governments increased deficit spending, which resulted in an upsurge in inflationary impulses, thus stimulating import demands. The combination of overvalued exchange rates with economic nationalism and state activism led to the emergence of state corporations on a large scale. African governments became active in many arenas of production and distribution in both statist "socialist" regimes and in capitalist ones, such as Ivory Coast, Nigeria, Cameroon, and Kenya.[16] The more sub-Saharan African states participated in the world economy, the less they received in value in return.

During the 1970s, a number of African and other Third World regions began to adopt protectionist policies rather than support capital accumulation policies. Still others were economic nationalists but sought to cultivate capital through a stronger role for indigenous capital. Nationalization occurred throughout Africa and other Third World regions that mounted opposition to foreign and domestic capital, for example, Tanzania, Mozambique, Angola, Algeria, and Ethiopia, after 1975. These domestic efforts reinforced the policy position on international economic issues adopted by the Group of 77 in UNCTAD and the nonaligned movement throughout the 1970s as these two Third World organizations launched their quest for a new international economic order. Other states adopted limited nationalization schemes, or state equity purchases occurred to give states a major role in major industries, for example, Zambia and Chile[17] in copper; Nigeria, Venezuela, and Saudi Arabia in the oil industry; and Ghana in gold, bauxite, and banking. In some African and Third World states certain sectors became the preserve of state and indigenous entrepreneurs.

Africa's per capita income levels and growth rates have continued declining since the first oil crisis of 1973, while its percentages of worldwide official development assistance have risen from 17 percent in 1970 to around 30 percent in 1987. In comparison with other regions, nominal GDP has risen very slowly since 1970 despite terms of trade and export prices that have been, on average, slightly better than for other developing areas. Africa's real GDP growth rates have fallen drastically since the mid-1960s. Other Third World regions have fared better despite the global economic downturn in the world economy, especially during the 1980s. Africa's export levels have remained low, in some cases actually declining after 1970, while those of other Third World regions have recorded significant growth. Africa's world market share of non-oil primary products declined from 7 to 4 percent between 1970 and 1985.[18] In comparison with other regions, Africa's annual growth rates for exports have performed very poorly.

Africa's economic marginalization becomes more obvious in comparison with other peripheral countries, especially in South Asia. The African continent has continued to decline with reference to per capita GNP while South Asia has exhibited modest growth. In terms of investment environment, South Asia's record has been extraordinary in comparison with Africa, despite the global economic crisis. South Asian economic policies were more successful in providing a hospitable climate as well as the political and administrative context for foreign investment. This is vividly demonstrated in the comparison rates of return on investment. Africa fell from 30.7 percent in the 1960s to just 2.5 percent in the 1980s. South Asia's increased gradually but steadily, if not minimally, from 21.3 percent to 22.4 percent. Compounding the investment problems, Africa's population growth rate continues to climb while South Asia's population is declining. In terms of per capita GDP, Africa has declined dramatically while South Asia has maintained slow but steady growth rates.[19] The African continent has become increasingly peripheral in the world economy.

The African continent suffered from the second oil crisis in 1979–80 at the same time that export commodity prices were already declining, ushering in a more severe crisis than that of the 1970s. At this juncture, most African states experienced huge balance of payments deficits as they confronted higher oil imports. In 1981–84 a major recession occurred in the industrial heartland of the capitalist world system, creating dramatic declines in export volume and in commodity prices to levels not seen since the 1930s. In addition, there was a massive increase in real debt as the United States and other advanced capitalist states used monetarist policies to choke off inflation.[20]

In the 1980s, the terms of trade[21] for sub-Saharan Africa fell sharply, although the decline was from the historically high level achieved in 1981. Nevertheless, the declines in the terms of trade were still higher during the first half of the 1980s than in the 1960s, although by 1986–87 they were lower. Per capita income growth was very modest, averaging less than one-tenth of a percentage point a year during the entire period 1961–1987, with the exception of 1986–87. Price volatility has wreaked havoc on economic management and planning throughout this region.[22] The overall decline in the terms of trade during the 1980s spurred African governments to seek additional loans in order to finance minimal import levels (with the poorest countries being eligible for International Development Association soft loans). During the 1980s, borrowing escalated for most sub-Saharan African countries. Starting in 1975, sub-Saharan African debt reached nearly $20 billion. By the 1980s, debt obligations climbed to $56 billion, nearly a three-fold increase in five years. Interest rates turned from negative to positive over the same period.[23]

Starting in the 1980s, sub-Saharan Africa's debt obligation has grown faster than that of any other Third World regions. According to the World

Bank, long-term debt has increased 19-fold since the 1970s and now is the heaviest among developing regions. Latin American debt is only 59 percent of GNP. Sub-Saharan African nations owe less to private creditors (39 percent compared to 73 percent) than do their Latin American counterparts. Approximately one-third of their private debt was guaranteed by creditor governments. Sub-Saharan Africa's problem in servicing its commercial debt has received scant attention because its share of total Third World debt is small (approximately 10 percent) and poses no threat to the international banking system.[24] Africa's debt rose sharply in the 1980s as its economic problems accelerated. By 1990 the continent's total debt had risen to $190 billion, over three times the 1980 level of $56 billion. In 1995 the region's debt stock had reached $223 billion.

Although the African continent has the lowest debt ratio among developing areas, the region faces some of the harshest difficulties in servicing its debt. This state of affairs applies to the majority of states on the continent whose economies are classified as low − income with a per capita income of $580 or less. The external debt/GDP ratio for these countries is just short of 100 percent on the average, and is twice that for some countries like Congo, Guinea, Bissau, Sao Tome, and Somalia (Latin American debt by comparison is about 40 percent of GDP.) African states' debt service ratio is nearly 20 percent and would have been higher if the full payments had been made as scheduled and if there had been no new debt cancellation.[25] Debt service obligations have been impossible for many African countries to meet. Over half of the sub-Saharan African countries have had their debt rescheduled a total of 121 times; some countries have had to reschedule their payments' four, six, and eight times.[26] The gravity of this debt crisis became clear with the soaring liability in interest payments to creditors. These obligations were $1 billion in 1982. By 1991, interest payments to creditors soared to approximately $11 billion.[27] The inability of African countries to meet their debt obligation during the 1980s was not unrelated to the major declines in export commodity prices, for example, oil, cocoa, coffee, and copper.

Because most of the Africa's creditors are Western governments (France, the Netherlands, Britain, the Scandinavian countries) and international financial institutions (primarily the IMF and the World Bank), one would expect general agreement on lowering the debt burden in order to stimulate economic growth in Africa. To date, no general consensus has emerged to resolve the African debt predicament. Several European states (France, the Netherlands, Britain, the Scandinavian countries), as well as Canada and the United States have canceled an estimated total of $7.6 billion that was owed by the poorest reforming African economies. The Group of Seven Toronto Summit of June 1988 agreed on a relief program that includes partial write-offs, longer maturity periods, and enhanced concessional rates of interest. African states' economic development policies must be informed by the norms of a free market, including private ownership of the means of production and reduction of the state role in the economy. Structural Adjustment programs under the instrument of the IMF and the World Bank have facilitated the implementation of economic reform. Since the Toronto Summit, 20 African states have benefited from the new facility; however, this has not reduced the debt burden enough to meet the estimated net resource inflows consistent with a 4 to 5 percent growth rate.[28] The African continent has been unable to participate fully in the unfolding technological and managerial revolution developing in the world economy since the 1970s.

Development efforts came to a halt as nations throughout the African continent struggled to survive the worst economic crisis since their independence. Civil wars and interstate conflicts accelerated in the 1980s in such diverse places as Angola, Mozambique, Ethiopia, Somalia, Chad, Liberia, and the Sudan. Many of these militarized conflicts endure notwithstanding the end of the Cold war era. Civil strife on the continent further exacerbated the economic crisis as money was spent on arms rather than allocated for human capital.[29]

The African continent was not the only Third World region to experience serious economic marginalization in the 1980s and the 1990s. For example, the growth in per capita output of the industrial market economies was 1.7 percent per annum from 1973 to 1982, compared to 3.7 percent in the 1963–72 period. Oil-exporting countries, in contrast, fell from 5.6 to 3.8 percent in the two periods. The non-oil developing countries' per capita growth rates fell from 3.6 to 2.7 percent in the two periods. In the Western Hemisphere, growth in per capita output in 1973–82 was 2 percent, compared with 3.3 percent in the previous decade. In the United States, the 1979–82 recession was the worst since the 1930s. The effects of the global economic crisis were particularly severe for less developed and indebted nations, notably in Latin America and to some extent on the African continent.[30] (See Tables 6.1, 6.2, and 6.3 for details.)

Table 6.1

GDP and GDP Growth in Seven Third World Regions, 1970-1992

Regions	1992 GDP (billions of dollars)	1992 Population (millions)	1992 GDP per capita (dollars)	Average Annual GDP Growth Rate (percent)		
				1970-80	1980-90	1990-92
East Asia	631	74	8,527	9.1	8.3	6.5
Southeast Asia	347	325	1,068	6.9	5.8	6.3
Latin America	1,219	453	2,691	6.2	1.3	3.1
Sub-Saharan Africa	166	503	330	3.5	1.9	1.7
South Asia	297	1,178	252	3	5.5	3.3
Middle East	366	211	1,735	5.5	3.6	3.6
Eastern Europe	187	96	1,948	n.a.	0.9	-7.2

Source: Barbara Stallings, "Introduction, Global Change, Regional Response," *Global Change, Regional Response: The New International Context of Development* (New York: Cambridge University Press), pp. 24–25. *n.a.* indicates that figures are not available.

Table 6.2
Net Long-term Resource Flows and Transfers in Seven Third World Regions,
1970–92 *(millions of U.S. dollars)*

Regions	*1970*	*1980*	*1985*	*1990*	*1992*
East Asia					
Net resource flows	455	2,440	2,979	2,979	5,899
Long-term loans	271	2,426	2,649	59	2,923
Grants	119	8	2	6	6
DFI	66	6	328	1,461	2,970
Interest and profits	-81	-1,701	-2,894	-2,001	-2,226
Net transfers	374	740	85	2,979	3,673
Southeast Asia					
Net resource flows	1,069	7,307	5,773	14,915	20,249
Long-term loans	765	5,859	4,148	6,586	10,227
Grants	110	249	404	878	945
DFI	195	1,198	1,180	7,454	9,077
Interest and Profits	-485	-7,193	-8,868	-11,872	-13,244
Net transfers	584	114	-3,135	3,044	7,004
Latin America					
Net resource flows	4,163	29,353	13,239	19,272	20,796
Long-term loans	2,945	22,878	7,691	8,012	5,317
Grants	130	360	1,258	2,492	3,089
DFI	1,087	6,115	4,290	9,111	22,389
Interest and profits	-3,381	-22,127	-32,917	-25,270	-25,263
Net transfers	782	7,226	-19,678	5,443	5,443
Sub-Saharan Africa					
Net resource flows	1,277	11,008	9,364	16,503	17,260
Long-term loans	821	7,899	3,765	3,801	2,089
Grants	363	3,089	4,559	11,846	13,413
DFI	92	20	1,040	856	1,757
Interest and profits	-180	-2,172	-3,427	-10,148	-10,181
Net transfers	373	5,946	4,417	6,355	7,079
South Asia					
Net resource flows	1,320	5,465	5,748	9,434	10,126
Long-term loans	1,007	3,217	4,010	6,135	5,360
Grants	284	2,441	1,581	2,725	3,949
DFI	29	106	157	574	818
Interest and profits	-299	-929	-2,047	-4,230	-4,009
Net transfers	1,021	4,836	3,701	5,204	6,116
Middle East					
Net resource flows	929	11,605	9,757	8,130	11,450
Long-term loans	484	6,414	6,721	-1,000	4,239

Table 6.2, continued
Net Long-term Resource Flows and Transfers in Seven Third World Regions,
1970–92 *(millions of U.S. dollars)*

Regions	1970	1980	1985	1990	1992
(Middle East, continued)					
Grants	334	3,805	1,540	7,534	5,647
DFI	111	1,387	1,495	1,596	1,564
Interest and profits	-1,110	-4,923	-4,688	-7,107	-6,732
Net transfers	-180	6,683	5,068	1,023	4,718
Eastern Europe					
Net resource flows	n.a.	n.a.	2,383	1,361	4,573
Long-term loans			2,368	911	1,129
Grants			0	0	0
DFI			0	450	3,444
Interest and profits			-3,357	-2,526	-3,223
Net transfers			-974	-1,165	1,352

Source: World Bank, *World Debt Tables, 1991–92, 1993–94. n.a.*: Figures are not available

The vast majority of the nations that comprise the Third World make up the peripheral sector of the capitalist world economy. Many of these nations are mere consumers of the technological revolution that has been bursting forth during this cycle of global economic restructuring. Most are primarily purchasers of military hardware and consumer goods for their small middle class. Hence, technological development that is germinating in the upper tier of the semiperiphery (the newly industrializing countries) has simply bypassed this sector of the Third World. The periphery has lost more ground as a direct consequence of the changing global division of labor between the North and South. Most of the states in Africa, the Caribbean, and Central America, and several states in Latin America find themselves at an alarming competitive disadvantage.

The decline in economic growth among the industrial market economies had a serious effect on the demand for, and prices of, commodities exported by developing countries. The price of commodities other than oil fell 21 percent in real terms from 1980 to 1982. During this same period, international interest rates experienced rapid growth. The six-months' Eurodollar rate grew an average of 8.3 percent in 1975–79. In the 1980–82 period, it increased to 14.2.[31]

The pressure of the recession and an acceleration in the fall of real prices of commodity exports, coupled with extremely high real interest rates in the late 1970s and the early 1980s, forced many indebted nations to turn to the IMF, which in turn pressed these nations to liberalize their economies and cut the overall size of the public sector.[32]

Beginning in 1983 the U.S. economy began a dramatic recovery that had consequences for the world system. From 1983 to 1988, industrial market

Table 6.3

Growth of Export Value in Seven Third World Regions, 1972–92

Regions	Exports (billions of U.S. dollars)				Real growth rate (percent per year)		
	1972	1980	1990	1992	1972–80	1980–90	1990–92
East Asia	9.5	69.8	213.7	251.5	16.8	9.4	7.4
Primary Goods	1.7	11.2	20.3	21.5	3.9	9.5	7.5
Manufactures	7.8	58.6	193.4	230.0	19.6	9.5	7.4
Southeast Asia	5.6	47.0	86.1	116.8	10.6	8.0	17.4
Primary Goods	5.1	40.1	40.7	47.1	8.0	3.0	11.9
Manufactures	0.5	6.9	45.4	69.7	29.5	17.3	22.0
Latin America	17.4	91.5	122.2	125.3	4.4	4.4	3.1
Primary Goods	14.6	75.0	81.5	77.3	1.9	3.7	1.4
Manufactures	2.8	16.5	40.7	48.0	16.1	6.3	7.0
Sub-Saharan Africa	7.7	45.3	34.6	34.3	2.7	0.3	3.8
Primary Goods	7.1	43.4	31.3	30.9	2.4	0.1	4.0
Manufactures	0.6	1.9	3.2	3.5	7.9	2.2	3.1
South Asia	3.7	12.0	26.8	31.8	5.3	7.2	8.4
Primary Goods	1.8	5.6	7.3	8.4	1.5	4.3	10.1
Manufactures	1.9	6.4	19.5	23.4	8.1	8.6	7.8
Middle East	12.2	152.0	90.7	92.7	3.7	-0.7	7.0
Primary Goods	11.5	148.6	81.6	83.2	3.3	-1.2	7.8
Manufactures	0.7	3.4	9.1	9.5	13.4	7.4	0.5
Eastern Europe	11.9	36.9	29.1	28.3	2.9	-3.7	-1.0
Primary Goods	3.7	12.7	9.7	10.7	-4.2	-0.3	9.2
Manufactures	8.2	24.2	19.4	17.6	6.4	-5.0	-6.3

Source: World Bank, *World Tables, 1994;* Republic of China, *Taiwan Statistical Data Book, 1994.*

economies grew at an annual rate of 3.5 percent, with the volume of imports expanding only 8 percent a year and the inflation rate remaining at a moderate rate on the average. The recovery was recognized in the North as the beginning of another economic boom for the world economy. This optimism was short lived, as this recovery remained modest in comparison to the 1960s. However, it bypassed the vast majority of the periphery and semiperiphery (with the exception of the East Asian Pacific rim) of the Third World, as these actors did not see any appreciable improvement in the international economic environment in which they had become expected to operate. From 1983 onward, debt service repayments of principal and interest exceeded loan disbursements. Third World nations transferred $163 billion to the North from 1984 to 1988.[33]

Furthermore, prices of non-oil commodities, which had recovered slightly in 1983–84, fell by a further 23 percent from 1984 to 1988. The price of petroleum fell an additional 65 percent. In addition, prices of thirty-three commodities of special interest to the peripheral sectors of the Third World (excluding petroleum) were 30 percent lower in real terms in 1988 than the average for 1979–81. In comparison, for food and tropical beverages the fall was 37 percent. Petroleum prices slid 64 percent. Therefore, the terms of trade for developing countries had declined by 29 percent as compared to 1980, and those of oil exporters among them by 49 percent. The average real price of non-oil commodities for the whole period 1980–88 was 25 percent below that of the previous two decades and the terms of trade of non-oil developing countries were 8 percent below those of the 1960s and 13 percent below those of the 1970s. For those Third World states still relying heavily on commodity production, rewards for their efforts since the 1980s have been inadequate.[34]

The global economic crisis of the 1980s forced a large number of states on the periphery to turn to the IMF for help with their economic problems. The IMF, through its adjustment policies, pressed these peripheral states to liberalize their economies, reduce the size of the public sector, and refrain from employing OPEC-style remedies by opening up their economies and allowing the magic of the marketplace to dictate economic policies. Economic development policies emphasizing an important role for the socialist and capitalist states were blamed for the economic stagnation in sub-Saharan Africa, South and Central America, and the Caribbean. Industrial policies that relied on import substitution suffered criticism for cultivating a state of encumbrance that put economic growth at a disadvantage, and distorted market forces. Increasingly in the aftermath of the global economic crisis of the 1980s, Third World states in the periphery began to adopt more unilateral approaches toward solving their economic woes.

The wheels of fortune for the peripheral sector of the Third World became increasingly tied to their performance in the world economy. The more these nations participated in the world economy the less they earned for their labor. The nations of sub-Saharan Africa, Central and South America, and the Caribbean were unable to complete the transition from agriculture and commodity production to manufacturing during this period of global restructuring. They remained on the periphery of the global commodity chain. The new global division of labor bypassed this sector of the Third World as new microelectronics technology transformed the world economy. At this juncture, the World Bank and the International Monetary Fund employed structural adjustment policies that undermined the state role in economic decision making. As the Cold War came to an end, even the military could no longer avoid spending cuts imposed from the World Bank and the IMF.

NEW POLICIES AT IMF AND THE WORLD BANK

In exchange for restructuring the massive debt loads of various developing states, the IMF and the World Bank have become increasingly involved in these states' internal policies. Structural adjustment programs (SAPs) have primarily stressed privatization, a reduced state role in the economy, support for local and foreign entrepreneurs, the creation of a better business environment, the reduction in inflation and the role of the state in economic development, and in recent years, political reform and movement toward multiparty democracy. Though the discipline in government expenditures demanded by SAPs drastically reduced funds available for social services, international lending agencies were reluctant to interfere with many governments' continued high military spending. They were far more likely to recommend cuts in food subsidies and education than military cutbacks, for example, in Zaire and Liberia in the 1980s.

Whereas defense was regarded as strictly "political" and therefore not a legitimate area of interference, in the 1990s the IMF and World Bank began to acknowledge that high military budgets could undermine the success of structural adjustment programs. Consistent with this new approach of holding Third World governments accountable for "good government," these agencies are now seeking to scrutinize military expenditures more directly, especially on the African continent. The subject is still being discussed with tact and political sensitivity between the Bretton Woods institutions and African government officials. However, there is little doubt that global leaders will no longer write blank checks for African, South American, and Central American military buildups.

The IMF, the World Bank, and other Western donors are using economic aid as a carrot to encourage new approaches toward economic development policies. The structural reforms being called for by the Bretton Woods institutions, observes the IMF's managing director, Michael Camdessus, are as far-reaching in economic culture as anything being undertaken in Eastern Europe or Latin America.[35] African states are under intense pressures to move speedily toward "democratic capitalism." British Foreign Secretary Douglas Hurd outlined this new policy in mid-1990 in the following manner:

> Countries which tend towards pluralism, public accountability, respect for the rules of law, human rights and market principle should be encouraged. Governments which persist with repressive policies, corrupt management and wasteful, discredited economic systems should not expect us to support their folly with scarce aid resources which could be used better elsewhere.[36]

The dilemma for African leaders is that while lending agencies are pressuring them to reduce military spending, the main effect of structural adjustment programs may be to increase their insecurity dilemmas and thus encourage a new wave of militarization. The vast majority of states located in this zone of the world system are undertaking adjustment programs of some kind either through the sponsorship of the World Bank or the International Monetary Fund (IMF). These countries are altering their economic policies and development strategies to make their economies more open and flexible and, therefore, growth-oriented and more resilient to both internal and external shocks. Since the upsurge of the international debt crisis two decades ago, African economies continue to wobble under the huge debt burdens and negative impacts of economic adjustment imposed to cope with such crises. One way to estimate the magnitude and unmanageability of these burdens is to apply the conventional debt-cum-growth model. This model states that in order for debt accumulation to be sustainable, growth rate of external debt must not be higher than that of domestic output, exports, or tax revenues. Employing the domestic output measure, this implies that the ratio of external debt stock to domestic output should either remain constant or decline over time. Africa's debt-GDP ratios have experienced neither a constant nor declining trend. In fact, the average ratios, calculated from IMF's own publication, *World Economic Outlook,* indicate an increasing trend upward (from 27.5 percent in 1973–83, to 53.7 percent in 1985–90, and to 60.5 percent in 1990–98). Thus, measured against productive capacity, Africa's debt burdens have been severely unsustainable, even though the absolute amounts of debt stocks (287 billion in 1998) have been lower than those in East Asia and the Latin America and Caribbean regions.[37]

Under IMF/World Bank-supported adjustment, African economies have been compelled to produce trade surpluses by reducing imports and domestic absorption and expanding primary exports. A 1996 report by Anne Pettifor and Angela Wood of the Debt Crisis Network (DCN), entitled *A Fresh Start for Africa,* shows that in order for African countries to overcome debt repayment difficulties they need to achieve a fifty percent increase in export volumes. At the same time it would require a far-reaching reduction in purchases of imports after 1985. By 1992 the volume of imports per head had declined by twenty percent of its 1980 level. These efforts at spawning trade surpluses were frustrated, however, by the weakening in Africa's terms of trade so that by the early 1990s many African countries began to accumulate large debt payment arrears. Whereas 38 percent of debt services due in 1989–90 went unpaid, 54 percent of debt services went unpaid in 1994.

Countries such as the Sudan, Somalia, Liberia, Zambia, and Sierra Leone had their drawing rights suspended due to large accumulated arrears to the IMF. Economic adjustment spawned by international financial institutions (IFIs) failed during the last decades to achieve even its basic objectives of compelling indebted African economies to produce ample foreign exchange for sustainable debt servicing. Nevertheless, it has led to large capital outflows from these economies. Between 1986 and 1990 the IMF alone extracted over $3 million in debt service payments from low-income sub-Saharan African countries.

Countries such as Zambia and Uganda, which have been classified as heavily indebted poor countries, have made huge net transfers to the IMF during the 1990s. The DCN report estimates that between 1984 and the mid-1990s governments of the poorest African countries transferred $96 million to rich industrialized countries, which was one and a half times the amount they owed them in 1980. In 1993 alone, sub-Saharan African governments paid $196 million more to the IMF than they received from it.[38]

Though the austerity discipline of SAPs may lead to stronger economies in the long run, in the short-term their primary impact is to reduce the ability of governments to meet their citizens' needs. As a result, these policies may intensify conflicts between divergent communal groups, clans, and religious communities as they fight over diminishing state resources. This political milieu may hasten new civil wars or old conflicts may be resumed. With or without official sanction, African regimes will no doubt put guns ahead of grain if their own survival is at stake. Examples abound on the continent, from Somalia and the Sudan to Angola, Mozambique, and the Republic of South Africa.

On the other hand, subsidized grain has been a matter of political survival for some regimes in Africa. Zambia's quarrels with lending institutions in the 1980s often focused on the issue of subsidized maize. Lending institutions were eager to see such subsidies removed as a pre-condition for aid. Western donors did not directly challenge Zambia's support for wars of liberation.[39]

THE CHANGING GLOBAL DIVISION OF LABOR AND THE SEMIPERIPHERY

Semiperipheral states have evolved into an important sector in the world system. These states emerged as the new pole of growth during the current downswing in the world economy, providing operational space in the world economy for competitive pressures among capitalist business enterprises that were unleashed during this cycle of global restructuring.

Ten Third World states earned 90 percent of the increase in the developing countries' share of total world manufacturing value from 1966 to 1978. Eleven Third World countries had more than half of the LDCs industrial production and more than 75 percent of the LDCs manufacturing exports. The newly industrializing countries also had very high gross domestic product growth rates (7 to 10 percent per annum before 1973), export growth rates of 16 to 20 percent per annum, very high domestic investment rates, and an increasing share of OECD import markets for manufactured goods (it more than tripled from 1963 and 1976), but this still amounted to only 8.1 percent of OECD imports.[40]

In this study, the semiperiphery comprised the following countries: Portugal,[41] Turkey, Mexico, Brazil, Chile, Peru, Malaysia, Taiwan, Algeria, South Korea, Zimbabwe, and South Africa. These twelve states are similar in rank in terms of strictly economic criteria: GNP per capita (GNPPC) plus a manufacturing sector of some significance.[42] The list crosses parts of Africa, Asia, Latin

America and Europe. South Korea's stellar economic performance as a manufacturing center in the East Asian Pacific rim in the 1980s warranted its inclusion despite Seoul's lower GNPPC as of 1970. Likewise, Zimbabwe was included although it has a lower GNPPC, but is a Southern African country with a significant manufacturing sector and has actively competed with South Africa for markets in Southern Africa. Hong Kong and Singapore were excluded as a result of their small population and political status as microstates. Other countries often mentioned in the 1970s as potential candidates for the semiperiphery were Egypt, Pakistan, India, the Philippines, Argentina, Nigeria, the Ivory Coast, Kenya, and Mauritius. With the possible exception of Mauritius, which has an important export processing zone, most of these actors have experienced sluggish growth that has left them near the fringes of the world economy in the 1980s.[43] There is a growing hierarchy developing within the Third World semiperiphery that has threatened to undermine the political efficacy of a united front on North-South issues. As these actors have become more integrated into the capitalist world economy, they frequently have chosen a unilateral approach to international economic issues. Increased participation by the semiperiphery in the capitalist world economy has resulted in these nations becoming silent partners in the new global division of labor. Thus, the semiperiphery has become dependent upon the advanced market economies during this cycle of global restructuring.

Taking this group of states as a point of departure, our question remains, which region or sector of the Third World semiperiphery has diverged dramatically from the norm of the common effects of the world economic downturn since the early 1970s? How has the change in economic fortunes forced the semiperiphery as a group to choose the unilateral approach to the North-South conflict? In what ways has the monetary crisis that has accompanied this downturn in the world economy limited the policy options on international economic issues for the semiperiphery and the Third World?

Transnational corporations have played a pivotal role in the rise of the Third World periphery as an important force in the world economy. They have built entire factories, at first taking advantage of the lower wages in countries like South Korea, Malaysia, and Taiwan. These countries are following a strategy of competing in the world market based on the comparative advantage of their low production costs.[44] Semiperipheral states compete with advanced capitalist states for transnational corporations' markets on a global scale. The debt crisis and the downturn in the world economy since the early 1980s have dampened the ability of a number of these states to expand their operations in the periphery, thus undermining collective self-reliance within the South.

Transnational corporations have invested in more integrated, basic manufacturing industries, seeking to gain access to low-cost labor, valuable mineral resources, and broadened markets of entire regions such as the East Asian Pacific rim, South and Central America, and Southern Africa. Corporate leaders viewed countries such as Brazil, South Korea, South Africa, Taiwan, and

Malaysia as hospitable investment environments where markets are protected, wages are low, and governments refrain from expropriating foreign assets. Profits are high enough for local partners to share, including the local state in the form of additional revenues and/or taxes, and to still send home a percentage large enough to offset declining rates of capital accumulation in the North.[45]

Reductions in the costs of production take place with the transfer of labor-intensive industries such as textiles and certain types of electronics equipment to cheap labor zones. In recent years, capital-intensive industries such as the steel and automotive industries have been located in the Third World. The automobile industry offers a classic example of this process. Transnational corporations have opened factories in the Third World in order to penetrate markets protected in the first stage of import substitution. This objective expanded rapidly to include reexport of vehicle parts to the center (from the Iberian peninsula of Eastern Europe to Northwest Europe or from Mexico to the United States). In exchange for this reexportation, protectionism against other manufactured goods are reduced. Similar conditions exist in other sectors such as steel and textiles.[46]

Massive rationalization of production systems are under way in advanced market economies of the North. Manufacturing processes are being combined and divided into new units of production. Capitalist business enterprises have embarked on a perennial search for new motors of capital accumulation. This trend has accelerated, increasing the supply of low-cost labor throughout the Third World. Increasingly the newly industrializing countries have relied on exports to build their manufacturing capacity and to expand their domestic markets.

One major result of the growth of manufacturing production in the Third World has been an intensification of dependent relationships in the trading arena between advanced market economies and the semiperiphery. Over the last three decades there has been a fundamental shift in the composition of trade away from agricultural goods, minerals, and other commodities toward manufacturing. Starting in the 1970s, industry outstripped agriculture as a source of economic growth in all regions of the Third World. From 1965 to 1990, industry share of GDP grew by 13 percentage points in East and Southeast Asia, by 10 percent in Sub-Saharan Africa, 5 percent in South Asia, and 3 percent in Latin America.[47]

As Gary Geriffi observes, manufacturing has emerged as the cornerstone of development in East and Southeast Asia. In 1990, 34 percent of the GDP of East and Southeast Asia was in the manufacturing sector, compared with 26 percent for Latin America, 17 percent for South Asia, and only 11 percent for Sub-Saharan Africa. The manufacturing sector's share of GDP in some developing nations such as China (38 percent), Taiwan (34 percent), and South Korea (31 percent) was even higher than Japan's manufacturing/GDP ratio of 29 percent.[48] There is a new division of labor emerging among the semiperipheral states separating them further from the rest of the Third World.

Since the 1970s, the relative importance of primary commodities in exports as well as GDP usually has decreased quite sharply. The semiperiphery in Asia has moved fastest and furthest toward manufacturing export during this period. Sub-Saharan Africa and Latin America are still mostly primary commodity exporters, although to a lesser degree than in the past and with significant subregional variation.

Countries and regions are linked to the global commodity chain through the goods and services that they supply in the world economy. These trade linkages can be conceptualized into five major export roles: (1) primary commodity exports; (2) export processing (or in-bond) assemblage operations, (3) component supply sub-contracting, (4) original equipment manufacturing (OEM), and (5) original brand name manufacturing (OBM). Each type of manufacturing (roles 2–5) is sequentially more complex to establish because it implies a higher degree of domestic integration and local entrepreneurship. Therefore, economic development is strengthened as countries move from the second to the fifth option.[49] These roles are not mutually exclusive. Most nations exhibit multiple roles in the world economy. The East Asian NICs employed all export roles from the 1960s to the mid-1990s, although they are currently focusing almost without exception on component supply – subcontracting, OEM, and OBM. Most of the countries of Southeast Asia and Latin America are involved in the first three roles. More than half of the exports in South Asia and Sub-Saharan Africa fit the first two roles, with many African nations limited to only primary commodity exports. See Table 6.4.

Table 6.4
Export Roles in the Global Economy Occupied by Major Third World Regions

	Primary Commodity Export	Export Processing Assembly	Component Supply Sub-contracting	Original Equipment Mfg.	Original Brand-name Mfg.
East Asia	X	X	X	X	X
Southeast Asia	X	X	X		
Latin America & Caribbean	X	X	X		
South Asia	X	X			
Sub-Saharan Africa	X	X			

Source: Gary Gereffi, "Global Production System and Third World Development," in James H. Mittelman, *Globalization: A Critical Reflection* (Boulder, CO, Lynne Rienner, 1996).

Divergent trends in manufacturing emerged prior to the economic slowdown of the 1980s. Nevertheless, the sluggish performance in manufacturing has not reached the severity in the terms of trade experienced in agriculture and commodity sectors. Prices of agricultural raw materials, metals, and minerals have decreased over time relative to the prices of manufactured goods and services, resulting in an increased deterioration in the terms of trade for the Third World as a whole.[50]

Policy makers have taken decisive roles in transforming their economies from mere producers of commodities to important exporters of manufactured goods. These policy makers have employed either import substitution or export promotion industrial policies in order to stimulate their manufacturing sector. Initially, most Third World states, following the advice of Raul Presbisch, adopted the import substitution policy in a bid to make the transition from commodity production to manufacturing. Over time, as some of these states began to experience bottlenecks in their development as a result of import substitution policies, they began to implement an export promotion policy. States in the East Asian Pacific rim, following the Japanese model, accelerated production for the world market in the 1960s. Semiperipheral states in Latin America and Southern Africa continued tenaciously employed import substitution policies. Policy makers in Latin America remained steadfastly committed to this model of industrialization as a result of their historical suspicion of American-based multinational corporations.

Starting in the 1970s, Brazil, Mexico, and to some extent, Chile and Peru, began to integrate an export promotion approach toward industrialization into their import substitution policies. One result of this deliberate change in policy to stimulate manufacturing within the Third World has been a dramatic increase in trade within certain product groups between the North and South. Table 6.5 demonstrates the declining significance of agriculture for this group of states from 1980 to 1986. Although the structure of trade between the North and the South does not approximate the consistency in product mix that characterizes commerce between advanced market economies, there is a growing movement toward international specialization within specific economic sectors. The classical unequal exchange between manufactured goods and commodities is being replaced by an unequal exchange between high-valued and low-valued goods and access to markets.[51]

In the clothing and textiles sector the semiperipheral states from the Third World have developed a niche in the world market, making these actors competitive with their Northern counterparts in this arena. In the fifties and sixties, the East Asian Pacific rim countries revived an industry in long-term decline and made it into a growth sector and a base for further industrialization. By the 1970s other Third World countries were following the Asian example in this sector, actively duplicating and to some extent displacing their Asian counterparts.

Physical quotas restricting exports helped the process by forcing the leading exporters into higher value lines, leaving the lower value products to newcomers. One of the countries that benefited from this policy was China. Its garment exports increased 18 percent annually beginning in 1977, and by 1981 China had become the third largest exporter among the less developed states.[52]

Changes in the spatial dimension of the international division of labor had their origins in the postwar period of rapid growth that reached its climax in the late 1960s. Manufacturing in advanced market economies continued to grow quite rapidly in the 1960s, with most countries experiencing annual rates of growth in manufacturing in the 5 to 8 percent range. The United Kingdom was the first advanced market economy to display signs of the coming crisis. Growth rates were only 3.3 percent. Throughout the 1970s manufacturing actually fell in the United Kingdom. The number of workers in industry, which had been growing until the early 1970s, stabilized in the mid-1970s and then fell in the late 1970s and 1980s. Traditional industrial regions exhibited the sharpest decline in industrial employment: Belgium and the United Kingdom lost 28 percent of their manufacturing employment from 1974 to 1983; West Germany lost 16 percent of its manufacturing employment.[53]

Manufacturing grew more rapidly in the semiperipheral zones of the Third World as a result of the decentralization process carried out by Northern-based transnational corporations, especially in the East Asian Pacific rim, Southern Europe, Latin America and Southern Africa. The result for many of the NICs during the 1950s and 1960s was a quickened pace in domestic production for the ten countries in our study. Table 6.5 draws attention to the rate of growth in GDP and demonstrates the roller-coaster nature of the boom and bust cycle that has plagued these countries from the 1950s to the 1980s. Their fortunes became increasingly tied to the fate of the world economy. South Korea and Taiwan exhibited much higher growth rates than the other states

Table 6.5

Growth in Gross Domestic Product in the Semiperiphery

Country	1950–1960	1960–1970	1970–1980	1980–1987
Algeria	2.1	4.3	7	3.8
Brazil	3.1	5.4	8.4	3.3
Chile	2.2	4.5	2.4	1
Malaysia	2.5	6.5	7.8	4.5
Mexico	3.2	7.2	5.2	0.5
Peru	2.6	4.9	3	1.2
Portugal	0.7	6.2	4.6	1.4
South Africa	3	6.3	3.6	1
South Korea	2	8.6	9.5	8.6
Taiwan	7.6	9.2	n.a.	n.a.
Turkey	2.8	6	5.9	5.2
Zimbabwe	4.1	4.3	1.6	2.4

Source: World Bank, *World Tables, 1950–1960, 1960–1970, 1970–1980 and 1980;* and World Bank, *World Development Report 1975, 1980–87, and 1982;* World Bank, *World Tables, 1989;* South Africa, *South African Institute of Race Relations Survey, 1989;* Taiwan, *Asian Development, 1986 and 1989. n.a.* indicates that figures are not available.

Table 6.6

Percentage of GNP: Agriculture
Semiperipheral States, 1955-1987

Country	1955	1960	1970	1975	1980	1987
Algeria	n.a.	16	10	9	6	12
Brazil	21	16	10	9	10	11
Chile	n.a.	9	7	7	7	n.a.
Malaysia	36	36	31	28	23	25
Mexico	18	16	11	11	10	9
Peru	24	18	16	14	8	11
Portugal	30	25	18	14	13	9
South Africa	15	12	8	8	7	6
South Korea	n.a.	37	27	24	16	11
Taiwan	29	28	15	11	8	5
Turkey	43	41	30	27	23	17
Zimbabwe	n.a.	18	15	16	12	11

Sources: 1955, 1960, 1970, *World Bank, 1984;* with the exception of Taiwan, from *World Bank, 1982;* 1987: *World Bank, 1989. n.a.* indicates that figures are not available.

under review, demonstrating that the East Asian Pacific rim has been more successful in gaining a command over global resources. Brazil, Peru, and Mexico made modest gains but were unable to replicate the performance of their Asian counterparts. The move toward manufacturing by semiperipheral states in Latin America and Southern Africa was not as spectacular as South Korea's and Taiwan's. These actors still had a large stake in commodity production, although most had made investments in processing their metals and minerals locally.

Semiperipheral states in the East Asian Pacific rim made a greater transition from agricultural production to manufacturing than did their counterparts in Latin America, Southern Africa, and to some extent, Southern Europe. The percentage of GDP in the manufacturing sector is much higher in South Korea, Taiwan, and Malaysia. (See Tables 6.6 and 6.7) This transition to manufacturing became a matter of policy in Portugal, Brazil, Mexico, and South Africa. Peru and Chile made modest progress in this arena. Gradual policy changes took place in Turkey, Algeria, and Zimbabwe. South Africa has maintained a steady state between its agricultural and manufacturing sectors from the mid-1950s to the 1980s. In the 1970s South Africa's manufacturing sector began to decline as a result of the increased cost of importing capital goods (between 1957 and 1970 these costs had risen between 30 to 45 percent). Failure of the apartheid regime to increase the skills of its labor force, along with the increasing level of domestic and international conflict over the continuation of racial oppression, contributed to instability and decline in the manufacturing sector. For most of these semiperipheral states the percentage of their GDP accounted

Table 6.7

Percentage of GNP: Manufacturing
Semiperipheral States, 1955-1987

Country	1955	1960	1970	1975	1980	1987
Algeria	n.a.	8	14	10	14	12
Brazil	2	26	27	24	n.a.	28
Chile	n.a.	21	26	20	21	n.a.
Malaysia	9	9	13	16	24	23
Mexico	24	19	24	23	24	25
Peru	23	24	23	25	27	23
Portugal	26	29	33	31	36	n.a.
South Africa	20	21	23	23	23	23
South Korea	n.a.	14	21	21	28	28
Taiwan	19	21	33	33	35	39
Turkey	11	13	17	17	21	26
Zimbabwe	n.a.	17	21	21	25	31

Sources: 1955, 1960, 1970, *World Bank, 1984;* with the exception of Taiwan, from *World Bank, 1980.* 1975: *United Nations, 1986:* pp. 122–139. 1980: *World Bank, 1989. n.a.* indicates that figures are not available.

for by the agricultural sector was below 15 percent, although South Africa and Chile were well below this figure fifteen years earlier.

The change in the distribution of labor force was an important indicator of the transition to manufacturing among semiperipheral states during the 1960 to 1980s. Table 6.8 provides evidence on both the individual nation and regional variation in labor distribution by sector (agriculture and industry). As this table demonstrates, Algeria, Brazil, Mexico, Portugal, Taiwan, and South Korea started with 50 percent of the labor force involved in the agricultural sector. Industry had a modest representation in the 1960s. By the 1980s most of these nations had increased their labor force representation in the industrial sector to slightly over 25 percent, with Taiwan achieving a 42 percent representation. South Africa and Chile maintained almost the same ratio in agriculture and industry with only slight variation. Four countries – Peru, Malaysia, Turkey and Zimbabwe – maintained a high concentration of their labor force in agricultural production. At the same time, three nations became the most rapidly industrializing nations within the semiperiphery: South Korea, Taiwan, and Brazil. During this same period (1960s–1980s), South Africa failed to maintain its competitive advantage in manufacturing.

Over the last twenty years we have also witnessed spectacular changes in the relationship among trade, production, and exchange with reference to North-South relations. The semiperiphery has played a pivotal role in the changing international division of labor in these arenas. The structure of data on imports demonstrates the growing importance of the price of oil to the world economy. Table 6.9 demonstrates that the dramatic increase in oil prices

Table 6.8

Distribution of Labor Force: Agriculture and Industry
Semiperipheral States, 1960-1980

Country		1960	1970	1975	1980
Algeria	Agriculture	n.a.	50	41	31
	Industry	12	13	n.a.	27
Brazil	Agriculture	52	44	38	31
	Industry	15	18	n.a.	27
Chile	Agriculture	28	21	20	17
	Industry	28	25	n.a.	25
Malaysia	Agriculture	63	56	53	50
	Industry	12	14	15	16
Mexico	Agriculture	55	45	40	36
	Industry	20	23	24	26
Peru	Agriculture	53	48	44	40
	Industry	20	18	19	19
Portugal	Agriculture	44	33	31	28
	Industry	29	33	34	35
South Africa	Agriculture	32	31	31	30
	Industry	30	29	29	29
South Korea	Agriculture	66	50	42	34
	Industry	9	17	23	29
Taiwan	Agriculture	50	37	30	19
	Industry .	18	30	36	42
Turkey	Agriculture	70	68	61	54
	Industry	11	12	13	13
Zimbabwe	Agriculture	69	64	62	60
	Industry	11	12	14	15

Sources: All figures are from the World Bank, *World Tables, 1983,* Vol. 2, with the exception of data from Taiwan: *World Tables, 1976. World Development Report 1988: Taiwan, Statistical Yearbook of the Republic of China, 1988. n.a.* indicates that figures are not available.

(1973–74, 1979–80) raised significantly the percentage of imports accounted for by fuels (with the exception of the oil exporters), which then fell as oil prices declined in the 1980s. The same trend was present in South Africa, although we lack reliable data due to the oil embargo against Pretoria. Despite the oil crisis, manufactured goods continued to account for an overwhelming and surprisingly steady proportion of the value of imports throughout the 1970s and 1980s.

The volume of imports became increasingly constrained as a result of the unfolding debt crisis. The terms of trade declined significantly following the short-lived commodity boom of the 1970s (see Table 6.10). South Africa was able to weather the global economic crisis for a short period of time as a result of the countercyclical trend in gold prices, which peaked in 1974 ($194) and early 1980 ($850), only to decline substantially thereafter.[54]

Table 6.9

Percentage Share of Merchandise Imports:
Foods, Fuels, and Other Primary Commodities
Semiperipheral States, 1960-1987

Country		1960	1970	1975	1980	1987
Algeria	Foods	26	13	n.a.	21	27
	Fuels	4	2	2	3	2
	OPC	14	11	n.a.	10	9
Brazil	Foods	14	11	n.a.	10	9
	Fuels	19	12	26	43	27
	OPC	13	7	n.a.	6	8
Chile	Foods	n.a.	15	n.a.	14	12
	Fuels	n.a.	6	20	21	10
	OPC	n.a.	7	n.a.	4	4
Malaysia	Foods	29	22	n.a.	12	10
	Fuels	16	12	12	15	6
	OPC	13	8	n.a.	6	4
Mexico	Foods	4	7	n.a.	8	11
	Fuels	2	3	6	2	1
	OPC	10	9	n.a.	7	8
Peru	Foods	16	20	n.a.	20	13
	Fuels	5	2	12	2	1
	OPC	5	5	n.a.	14	13
Portugal	Foods	15	14	n.a.	14	13
	Fuels	10	9	15	24	12
	OPC	28	13	n.a.	5	3
South Africa	Foods	6	6	n.a.	5	3
	Fuels	7	5	0.25	0.6	0
	OPC	9	4	n.a.	4	4
South Korea	Foods	10	17	n.a.	10	6
	Fuels	7	7	19	30	15
	OPC	25	21	n.a.	17	17
Taiwan	Foods	n.a.	9	10	7	6
	Fuels	n.a.	5	14	28	11
	OPC	n.a.	1	17	14	12
Turkey	Foods	7	8	18	4	4
	Fuels	11	8	n.a.	49	23
	OPC	16	17	n.a.	3	13
Zimbabwe	Foods	10	17	n.a.	10	8
	Fuels	7	7	19	30	17
	OPC	25	21	n.a.	17	17

Sources: 1960: *World Bank, 1982.* 1975: *United Nations, 1983.* Taiwan, *World Bank 1981.* 1970, 1980: *World Bank, 1984.* 1987: *World Bank, 1989. n.a.* indicates that figures are not available.

Table 6.10

Terms of Trade
Volume Comparisons, 1967–1987
Semiperipheral States

1980=100

Country	1967	1970	1975	1980	1987
Algeria	18	19	157	100	54
Brazil	190	189	126	100	97
Chile	227	237	107	100	84
Malaysia	161	103	75	100	72
Mexico	97	108	94	100	70
Peru	129	131	94	100	69
Portugal	129	131	107	100	100
South Africa	126	122	115	100	71
South Korea	149	122	115	·100	71
Taiwan	157	157	124	100	100
Turkey	167	160	110	100	101
Zimbabwe	161	178	111	100	84

Sources: World Bank, *World Tables, 1989.* Taiwan: *Yearbook of the Republic of China, 1988.*

Most semiperipheral states were very successful in carving out a niche in the export of manufacturing goods despite the global economic crisis. As Table 6.11 demonstrates, most of the countries under review were able to expand their manufacturing exports throughout the 1970s and 1980s. Portugal, Taiwan, South Korea, and to some extent South Africa (although Pretoria's exports were largely confined to the Southern African region) made great strides in the export of manufactured goods. Mexico, Brazil, and Turkey made modest gains, while gains by Peru, Malaysia, and Chile were not exemplary. Algeria's and Zimbabwe's exports in this arena were negligible. An examination of the structure of exports in fuels, minerals, and metals demonstrates the degree to which some semiperipheral nations remained commodity producers. Table 6.12 provides evidence of the constancy of commodity production in Algeria, Brazil, Chile, Malaysia, Mexico, and Turkey. Likewise, South Africa, Peru, and Zimbabwe also maintained a moderate level of export in fuels, minerals, metals, and other commodities.

Pretoria was unable to develop an export market for manufactured goods beyond the Southern African region, attesting to the apartheid regime's lack of competitiveness on a global scale. Manufacturing exports in most of these states consisted primarily of semiprocessed minerals and agricultural products. South Korea and Taiwan export a smaller quantity of commodities, having aimed their expansion at the manufacturing arena abandoned by the core. Chile, on the other hand, has relied more on revitalizing its agricultural production as a motor of economic growth.

The semiperiphery has demonstrated that dynamic integration in the capitalist world economy can lead to economic development. Nevertheless, economic growth in Brazil and Mexico has sharpened social inequality and uneven regional development.[55] These pioneering states have responded to the technological demands of a changing world economy by making significant investments in their educational systems and developing a domestic basis for manufacturing. South Africa entered the 1960s with a competitive advantage in manufacturing but was unable to sustain this lead in the 1970s and 1980s. Likewise, most of the other states under review were unsuccessful in duplicating the export performance of these leading states (South Korea, Taiwan, Portugal, Brazil, and Mexico).

After two decades of stellar economic performance, the semiperiphery throughout the Third World began to experience sluggish economic growth as the 1980s began to unfold. A series of shocks penetrated the economies of these advanced developing countries, undermining policy makers' goals of self-sustaining economic growth. Most of these semiperipheral states had to adjust their economies to new "ecological disturbances." The primary external disturbances were the oil price increases in 1973–74 and 1979–80, the extreme deterioration in the terms of trade experienced after 1980 (see table 6.11), and the steep rise in world interest rates in 1980–82, which ushered in the debt crisis throughout the semiperiphery and the periphery. Developing countries had to expend more resources in order to service their foreign debt.

The debt crisis had negative consequences for the semiperiphery and the periphery alike. The world economy shifted to a much slower pace. Direct investment into the semiperiphery and especially the periphery took a nose dive. Foreign capital sought safer havens in core states. Both the public and private sector became more dependent on petrodollars from Northern banks. Short-term loans proliferated. With the rise in interest rates the semiperiphery and the periphery found it increasingly difficult to repay their rising debt. The 1982 Mexican moratorium on debt repayment plunged the world economy into a debt crisis as core states began to restrict capital outflows to the South, while other semiperipheral and peripheral states sought to reschedule or defer payments over a much longer term. Still others sought to halt repayment altogether (Peru), which was detrimental to their economy. As Table 6.13 reveals, most of the semiperiphery (Algeria, Chile, Malaysia, Mexico, Peru, Portugal, Turkey, and Zimbabwe) encountered problems in servicing their foreign debt, as the percentage of total debt to GNP hovered near or above 50 percent throughout most of the 1980s. Again, South Korea and Taiwan were the exceptions. Brazil has managed, at an astronomical cost to its citizens, to keep the percentage of total debt to GNP in the 30 to 40 percent range.

The debt crisis has forced the majority of the semiperiphery to seek unilateral rather than multilateral solutions to their economic problems, as the North, led by the United States, has refused to participate in any multilateral forum calling for negotiation, rescheduling, or moratorium on foreign debt.

The United States has insisted on a case-by-case approach to the debt ques-

Table 6.11

Percentage Share of Merchandise Exports:
Machinery, Transport, and Other Manufactures
Semiperipheral States, 1960-1987

Country		*1960*	*1970*	*1975*	*1980*	*1987*
Algeria	Machinery, transport, & equipment	1	2	1	0	0
	Other manufactures	6	5	0.7	0	1
Brazil	Machinery, transport, & equipment	n.a.	4	10	17	17
	Other manufactures	3	11	13	22	28
Chile	Machinery, transport, & equipment	0	1	1	1	3
	Other manufactures	4	4	7	19	6
Malaysia	Machinery, transport, & equipment	n.a.	2	6	12	27
	Other manufactures	6	7	11	8	13
Mexico	Machinery, transport, & equipment	1	11	9	19	28
	Other manufactures	11	22	20	21	19
Peru	Machinery, transport, & equipment	0	0	1	2	3
	Other manufactures	1	1	2	5	16
Portugal	Machinery, transport, & equipment	3	8	13	13	16
	Other manufactures	52	56	55	58	64
South Africa	Machinery, transport, & equipment	4	7	6	5	3
	Other manufactures	24	34	19	4	n.a.
South Korea	Machinery, transport, & equipment	3	7	14	20	33
	Other manufactures	n.a.	70	63	70	59
Taiwan	Machinery, transport, & equipment	2	17	20	25	32
	Other manufactures	n.a.	60	62	63	60
Turkey	Machinery, transport, & equipment	0	0	1	3	7
	Other manufactures	3	9	21	9	60
Zimbabwe	Machinery, transport, & equipment	n.a.	n.a.	3	2	3
	Other manufactures	3	n.a.	11	26	37

Sources: 1960, 1970: *World Bank, 1980.* 1975: *United Nations, 1963.* 1980: *World Bank, 1984.* 1987: *World Bank, 1989.* Taiwan, except 1960: *Taiwan, 1988; World Bank, 1989.* 1987: *World Bank, 1989. n.a.* indicates that figures are not available.

Table 6.12

Percentage of Merchandise Trade:
Fuels, Minerals, and Other Commodities
Semiperipheral States, 1960-1987

Country		1960	1970	1975	1980	1987
Algeria	Fuels, minerals, & metals	12	73	94	99	98
	Other commodities	81	21	5	1	0
Brazil	Fuels, minerals, & metals	8	11	15	11	22
	Other commodities	89	75	58	50	33
Chile	Fuels, minerals, & metals	92	88	75	59	69
	Other commodities	4	7	17	21	23
Malaysia	Fuels, minerals, & metals	20	29	25	35	25
	Other commodities	74	61	67	46	36
Mexico	Fuels, minerals, & metals	24	19	35	39	44
	Other commodities	49	49	38	22	9
Peru	Fuels, minerals, & metals	50	49	50	19	11
	Other commodities	8	5	6	7	3
Portugal	Fuels, minerals, & metals	37	31	26	23	12
	Other commodities	42	32	40	23	9
South Africa	Fuels, minerals, & metals	28	27	26	23	12
	Other commodities	42	32	40	23	9
South Korea	Fuels, minerals, & metals	n.a.	7	8	1	2
	Other commodities	56	17	15	9	5
Taiwan	Fuels, minerals, & metals	n.a.	2	1	2	1
	Other commodities	n.a.	22	17	10	7
Turkey	Fuels, minerals, & metals	8	8	12	9	6
	Other commodities	89	83	66	65	27
Zimbabwe	Fuels, minerals, & metals	71	n.a.	41	22	17
	Other commodities	25	n.a.	45	0.49	43

Sources: 1960: *World Bank, 1982.* 1970: *World Bank, 1980.* 1975: *United Nations, 1983.* 1980: *World Bank, 1980.* 1987: *World Bank, 1989.* Taiwan: *Taiwan, 1988.* Zimbabwe: 1980 and 1987: *World Bank, 1989. n.a.* indicates that figures are not available.

Table 6.13

Total Earned Debt as a Percentage of GNP
Semiperipheral States, 1970-1988

Country	1970	1980	1983	1986	1987	1988
Algeria	19.3	46.8	33.7	34.1	39.4	47.6
Brazil	12.2	30.6	50.1	41.7	39.4	30.7
Chile	32.1	45.2	98.9	142.0	124.0	96.6
Malaysia	10.8	28.0	63.6	85.3	75.9	66.0
Mexico	16.2	30.1	66.4	87.3	77.8	58.0
Peru	37.3	51.0	63.5	61.0	41.5	47.3
Portugal	12.1	40.4	74.0	58.4	51.3	42.3
South Africa	n.a.	27.6	32.3	n.a.	36.3	n.a.
South Korea	22.3	48.7	50.8	45.5	31.5	22.0
Turkey	15.0	34.4	40.8	58.0	62.0	57.7
Zimbabwe	n.a.	14.9	39.2	53.0	51.5	43.5

Sources: South Africa: *Hirsch, 1990;* percentage calculated with GNP figures from *World Bank, 1989;* refers to only long-term debt, i.e., excludes IMF credits, short-term debt; see text. All others: from *World Bank, 1990. n.a.* indicates that figures are not available.

tion. The adoption of a unilateral approach on the debt crisis and other international economic issues has had serious ramifications for Third World solidarity. This policy approach toward North-South issues began to undermine cooperation dramatically between the moderate and radical states within the periphery.

Even South Africa, a country endowed with mineral wealth ranging from gold to diamonds, as well as a modest manufacturing base, felt the shocks of this crisis. Although data on debt from South Africa are very sparse, Pretoria has also encountered enormous difficulty since the mid-1980s in servicing its debt because capital and financial markets became closed to the former apartheid regime. Starting in the mid-1980s, South Africa experienced some difficulty in accelerating its economy as a result of the lack of both foreign and domestic investments. The post-apartheid government has been able to attract foreign capital, but not in the quantity that Pretoria requires to move up the ladder among semiperipheral states. South Africa's labor force is less competitive than their counterparts in East and South Asia. Nevertheless, South Africa historically has been in a more competitive position to service its debt.

What emerges from these trends is a new hierarchy within the semiperiphery, with South Korea and Taiwan taking the lead among these advanced developing countries. Brazil, Portugal, and Mexico make up the second tier, with the other states comprising the bottom tier. As the semiperiphery sought remedies for the economic maladies that affected their economies, they began to withdraw support from many of the major tenets of the quest for a new international economic order. These actors were playing a significant role in the new international division of labor that was evolving during this cycle of global restructuring, dramatically diversifying the economies within the Third World. Indeed, they became silent partners in this restructuring process. The Third World periphery experienced negative consequences of the worldwide economic crisis. This crisis had the effect of undermining the Third World coalition on the North-South conflict as these actors were increasingly forced to adopt unilateral rather than multilateral actions to resolve their economic and fiscal problems.

The advanced developing countries in East Asia fared better than their counterparts in Latin America, Southern Africa, and Southern Europe. This latter group was less successful in shaking off the effect of the global economic crisis. The ensuing debt crisis forced these actors to abandon their efforts to upgrade their niche in the competitive manufacturing market by investing in newer technology and by sharpening the skills of their labor force.

MEXICO, NAFTA, AND THE 1995 CRISIS IN EMERGING MARKETS

Starting in the early 1990s Mexico emerged as an important trading partner with the United States. In 1992 President George Bush proposed a North American Free Trade Association between the United States, Canada, and Mexico. After two years of debate in the United States, the NAFTA Treaty was signed by the three countries and ratified by the U.S. Congress in Fall 1994. By then, Mexico had evolved into a Third World star with reference to free trade and market-based financial and economic polices. Under President Carlos Salinas de Gortari, Mexico had become the darling of international investors seeking profits in this country's emerging financial market. It had a large current-account deficit, but since this reflected private (as opposed to public sector) decisions about saving and investment, it initially appeared less threatening. This deficit was not driven by heavy government borrowing, but by a large increase of profit-seeking foreign capital. At this juncture, Mexico's public debt, at 40% of GDP, was small by international standards.[56]

The Clinton administration defined this crisis as a global economic security issue with direct impact on the U.S. economy and pressed hard for U.S. legislation and for governments of other highly developed countries to come to Mexico's rescue. However, the U.S. Congress refused to cooperate with President Clinton despite the support of Republican leadership in the House and Senate. The administration changed to a joint executive branch-IMF rescue package, based on a Treasury Department Stabilization Fund, to provide Mexico with the necessary funds. In January 1997, Mexico paid the final $3.5 billion of the U.S. $13.5 billion it had borrowed from the United States, thereby repudiating the distressing prediction of opponents of the bailout.

The Mexican financial crisis spread to other emerging markets in Latin America and other regions of the world system. During the first couple of months in 1995, Argentina, Brazil, and Mexico all tumbled by 50–70% in dollar terms. Other emerging markets experienced similar declines: China, the

Czech Republic, Hungary, India, and Taiwan fell by a fifth or more. Starting in the Spring of 1995, the Latin American stock market experienced a rebound. Mexico and Argentina rose 50% or more in dollar terms, while Brazil leapt by 90%. Domestic rather than foreign investors propelled this renewed drive.

Despite the recent Mexican devaluation of the peso, which was partially responsible for starting this crisis, the prognosis for emerging markets became very robust in 1996. Global financial markets recovered and sought new avenues of investment in the emerging markets of East and Southeast Asia. Starting in 1997, East and Southeast Asia experienced the perils of direct foreign investment in their financial markets as Thailand's economy began to plummet.

THE 1997–98 FINANCIAL CRISIS IN ASIA

Starting in mid-1997, a thorny currency crisis gripped several high-flying economies in Southeast Asia — Indonesia, Malaysia, the Philippines, and Thailand, sending the region into a major financial dilemma. As our foregoing analysis of the semiperiphery in divergent Third World regions has demonstrated, East and Southeast Asia leaders have carved out their own niche in the global commodity chain and the international division of labor. Until recently, these states were considered the favorite of the international investment community, and these actors have taken a beating at the hands of money managers inside and outside of their countries. The Southeast Asian countries attracted considerable foreign capital investments in the 1990s. Many of these investments enhanced export potential and thereby contributed to long-term economic growth. Increasingly, in the mid-1990s, a mounting share of foreign flows appears to have headed for speculative investments in real estate properties. After financial markets deregulated in many countries, commercial banks got into the act by borrowing dollars abroad and lending the funds domestically to real estate developers. As the bankers made these loans in local currency, the banks exposed themselves to the risk of currency depreciation, since the value of such loans would fall relative to the value of their dollar borrowing. According to Steven Radelet and Jeffrey Sachs, even when domestic real estate loans were in dollars, however, the banks were at risk, since domestic property developers would be unable to repay the dollar-dominated loans in the event of weakening domestic currency.[57] The crisis that started in Thailand soon spread to South Korea, Malaysia, and Indonesia, requiring IMF intervention into the region's financial markets.

The resulting crisis eventually contributed to a new wave of protest in Indonesia, as students and workers protested the IMF-imposed stabilization policies. The property of the Chinese ethnic minority became the target of rioters, sending the country into a political and economic quandary. Eventually President Suharto was forced to leave office, leading to more assistance from the IMF. The prospects for increased destabilization continue in Indonesia despite the recent change in government. Until the recent Asian crisis aroused the public to the reality that capital movements could generate crisis repeatedly, many assumed that free capital mobility among all nations was exactly like free trade in goods and services, a mutual gain hypothesis. Likewise, restricted capital movement was perceived, just like its twin, protectionism, as harmful to the economy of each country, whether rich or poor. This debate increasingly pits supporters of economic liberalization and privatization against economic nationalists of a variety of stripes.

Jagdish Bhagwati observes that the current Asian financial crisis cannot be separated from excessive borrowing of foreign short-term capital as Asian economies loosened up their capital account controls and enabled their banks and firms to borrow from abroad. In 1996, total private capital inflows to Indonesia, Malaysia, South Korea, Thailand, and the Philippines were $93 billion, up from $41 billion in 1994. In 1997, that suddenly changed to an outflow of $12 billion.[58] The increased mobility of capital has also accelerated financial crisis, particularly in developing countries.

During each cycle of financial and currency crisis that is related to capital inflows, a country normally follows a set of standard operating procedures. The debt crisis of the 1980s cost Latin America a decade of growth. The Mexicans, who were vastly overexposed through short-term inflows, were devastated in 1994. The Asian economies of Thailand, Indonesia, and South Korea, all seriously disadvantaged with short-term debt, went into a descent in 1997, their growth rates decreasing drastically.[59] Capital mobility has emerged as an important component of economic globalization. We will examine the political and social ramifications of globalization in the concluding chapter.

DEMISE OF PAN-PROLETARIANISM IN THE THIRD WORLD

The Group of 77 and the nonaligned movement achieved modest success in placing NIEO issues on the agenda of most international institutions in 1974. Nevertheless, both organizations failed in their attempts to implement NIEO issues in concrete policies that governed North-South relations. Many of the components of the Action Programme had not materialized. Third World states were unable to compel the advanced market economies to establish a new international economic order either through UNCTAD or through the nonaligned movement. These actors lacked the political, economic, and military requisites of power to enforce their demands on a recalcitrant North. Unity among Third World states became weakened by the 1980s.

The seeds of Third World fragmentation have been present since the historic Bandung Conference of 1955. Economic diversity among Third World states has increased the difficulty of maintaining a united diplomatic front on international economic issues. Several factors contributed to fragmentation among these actors. One major issue that threatened solidarity was the increased economic gap between OPEC and non-oil developing countries (NOLDCs) and the potential conflict over the price that these states had to pay for oil. Since 1974 a number of Third World leaders have called for a two-tier price system. This proposal envisions a lower price for developing countries and a higher price for the industrial developed countries. Venezuela and Algeria were the only OPEC member states to offer preferential pricing policies to select Third World states. In the Americas, only Venezuela and Mexico[60] offered a preferential price. Algeria worked out a plan with Libya, Nigeria, and Gabon to sell oil to other African states at a discount. However, the majority of OPEC members did not support a cartel-wide price reduction to the Third World. As a result of this posture, OPEC was accused of exploiting the least developed countries. The global energy crisis that accompanied the introduction of oil power in world politics contributed to increased Third World fragmentation.

Conflict evolved in the 1970s between OPEC and the advanced developing countries (ADCs) from Latin America and Asia over the price of petroleum. As a number of ADCs in Latin America and the East Asian Pacific Rim began to export manufactured goods, their appetite for petroleum and petroleum-based products accelerated, adding substantial financial burdens to these states. Third World ADCs became increasingly vulnerable to fluctuations in the price of oil. OPEC members also correctly recognized their inherent weakness in relying on a commodity as critical to the world economy as oil and refused to employ any additional oil boycotts against the advanced market economies for fear that these actors might devise an alternative product that would reduce their dependency on petroleum. By the late 1970s, oil was no longer a viable weapon in the Third World arsenal for establishing a new order. As OPEC members and other oil producers became more integrated into the world economy, they began to adhere to the rules and norms of supply and demand. Western financial institutions recycled oil-surplus capital as loans to Third World NICs and resource-rich states. The oil-producing states also imported turn-key factories, military hardware and manufactured goods from the North.

Over time, a number of OPEC member states became more integrated into the Western security system, among them Saudi Arabia, Kuwait, the United Arab Emirates, and the Gulf states. U.S. policy makers were very successful in getting such states as Saudi Arabia, the United Arab Emirates, Egypt, Kuwait, Iran (before the fall of the Shah), and Iraq (before Desert Storm in 1990) to play the international economic and political game according to Northern rules and norms. In recent years, Third World NICs have also begun to move away from some of the interests and objectives of the nonaligned movement and the Group of 77's efforts to create a new international economic order. The growing economic and political diversity in the Third World coalition accounts for some of these changes. Likewise, the changing spatial dimension in the global division of labor between the North and the South has influenced the NICs to seek unilateral solutions to their economic problems.

By the late 1980s, the nonaligned movement and the Group of 77 had lost their enthusiasm for collective self-reliance and the major tenets of their quest for a new international economic order as their members sought greater integration into the new international division of labor that was developing between the North and South. The worldwide economic crisis has reduced the capacity of the Third World to act as a diplomatic unit on North-South concerns. Throughout the 1980s, from Cancun, New Delhi, Harare, and Belgrade,[61] Third World leaders were unsuccessful in their bid to keep the North, led by the United States, from moving the locus of decision-making on North-South issues away from the United Nations General Assembly, UNCTAD, and UNIDO, where the Group of 77 had the majority of votes and where the principle of "one nation, one vote" would prevail, and toward the Bretton Woods international institutions (the IMF, the World Bank, OECD, and GATT), where the United States and the industrial market economies prevailed.

Although Fidel Castro of Cuba has repeatedly called for a debtor alliance as a strategy to combat the debt crisis of the 1980s, Third World states were unsuccessful in developing a collective response as individual states entered into negotiations on a case-by-case basis. This approach to the debt crisis and other international economic concerns became the preferred remedy of the United States and the industrial market economies.

Conflict among Third World states accelerated throughout the 1980s, calling into question the ability of the nonaligned movement and Southern regional institutions ranging from the OAU, the Arab League, and the Eastern Caribbean Community to the OAS to resolve disputes in their sphere of influence. The nonaligned movement became paralyzed over Vietnam in the late 1960s and was divided again by the Vietnam-Cambodia conflict of 1978-79. The decolonization process unleashed new conflicts in the South including ethnic, communal, religious, secessionist, and social conflicts that at times escalated into full-scale civil wars with intervention from the superpowers and other external forces. Third World regional institutions ranging from the OAU to the Arab League, were unable to resolve peacefully a number of these inter-Third World conflicts in the Sudan, Ethiopia and Somalia, Chad, Angola, Mozambique, Nicaragua, and Lebanon. The Iran-Iraq war played a pivotal role in reinforcing divisions within the Third World and reducing the legitimacy of the nonaligned movement.[62]

Socialism was on the defensive in Eastern Europe and the Soviet Union in the mid-1980s. In 1990 the Third World could no longer count on the Soviet bloc as a counterbalance against the United States and the industrial market economies in the Northwest. The socialist world was marching down the path of democratic capitalism. The noncapitalist route to development was in full retreat as these actors sought a market economy, Western capital investment, new microelectronic technology for their ailing industries, and membership in GATT and the IMF.

By the early 1990s, the NIEO package, put on the agenda at Algiers in the

1970s, seemed no closer to realization. Global negotiations, written into the Havana Declaration by Algeria, did not move beyond the status of an agenda item in international institutions. Third World states borrowed over a half billion dollars, most of it from commercial banks. A number of countries have been near bankruptcy, thereby contributing to a decrease in the flow of capital to the South. In 1990 the United States offered the Brady Plan, named for Secretary of the Treasury Nicholas F. Brady, which encourages banks to forgive some debt in return for economic reform to improve the environment for private investment.[63] To date, only Mexico has followed the guidelines outlined in this plan. Argentina and Brazil are still trying to qualify for this plan. At the very time Third World solidarity was in retreat (the 1980s), unity of purpose among the industrial market economies was developing into a new and dynamic force. Prompted by the growth in complex interdependence of their national economies, the major industrialized countries of the North accepted the need for a degree of institutionalized coordination of their separate policies – hence the annual Group of Seven meetings. The evolution of the summit and its supporting structures has encouraged this group to perceive themselves as the guardians of world economy and to ignore the multilateral discourse and decision-making processes embedded in the United Nations Charter. Because the combined economic and political powers of these countries are so great, their decisions have serious ramifications for the rest of the world, which has little to no influence on the agenda or decisions of this body.[64] The Group of Seven symbolizes the continuation of global apartheid in the world system in the postwar era.

Under American leadership, the Group of Seven has rolled back the anti-statist posture and nationalism in the Third World. The old orthodoxy of development being guided by the state is being replaced by a new orthodoxy. Increasingly, developing nations are focusing on building a market economy, creating a hospitable environment for private capital, closing the state out of the economic arena and opening their political system to democracy. The advanced market economies have been able to use international financial institutions to impose their solutions on the Third World and demand that developing countries adjust their economies through keeping the state out of economic policy-making processes. The World Bank, the IMF, and other multilateral institutions have become instruments of Northern states.

Since the 1980s collective self-reliance has taken a variety of shapes reflecting the ideological and economic plurality in the Third World. Economic cooperation among Southern states has taken a divergent path in recent years as a result of the systemic changes in the capitalist world system. In Asia, ASEAN is becoming more economically integrated with South Korea, Taiwan, China, and to some extent Malaysia. As these advanced developing countries shed low-wage manufacturing and attempt to move up the ladder to higher-scale production, they will downgrade low-wage production to their neighbors. Mexico has negotiated a common market arrangement with the United States and Canada. The new North American Free Trade Area will increase substantially the size and scope of manufacturing in this semiperipheral nation and provide the United States with new operational space and new niches in the world economy in which to compete with the Japanese and East Asia. Brazil is seeking to move up the ladder to higher-valued manufacturing and is opening its economy to transnational corporations from the United States and Japan. Thus, nations of the semiperiphery are seeking a greater degree of integration into the new international division of labor between the North and South. These actors have become silent partners in the global restructuring process. Their alliance is with the North rather than the South.

The quest to overcome inequality at the international level in terms of race, and cultural, economic, and political power by the Third World will continue into the twenty-first century. The Third World will need to develop its own counterbalance of power in order to change the status quo. The rules of the game for the present world economy were established by countries with the prerequisite military and economic power. It is not in the interest of these actors to change the system. Third World states will need more than solidarity to alter the distribution of power in the capitalist world system. At this juncture, the semiperipheries have been compelled by the global economic crisis and industrial market economies of the North to abandon multilateral, collective self-reliance and the statist orientation of the Third World toward the North-South conflict.

NOTES

1. David Truman, *The Governmental Process: Political Interest and Public Opinion* (New York: Alfred A. Knopf, 1951).

2. Ibid., p. 27.

3. Mancur Olson, *The Logic of Collective Action: Public Goods and The Theory of Groups* (Cambridge, MA: Harvard University Press, 1975).

4. Ibid., p. 21.

5. Ibid., p. 30.

6. Ibid., p. 127.

7. Bruno S. Frey, "The Public Choice View of International Political Economy," in *The Theoretical Evolution of International Political Economy: A Reader,* ed. George T. Crane and Abla Amawi (New York: Oxford University Press, 1991), pp. 220–221.

8. See Robert Rothstein, *Global Bargaining: UNCTAD and the Quest for The New International Economic Order* (Princeton: Princeton University Press, 1979); Robert Rothstein, "Global Bargaining: UNCTAD and the Quest for A New International Economic Order," in *International Political Economy: A Reader,* ed. K. W. Stiles and T. Ahaha (New York: Harper-Collins, 1991), pp. 385–396.

9. See Stephen Krasner, *Structural Conflict: The Third World Against Global Liberalism* (Berkeley: University of California Press, 1985).

10. See G. Arrighi and Jessica Drangel, "The Stratification of the World Economy: An Exploration of the Semiperipheral Zone," *Review* 10, no. 1 (Summer 1980): 9–74.

11. F. Frobel, "The Current Development of the World-Economy: Reproduction of

Labor and Accumulation of Capital on a World Scale," *Review* 12, no. 4, (Spring 1982): 507.

12. J. Nyerere, "Address by the President of the Republic of Tanzania to the 4th Ministerial Meeting of the Group of 77, Arusha 12–16 February 1979," in *The Group of 77: Evolution, Structure, and Organization,* ed. K. P. Sauvant (New York: Oceana Publications, Inc., 1979), p. 6.

13. Ibid., p. 7.

14. Ann Seidman and Frederick Anang, eds., *Towards A New Vision of Self-Sustainable Development* (Trenton, NJ: Africa World Press, Inc., 1992), p. 24.

15. Lance Morrow, "Africa: The Scramble for Existence," *Time* (September 7, 1992): 42.

16. Jon Kraus, "Debt, Structural Adjustment, and Private Investment," in *Privatization and Investment in Sub-Saharan Africa,* ed. R.A. Ahene and B. A. Katz (New York: Praeger Publishers, 1992), pp. 75–76.

17. Even after Allende was overthrown and killed in a bloody coup, the military leaders continued nationalization of the copper mines as a matter of policy.

18. T. R. Callaghy, "Vision and Politics in the Transformation of the Global Political Economy: Lessons from the Second and Third Worlds," in *Global Transformation and the Third World,* ed. Robert O. Slater, et. al. (Boulder, CO: Lynne Rienner Publishers, 1993), p. 210.

19. Ibid., p. 210.

20. J. Kraus, "Debt," p. 76.

21. The terms of trade is the total value of export earnings not only on the volume of these exports sold abroad but also on the price paid for them. However, if export prices decline, a greater volume of exports will be have to be sold merely to keep total earnings constant. Similarly on the import side, total foreign exchange expended depends on both the quantity and price of imports. Clearly, if the price of a country's exports is falling relative to the prices of the products it imports, it will have to sell much more of its export product and enlist more scarce productive resources merely to secure the same level of imported goods that it purchased in previous years. See Michael P. Todaro, *Economic Development in the Third World* (New York: Longman, Inc., 1985), pp. 370–374.

22. World Bank, *Sub-Saharan Africa: From Crisis to Sustainable Growth* (Washington, D. C.: International Bank for Reconstruction and Development, 1989), p. 25.

23. J. Kraus, "Debt," p. 76.

24. World Bank, *Sub-Saharan Africa,* pp. 20–21.

25. World Bank, *World Debt Tables, 1993–94.*

26. J. Kraus, "Debt," p. 77.

27. United Nations, *African Debt: The Case for Debt Relief* (New York: 1992, a pamphlet produced by the African Recovery Unit/CPMD, Department of Public Information, United Nations, New York).

28. Michael Chege, "Sub-Saharan Africa: Underdevelopment's Last Stand," in *Global Change, Regional Response: The International Context of Development,* ed. Barbara Stallings (Cambridge: Cambridge University Press, 1995), pp. 332–333.

29. See Darryl C. Thomas and Ali A. Mazrui, "Africa's Post-Cold War Demilitarisation: Domestic and Global Causes," *Journal of International Affairs* 46, no. 1 (Summer 1992): 157–174.

30. S. Gill, *American Hegemony and the Trilateral Commission* (Cambridge: Cambridge University Press, 1990), p. 101.

31. South Commission, *The Challenge to the South* (New York: Oxford University Press, 1990), p. 57.

32. S. Gill, *American Hegemony,* pp. 101–102.

33. South Commission, *The Challenge of the South,* pp. 58–59.

34. Ibid., p. 60.

35. "Democracy in Africa," *The Economist* (February 22–28, 1992): p. 18.

36. Ibid., p. 18.

37. See Geepa Nah Tiepoh, "Debt and Adjustment Under the New Globalization," *African News* (April 24, 2000): p. 2.

37. Geepa Nah Tiepoh, op. cit., p. 5.

38. Jonathan Kydd, "Zambia in the 1980s: The Political Economy of Adjustment," in *Structural Adjustment and Agriculture: Theory and Practice in Africa and Latin America,* ed. Simon Commander (London: Overseas Development Institute, 1989) pp. 127-144.

40. R. Rothstein, *The Third World and U.S. Foreign Policy: Cooperation and Conflict in the 1980s* (Boulder, CO: Westview Press, 1981), p. 141.

41. Although Portugal is a European nation, its economic performance conforms to the Third World semiperiphery.

42. This list was generated by taking all countries within 50 percent (above or below) of South Africa's GNPPC circa 1973, and eliminating small countries with a population below 10 million, oil-exporting countries, and members of COMECON (data absent, state structure different). Algeria might have been excluded as an oil exporter, but is included because of its significant manufacturing capability. This list was also the result of consultation with Immanuel Wallerstein and William Martin as part of the Research Working Group at the Fernand Braudel Center for the Study of Economics, Historical Systems, and Civilizations. See Darryl C. Thomas and William Martin, "South Africa's Economic Trajectory: South Africa's Economic Crisis or World Economic Crisis?" in *How Fast The Wind? Southern Africa 1975–2000,* ed. Sergio Vieira et. al. (Trenton, NJ: Africa World Press, 1992), pp. 165–196. Two states, Argentina and Nigeria, had the potential of becoming part of the semiperiphery. However, both experienced stagnation, and the manufacturing sector lost substantial ground in the late 1970s and 1980s. Many were called but few were chosen for this new international division of labor.

43. A. Lipietz, *Mirages and Miracles: Crises of Global Fordism* (London: Verso Press, 1987), pp. 87–89.

44. J. Browett, *Industrialization in the Global Periphery: Significance of the Newly Industrializing Countries* (Adelaide: Flinders University of South Australia, School of Social Science, 1986); E. K. Y. Chen, *High Growth in Asia's Economies: A Comparative Study of Hong Kong, Japan, Korea, Singapore, and Taiwan* (London: MacMillan, 1979); N. Harris, *The End of the Third World: Newly Industrializing Countries and the Decline of Ideology* (London: Penguin Books, 1986).

45. A. Seidman and N. S. Makgetla, *Outpost of Monopoly Capitalism: Southern Africa In A Changing World Economy* (Westport, CT: Lawrence Hill Company, 1980), pp. 9–10.

46. A. Lipietz, *Mirages and Miracles: The Crisis of Global Fordism* (London: Verso Press New Left Books, 1987).

47. Gary Gereffi, "Global Production System and Third World Development," in *Global Change, Regional Response: The New International Context of Development,* ed. Barbara Stallings (Cambridge: Cambridge University Press, 1995), p. 106.

48. Ibid., p. 106.

49. Ibid,. p. 121.

50. M. Castells and L. D. Tyson, "High Technology and the Changing International

Division of Production, in *The Newly Industrializing Countries in the World Economy: Challenges for US Policy,* ed. Randall B. Purcell (Boulder: Lynne Rienner Publishers, 1989), pp. 9–10.

51. R. W. Cox, *Production, Power, and World Order: Social Forces in the Making of History* (New York: Columbia University Press, 1987); M. Castells and L. D. Tyson, "High Technology," pp. 9–10.

52. N. Harris, *The End of the Third World,* pp. 104–105.

53. See J. Henderson and M. Castells, *Global Restructuring and Development* (London: Sage Publication, 1986); A. Lipietz, "Toward Global Fordism," *New Left Review* 132 (1982): 33–47.

54. D. C. Thomas and W. Martin, "South Africa's Economic Trajectory," p. 8.

55. M. Castells and L. D. Tyson, "High Technology," p. 21.

56. "The Mexico Syndrome, and How to Steer Clear of It," *The Economist* (March 18–24, 1995): pp. 73-74.

57. Steven Radelet and Jeffrey Sachs, "Asia's Resurgence," *Foreign Affairs* 76, no. 6 (November/December 1997): 44–59.

58. Jagdish Bhagwati, "The Capital Myth: The Differences between Trade in Widges and Dollars," *Foreign Affairs* 77, no. 3 (May/June 1998): 7–12.

59. Ibid., p. 8.

60. Mexico is not a member of OPEC but has emerged as an important producer of petroleum in the Western Hemisphere.

61. These were cities in which the nonaligned movement held their meetings in the 1980s and attempted to bargain for a new order.

62. Fred Halliday, *Cold War, Third World: A Essay on Soviet-US Relations* (London: Hutchinson Radius, 1989), p. 22.

63. "Third World Embracing Economic Reform," *New York Times,* 8 July 1991, p. D3.

64. South Commission, *The Challenge of the South,* p. 72.

Part IV

Pan-Proletarianism Phase II:
Race Consciousness in the North
and the New Era of Global Apartheid

7

The Political and Military Dimensions of Third World Fragmentation

On August 2, 1990, Iraq invaded Kuwait after failing to resolve a conflict over past debt that began accumulating during the first Persian and Arabian Gulf War (involving Iraq and Iran from 1981–1987). This second Persian and Arabian Gulf War placed Iraq at the arc of the crisis between the North and the South, especially with reference to the industrial democracies' access to petroleum, a vital commodity in the world system. The militarization of this conflict became a major test of the Carter Doctrine concerning the Persian Gulf and the new post-Cold War alliance between Washington and Moscow. The Middle East crisis that ensued signaled the outline of a new world order in several ways. This evolving new order represents a concert of Great Powers, essentially status quo nations that believe in liberal capitalist democracy and support the international regime against a small group of nations with radical and antisystemic goals. This conflict provided more evidence that the former Soviet Union and Warsaw Pact nations were ready to abandon their commitment to defend Third World states from the United States and the Northwest coalition. At this juncture, the Russians gave a higher priority to domestic restructuring, behaving like a status quo power throughout the duration of the conflict. It was surprising to hear the Soviets condemn Iraq's aggression and violation of Kuwait's sovereignty, given their history of annexation of Estonia, Latvia, Lithuania, and portions of Finland, Poland, Germany, Rumania, and Czechoslovakia in the 1940s and their violation of the sovereignty of Eastern European nations as late as the 1980s. At the same time, it was surprising to find the United States enlist the United Nations Security Council to mobilize a multinational force against Iraq, given the level of American hostilities toward this international institution in the 1980s.

The aftermath of the Persian Gulf War of 1991 ushered in a new era of world politics, replacing the Cold War that had long defined the discourse between the North and the South. This new mandate, proclaimed by both former President George Bush and his new Russian counterpart, President Boris Yeltsin, is based on an intensification in cooperation between the Northeast – the former Soviet Union and the Warsaw Pact nations of East Central Europe – and the Northwest – the United States, Western Europe, and Japan. Since 1991, both blocs have sought to resolve all outstanding regional conflicts in the Third World and to reduce the flow of arms to the most volatile regions. In addition, the United Nations' collective security apparatuses are being rediscovered as new diplomatic tools in conflict resolution. However, if the collective machinery of the United Nations should fail, the United States would act as "police force of last resort." In December 1992, U.S. military forces were dispatched to Somalia, after the United Nations peacekeeping troops failed to restore order and protect relief workers in that troubled African state. Likewise, the Northeast and Northwest are emerging as partners in this new dispensation, in which democratic capitalism is held up as the only viable political, economic, and cultural answer to the age-old problem of how to build political and economic institutions that can contribute to human development and simultaneously protect individual liberties. As this process of convergence accelerates between the Northeast and the Northwest, a new global rift is emerging along North-South lines.

This chapter will analyze the extent to which the new world order is taking on a decisive racial character and is ushering in a new era of global apartheid. It will examine the role of Third World states' insecurity dilemmas, which have generated political instability as well as the role of Third World arms sales in fueling interstate tensions, provoking communal and ethnic tensions, and at times prolonging civil wars. It will also examine the impact of the Second Cold War on Third World solidarity, the decline of socialism and the noncapitalist path to development advanced by the former Soviet Union, and the renunciation of revolutionary and antisystemic movements in the developing world by Moscow. This inquiry will explore the implications of democracy and majority rule in the new postapartheid South Africa and the "ballot versus the bullet" concept in the transitional processes between the Palestinians and Israelis. The ballot versus the bullet scenario has implications for democratic consolidation as well as Third World solidarity as we approach the twenty-first century. Finally, this chapter will also examine how states in the Northeast and Northwest have monopolized the levers of power within international institutions, thus verifying the codification of global apartheid through a new international regime governing interstate relations. These issues have ramifications for globalization, democratization, and transitions in the Third World.

THIRD WORLD SECURITY DILEMMAS AND THE SECOND COLD WAR

In recent years a proliferation of studies has drawn attention to the security dilemma facing developing countries, emphasizing the array of domestic factors that contribute to interstate and intrastate conflicts that have over time escalated into full-blown wars in such diverse places as Afghanistan, Angola, El Salvador, Chad, and the Sudan.[1] First, instead of facing an anarchic international system, a large number of African and Third World decision makers face domestic anarchy as a result of lack of social cohesion and state incapacity to provide for basic needs: food, shelter, economic well-being, political participation, and a methodical process of selecting leaders. This lack of state capacity to provide domestic order and tranquillity has also contributed to a serious question of legitimacy.[2] Most African and Third World leaders face a domestic source of the "security dilemma" rather than an anarchic international system. In a word, most African and Third World societies are not unitary actors.

Second, most African and Third World states came forth in a world system in which their borders were sheltered from external infringements, violations, or modification by international law and international institutions under the leadership of Pax Americana. Earlier attempts to alter borders and create new states in Nigeria, Zaire (the former Belgian Congo, and as of 1998, the Congo again), and Chad and, more recently, in Kuwait with the Iraq intervention in August 1990, failed through a combination of local, regional, and global forces. In the process of state-building, African and Third World decision makers have not had the option of increasing their territorial boundaries that their Northern counterparts had prior to the Second World War.[3] Indeed, there are approximately eighty contested boundaries and territorial claims currently on the international agenda, although most of them are dormant. Until the breakup of the former Soviet Union and Yugoslavia in 1991 and 1992, there was less willingness to use force to solve these problems.[4] The postwar international regimes[5] against territorial expansion in Africa and the rest of the Third World became enshrined in international law through the United Nations and the Organization of African Unity (OAU).[6] Both superpowers supported this principle at key junctures during the Cold War.

Third, perhaps the most critical element governing the insecurity dilemma for most African and Third World decision makers revolves around the nation-building process itself. Most new and old historic states, setting aside Latin American states, possess one common denominator: they emerged from the disintegration of imperial empires. The majority of new states made the transition from colony to nation under U.S. global leadership in the postwar era. In most Third World societies, the state came before the nation. Most African leaders inherited the colonial state, which did not create a unitary state. The colonial state emphasized differences between groups in order to facilitate their rule. Mohammed Ayoob makes the observation that political and administrative boundaries served the purposes of colonial convenience, arbitrarily cutting across ethnic, religious, and linguistic ties, dismembering established political units, and joining diverse precolonial entities into uneasy administrative units.[7] Traditionally, the concept of *nation* was defined as a collectivity of persons whose self-identification on the basis of common ethnicity, language, race, and historical experience became the raison d'être for expression of political identity and power. Commenting on the impact of colonialism and system of indirect administrative rule on state-building in Africa, Ali Mazrui observed that it

> aggravated the problem of creating a modern nation-state after independence. The different groups in the country maintained their separate ethnic identities by being ruled in part through their own native institutions . . . different sections of the population perceived each other as strangers, sometimes as aliens, increasingly as rivals, and ominously as potential enemies.[8]

Starting in the postwar era, African and other Third World leaders began struggling to create one nation out of many, seeking to establish legitimacy and loyalty to one state in a political milieu in which the juridical state became an outside and occupying force.

This competing justification for the legitimacy of the state became hostage to ethnic, religious, and ideological factors in such diverse places as Vietnam, Kampuchea, the Sudan, Sri Lanka, Afghanistan, and Lebanon. In such an environment, minorities become restive and seek what the majority has already achieved: a state of their own. Armed struggles were launched by the Shans, Karens, and Chin in Myanmar (Burma); the Sikhs and Kashmiris, among others, in India; the Bengalis in Pakistan (Bangladesh); the Tamils in Sri Lanka; various groups in what is called Afghanistan; the Eritreans in Ethiopia, and the list goes on.[9] With few exceptions, most Third World states must compete for loyalty and resources with other social institutions such as families, clans, transnational corporations, domestic enterprises, tribes, religious communities of various stripes, and patron-client dyads.[10] For the most part, Third World leaders lack the ability to use state agencies to compel their citizens to do what they want them to do. Citizens all across the Third World give their loyalty and support to other social institutions and thus undermine the very legitimacy of the state.

Third World insecurity dilemmas fall into four arenas. First, there are a variety of communal groups fighting for their own security and for hegemony over their competitors. Second, most regimes in power, representing the interests of a particular ethnic or social stratum, or an economic or military elite that has taken control of the reins of the state, lack support from significant sectors of the population. Third, a large number of Third World states lack the capacity to provide for the basic needs of the population and to maintain political order. Fourth, the real threat to the regime or leader is often domestic, thus distinctions between threats to the leader and threats to the state become blurred in such an environment.[11]

Since a number of Third World leaders have conceptualized domestic threats to their continuation in power as challenges to the state itself, this state of affairs has led decision makers throughout the developing world who face similar insecurity dilemmas to adopt three strategies: (1) militarization, i.e., developing and arming sizable military and police forces; (2) repression and state terror, that is, waging a battle against the alleged "enemy within"; and (3) diversionary tactics – identifying external enemies to distract attention from the situation at home.[12] Third World leaders have used these strategies to rationalize their purchases of conventional arms from the superpowers and their allies.

Domestic conflicts ranging from ethnic and religious conflicts to civil and interstate wars provided fuel for extending the Cold War into this Third World. During the 1980s, Africa, Asia, the Middle East, and other Third World regions became vital battlegrounds in the superpower rivalry. On the African continent, Angola and Ethiopia became the arena of competition between Washington and Moscow as both superpowers increased their support to their clients in this zone of the world system. El Salvador and Nicaragua also became the superpowers' theater for low-intensity conflict. By the mid-1980s, the civil war in Afghanistan became the Soviet Union's Vietnam. Both superpowers increased their export of conventional arms throughout the developing world as they competed for the ideological soul of the South. During the 1980s President Ronald Reagan sought to enlist Third World anticommunist groups in his coalition against the "evil empire" of Marxist-Leninism. After the Cuban missile crisis of 1962, the superpowers became reluctant to integrate regional conflicts into military conflicts between Washington and Moscow. Starting in the 1970s, Third World conflicts became fodder for increased Soviet-American rivalry.

Wars of national liberation, territorial and civil wars in Vietnam, North and South Korea, as well as the Congo and Cuban crises, influenced both Washington and Moscow to deploy diplomatic instruments and to rely more on their Third World allies to protect their ideological and strategic interests in the developing world. In the 1960s, Moscow lacked the military means to reach beyond Central and Eastern Europe. Military coups in Portugal and Ethiopia in 1974 provided a window of opportunity for Soviet expansion into Eastern and Southern Africa by providing military assistance to several client states. Moscow's fortunes soared as Ethiopia struggled to maintain its territoriality against an encroaching Somalia and the Eritrean liberation movement sought self-determination and sovereignty. Wars of national liberation in Southern Africa and struggles against white minority rule helped Moscow recruit new allies in Angola, Mozambique, Zimbabwe, and Namibia. As the battle against apartheid gained momentum in South Africa, Moscow became a major actor in that arena.

In the early 1980s the United States began to respond to these new Third World initiatives of the Soviet Union by seeking new alliances of its own and by showing a greater determination to use military force, especially in low-intensity conflicts in the developing world, as a challenge to Moscow. These new levels of intensity governing relations between Washington and Moscow over the Third World led many analysts to refer to the 1970s and 1980s as the Second Cold War.

As the Second Cold War began to unfold in the late 1970s, it became apparent that it was fundamentally different from the earlier Cold War in geopolitical focus. The Second World War had frozen the boundaries of Europe, dividing the majority of states between one of the two political and economic systems organized by the superpowers. This partition held without fundamental change for approximately four decades, until 1989. Efforts were made in Germany (1953), Hungary (1956), Czechoslovakia (1968), and Poland (1981) to change their subordinate position vis-à-vis the superpowers; however, local and external forces successfully maintained the status quo. In the Northwest, attempts to change borders were mounted in France and Italy (1946–48) and Portugal (1974). In the Northeast it was easier for select states (Albania, Yugoslavia, and Rumania) to change their strategic alliances; for those in the Northwest it was much easier to vary their domestic political orientation (Greece and Spain). While some states moved toward exercising greater autonomy, the core blocs remained solid.[13] This left the Third World as the new arc of crisis in the Cold War.

In the Third World there were no lines of demarcation that the superpowers recognized as limiting their respective spheres of influence. The political landscape in this vast zone of the world system was fluid. Following the Second World War, boundaries in the Far East remained highly contested, down to 1949 with the Chinese Revolution and through 1954 with the Korean and the first of the Indochinese wars. Subsequently, the Third World became the zone of conflict with over 140 conflicts costing over twenty million lives, a zone in which the United States and the Soviet Union remained as active participants in intrastate and interstate disputes.[14]

Civil strife, wars of national liberation, and interstate conflicts resulting from Third World state insecurity dilemmas provided the raw material sought by the superpowers to achieve their ends. Starting with the first and second Indochina wars of the 1950s and 1960s, Asia emerged as the arc of crisis as Washington and Moscow competed for the soul of the Third World. Africa and other developing areas received less attention from the superpowers. The Middle East was possibly the only exception to this rule prior to the 1970s. Both superpowers exported arms and provided military training to Arab and Israeli combatants in this volatile region. The Portuguese military coup in 1974 resulted in civil wars and ethnic conflict in Angola, thus giving the Soviet Union another opportunity to expand its influence. Similarly, the Afghanistan coup of 1979 increased Kabul's arms dependency on Moscow. Struggles erupted in Namibia and Zimbabwe against colonialism and white minority rule in Southern Africa, leading each superpower to fear that Africa might swing decisively to the opposite camp. A new phase of superpower conflict in Africa began in the 1980s as President Reagan sought to enlist a number of African domestic groups to undermine Soviet-sponsored states such as Angola and Mozambique, or to prop up Western-sponsored states such as Zaire, Kenya, and at times Somalia. Superpower competition for influence was also evident in other developing regions of the Third World.

The successes of antisystemic struggles in Iran, Nicaragua, and Grenada in 1979 brought to power new regimes that were friendly toward the Soviet Union and its ally, Cuba. Following leftist success in Nicaragua and Grenada, conflict in El Salvador intensified between governmental authorities and the Salvadoran Democratic Front. American policymakers also provided support to such allies as Pakistan and Turkey. These states became channels for arms and military assistance to the Afghan mujahideen rebels combating the Soviet-sponsored regime in Kabul. Military assistance became a critical component in the Caribbean and Central American basin, as U.S. policymakers sought to isolate Cuba, Nicaragua, and Grenada and to neutralize rebel forces in El Salvador. Increasingly in the 1980s, arms exports replaced foreign aid as the chief, if rather blunt, instrument of Soviet and American policy toward the Third World.

As Michael Klare argues, arms transfers give the supplier considerable influence over the political behavior of the recipient.[15] Arms exports have emerged as an instrument for delineating and reinforcing spheres of influences serving as commitments by major powers to particular states. In this regard, Third World recipients are not valued for the resources they bring to bear in a conflict, but are conceptualized abstractly as objects of East-West rivalry. Such an approach reinforces a zero-sum analysis of geopolitical competition.

In this arena, the Soviets operated at a great disadvantage since they held primarily the military card. The United States had other means of exerting influence, such as economic aid and the ability to supply highly valued manufactured goods.[16] American policy makers exercised influence in such international institutions as the World Bank, the IMF, and the General Agreement on Tariffs and Trade (GATT). Washington could pull additional levers of influence in various regional financing agencies, as well as the Group of Seven. Countries in sub-Saharan Africa received approximately $420 million in economic assistance from 1965 to 1974, while the Soviets provided $240 million in arms supplies. The states in North Africa obtained $740 million in economic credits and $2.9 billion in arms deliveries and equipment.[17] In short, the Soviets were a one-dimensional superpower, and this limited their influence in Africa and other developing regions, despite high levels of arms exports. Military assistance to allies such as Ethiopia, South Yemen, Afghanistan, and Angola contributed to a fatal drain on the Soviet Union's already shaky economy.

THIRD WORLD-ORIENTED DEADLY QUARRELS

Militarized conflicts in the Third World have taken the form of wars of national liberation, ethnic and communal violence, civil wars, and of interstate conflicts. These militarized disputes in the developing countries provided fertile ground for outside intervention in the 1970s and 1980s. During the postwar era, Africa, Asia, and other developing regions have emerged as critical zones of militarized conflict.

Between 1945 and 1965 most of the militarized conflicts in the Third World were anticolonial struggles that involved military intervention by states from the Northwest. Most of these anticolonial battles took place in Africa and Asia. For those anticolonial battles that had a short duration, most of the casualties were in the 1,000 to 5,000 range. However, for anticolonial struggle that had a long duration — ten to fifteen years — the casualties ranged from 15,000 in Kenya and Madagascar, to 100,000 in Algeria, to 600,000 in Vietnam (Far East) and 800,000 in India. Higher casualties occurred in Algeria and Vietnam, where the struggles for liberation became fodder for the continuation of the East-West conflict within a North-South context. The conflict in India had a religious dimension, involving a dispute between Muslims and Hindus as well as with the British. Perhaps the Korean War (1950–1953) was the most brutal interstate dispute early in the Cold War. With the intervention of the United States and the People's Republic of China, approximately 3 million civilian and military casualties occurred.[18]

Civil wars in the Third World were very deadly affairs during the 1945-1965 period. Most involved outside intervention by the Northwest, usually supporting separatists, especially when strategic raw materials were at stake, as for example, Biafra in the Nigerian civil war and Katanga in the Congo crisis. The Lebanese civil war of 1958 resulted in 2,000 casualties and included American military intervention. The Soviets lacked the military means to achieve global reach and became only modestly involved in such disputes. Moscow did provide military assistance to the Nigerian government and supported its efforts to maintain its territory. The casualty rates were very high, ranging from 300,000 to over 2 million civilian and military casualties in Nigeria. Civil wars took place during this period in the Congo (Zaire), Nigeria, the Sudan, and Vietnam. The Arab-Israel conflict in 1948 cost approximately 8,000 military casualties, while British and French intervention in the Suez Canal crisis resulted in 4,000 civilian and military deaths. Again, there is a high correlation between the duration of these militarized conflicts and the severity of the casualties.

Ethnic and communal violence escalated during the 1945–1965 period. However, most of the casualties remained in the 1,000 to 2,000 range, the lone exceptions being Pakistan versus Kashmir — with India's intervention in 1965, 20,000 casualties, and Rwanda where 105,000 deaths due to ethnic violence were recorded. In Latin America, U.S. intervention into the Dominican Republic (1965) and Guatemala (1954) led to 1,000 and 3,000 casualties respectively. Casualties in revolutions in Bolivia (1952) and Cuba (1958) ranged from 1,000 to 5,000.[19]

The decades of the 1970s and 1980s witnessed an increase in outside intervention in Third World militarized disputes. Both superpowers and their allies began to take sides in these local and regional conflicts, thus intensifying their duration and severity. Civil wars and wars of national liberation were also attractive to Washington, Moscow, and their respective allies. Military coups in

Portugal and Ethiopia in 1974 provided windows of opportunity for Moscow and Cuba to get involved in militarized disputes in the developing world, especially in Africa – Angola (1975–90), Ethiopia and Somalia (1976–83), Mozambique (1981 and 1994), the Sudan (1984 and continuing) – and in Central America – El Salvador (1979–90) and Nicaragua (1981–88). These interstate conflicts and civil wars became part of the competitive rivalry between Washington and Moscow. The Sudanese civil war remained primarily a regional affair. The United States and its allies began to renew their activities in Africa, Central America, and South Asia as Washington sought to roll back an expansionist Soviet bloc.

Civil wars also were deadly throughout the Third World during most of the 1970s, 1980s, and the 1990s, especially in sub-Saharan Africa and South Asia. Civil wars in Angola (750,000 casualties) and the Sudan (1,500,000 casualties) were very costly with reference to civilian and military casualties. Perhaps the civil war in Afghanistan was the most costly, incurring 1,500,000 casualties from 1978 to 1992, and later fighting between the various factions resulted in over 500,000 casualties. The Liberian civil war resulted in 150,000 casualties between 1990 and 1995.

In Central America, civil wars in El Salvador (1979–90) and Nicaragua (1981–88) accounted for about 75,000 and 30,000 casualties, respectively. The conflict between the Shining Path and the Peruvian government (1980 and 1995) has led to approximately 35,000 casualties despite efforts to neutralize this radical national liberation movement. The killing field of Kampuchea (Cambodia) was the only internal war with casualties over 1 million. The Pol Pot regime instituted a campaign of systematic genocide (1975–78) against large segments of the population. This campaign included the forceful removal of the population from the urban centers. In Myanmar (Burma), the civil dispute between the government and opposition groups cost over 9,000 lives from 1985 to 1988.[20] Most of these internal wars in the Third World were fueled by external intervention and arms sales from the superpowers and their allies. Foreign intervention increased both their duration and their severity. Combatants in these civil conflicts did not make distinctions between civilian and military targets. This policy played a key role in increasing the severity of the casualties.

Interstate militarized disputes were also on the rise during the 1970s and 1980s. These conflicts were very low-level affairs and resulted in smaller numbers of civilian and military casualties when the superpowers and their allies remained on the sidelines. The Tanzanian-Ugandan war of 1978–79 is an example of this phenomenon. However, the number of civilian and military casualties rose with the participation of the superpowers and their allies, for example, in Chad (1980–87), 7,000; South Yemen (1986–87), 11,000; Somalia-Ethiopia (1976–83), 39,000; Vietnam-Kampuchea (1978–89), 65,000; and the China-Vietnam border skirmish (1987), approximately 1,000. In the Middle East, interstate conflict became more prevalent in the 1980s. The Israeli invasion and occupation of southern Lebanon (1982–90) resulted in approximately

100,000 casualties, while the Iraq-Iran War (1980–88) resulted in 500,000 casualties. The Yom Kippur War of 1973 involved Egypt, Syria, and the Israelis plus the two superpowers, and accounted for only 16,000 casualties.[21]

Wars of national liberation against Third World states produced modest casualty rates when the superpowers and their allies remained on the sidelines, for example, 16,000 in the Western Sahara (1975–87). The participation of the superpowers and their allies increased the severity of the casualties in such conflicts, as for example, 575,000 casualties in Eritrea and Ethiopia (1974–92). Communal and ethnic disturbances were also very violent affairs during the 1970s and 1980s. Ethnic and communal violence resulted in 600,000 casualties in Uganda during the 1970s and 1980s, while Burundi (1988) and South Africa (1983–90) recorded 1,000 and 10,000, respectively. Ethnic conflicts in Rwanda reached new levels of destruction in this East African country. A United Nations spokesman estimates that at least 500,000 people are believed to have died in ethnic massacres and fighting between the rebel Rwandan Patriotic Front and government forces between 1994 and 1995. Violence began April 6, after President Juvenal Habyarimana, a Hutu, was killed in an apparent rocket attack on his plane as it landed at the Kigali airport. The Hutu-dominated interim government has blamed the massacres that followed on tribal passions inflamed by suspicions that the late President's plane was downed by Tutsi rebels. The histories of Burundi and Rwanda have been riddled with conflict between the Hutu, who comprised approximately 85 percent of the population, and the Tutsi, who make up a 15 percent minority.[22] Rwanda emerged as another killing field, and the United Nations and the international community appear unable to stop the genocidal tendencies that continues to ravage this East African nation. The United Nations has established an international tribunal to bind over to trial those individuals responsible for genocide. To date, only a small number of individuals have been tried, found guilty, and executed.

Ethnic and communal violence had a strong religious dimension. Conflict over the rise of Islamic fundamentalism exemplified this trend. In Syria (1982) approximately 20,000 conservative Muslims were massacred, while Iraqi authorities killed approximately 10,000 Kurds in 1988, approximately 30,000 Kurdish and Shiite rebels in 1991–92, and factional fighting among Kurds resulted in 2,000 casualties. The conflict between the Tamils, Sinhalese, and the Sri Lankan authorities has cost approximately 50,000 lives from 1984 to 1995.

Algeria, once revered as the fulcrum for Third World solidarity, has been embroiled in a major militarized internal conflict after rejecting the ballot and election results that would have ushered the Islamic Salvation front into power. At this juncture, actors in this conflict consider bullets and violence preferable to the ballot and conciliation in resolving this political conflict. Islamic guerrilla warfare broke out in January 1992, after the army canceled elections won by the FIS. The army refused to allow the FIS to form a government and banned this organization from legitimate participation in the Algerian political system. A subsequent crackdown drove moderates to join forces with radicals who resorted to violence after the election's nullification. The Islamist insurgents have targeted military vehicles, barracks, the police, and government buildings. Another Islamist organization, the Armed Islamist Group (GIA), then appeared and intensified the casualties by killing intellectuals, journalists, women, and foreigners, and massacring villagers in western Algeria. At the same time, the Algerian government has not allowed international inquiry into the massacres. Since 1992 approximately 100,000 people have died from the violence.[23]

There were several episodes of state-directed violence and right-wing death-squads attacks against citizens calling for democratization or political reform in diverse Third World states. These incidents of state-sanctioned violence took place in Argentina, Brazil, Chile, and the People's Republic of China. In Argentina, from 1976 to 1979, nearly 12,000 civilians and 3,000 military personnel disappeared without a trace. In Brazil, around 1,000 casualties resulted from right-wing terrorism. In Chile, nearly 20,000 civilians became casualties to the new military junta in 1974. In Beijing, nearly 1,000 student activists lost their lives in China's pro-democracy movement. In 1990, nearly 2,000 dissidents were executed.[24]

Militarized disputes throughout the Third World took the form of civil wars, ethnic and communal violence, and intrastate and interstate conflicts. These incidents of civil violence confirm our hypothesis concerning insecurity dilemmas. These militarized conflicts were ignited by the arms race that accompanied the escalation of Third World-oriented conflicts. Africa, South Asia, the Far East, and the Middle East evolved into important zones in the global arms market.

In the 1970s and 1980s, Third World leaders found it increasingly difficult to find peaceful solutions to domestic and regional conflicts, especially with the advent of foreign intervention, which came in a variety of guises. Diplomatic and military support through arms sales became the most important means for the superpowers and their allies to become participants in regional conflicts. Regional organizations including the Organization of African Unity (OAU), the Arab League, the Association of Southeast Asian Nations (ASEAN), and the Organization of American States (OAS) found it almost impossible to get warring parties to meet at the peace table and make dramatic efforts to resolve their outstanding conflicts. Examples of such impasses took place in the Iraq-Iranian war (1981–88), Mozambique and RENAMO (1976–1992),[25] Ethiopia and Eritrea (1960s–1992), and the Iraq-Kuwait conflict (1990–91). Perhaps leaders in Central America were the only exception to this pattern, as Costa Rica was successful in brokering a settlement between the Sandinistas and the Contras in Nicaragua with the assistance of Mexico and other states in the region.[26] In February 1990 Violeta Chamorro, head of the National Opposition Union (UNO), defeated Sandinista leader Daniel Ortega for the presidency by a fifteen percent margin. UNO captured 51 of the 92 Assembly seats.[27] Even the nonaligned movement was ineffective in resolving militarized disputes between Third World states during this same time period. Archie

Singham and Shirley Hune, in their seminal work on nonalignment, identified Third World-oriented militarized disputes as the most difficult conflicts for the nonaligned movement to resolve. Singham and Hune argued that such conflicts can easily escalate to include the superpowers and their allies. Likewise, civil wars, internal wars, and interstate conflicts in the Third World escalated after arms sales from both Cold War coalitions, thus aggravating the situation and increasing the number of actors involved as well as the complexity of these disputes.[28]

PATTERNS IN THIRD WORLD ARMS IMPORTS 1970s–1990s

The advent of the Second Cold War[29] in the 1970s played a critical role in fueling arms sales throughout the developing world, with Africa, the Far East, and the Middle East emerging as the most dynamic arenas for competition among the superpowers. The superpowers dominated the arms trade to the Third World during the 1970s and 1980s. In the early 1970s the Soviets sold approximately $30 billion in arms to Third World regions, averaging approximately $6 billion a year from 1971 to 1976. At the same time, the United States exported approximately $27 billion of arms to the developing world, averaging around $5.5 billion a year. From 1976 to 1980 the Soviets sold approximately $43 billion of arms to the Third World, averaging around $8.6 billion in sales annually. The United States exported approximately $33 billion of arms from 1976 to 1980, averaging around $6.6 billion in sales annually.[30] Between the early and mid-1980s the Soviets continued to dominate the arms market in the Third World. Soviet sales to this zone reached approximately $41 billion, averaging $8.2 billion a year from 1981 to 1985. The United States exported approximately $28 billion, averaging around $6 billion annually during the same time period. Moscow exported approximately $43 billion to the developing world, averaging around $8.8 billion annually during the 1986–90 period. The United States sold approximately $21 billion of arms to the developing world between 1986 and 1990, averaging approximately $4.2 billion annually.

The Soviet Union took advantage of a number of opportunities to increase its influence in divergent Third World regions including the Horn of Africa, southern Africa, South Asia, and North Africa. Soviet arms sales to the Third World reached their peak in 1987, when Moscow became deeply involved in supporting militarized conflicts in Afghanistan, Angola, Ethiopia, Namibia, and Nicaragua. Perhaps 1978–1988 marked the high point in Soviet arms sales to the Third World. Sales to the Third World began to decline after 1989. Gorbachev's new thinking included reevaluation of regional conflicts in U.S.–Soviet relations. His gradual retreat from supporting antisystemic forces in the Third World became an important ingredient in the winding down the Cold War.

In response to Soviet successes in South Asia, North Africa, and sub-Saharan Africa, Washington stepped up its own military involvement in the Third World, expanding its operations into Central America, eastern and southern

Africa, and the rest of the Third World in the mid-1970s. In 1979 President Jimmy Carter enunciated the Carter Doctrine that committed the United States to defend Western interests in the Persian Gulf from Soviet encroachment.

The 1980s were a period of decisive competition between the United States and the Soviet Union throughout the Third World, but especially in Central America, the Caribbean, eastern and southern Africa, and the Middle East. Washington could count on regional allies whose goals paralleled its own. For example, in the early 1980s, Egypt provided military assistance and training to Somalia in its conflict with Ethiopia. Zaire became a political sanctuary for the National Union for the Total Independence of Angola (UNITA) in the continuing Angolan civil war. The Republic of South Africa helped Washington through its "destructive engagement" policy toward Angola, Mozambique, and the Southern African Development Coordination Council (SADCC).[31] In South Asia, Pakistan provided a base for supplying the mujahideen rebels in Afghanistan in their bid to oust the Soviet-backed regime in Kabul. In Central America, Washington could rely on Honduras as a base of support for the Contras in their bid to oust the Sandinistas in Nicaragua. The Organization of East Caribbean States (OECS)[32] supported the American invasion (1982) that aborted Maurice Bishop's New Jewel Movement revolution in Grenada. Jamaica also became an ally in this military incursion.

In recent years a number of arms exporters have emerged from the ranks of the developing world. Any serious attempt to reduce arms transfers would have to involve arms sellers from Eastern and Western Europe, as well as the developing world. Third World arms exporters have increased their sales during international conflicts. Arms exports by developing countries such as China, Brazil, Libya, and Syria to zones of conflict constituted a much higher percentage of their total exports than was the case for major suppliers, especially with reference to the Iraq-Iranian war.[33] Between 1978 and 1988, arms sales by the three major exporters fell in real terms or increased much less rapidly than did sales from Third World countries, including China. The largest arms market during this period was the Middle East, which became dominated by the demand generated by the Iraq-Iranian war.[34]

The concentration of global arms exports by the five permanent members of the UN Security Council (the United States, the Soviet Union, France, Great Britain, and China) continued a long-term trend in the sale of conventional weapons. During the second half of the 1980s exports by the USSR to the Third World began to decline, while the U.S. exports increased.

Arms export trends document the emergence of the Middle East, the Far East, and South Asia as important markets between 1960 and 1990. North Africa and sub-Saharan Africa loomed large in the arms market during the late 1970s and mid-1980s. This intensification of arms imports to North Africa and sub-Saharan Africa resulted from the growth of interstate conflicts, as well as civil wars in Angola, Mozambique, Somalia, Chad, and Ethiopia. Wars of liberation in Ethiopia between the government and the Eritrean Liberation Front also contributed to arms imports. Growth in the intensity of militarized disputes correlates highly with the increase in flows of conventional weapons to volatile regions.

American arms exports to the Third World were targeted primarily toward the Middle East, the Far East, and to some extent North Africa and Central America. American exports to these regions accelerated during the late 1970s and 1980s in direct competition with the Soviets and their regional allies for influence. Soviet exports to the Third World were predominantly to the Middle East, North Africa, South Asia, followed by sub-Saharan Africa and the Far East. Arms sales by the United States and the USSR remained very modest in Central and South America. Arms exporters from Europe and the Third World (including Brazil and Israel) emerged as important suppliers in the Far East, Central and South America, and in South Africa during the 1980s. See Tables 7.1 and 7.2.

Since 1990, the United States has replaced the Russians as the largest exporter of major conventional weapons. This change has been another important result of the end of the Cold War and Mikhail Gorbachev's new policy toward Third World regional conflicts. The United States delivered over $8.7 billion of arms in 1990, representing 40 percent of the worldwide trade, although this total world figure represented a 25 percent decrease from the 1989 level. American arms exporters sold most their arms to other industrialized countries, with Japan by far the largest U.S. customer. At the same time, the United States exported $3 billion in arms to the Third World, making it second only to Moscow and accounting for over one-quarter of the global trade in this category. The United States exported conventional weapons worth over $54 billion to 77 countries, representing the largest arms clientele for any country from 1986 to 1990. Industrial countries still represented the majority of the American arms market, importing $32 billion in weapons and constituting half

Table 7.1
Ten Leading Suppliers of Conventional Weapons to the Third World, 1986–1990

Country	1986	1987	1988	1989	1990	1986–1990
1. USSR	10,440	10,936	8,658	8,862	4,273	43,169
2. USA	4,981	6,328	3,939	3,465	3,049	21,761
3. France	3,446	2,659	1,413	1,642	1,330	10,490
4. China	1,463	2,553	1,810	817	926	7,569
5. UK	1,091	1,681	1,281	1,187	971	6,210
6. Germany, FR.	661	254	367	168	496	1,946
7. Netherlands	132	263	402	661	125	1,583
8. Italy	399	320	362	49	39	1,169
9. Brazil	134	491	338	151	22	1,136
10. Israel	261	267	111	241	31	912

Source: SIPRI, 1991. Figures are in millions of U.S. $ at constant (1985) prices.

of the global trade. During the same period, the United States exported $21.8 billion in arms to the Third World, second only to the Russians.[35]

U.S. conventional weapons exporters specialize in high-tech products, especially in the aerospace industry, dominating in such market niches as aircraft, air-launched weapons, and avionics equipment. The Middle East and South Asia are important customers of the United States in the arms market. Third World states from these regions are more likely to be able to afford such products than their African, Central and South American counterparts. The values of new arms export contracts signed by major arms exporters in France, Britain, and the former Soviet Union has fallen significantly since 1988. The French and British decline ranges from 30 to 35 percent, while the former Soviet Union's decline hovers around 50 percent.[36]

In 1990, Moscow exported conventional arms worth $6.3 billion, accounting for nearly 30 percent of the world's total, making the Russians the second major exporter behind the United States. The Soviet's former allies in the Warsaw Pact and other longtime recipients, India, Iraq, and Afghanistan, have substantially reduced their orders for conventional weapons. In 1990, arms sales fell dramatically from the 1989 total by $12.2 billion, representing a 48 percent decrease. Soviet arms transfers ($4.3 billion) to the Third World accounted for roughly two-thirds of their total arms sales. These arms transfers account for 36 percent of global deliveries to the developing countries. Thus Moscow remained the leading arms exporter to the southern hemisphere. The Soviets exported $60.8 billion in conventional weapons to 38 countries from 1986 to 1990, giving it the fourth largest clientele in the world. During this period, five countries received over three-quarters of all Soviet exports: India (29 percent), Iraq (15 percent), Afghanistan (13 percent), North Korea (10 percent), and Syria (10 percent).[37]

Arms sales to the Third World reached a peak in the mid-1980s and began

Table 7.2

Ten Leading Third World Importers of Conventional Weapons, 1986–1990

Country	1986	1987	1988	1989	1990	1986–1990
1. India	3,729	4,582	3,382	3,754	1,541	16,989
2. Saudia Arabia	2,413	2,400	2,046	1,427	2,553	10,838
3. Iraq	2,484	4,440	2,155	1,177	59	10,314
4. Afghanistan	692	768	1,009	2,183	1,091	5,742
5. Korea, North	1,019	631	1,458	1,276	516	4,900
6. Egypt	1,645	2,379	348	139	206	4,717
7. Syria	1,511	1,172	1,172	336	0	4,191
8. Angola	980	1,140	889	74	508	3,592
9. Korea, South	287	604	987	997	249	3,125
10. Iran	738	704	558	336	578	2,913

Source: SIPRI, 1991. Figures are in millions of U.S. $ at constant (1985) prices.

to decline after 1988. At this juncture, both superpowers moved toward reducing arms sales to volatile regions, seeking to diminish the possibility of a major showdown between themselves in such regions as eastern and southern Africa, South Asia, Central America, and the Middle East. Washington and Moscow began taking important steps toward resolving the remaining outstanding conflicts in Third World regions. The reductions in arms transfers were an important consequence of the end of the Cold War. A new world order emerged in the aftermath of the Second Persian-Arabian Gulf War of 1990–91. See Figures 7.1, 7.2., 7.3, and 7.4.

Nevertheless, the regional dimension of the reduction in arms transfers has been uneven, with some Third World zones experiencing a greater decline than others. The Middle East saw a very steep drop in arms imports from their peak in 1984. The initial decline was attributed to the reduction in arms imports by Iraq and Iran as their interstate conflict came to an end in 1988. Arms imports from Iran and Iraq declined 50 percent after 1988. Arms sales to the Middle East rose by $11.7 million in 1990, partially in response to the Second Persian-Arabian Gulf War. (See Figures 7.5 and 7.6) Arms sales to this volatile region continued to rise despite President George Bush's pledge to reduce the arms flow. Most nations in the region are buying more sophisticated, high-tech conventional weapons as a response to Iraq's resounding defeat.

In the aftermath of the Gulf War, the economic and to some extent the military burden for a regional security system will more than likely fall on the Gulf Cooperation Council (GCC), in which Saudi Arabia is the most powerful member.[38] Preliminary arms sales data for 1991 and 1992 suggest that Saudi Arabia has continued to purchase more sophisticated military hardware from the United States and other arms suppliers. The Saudis emerged from the Gulf War as an important market for American high-tech weapons. The 1991/92 recession in the United States provided additional incentive for the arms industry to continue selling more weapons to this region in order to forestall a rise in unemployment in this key manufacturing sector. The former Soviet Union, in making the transition to a market economy, has a pressing need for hard currency and continues its export of weapons to this volatile region.

During the 1970s and 1980s East Asia and the Far East have also evolved into a very lucrative arms market. In South Asia, India and Pakistan are major military powers. The regional arms race between New Delhi and Islamabad has been partially responsible for the growth in arms sales to this region. The Afghanistan civil war (1978–1992), which began to wind down in 1990 and came to an end in May 1992, also contributed to the increase in regional arms imports. Both superpowers and their European allies became involved in arms transfers to this militarized dispute between the mujahideen rebels and the Soviet-backed regime in Kabul. Arms transfers to South Asia surpassed those to the Middle East by as much as 50 percent in 1989. Starting in 1990, arms sales to Afghanistan declined by the same amount, reflecting decisions by the USSR and the United States to cease supplying arms to their allies in this

Figure 7.1 – Imports of Major Conventional Weapons in the Developing World, 1982–1991

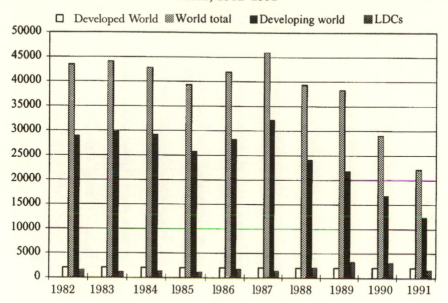

Figure 7.2 – Regional Variance in Import of Conventional Weapons in the Developing World, 1982–1991

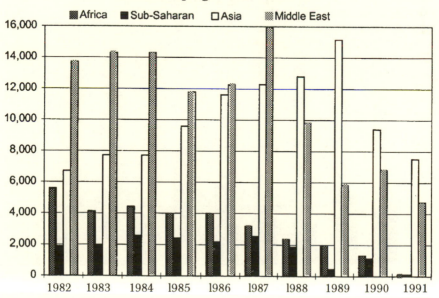

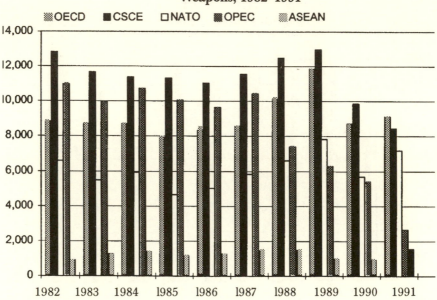

Figure 7.3 – Global Regional Variance in Import of Conventional Weapons, 1982–1991

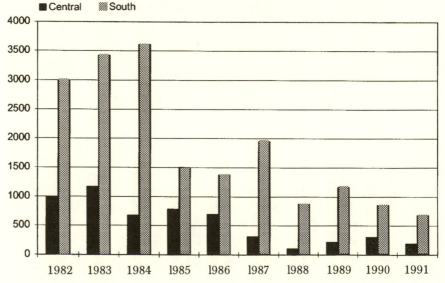

Figure 7.4 – Imports of Conventional Weapons in South and Central America, 1982–1991

Figure 7.5 – Imports of Major Conventional Weapons, 1982–1991

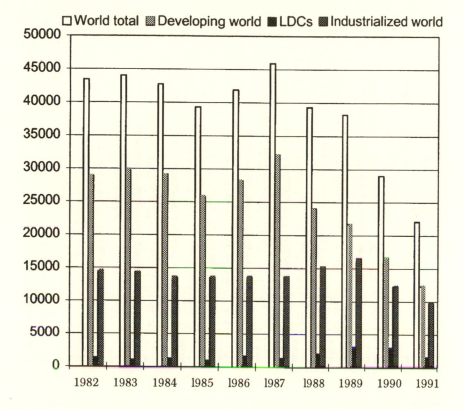

divided nation.[39] (See Figures 7.7 and 7.8.) Nevertheless, the arms race between India and Pakistan reached new levels of intensity after 1990. India and Pakistan announced their membership in the nuclear club, but even so, India and Pakistan have maintained their status as major Third World markets of major conventional weapons.

In the Far East, arms transfers continued to rise during the 1960 to 1990 period. Arms sales reached their peak in this region in 1988 and began to decline thereafter. Some of the fast-growing economies in the Far East (the Republic of Korea, Singapore, and Taiwan) increased their defense spending without expanding their share of military spending in output. The Republic of Korea and Taiwan became important shipbuilders, thus joining another very lucrative arms market. North Korea and Thailand have also evolved as important Third World arms producers. The member states of the Association of Southeast Asian Nations (ASEAN) have also become major importers of arms even as the Cold War came to an end. These nations[40] reached their peak with reference to arms imports in 1988, then continued to reduce their demand for

Figure 7.6 – Exports of Major Conventional Weapons, 1982–1991

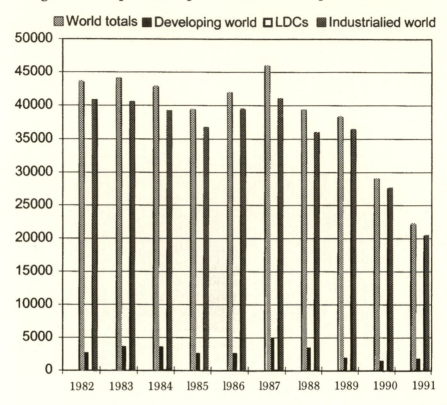

weapons over the next two years. However, arms imports surged among this collectivity of states in 1991, breaking the global pattern of arms reduction. Although there were other regions and alliance systems that increased their arms imports, including NATO, OPEC, and OECD, ASEAN growth in this arena represents a departure from past military posture. These nations are pursuing the development of modern multi-service military forces with significant power projection capabilities. Nations in the Far East and South Asia have become major consumers of high tech and more sophisticated conventional weaponry. All the Asian NICs, plus China, Japan, and North Korea are now producers of at least some military equipment, and many have invested substantial capital in the establishment of modern naval and aerospace production facilities. These actors are becoming increasingly self-sufficient in the production of advanced weapons, and in some cases, have become major arms exporters. Likewise, countries from the Asian Pacific rim are also developing domestic arms industries which by the early 21st century may approach the

Figure 7.7 – Imports of Major Conventional Weapons, 1985–1994

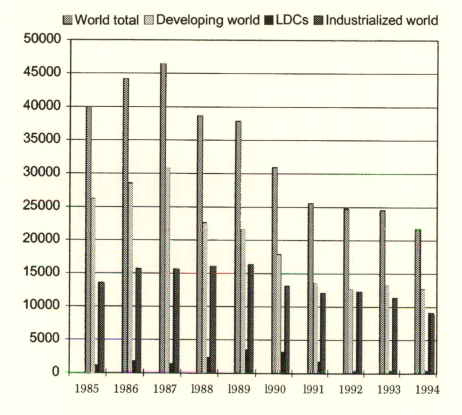

level of those in the advanced industrial countries. These actors possess the combination of growing economic resources with which to pursue building a military industrial complex and the emergence in many of these countries of civilian industries with considerable scientific and technological expertise.[41] Although states in this region are developing an inclination for more sophisticated weaponry, they have continued the downward trend in importing major conventional weapons in the 1990s.

Arms transfers to North Africa and sub-Saharan Africa reached their peak in 1986 and 1988 respectively. At this juncture, both superpowers began to negotiate an end to the Angolan civil war. In 1988, they pressured their regional allies to make concessions at the peace conference that convened in London.[42] In Ethiopia, both superpowers sought a peaceful resolution of this conflict. However, Washington and Moscow failed to persuade the combatants in this militarized dispute to negotiate an end to their hostilities. Resolution of civil wars in Ethiopia and Chad have been resolved on the battlefield. In

Figure 7.8 – Regional Variation in Imports of Major Conventional Weapons, 1985–1994

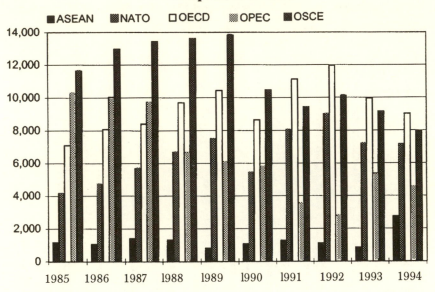

Figure 7.9 – Import of Major Conventional Weapons by Region, 1985–1994

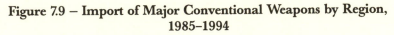

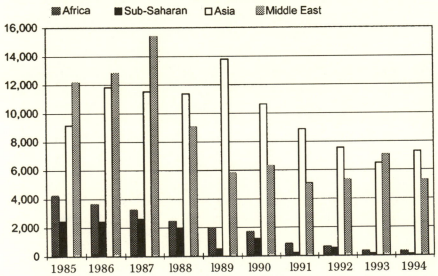

Liberia and Somalia, civil wars were resolved through additional military battles in the capital cities. Peacekeeping troops from the Economic Community of West African States (ECOWAS) have been in Liberia since 1991, attempting to resolve the ongoing civil war and restore order.

The Somalian civil war further deteriorated into violence and open warfare between various clans. Starting in 1992, Mogadishu became the battleground of more intensified clan violence. Throughout Somalia, civil society broke down as the state ceased to function. Starvation, looting, and anarchy followed as the warlords meted out their brand of justice. In December 1992, former President Bush dispatched U.S. troops to this African nation as part of a UN effort to restore order, guide the Somalis toward democracy and nation-building, and protect humanitarian groups and international relief agencies who were attempting to stop the massive starvation in this African nation. The Somalian intervention had far-reaching consequences, because American policy makers aimed to incorporate United Nations peacekeeping operations as an integral part of the U.S. policy of "assertive multilateralism." By June 1993, civil disorder returned as forces loyal to General Muhamed Farah Aideed led an assault on Pakistani UN peacekeeping troops, killing twenty-four. The United Nations shifted its policy toward war making and actively engaging General Aideed. Arms imports into sub-Saharan Africa reached their peak in 1988, declined in 1989, surged again in 1990 and plunged in 1991. Since 1988, African states have been under increasing pressure from the United States, the Russians, and Western Europe to aggressively pursue economic and political reforms and join forces with democratic capitalism. African states are being urged to abandon the military card in the post-Cold War era. (See Figures 7.8 and 7.9.)

Over the course of the last two decades the African continent has not fared very well during this period of global economic restructuring and crisis. The growth rate in sub-Saharan Africa has hovered around -2.4 and in 1989 only achieved a 0.3 growth rate for the 1980–1988 period. Sub-Saharan Africa had an overall growth rate of -17.4 during the 1980 to 1990 period. As a result of this dismal economic performance, the debt crisis is now plaguing leaders throughout the continent and constraining their decision making with reference to arms imports.

The debt crisis also began to affect arms sales to South and Central America as these two regions began to cope with the global economic crisis. The 1980s became the lost decade as a result of accumulated debt and the brake on development that ensued as leaders in these two regions sought to service their outstanding debt.[43] Arms sales reached their peak in 1986 and 1987, respectively, in Central and South America, and continued to decline throughout the rest of the decade. The South American region did experience a modest growth in arms imports in 1989. Thereafter, arms transfers to this region continued their descent. (See Figures 7.10 and 7.11.)

Regional variations in arms transfers resulted from several factors, including the end of the Cold War era and the global economic crisis. Other con-

Figure 7.10 – Regional Variation in Exports of Major Conventional Weapons in the Americas, 1982–1991

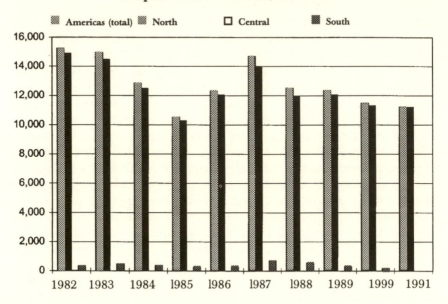

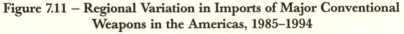

Figure 7.11 – Regional Variation in Imports of Major Conventional Weapons in the Americas, 1985–1994

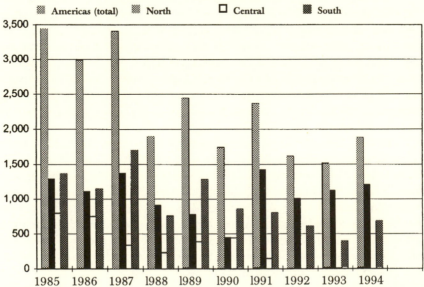

tributing factors were increased arms production in the Third World, the pro-liferation of ballistic missiles and nuclear technology, and weapons sent to select developing countries. The Second Persian-Arabian Gulf War has also encouraged a rise in sales of more sophisticated conventional weapons to the Middle East as states in this zone of the developing world attempt to cope with their new security dilemmas.

In 1990, Third World states imported $11.8 billion in major conventional arms, which represented a 35-percent reduction from the 1989 level. Nations from African, Central America, and South America failed to rank among the top five Third World arms importers, Saudi Arabia, India, Afghanistan, Iran, and Thailand, whose arms transactions were worth $6.3 billion, accounting for over half of the Third World total. Two African states did rank among the top ten arms importers which included the above-mentioned five plus North Korea, Angola, Pakistan, South Korea, and Egypt; arms imports accounted for approximately 70 percent of the developing world market.

Since the Gulf war, the United States has maintained its position as the world's largest arms merchant, providing the Third World with billions of dol-lars of weapons. In 1991 the United States held on to its position by selling $15.2 billion worth of weapons, a 44-percent share of a shrinking global arms market. In recent years, both France and Russia have intensified their efforts in this market and are threatening to offer stiff competition to the United States as the world system enters the new millennium. The arms bazaar milieu of the 1980s and early 1990s has relaxed, in part as a result of the Asian economic and financial crisis, which has dampened nations' appetites for entering costly new deals. Sanctions have effectively shut out Libya and Iraq from conven-tional arms markets. Another factor has been the slump in crude oil prices, influencing Saudi Arabia's decision to slow its acquisition of new weapon sys-tems, particularly from the United States. Developing nations remained the pri-mary consumers of U.S. weaponry. Saudi Arabia, with $11 billion in new weapons delivered, and Taiwan, with $9.3 billion, were by a 10-fold factor the largest buyers among developing nations in 1997, far outstripping their nearest competitors, Egypt, Iran, and Kuwait.[44]

The Russian Republic has been struggling to sign new arms deals in order to earn hard currency. Increasingly, Third World nations are perceiving the Russians as unreliable suppliers because of their chronic economic problems. Russia's best customers are India, which bought 40 Russian fighters in 1997, and China, which purchased two destroyers. In 1990, Iran was a major buyer of Russian fighter jets, bombers, tanks, and submarines. Currently, Iran has ceased to be a major purchaser of Russian weapons as a result of U.S. pressure and its own economic problems. Russia delivered $2.7 billion of arms from 1990 to 1993, but $700 million from 1994 to 1997. China has replaced Russia as a major arms supplier to Iran. China's deliveries have also declined, from $1.8 billion from 1990 to 1993 to $800 million from 1994 to 1997. The Middle East prevails as the focal region for arms purchases in the post-Cold War era, and the Unites States continues as its most stable supplier. American allies in the region have received, among other weapons, 116 supersonic aircraft, 1,358 surface-to-air missiles, 1,332 tanks and self-propelled guns, and 72 helicopters in the last four years, according to a Congressional Research Service report. From 1990 to 1997 the U.S. signed contracts to sell $44.1 billion of weapons to the Middle East. France is in a position to overtake the U.S. as the region's biggest arms supplier, according to this report.[45]

Asia continues its distinction as the second largest regional market for conventional arms; Russian sales to India, China and Vietnam have given it the biggest share of arms-transfers agreements in the region. From 1994 to 1997 Russia concluded $29.6 billion in agreements with Asian nations, more than 40 percent of that market. During the 1990s, the United States dominated the conventional arms market to the Third World. The Congressional Research study shows that from 1990 to 1997, the U.S. delivered $53.4 billion of weapons to the Third World, far outstripping Britain, Russia, and France.[46]

At this juncture, the ideological justification for escalating conflicts in sub-Saharan Africa, Central America, the Caribbean, and the rest of the Third World beyond the Middle East and East Asia no longer exists. In the context of the new world order, several Third World regions are no longer part of the Great Powers alliance systems and their national security equations. At the United Nations, the nonaligned movement's votes are becoming less relevant in a world system with only one superpower and ideology, that is, democratic capitalism. Likewise, developing countries who joined the superpowers' coalitions during the Cold War era are also becoming less relevant to their former allies in a world system in which the interests of the Northeast and the Northwest are converging. However, while the justification for outside intervention in Third World affairs no longer exists, it is quite another matter whether or not the self-destructive conditions that fuel these conflicts will necessarily disappear. Benign neglect may prove just as malicious as outright intervention.

GORBACHEV'S NEW THINKING AND THIRD WORLD RADICALISM

The fall of the Berlin Wall on November 9, 1989, marked the end of the Cold War which had dominated the discourse of world politics since the end of the Second World War. Soviet dominion in Eastern and Central Europe began crumbling after 1989. The fall of the Berlin Wall ignited similar revolts and nationalist stirrings in Central Asia and the Soviet Union. A new revolution was brewing throughout the socialist bloc as people and nations struggled to be free. Borrowing from the pages of the African American civil rights movement, people from Latvia, Lithuania, and Russia initiated nonviolent direct action tactics challenging the legitimacy of the Communist Party. As these new freedom fighters marched on their respective capitals, they demanded freedom, self-determination, and sovereignty. By 1991 the walls surrounding the Communist bloc came tumbling down as a new wave of democratic capitalism and nationalism began to replace Marxist-Leninism. The new revolution in the Soviet bloc began in part as a response to President Mikhail Gorbachev's new thinking on economic and political restructuring. The processes of global restructuring that rendered the socialist economic policies ineffective for the unfolding microelectronics and information revolution contributed to the demand for change.

In the early 1980s, the Soviet Union stood by its commitments to defend antisystemic movements in the Third World, ranging from Cuba and Nicaragua in the Americas, to Angola, Ethiopia, and Mozambique on the African continent, to Afghanistan and Vietnam in the Far East and South Asia. The Soviets supported the antiapartheid movement in the Republic of South Africa and the anticolonial movement in Namibia as well as antisystemic forces in El Salvador. At the twenty-sixth Party Congress in 1981, neither the commitment to détente nor Soviet support to radical Third World states was questioned. Brezhnev committed Moscow to combating the new counterrevolution being launched by the Reagan administration. During the interim between Brezhnev's death in November 1982 and the election of Mikhail Gorbachev in February 1985, Soviet leadership was rethinking Moscow's role in Third World-oriented conflicts. President Yuri V. Andropov announced some initial steps toward reducing Moscow's exposure to Third World regional conflicts; however, he died before a number of these policy initiatives were implemented. With Gorbachev's rise to power in 1985, Soviet Third World policy underwent a dramatic transformation. During the first Reagan administration the conflict between the two superpowers in the Third World was so intense that it was virtually impossible to schedule any summits between these two antagonistic blocs. Since 1985 there have been several such gatherings between Washington and Moscow. In July 1991, the Soviets participated in the Group of Seven meeting for the first time. This momentous event came as result of meetings between President Bush and President Gorbachev. During this period Washington and Moscow laid the groundwork for a massive reduction in the arms race, conflict resolution with reference to Third World regional militarized disputes, and a comprehensive Middle East conference in the wake of the Gulf War of 1991. This new approach toward Third World regional conflict became known as international glasnost.

International glasnost involved a broad rejection of Soviet commitments to support antisystemic movements in the Third World that were supporting the cause of socialism. In the Soviets' new view, Third World regions constituted zones of instability and crisis where superpower confrontation had the potential of escalating into full-blown nuclear war, threatening the very survival of spaceship earth. Therefore, the greatest cost of Third World regional conflict was military rather than economic, although socialist regimes were becoming a fiscal burden by the mid-1980s. This state of affairs led Soviet leaders to seek resolution of a number of regional conflicts throughout the Third World. At this juncture, the Soviets entered a number of discussions through the United Nations that eventually led to the Soviet withdrawal from Afghanistan; a negotiated settlement among Angola's Marxist-Leninist government, UNITA, South Africa, and the United States; the Cuban departure from Southern Africa; and the independence of Namibia. Similar discussions took place over the civil war in Cambodia and other hot spots in the Third World. Washington and Moscow began reducing their arms transfers to the Third World with the exception of the Middle East.

This new collaboration between Washington and Moscow resulted in a dramatic decline in Soviet support for radical Third World antisystemic movements. The growing economic crisis in the Soviet Union as well as in Eastern and Central Europe reduced the ability of these actors to engage in global revolutionary reach in the developing world. The ideological and cultural division that once defined relations between the Northeast and the Northwest underwent a dramatic change in the 1980s. As the convergence of interests within the North moved forward, a new world order evolved redefining North-South relations. Gorbachev and his allies also developed new thinking about the historical and contemporary role of capitalism in economic development.

THE DEMISE OF THE NONCAPITALIST PATH TO DEVELOPMENT

Starting in the 1960s, Third World leaders were drawn to socialism as an alternative path to economic development. Initially, the socialist model was conceptualized as a plausible solution to the twin problems of development and industrialization with equity. Starting in the 1970s, a number of Third World states began to emulate the Marxist-Leninist theory and practice of development. This model supposedly offered new nations a variety of benefits: through nationalization of the means of production it allowed them to gain control over the commanding heights of their economies; through planning, it permitted the rational distribution of scarce resources to allow rapid socioeconomic development; its policy priorities permit a rapid improvement in the quality of life for all citizens, including the poorest; and education, health, and welfare provisions received high priority.[47] Authoritarian political structures also accompanied egalitarianism in the economic and social spheres. This model was very effective in material terms, offering a shortcut to modernization: the USSR claimed annual growth rates of 10 to 20 percent in the 1930s and 1950s. Accordingly, new industrial cities emerged from the bare ground in the Urals and the Far East; totally new industries evolved. Large-scale public works projects began; canals, railway lines, and roads were constructed; mines were sunk; power stations and dams to generate hydroelectricity were built to bring power to the economy.[48]

The Stalinist growth model was very successful in mastering relatively unsophisticated technologies and producing goods on a massive scale. The

Soviets were able to extract capital from the agricultural sector in the 1930s, which they then used to build up heavy industry. In the postwar era, when labor became plentiful, this model successfully mobilized resources in reconstructing a war-torn society.[49]

The Soviet Union also constructed a massive security state to protect its socialist experiment. Since the mid-1980s, the noncapitalist approach to development has been on the defensive as the People's Republic of China, Eastern European nations, and the Soviet Union have moved away from socialism. The massive security state of the Soviets became a shield for developing states' adopting socialist economic policies which was effective until the end of the Gulf War. The global economic crisis of the 1980s reduced the amount of foreign exchange that could be earned as their products became increasingly obsolete and the prices of their commodities declined significantly in the world economy.

During this cycle of global restructuring, the Soviet noncapitalist model of development sputtered as microelectronics emerged as the driving force behind the third industrial revolution. The authoritarian nature of the central planning apparatus in the Soviet Union reduced the capability of this society to respond to the technological revolution being unleashed in a changing information-based world economy. As computers and microchips have become not merely tools of production but integrated into products, the life cycles of goods become shorter. Many products and production processes are becoming obsolete in a few years.[50] In the age of personal computers, Soviet industries lost their ability to compete on a global scale. The ongoing technological revolution unleashed during this cycle of global restructuring also played a role in weakening the noncapitalist route to development.

Emerging Marxist-Leninist states in the Third World rejected any notion of externally generated growth or infusion of foreign capital, preferring instead to overcome underdevelopment and dependency by adopting a more self-reliant strategy. Third World Marxist-Leninist leaders proposed self-reliance rather than incorporation, autonomy rather than increased integration into the capitalist world economy. At the local level, self-reliance required restructuring domestic relations with an emphasis on rural development, a reduction in income inequality, and a decentralization of administration. Village management in China and the *Ujaama* movement in Tanzania were among the best and worst examples.[51] At the international level, self-reliance implies shifting economic interactions away from northern states, the multinational corporations, and the Western aid-giving agencies, thus cutting the ties of foreign penetration and dependence.

For some Third World states, self-reliance implied total withdrawal from the world market and a reduction of exports and imports (both goods and services) to a minimum.[52] Albania and Burma are examples of this extreme posture. Burmese political authorities ordered restrictions on domestic and foreign travel. Both countries have experienced economic stagnation as a result of adopting this policy option. The situation has grown so grave in Albania that people have fled by the thousands, seeking political and economic haven in Italy and other European nations.

The impracticality of totally withdrawing from the capitalist world economy was brought home to most of these actors in the 1980s. Angola's economic livelihood depends on foreign exchange payments that Gulf Oil of the United States makes for the petroleum produced in Cabinda. Cuban troops provided protection to this contested region in Angola until very recently. Angola began departing from socialist approaches to economic development in 1985. Collective farming lost its policy glitter as peasants resisted this foreign imposition, and agricultural productivity fell. Dos Santos increased Angola's ties with the West as the United States, Portugal, Brazil, France, and the Bahamas replaced the Soviet Union and Eastern Europe as Angola's chief economic partners. New policies were developed beginning in 1985 in order to improve the availability and quality of consumer goods and improve confidence in the rural areas. Following the Second Congress, Angola's leaders moved to adjust their socialist policies to Angolan realities. Angola made overtures to the West and joined the Lomé Convention.[53] Foreign investment was encouraged as the Congress moved to revamp its policies on such investments.[54]

Mozambique and Angola failed to consolidate their socialist experiment as a result of their continuing military engagement with rival forces supported by the Republic of South Africa. The Mozambique National Resistance (RENAMO), numbering over 10,000 fighters, received its training from South Africa and developed into a formidable war machine that terrorized citizens of Mozambique throughout most of the 1980s. In 1984, faced with disorder and widespread anarchy, Samora Machel signed the Nkomati Accord. Mozambique agreed to cease providing support and sanctuary to the African National Congress (ANC).[55] In exchange Pretoria agreed to cease supporting and arming RENAMO. Mozambique's leaders have also joined the Lomé Convention and have attempted to increase economic intercourse with the West.

The self-reliance model adopted in Tanzania had its problems as well. Former President Julius Nyerere declared in 1977 that "Tanzania is neither socialist nor self-reliant . . . Our nation is still economically dependent. . . the goal of socialism is not even in sight."[56] After ten years of self-reliance Tanzania had not achieved economic independence. Robert Mugabe and his ruling party still conceptualized socialism as a long-term goal, but borrowed from the Soviet Union's New Economic Policy of the 1920s and provided support to peasant farmers who preferred private ownership of the means of production. Likewise, Zimbabwe's leaders decided against nationalizing either the agricultural or the industrial base in this society. Nevertheless, the economic crisis of the 1980s forced the leadership to seek relief from the IMF, thus reinforcing this actor's position in the capitalist world economy. Third World states opting for the socialist or self-reliant model of development found themselves on the defensive as their economies stagnated and the global economic crisis increased misery in their societies. Starting in the 1980s, several Third World states operating within the socialist camp faced chronic economic problems and even food shortages as a result of economic isolation, wars, and policy blunders.[57]

Throughout the 1980s the downturn in the world economy and the accompanying fall in the price of commodities resulted in an economic nightmare for most of the Third World states opting for the socialist model. These states could no longer count on the Socialist bloc for the economic aid and technical assistance required by their economies in order to survive in a world hostile to nontraditional economic experiments. Abandoned by their traditional supporters in the Soviet bloc, these socialist nations experienced the pains of the global economic crisis and a new thinking toward Third World capitalism.

The noncapitalist path to development encountered a number of bottlenecks in the Eastern bloc during the 1960s and 1970s. Premier Khrushchev sought to inject life into the Northeast by promoting intra-Comecon trade. At this juncture, greater policy coordination, standardization of industrial products, emphasis on long-term trade agreements, establishment of an international bank for socialist countries, and increased specialization and division of labor among Comecon countries became primary objectives to complement the expansion of trade. The results were disappointing because of the persistence of a previous bias toward economic self-sufficiency, rigid central planning instead of reliance on the market, scarcity of goods, and poor quality of those available.

In the 1970s the Soviet Union and Eastern European nations sought access to Western markets for capital and technology. Most Eastern bloc countries (including the Soviet Union) faced the problems of currency inconvertibility in their trade with the West. Socialist governments' fiscal policies and limited participation of these states in the world economy contributed to currency incompatibility between East and West. During the 1970s, this situation changed for most Eastern European nations as they began to borrow from the West. By the end of the 1970s the Eastern bloc debt to the West was in excess of $50 billion.[58]

In the past, the Soviet Union had allowed some tinkering around the edges of the socialist system. Socialist experiments took place in Hungary in 1968, the People's Republic of China in 1978 and the former Soviet Union in 1986. Side by side with the introduction of market mechanisms, a number of Eastern European nations experimented with cooperative and private enterprises and experienced some degree of success. These actors have pursued their goal of trying attract foreign capital as a means of acquiring managerial expertise and advanced industrial technology.[59] The advent of these experiments in the Soviet bloc undermined the long-term survival of the noncapitalist model of development.

Eastern Europe has been undergoing a profound political and economic revolution since 1988. The logic of socialism and the politics of communism are being abandoned for democratic capitalism. Dramatic structural transformation in this zone of the world system took place in 1989 as the German Democratic Republic, Czechoslovakia, Bulgaria, and Rumania followed the lead of radical reformist countries such as Poland and Hungary. Mongolia also began to experiment with democratic political procedures. In country after country, the Communist Party lost its constitutional monopoly on power, and new parties emerged to participate in the first freely contested elections since the 1940s. The result in a number of places was the resounding defeat of the Communist Party, while in other cases the party split and changed its name, as a means of symbolically separating itself from the past.[60] Toward the end of 1989, the Berlin Wall came tumbling down as the East Germans were unable to stop the flood of dissidents trying to escape the economic wretchedness brought on by their failed socialist experiment.

THE END OF THE SOVIET EMPIRE, 1989–1991

In 1989 the German Democratic Republic became part of the Federal Republic of Germany. Poland moved toward implementing a market economy, Hungary abandoned the Communist Party and the remnants of socialism, and even Russia made overtures toward a market economy and applied for membership in the IMF. Yugoslavia and Russia are being threatened from within by ethnic nationalist forces seeking self-determination and sovereignty. As the Russians make the transition to a market economy, the ruble will become a convertible currency. The People's Republic of China crushed its youthful democratic movement, thus supporting the status quo. Communists in North Korea, Cuba, and Vietnam did not retreat from orthodox Marxist-Leninism. Nevertheless, socialism is in full retreat and on the defensive in this era of global restructuring. As the East and West continue to wither away, the interests of the Northeast and Northwest continue to intersect and the world system becomes more polarized along economic, cultural, and racial lines.

This retreat of the socialist bloc reinforces the new thinking on the role of capitalism in the Third World. During the Cold War, the socialist bloc encouraged Marxist-Leninist states in the Third World to maintain their ties with the industrial market economies, and advised them to rely on these actors for trade, aid, and technology. First, Gorbachev and his chief theoreticians argued that modern capitalism is not necessarily antithetical to socialism and, under the proper conditions, may coexist with it. Second, capitalism can develop in the Third World, and may do better than a misplaced conception of socialism, for which the Third World has not reached the proper phase of development. Third, he urged Third World socialist states and other developing countries not to exit from the capitalist world economy, which provides an array of technological and trading opportunities. Fourth, Russia and the East European nations enhanced their ties with the capitalist world, as these former socialist states sought to jump-start their economies. They wanted their economies to benefit from the ongoing technological revolution during this era of global restructuring. Fifth, Third World antisystemic movements did not contribute to national security At this juncture, these movements had become an unnecessary economic burden.[61] Russia dramatically reduced its support to Third World radical regimes and to traditional allies in the South, including the Cubans. Nevertheless, a number of groups in Russia opposed the domestic and foreign policy changes introduced by former Premier Gorbachev. The military industrial complex in the Soviet Union and hard-liners in the Communist Party stood to be the greatest losers from these new policies. Gorbachev began moderating his liberalization in an effort to restore stability and appease the hard-liners. Nevertheless, these moves failed to satisfy the hard-liners, and they organized a coup in August 1991 to oust the Russian leader from power, with support from elements in the military and the KGB. The coup leaders seized power on August 17, 1991, in order to prevent Gorbachev from signing a pact granting the Soviet Republics more autonomy and independence. Coup leaders also sought to halt the movement toward a market economy and democracy. Gorbachev and his family were placed under house arrest, protest meetings became illegal, independent newspapers ceased to operate, and troops were put on alert in Moscow. Boris Yeltsin, who was president of the Russian Soviet Federated Socialist Republic (RSFSR), refused to recognize the legitimacy of the coup leaders and mobilized Soviet citizens against the plotters. The Soviet people opposed the coup and wanted to continue the democratic experiment. Soviet citizens became human cannons in the struggle to continue down the road to democracy. The military became divided and refused to take orders from the coup leaders. By the end of the week, the coup leaders faced arrest, and Gorbachev returned to power. The failed coup propelled the democratic movement to new heights as the Union of Soviet Socialist Republics began to disintegrate. From the Baltic states of Estonia, Latvia, and Lithuania to the republics of Armenia, Kazakhstan, and Uzbekistan, new nations struggled to be born.

The disintegration of the Soviet empire marked the final episode of the third wave of decolonization that began with the withdrawal of Eastern Europe from the Soviet bloc. People in Eastern Europe, the Russian Republic, and the emerging republics in Central Asia and elsewhere were seeking the benefits of democracy and market capitalism. The Communist Party was barred from political activities, and many symbols of Bolshevism faced attack. Traditional ideologies of communism and socialism lost legitimacy as the Soviet people sought alternative policies to solve their problems. By December 1991, Boris Yeltsin had taken over the mantle of leadership from Gorbachev. The Soviet Union continued to disintegrate into eleven new nation-states. A commonwealth of nations has replaced the Soviet Union as nationalism and self-determination have unraveled an imposing socialist fraternity of states. Gorbachev is no longer a power broker in the new Russian Republic. However, the revolution he unleashed is still unfolding, beckoning the Second World toward the ideological and cultural logic of democratic capitalism as we enter the twenty-first century. The city of Leningrad has changed its name back to St. Petersburg, and other symbols of Bolshevism and communism are under attack.

The new Russian Republic, the Commonwealth of Independent States, and the former Warsaw Pact nations are impressed by the spectacular economic performance of the developing states of the Third World semiperiphery and Japan over the last twenty years. These successful, dynamic economies of the late twentieth centuries have never subscribed to *laissez faire* or a simple free market doctrine as espoused by Margaret Thatcher and Milton Friedman. Japan, South Korea, and other economically vigorous semiperipheral states are following the model of the export promotion industrial policy to achieve economic growth during this cycle of global restructuring. The instruments that safeguard social health are largely cultural, but the state has played a critical role in targeting societal developmental efforts.[62] The former Soviet bloc has come to the conclusion that access to Western capital and technology can help Second and Third World nations resolve their economic woes. The jury is still out on the transformation of Russia from an authoritarian political system and command market to a democratic and free market society. The question still remains, will the Russians adopt American-style *laissez faire*, export promotion industrial policy as practiced in East Asia, or continue a modified command economy? Will the struggle over economic reform and the introduction of a free market intensify the conflicts within Russia and contribute to further political instability? Since Yeltsin's ascension to power in 1991, the new Russian Republic has been engaged in a struggle over the pace of political and economic reform.

On December 12, 1993, the Russian Republic held its first parliamentary election in the post-Soviet era. The election result did not provide President Boris Yeltsin the landslide victory that he had hoped would give him a national consensus to end the gridlock over political and economic reform. Vladimir Zhirinovsky, leader of the ultranationalist Liberal Party, received more votes but won fewer seats than the pro-reform Russia's Choice party in this critical election. The preliminary results gave the Liberal Democratic Party 22% of the vote, Russia's Choice 20%, Yabloko 11%, the Communist Party 9.5%, Women of Russia 8.0%, Agrarian Party 7.0%, Party of Russian Unity 6.5%, and Democratic Party of Russia 6.0%.[63] Russia remains divided over the political reforms to be undertaken and the speed with which to create a free market economy. Most analysts of the Russian vote attribute Zhirinovsky's success to his appeal to those Russians who have lost from the reduction of state subsidies and gain nothing from the introduction of market forces. Zhirinovsky also received support from the armed forces, from people living on the periphery of the Russian Republic (coal miners in the Arctic circle) where state subsidy for economic activity continues as an instrument of public policy, and from people who live in the rust bowls of Russia.[64] Mr. Zhirinovsky assured them that their economic nightmare was over. The composition of the new parliament includes ultra-nationalists, Communists, reformers and independents. President Boris Yeltsin had a difficult task in balancing these competing forces and forging a pro-reform coalition.

The Russian people approved the new constitution, thus giving the president greater flexibility in his dealings with a recalcitrant parliament. The new constitution creates a strong presidential government, granting the executive branch power of appointments and policymaking, subject to confirmation by parliament. In the case of discord, the president has the greater power, because he can employ decrees, directives, as well as call referendums, without legislative intervention. The constitution also gives the president power to define the basic domestic and foreign policy guidelines and to appoint a prime minister. The lower house, or state Duma, may reject the president's choice of premier, but if it does so three times the president must dissolve the Duma and call a new election.[65] The Constitutional Courts have the important task of interpreting and protecting the constitution. Judges are appointed for life, giving the judiciary political independence from the parliament and the president. Only time will provide the empirical evidence as to how independent Russia's judiciaries are from political interference and manipulation from the other branches of government.

Resurgence of Russian nationalism ignited fear throughout the commonwealth of new states. During the first few months of 1994, President Clinton proposed associate membership in NATO to the former Warsaw Pact nations who feared Zhirinovsky's call for restoring the Soviet empire. The Russians lobbied for associate status for the new Russian Republic as a way of alleviating the fears of its neighbors.

Since 1991 the new Russian republic has been undergoing a double transition. The Russians are pursuing democratization and the creation of a market economy. They have encountered a number of obstacles in this dual transition process. On December 17, 1995, state Duma elections were held and participating parties had to pass a 5% threshold in order to earn proportionate share of the 225 seats in the Duma. The results were Communist Party of Russian Federation 22.3% of the vote, Liberal Democratic Party of Russia 11.2%, Our Home Is Russia 10.1%, Yabloko Bloc 6.9%. The distribution of Duma seats by party affiliation were Communist Party of the Russian Federation 157, Independents 78, Our Home Is Russia 55, Liberal Democratic Party of Russia 52, Yabloko Bloc 45, Agrarian Party of Russia 20, Russia's Democratic Choice 9, Power to the People 9, Congress of Russian Communities 5, Forward! Russia 3, Women of Russia 3, and other parties 15. Most of the Duma members were opposed to the economic reforms outlined by President Boris Yeltsin. The political climate in Russia became increasingly antagonistic as Russians debated the benefits of the transition to a market economy and the disappearance of a social net. The presidential elections of 1996 became another critical battlefield between those who desired to return to the old system and those who wanted to construct a democratic and capitalistic Russian republic.

On June 17, 1996, the Russian Republic held its first presidential election under the new constitution. After the General Election Committee had completed processing the first-round votes, Boris Yeltsin had won 35.1 percent, Gennady Zyuganov 32.0 percent, and Alexander Lebed 14.7 percent. The other candidates were less convincing, but the liberal reformer Grigory Yavlinsky had attracted more votes — 7.4 percent — than the ultranationalist firebrand Vladimir Zhirinovsky, who had 5.8 percent of the votes.[66]

During his campaign for the presidency, Yeltsin used social spending to undermine the challenge of Zyuganov. Between March and May 1996, the central bank had to issue more than 25 billion rubles, and sell $3 billion of its reserves to support the ruble. Moscow's budget deficit accelerated to 9.6 percent of GDP in April, from 5 percent in the first quarter. Another 8 trillion rubles had to be paid out in inflation compensation to depositors of Sberbank, Russia's largest savings bank, and for wages and aid to teachers. Electoral politics also softened the federal government's resolve to collect taxes, and enterprises underpaid a total of 75 trillion rubles ($15 billion) in the first six months.[67]

General Alexander Lebed's performance surprised most observers of Russian politics. After he gave his support to Yeltsin in the second round, communist defeat was inevitable. In the second and final round of the presidential election, Yeltsin received 54 percent of the votes, Zyuganov 40 percent. Six percent checked off "none of the above." The Russian Republic had reached a turning point on the road to democracy and a market economy. The Russian people had voted for continuation of a dual transition.

Starting in December 1993, the political arena in Russia stabilized as politicians prepared for parliamentary and presidential elections in 1995 and 1996, respectively. Moscow returned to the good graces of the IMF thereafter, with the reduction of its budget deficit and stabilization of the ruble. In a key indicator of international confidence in the Russian economy, capital has been flooding back into the country in significant quantities throughout most of the 90s. The economic reform is moving forward as Russia continues to make the transition from communism towards a market economy. This change in Russian international financial status began in the spring of 1995 as the Russians liberalized the rules governing foreign exchange transactions. Western economists estimate that Russia's foreign exchange reserves are back up to $10 billion, from $2.5 billion at the beginning of 1995.[68]

Since 1996, Russia has had a bumpy road toward a market economy. The Russian financial ministry has had a difficult time achieving the goals laid out by the IMF. President Yeltsin and the Duma intensified their conflict over the pace of economic and financial reforms. The economic status of average citizens in Russia continues to worsen. The IMF and the Group of Seven have been less than enthusiastic about Moscow's progress. The Russian federation has arrived at an important fork in the road. It can continue on the road toward market economy or make a decisive change toward corporatism. We will examine this dilemma in the last chapter on globalization, democratization, and transitions in the world system.

A NEW WORLD ORDER OR A RETURN TO ANARCHY?

Increasingly the lines of demarcation between domestic and foreign policy are becoming blurred, especially when states break down and civil society ceases to function, leading to the intervention of regional states and international and regional organizations. The breakdown of civil society in such diverse areas as Haiti, Somalia, the Sudan, Angola, and former Yugoslavia are a few examples of this growing trend toward the disintegration of civil society in the world system. The Bush administration had proclaimed a new world order as a result of the U.S.-led multinational-force victory in the Gulf War. He envisioned Western-style democracy, a market economy, and increased convergence of interest between the Northeast and Northwest as the remedy to societal ills inflicting "failed societies." Failed societies are nations in which civil society has broken down and the state ceases to provide both security and political order. Haiti, Somalia, and Yugoslavia emerged as important laboratory studies for U.S. policy makers's new adventures into nation-building and state-restoration in the post Cold War era.

Fragmentation of the State and the Clash of Civilizations

Samuel Huntington contends that the clash of civilizations has replaced the conflict of interests between states as the deciding factor shaping post-Cold War international conflicts. According to Huntington,

> The rivalry of the superpowers is replaced by a clash of civilizations. In the New World order, the most pervasive, important and dangerous conflicts will not be between social classes, rich and poor, or other economically defined groups, but between people belonging to different cultural entities. . . . And the most dangerous cultural conflicts are those along the fault lines of civilizations.[69]

Huntington's classification of civilizations is problematical. He includes six to nine civilizations in the contemporary world system; they are Sinic (Chinese), Japanese, Hindu, Islamic, Western, Latin American, Buddhist, Orthodox, and African. Huntington is not very clear on his criteria for defining a civilization.

Nevertheless, even if we accept Huntington's taxonomy of civilization, there are serious gaps between this theory and the evidence when we examine recent international conflicts. The human

> torrent of foot-soldiers who perished in the Iraq-Iran war died in a conflict that occurred in a single civilization. . . . The genocide of the Tutsis by the Hutus was "intra-civilizational," as was Pol Pot's Cambodia. Even the First World War might aptly be described as a European civil war. At the same time, the Korean War and the Vietnam War were not civilizational or cultural conflicts;

they were strategic engagements between states, all of which justified their claims by invoking Western ideologies.[70]

At the moment, as in the past, wars are waged between peoples of different nationalities or ethnicities, not between members of different "civilizations." Whether sovereign states or irregular militias wage wars, the logic of military rivalry often compels coalitions that bring together different "civilizations." As John Gray has observed, "In the conflict between Armenia and Arzerbaijan, Iran has thrown in its lot with Christian Armenia, not with Islamic Arzerbaijan. The Byzantine kaleidoscope of shifting alliances in the Balkans and Central Asia offers no support for Huntington's grand theory."[71]

Disintegration of Yugoslavia

Starting in the 1990s, Yugoslavia became the battleground over competitive nationalism. People in power, fearing democracy could sweep them out of office, changed their allegiance from communism to nationalism. Slobodan Milosevic became the politician to exploit nationalist grievances. He began beating the Serbian nationalist drum in his bid to seize control of the Serbian branch of the Yugoslavian Communist party in 1987, leading to counternationalism in Croatia.[72] Counternationalism later developed in Bosnia and most recently among ethnic Albanians in Kosovo in direct response to the Serb nationalism that had its roots in the narcissism of minor differences that evolved in post-Cold War Yugoslavia.[73] We will define and expand this concept later.

The ethnic conflict between Serbia, Bosnia, and Herzegovina has all the features of the kinds of civil disputes that confront most Third World states. In the Third World where ethnic, communal, and religious communities feel insecure within their existing borders and are distrustful of political authorities, these domestic characteristics reinforce insecurity dilemmas facing these new nation-states. William Pfaff has argued that the very idea of an ethnic nation is a permanent provocation to war. This conceptualization of the nation-state (or state-nation) makes spies and prospective dissidents of those who have the misfortune of living outside the shifting boundaries identified with their nationality, inviting their oppression by the people among whom they live, and rationalizing national expansion by governments to which they are ethnically attached.[74]

Zaki Laidi has identified the breakup of the Soviet Union (the Soviet Empire as well as the Federation of Socialist states) and fear (ethnic hegemony) as two of the motivating forces that contributed to the decomposition of the Yugoslavian State. The phenomenon of contagion-panic was a critical ingredient that propelled the decomposition of the state. Political contagion from the former Soviet Union made it futile and false to imagine the continuation of the multi-ethnic Yugoslavian Federation. In a word, the dissolution of the Yugoslavian Federation was anticipated in many quarters within the bodies politic. If the conflagration of antagonism were kindled first in Slovenia when they had been predicted in Kosovo, it was precisely because the Slovenians – economically advanced and more ethnically homogeneous – anticipated the breakup. They disconnected themselves from the Yugoslavian Federation out of apprehension over the consequences of rupture. In stark contrast, the Bosnians who could not afford the economic cost of independence sought to maintain the federation. It was only after the survival of Yugoslavia became impossible that the fear of bearing the cost of Serbia-Croat disintegration forced Bosnians to think of themselves as a nation, even as an Islamic nation. Their nationalism, like most in the post-Cold War era, is not "genetic" because it was a conception of Tito or some other authoritarian leader.[75]

Once the leader dies or the regime loses its capacity to employ violence in order to get compliance and legitimacy, it ceases to exists. As Michael Ignatieff has observed, Communist regimes everywhere have shown no capacity to sustain electoral or political legitimacy once they loose their capacity to intimidate the population.[76] He contends that there is no other principle of legitimacy beyond nationalism for post-communist leaders to employ in order to stay in power and arrest reform and democratic revolution. He asserts that there is no other language that is capable of mobilizing people around a common project. The liberal alternative – which envisions Yugoslavia's peoples as equal juridical subjects, as citizens with an attachment of shared procedures, and the rule of law and democratic accountability – is inoperative as a principle of mobilization. After fifty years communist political rhetoric has discredited this bourgeois definition of democracy. In the space of three, five, and nine years, depending on the location of the "ethnic cleansing" (Croatia, Slovenia, Bosnia, and more recently, Kosovo), Milosevic has repressed development of the nation-state, setting it back 400 years, to the late feudal world before the European nation began. In this time period he has caused the state to retrogress from civilization – interethnic tolerance and accommodation – to barbarism.[77]

After reviewing the factors that contributed to the dismemberment of the Yugoslavian Federation, Michael Ignatieff asks the pivotal question concerning the Serbs:

> How did they began to conceive of their differences, which were always present, as being identities that seal them from everyone else in their midst? How did they begin to think of themselves as Serbs, above all else, Croats, above all else?

He declared

> that these were people who shared a common life, language, physical appearance, and a great deal of history. For approximately fifty years, being a Serb

or Croat, or Bosnian took second place to being a Yugoslav; sometimes it took third or fourth place to being a worker or mother or any other of the identities that constitute the multiple compass of our belonging. Hence, nationalism is a fabrication of identity, because it denies the multiple character of belonging, privileging one over others. For that reason how does this invention of the primacy of national identity manage to displace other identities?[78]

At this juncture, we come face to face with the fundamental contradictions that make nationalism problematic in the post-Cold War era. Nationalism in this context is not grounded in the quest for a clearly defined identity, easily available and directly operational. It is based rather on what Freud calls the "narcissism of small differences," that is to say, the glorification of anything that disconnects us from someone historically close to us. The conflict, in this instance, is expressed not so much in an unconquerable hostility as in the promotion of differences. This is what Samuel Huntington failed to acknowledge when he raised the convenient specter of the clash of civilizations.[79] Michael Ignatieff has observed that the forces of globalization have resulted in the integration of economies and culture, thus blurring the boundaries between societies. At the same time, the forces of globalization have magnified the caustic and violent fragmentation of identities. As consumption patterns and lifestyles converge among human groups, people insist ever more violently on the marginal differences that divide them.[80]

During the post-Cold War era, this militarized dispute received very little attention from Washington, Moscow, and most of Europe until the civilian casualties and war damage began to dominate the news. Unlike Kuwait, this zone of the world system does not possess any commodities such as oil that are vital to the world economy. Hence, the Great Powers and the lone superpower did not find it in their interest to get involved militarily in this protracted civil war. The U.S. and NATO allies failed to adopt any military or diplomatic initiative to resolve ethnic conflicts and prevent the disintegration of Yugoslavia.

Adam Zwass has observed that democracies have always had difficulties mobilizing their military potential (unless the risk is minimal as, say, in the case of the U.S. invasion of Grenada). This fact was reinforced not only by the United States' massive isolationist tendency following World War I up to the Japanese attack at Pearl Harbor. The trauma of Vietnam, the withdrawal of American forces after a suicide attack on U.S. marines in Lebanon, and the present unwillingness of all major democratic powers, except France, to engage in a land war in the former Yugoslavia attest to this tendency.[81] The United States military's recent departure from Somalia reinforced this inclination. At the same time, United States has faced difficulty in building consensus at home and abroad for forceful military intervention on the scale of the Gulf War.

The deployment of military force under U.S. leadership eventually led to the Dayton Accord. NATO, rather than the United Nations, sent a large military force to implement the Dayton peace agreement negotiated in 1996 between the parties. Nevertheless, distrust and antagonism still endure between the parties. Initially, NATO command took the position that it was not their duty to arrest key leaders accused of ordering ethnic cleansing and genocide. American troops, scheduled to come home in 1997, are still deployed as critical elements of the NATO forces. NATO has negotiated an agreement to maintain a military presence for awhile in order to restore legitimate political authority through a Bosnia-Serbia-Croatian federation. The restoration of democracy requires not only successful elections but also that the parties abide electoral results. The arrest of leaders who are accused of formulating and implementing ethnic cleansing is critical for restoration of political legitimacy. The issue of justice, human rights, and reconciliation between the adversaries remained unfulfilled. The Clinton administration and its NATO allies continued to go back and forth on the Mogadishu line between peace making and war making in conflict resolution. To date, they have refused to introduce ground troops into this conflict except as peacekeepers once an accord has been negotiated.

The militarized conflict (summer 1998) between the Serbs and the Kosovo Liberation Army over the fate of this province reinforced suspicion between the parties. The KLA sought independence and self-determination rather than to continue the road toward incorporation into "greater Serbia." The ethnic Albanians sincerely believed that NATO would rescue them if they failed to prevail in a war with the Serbs. Unlike Bosnia, where multi-ethnic life continued right through the war there, Kosovo — already riven by centuries of ethnic conflict and rivalry between Slavs and non-Slavs — was newly divided into two distinct and hostile cultures.[82]

The province of Kosovo has a population of approximately 2 million people with ethnic Albanians making up 90 percent of the population. The rise of the Kosovo Liberation Army in 1998 reflected a growing rejection of Rugova's peaceful resistance. Rugova had failed to secure any concessions from Milosevic and therefore more forceful action was required. The Serbs came to the conclusions that the KLA was a new challenge to their hegemony in the Kosovo province and the days of peaceful resistance were over. At this critical juncture, Milosevic faced armed radicals who resolved to seize independence rather than wait for it in the distant future. He embarked on a policy not only of destroying the KLA but also of destroying significant elements of the population that supported and protected the KLA. The mass murder of Albanians in the village of Racak in January 1999 was characteristic of this approach. The fighting intensified in 1998 and 1999 following, a government crackdown on rebel activities. Serbian forces replayed what happened in Bosnia and Croatia. The army acted first, and then Serbian citizens were armed in order to keep other ethnic groups from returning to the areas under dispute. However, Warren Zimmerman has observed that Milosevic intended to destroy the KLA and any resistance to his conception of Kosovo as part of Greater Serbia.

The dilemma in Kosovo inspired a decisive final solution for Milosevic. He not only sought to destroy the hydra's heads; he would destroy the beast altogether. If he failed to repopulate the province with Serbs, he would depopulate the Albanians. He was determined to get rid of the entire Albanian population of Kosovo. Again, the entire policy rested on forceful expulsion, requiring ethnic cleansing of cities and villages initiated through targeted murder and assassination of KLA members and their supporters. According to Zimmerman, the massive expulsion and in some cases the mass murder of the Albanian population was not the result of NATO bombing, but was part and parcel of a Serb plan meticulously prepared months in advance of the bombing.[83] Milosevic is directly and indirectly responsible for all four Balkan wars during the 1990s. His crimes against humanity are more apparent in Kosovo than in his previous wars in Slovenia, Croatia, and Bosnia, where he masked his role.

NATO bombing of Serbia in response to human rights violations in the Kosovo province symbolizes the last war of one era and the beginning of another. As Vaclav Havel observed:

> Clearly, blind love of one's own country – a love that defers to nothing beyond itself, that excuses anything one's own state does only because it is one's own country, yet rejects everything else only because it is different – has necessarily become a dangerous anachronism, a source of conflict and, in extreme cases, of immense human suffering.[84]

It was a war that validated the growing ascendancy of globalization and the declining idea that states can do anything they want within their own borders. The idea of sanctity of state sovereignty is dead. The whole concept of state sovereignty, enshrined at the Peace of Westphalia more than 350 years ago, became absolute this century. In the past, foreign governments were recognized when they controlled their own territories, and they were granted the right to do anything within their borders as long as they did not infringe the borders of their neighbors. As R. C. Longworth has noted, "violations of frontiers were a cause of war, violations within frontiers were not."[85] On one side was Serbia fighting for territory, frontiers, and sovereignty in a world swallowed up by the forces of globalization where such concepts were in retreat. The Serbs' cause was driven by memories of 600-year-old defeats, of blood grievances against neighbors, of a belief that ancestral lands were too important to be shared with tribes speaking a different language or professing a different religion. On the other side was NATO, a multinational alliance of 19 nations that had agreed to share, to a greater or lesser degree, their defenses, which is one of the key attributes of national sovereignty. NATO said it fought for human rights, or to eradicate an infection from European body politics, or to protect its own credibility, or out of simple repugnance at the sight of Europeans being jammed into railway cars 55 years after that sort of thing was allegedly to have ended forever. At this critical juncture, NATO was not fighting for land, or conquest, or oil, or empire.[86] The last empire, the Soviet one, had recently expired, and no one had sought to embark on a new project of empire building. The forces of globalization were transforming these primordial urges, as national borders became increasingly meaningless in a world of globalizing capitalism.

Nevertheless, we can not blame all of Serbia's problems on Milosevic. The Serbian people were given a choice during the past decade between the Balkan past and a European future. Three times, by voting for a Milosevic government, they chose the past. Nothing will change until the Serbs accept the enormity of their crimes and, like the Germans after the Second World War, opt for the new world, born of the end of the Cold War and the rise of the global economy. Although NATO bombing eventually led Milosevic to stop the war against the ethnic Albanians and to the withdrawal of Serbian troops from Kosovo, it has not ended the violence and counter-violence between these two ethnic communities. On July 24, 1999, fourteen Serbian farmers were killed in the deadliest attack since the war came to an end in June 1999. Approximately 80,000 of the estimated 200,000 Serbs living in Kosovo when NATO's bombing of Yugoslavia ended have departed since the alliance troops arrived in mid-June 1999. This tragedy will more than likely intensify Serb departures from Kosovo. To date, the soldiers have proved to be powerless to stop the violence against Serbs by ethnic Albanians. We still have not reached the "end of the nation-state constructed on the notion of national consciousness, i.e., the privileging of one ethnic or racial community culture over others." Franz Fanon warned us of the pitfalls of national consciousness in his celebrated book, *The Wretched of the Earth*. He observed, "National consciousness, instead of being the all-embracing crystallization of the innermost hopes of the whole people, instead of being the immediate and most obvious mobilization of the people, will be in any case only an empty shell, a crude and fragile travesty of what it might have been. . . . the nation is passed over for the race, and the tribe is preferred to the state."[87] His remarks were targeted primarily toward newly independent states of the Third World in the 1960s. His words resonate in the post-Cold War period and the era of globalization. At this juncture, we will turn our attention to Somalia where U.S. policy makers developed the Mogadishu line, delineating the policy not to commit American ground troops to ethnic-based conflicts.

Disintegration of Somalia

Former President Bush dispatched 28,000 marines and other troops in December 1992, to spearhead a multinational military force on a humanitarian mission aimed at opening up supply routes for food aid and wrestling control of the African state of Somalia from sparring warlords. The Somalia crisis was the result of a civil war that led to the fall of army dictator Mohamed Siad Barre in 1991. All factions in Somalia's internal conflict had employed starvation as a weapon, and by the time U.S. troops arrived, nearly 300,000 Somalis had died. Bush appointed Robert Oakley as special emissary to Somalia, and Marine Lt. General Robert B. Johnston as the leader of the intervention force. Major General Tony Zinni was appointed director of operations for the intervention forces during the first five months. Oakley, Johnston, and Zinni concluded that they had no choice but to establish relations with warlord General Mohamed Farah Aideed since he controlled most of Mogadishu, the Somali capital and the center of the U.S. operation. The three men attempted to implement an even-handed policy with respect to General Aideed and his competitors. The three men emphasized that they would not try to influence Somalia's form of government, or who the players would be. They made great efforts to make sure none of the factions would become ostracized.[88]

The Clinton administration came to power with the Somalia crisis already on the foreign policy agenda. Clinton envisioned the U.S. as an active participant in the post-Cold War world, with other nations, in promoting democracy and rescuing failed societies around the world. Somalia emerged as an important laboratory experiment where their theories of a new kind of peacekeeping mission would undergo testing. The Somalia experiment did not conform to their textbook hypothesis, as the U.S. and the United Nations increasingly became prisoners of the historical internal conflict. Adam Roberts observes that the Somali operation evolved without a clear overall purpose. The goal of feeding starving Somalis was soon confused with strategies to address the collapse of the state.[89]

The Clinton administration wanted to move quickly to reduce the size of the 28,000 troops and relinquish the responsibility of this operation to the United Nations. Policy makers in Washington welcomed the initial success as the first humanitarian phase had gone well; people were fed, inoculations were administered. Once the United Nations took control of the Somalia conflict, the Clinton administration paid little attention to this issue as a foreign policy issue and it receded to the back burner.

On March 26, 1993, the United Nations Security Council voted to extend the mission beyond feeding the hungry to include political reconciliation and helping Somalia reconstruct its national and regional institutions and civil administration. At the same time, Oakley departed Mogadishu with approximately 24,000 U.S. troops who were replaced by a multinational UN force. This change in policy led to attempts by United Nations officials to isolate General Mohamed Farah Aideed and freeze him out of reconciliation discussions. Retired Admiral Jonathan Howe, former deputy national security adviser to the Bush administration, was appointed as special representative of United Nations Secretary General Boutros Boutros-Ghali. Howe began working on an ambitious plan to disarm the warlords and to build grassroots regional councils to rule Somalia. These events did not sit well with General Aideed.

On June 5, 1993, Aideed forces attacked Pakistani peacekeeping troops, leaving twenty-four dead. The United States and the United Nations responded very quickly to this new crisis. On June 6, 1993, the Security Council, following a strong demand for justice by the Pakistani delegation, drafted and approved Resolution 837, demanding the arrest and trial of those responsible for the Pakistani deaths. By the middle of June, Admiral Howe placed a $25,000 bounty for the capture and arrest of General Mohamed Farah Aideed.

After the United Nations took over the Somalia operations in May 1993, the mission took a dramatic detour away from feeding the hungry to an armed conflict with the well-armed military forces in the capital's extensive streets. General Aideed's forces launched a major offensive against U.S.-led United Nations peacekeeping forces on October 3, 1993. As a result of this attack, 12 Americans were killed, 78 wounded, and others missing and held hostage. Brian Urquhart has observed that it is seldom recognized that the ill-fated raid by U.S. Rangers to capture General Muhammed Aideed in Mogadishu was conceived and commanded exclusively by the United States without the prior knowledge of the United Nations — or even senior U.S. officers in the UN headquarters in Mogadishu.[90] This event dramatically altered U.S. policy in this African nation, as President Clinton and his advisers began assessing the new situation in Somalia. On October 7, 1993, President Clinton declared that "it is not our job to rebuild Somalia's society, or even create a political process that can allow Somalia's clans to live and work in peace."[91] U.S. policy makers were abandoning the role of rebuilding "failed societies," especially when American national interest was not immediately at stake. After weeks of intensified conflict with General Aideed's military force that cost twenty-five American lives, President Clinton bowed to Congressional and public criticism by setting March 31, 1994, as the deadline for the departure of U.S. troops from Somalia. U.S. troops departed Somalia on schedule. The UN abandoned its main compound in Mogadishu to Somalia on February 1, 1995. The UN withdrew its last 8,000 troops with assistance from a U.S.-led multinational force that included 7,000 marines. The final withdrawal of UN forces was completed around March 6, 1995. At this juncture, U.S. policy makers abandoned "assertive multilateralism" through the United Nations.

Neither former President Bush nor President Clinton provided the U.S. public with real calculations of risk, cost, and potential loss of life that could arise with a humanitarian and nation-building project in nations where civil society ceases to exist and the state no longer functions. Both Bush and Clinton sought to mobilize the international community behind the banner of democracy and market economy. The United States lacks the resources to stay engaged in international affairs at the level and extent that it did during the Cold War. Borrowing from the Gulf War scenario, President Clinton sought to organize the United Nations as the international institution to foster nation-building and state restoration along democratic lines, introducing a market economy as well as recruiting others to help pay the expense for such operations.

Since the death of Muhammed Farah Aideed in August 1996, the violent conflict continues to afflict Somalia. The country is still divided into several warring factions. Hussein Aideed, a thirty-four-year-old former U.S. Marine, succeeded his father. The fighting escalated between Hussein Aideed and those of the three allied factions. President Daniel arap Moi of Kenya mediated peace talks between the factions in October 1996, when they agreed to end hostilities and remove road blocks and allow free movement of the people. This agreement faltered when the factions refused to remove the roadblocks, and Mr. Aideed insisted that he was the President of Somalia. Conflict between the various clans and sub-clans continue to poison politics in Somalia.

Increasingly the Great Powers are relying more on economic embargoes rather than armed intervention as an instrument of conflict resolution. During the Cold War, the United Nations employed economic embargoes in Zimbabwe and the Republic of South Africa. In both cases, the embargoes took a long time to compel these actors to change their policies and to return to the bargaining table in order to negotiate a peace agreement. The United States and its allies have intervened militarily in Third World states where their vital interests have been at stake, such as U.S., France, and Britain in Kuwait; the United States in Grenada and Panama; the British in the Falkland Islands; and the Israelis in Lebanon. These punitive operations have been successful in restoring order and protecting the vital interest of these powers.

Peace and Conflict Resolution in South Africa and the Middle East

In South Africa, Nelson Mandela and F. W. de Klerk successfully negotiated the end of apartheid and white minority rule. In December 1993 Mandela and de Klerk signed an agreement ending apartheid and ushering in a new era of multiracial democracy. The first multiracial and democratic elections were held April 27, 1994. Mandela and his associates aimed to create a unitary state rather than a federation which would give regional autonomy to the homelands and whites opposing the transition. Economic sanctions by the international community played a critical role in bringing the Nationalist party, the business community, the African National Congress, and other black liberation movements and political parties to the bargaining table in order to resolve this long-standing conflict. These protagonists were also influenced by the end of the Cold War and pressure from Washington and Moscow.

During April 27–29, 1994, South Africa held its first multi-racial elections for a new government to preside over the transition to a multi-racial democracy. F. W. de Klerk conceded the presidency to Nelson Mandela, acknowledging his defeat on May 3, 1993. The Mandela victory launched a new era in South African politics as black majority rule was finally achieved. Early voting projections indicated that the African National Council received 63.8 percent of the vote, and was trailed by the Nationalist Party which was led by F. W. de Klerk, at 23.0 percent, followed by the Inkatha Freedom Party led by Mangosuthu G. Buthelezi, with 5.8 percent of the vote, while the Freedom Front tallied 2.8 percent of the vote and other parties received 4.6 percent of the vote.[92]

Mandela invited F. W. de Klerk and Mangosuthu G. Buthelezi to join his cabinet as he initiated an era of racial reconciliation. President Nelson Mandela and his new government faced an awesome task in achieving political, economic, and social reconstruction of South Africa.

From 1994 to 1999 Nelson Mandela governed South Africa's transition to a multiracial democracy. He was successful in creating a new constitution in 1996. Under his leadership, ANC was able to win over support from the local and international business communities. However, the transition was marred by increased crime and violence related to crime. The status of the black majority did not improve substantially in the economic arena. The middle class did see some small growth in its membership and wealth. The status of the black majority is an important concern for Thabo Mbeki's administration which took over the reins of power following his electoral victory in June 1999. Mbeki served as Deputy President from 1994 to 1999, running the day-to-day governmental operations. Lacking the charisma of his predecessor, Mbeki will need political skills and a good economy to lead South Africa into the new millennium and hold back the pent-up demands of the black majority.

The Israelis and Palestinians reached an agreement in September 1993 to end their historic political and religious conflict. Yassir Arafat, leader of the Palestine Liberation Organization, and Yitzhak Rabin, the Prime Minister of Israel, signed an agreement on September 13, 1993, in Washington D.C., which was to grant the Palestinians autonomy and end the Israeli occupation of the West Bank and Gaza Strip. The Israelis were scheduled to turn over administrative and policing duties over the West Bank and Gaza Strip to the Palestine Liberation Organization on December 12, 1993, but violence by extreme groups on both sides and other disagreements led to postponement of the Israelis' release of their jurisdiction. Starting in December 1993 negotiations continued between the Israelis and Palestinians over the remaining thorny issues.

A new chapter was unfolding in the Middle East as Palestinians and Israelis made the difficult transition from crisis to reconciliation. Palestinian self-rule in the Gaza Strip and the Jericho region of the West Bank removed a primary source of tension in Arab-Jewish relations. The Middle East conflict had become a zero-sum game for both sides. Rabin and Peres embarked upon a peace initiative with the Palestinians that became the Oslo agreement. The Oslo agreement unleashed a wave of optimism that was unprecedented in this region. The assassination of Prime Minister Yitzhak Rabin and other acts of terror on both sides undermined the delicate steps toward peace. In May 1996, Peres was narrowly defeated by Benyamin Netanyahu. Under Prime Minister Netanyahu's leadership, the peace process ground to a halt as a result of bellicose policies toward the Palestinians. Jewish settlements are increasing in Jerusalem and in other vital sites. Prodding by the United States has not been adequate enough to return the peace process to the fast track. Deterioration of the Middle East peace process provides fodder for Hamas and other groups opposed to the peace agreement. In order for the Palestinians to achieve any degree of success they will also need financial support from the international community. Without economic and financial support Palestinian self-rule is doomed to failure.

The peace process in the Middle East became increasingly entangled in a web of mutual distrust between these historical adversaries. The Israelis found a number of Palestinian violations to prevent further steps toward reconciliation under the leadership of Prime Minister Netanyahu. The Wye Peace Accord of October 1998 did not prevent the peace process from becoming hostage to Israeli politics. The Netanyahu governing coalition crumbled following the "historic Wye Peace Accord," which swapped land for peace.

During the May 1999 elections, the Israelis elected Ehud Barak as the new Prime Minister by a vote of 58 percent, a huge majority by Israeli standards. He has put together a broad coalition that will provide support for making peace with the Palestinians and his Arab neighbors. During the month of July 1999, he made trips to the Middle East and the United States. His trips have reinvigorated the prospect for peace in the region. A new chapter is unfolding in this troubled region.

While the combatants in the volatile regions of the Middle East and South Africa are at least at the bargaining table and making some bold steps toward resolving their historic conflicts, ethnic, communal, and religious antagonism is ripping nations apart in other zones of the world system. At the present, political conflict in Somalia and Bosnia are being replicated in different guises in other regions as diverse as the Middle East – Egypt, Azerbaijan, Turkey, Afghanistan, and Tajikistan; Africa south of the Sahara – Mauritania, Senegal, Liberia, Mali, Togo, Nigeria, Chad, Djibouti, Uganda, Burundi, Kenya, Rwanda, the Sudan, and Zaire (Congo); Asia – Pakistan, India, Bhutan, Sri Lanka, Bangladesh, Myanmar, China, Cambodia, the Philippines, and Indonesia; and Latin America – Guatemala, Colombia, Peru, Brazil, and more recently, Mexico. The resurgence of ethnic, religious, communal, and political conflict in the world system undermines the notion that a new world order has come forth. We can also question the proposition that we have reached the end of history, as a number of regions confront the collapse of the state and the rise in ethnic, religious, and communal conflicts. The Angolan civil war resumed as Savimbi refused to acknowledge the results of the democratic election. Civil war that spread to Liberia and Sierra Leone in the early and middle 1990s began to wind down as the new millennium approached.

Leaders in the Northeast and Northwest concluded that with the end of the Cold War, Great Powers consensus would enhance the peacekeeping capabilities of the United Nations Security Council. The Second Gulf War of 1991–92 became the operative scenario for conflict resolution of volatile militarized disputes in the new world order. These leaders concluded that peacekeeping by the world body would enjoy broad international support, and conflict resolution would be easier to accomplish in the post-Cold War era. The

United Nations operated five peacekeeping engagements in 1987 with a combined manpower of 10,000 soldiers and an annual budget of $233 million. In 1993 the United Nations had 18 peacekeeping operations, and deployed some 75,000 troops at an annual cost of more than $3.1 billion. These post-Cold War operations are more dangerous and complex than classical peacekeeping, in which the United Nations forces supervised an agreed-upon truce, giving political leaders time to settle the dispute through peaceful means.[93]

Increasingly, post-Cold War peacekeeping forces are intervening directly by disarming guerrillas, monitoring elections, or escorting relief convoys, activities that might compromise their impartiality. Following the Somalia fiasco in October 1993, U.S. policy makers are retreating from "assertive multilateralism" through the United Nations Security Council's conflict resolution apparatus and have announced a new unsigned presidential directive outlining the parameters of what constitutes a threat to international peace and security. This new directive calls for United Nations Security Council intervention to include one or more combinations of the following scenarios: international aggression, a humanitarian disaster coupled with violence requiring urgent action, a sudden and unexpected interruption of an established democracy, or gross violation of human rights coupled with violence or the threat thereof.[94] U.S. policy makers also made it clear that when the Security Council intervenes in risky missions, Washington will increasingly require American officers in overall command or near the top of the command.

Starting in early summer of 1994, the American policy of avoiding any significant risk in UN operations had taken hold, and the Security Council not only refused to strengthen UN forces in Rwanda (April 1994) but timidly reduced it. This action laid the groundwork for the international community's inability to stop the genocidal violence that followed.

Many member states blamed United Nations Secretary General Boutros Boutros-Ghali for transforming UN Peacekeeping policy to peaceful enforcement. These actors are concerned about UN forces' employing military force in an early stage of military disputes before conflict resolution is achieved. These actors were critical of the Secretary General's lack of criteria for divining which conflicts are real threats to international peace and security. Britain's Foreign Secretary Douglas Hurd went further, arguing that conflicts in Bosnia, Somalia, the Sudan, and Angola are not real threats to international peace but just "tragedies" that did not require United Nations intervention.[95] This sentiment also reflects the extent to which the New World order is unable to tame the flames of ethnic violence. States in the Northeast and Northwest are moving toward a new international regime with reference to ethnic violence. The Kosovo conflict played an important role in eliminating the United Nations' doctrine on the sanctity of state sovereignty when states violate their citizens' human rights.

Initially, the new world order renewed the Northwest's confidence that the United Nations could be employed as an instrument of peace and conflict resolution under the leadership of the lone superpower – the United States. However, this international institution was plagued by the lack of consensus among the Great Powers, conflict over how best to deploy UN peacekeeping forces, and who should pay for these forces. At the same time, policymakers in the U.S. were blinded by their success in the Gulf War against Iraq. In recent international conflicts, it proved very difficult to generate global consensus. Although the United Nations enjoyed the fruits of victory in Angola, Cambodia, Mozambique, Namibia, and South Africa, its failures in Somalia, Bosnia, and Serbia undermined its legitimacy. The Russian and Chinese veto has undermined the capacity to employ the Security Council as an instrument of peace. The United Nations' operations engagements have always depended on consensus and support of the Great Powers. Domestic critics in the United States Congress used their opposition to the United Nations' activist policy as an excuse not to pay the United States' outstanding debt unless fundamental changes were made. U.S. debt to the United Nations stands at $1.3 billion. United Nations Secretary General Boutros Boutros-Gali became a sacrificial lamb for U.S. domestic critics of this international institution. The Clinton administration opposed the re-election of Boutros Boutros-Gali, whom critics blamed as the architect of a more interventionist policy. The United States threatened to employ its veto to sustain opposition to the Boutros-Gali's reelection. In December 1996, Kofi Anam of Ghana became the new United Nations Secretary General. In June 1999 the United States Congress finally passed the necessary legislation authorizing the U.S. government to pay its back dues to the United Nations. This action followed a threat to not allow the U.S. to have a vote in this international institution.

THE THIRD WORLD IN INTERNATIONAL INSTITUTIONS

With many Third World states gaining their sovereignty in Africa, Asia, South America, and the Caribbean in the 1950s, the United Nations General Assembly began to increase in size. For the Third World states, the United Nations became the preferred political area for fighting the battle against apartheid policies in South Africa and against colonialism. Third World leaders sought to make economic development a major agenda item in international institutions. These leaders also sought to challenge the decision-making apparatus in international institutions, employing the geographical representation concept as a mechanism to challenge northern predominance in international institutions. These actors also attempted to employ the "one man, one vote" formula as an answer to the North-South conflict over the structure of decision making in international institutions.

The United States and the industrial democracies gave in to the notion of geographical representation in international institutions. However, exceptions were made with reference to the International Monetary Fund (IMF), the World Bank, the General Agreement on Tariffs and Trade (GATT), the United

Nations Security Council, and the Governing Board of the International Labor Organization. The United States and the industrial democracies operated on the premise that those actors with the greatest economic and military power or contributions should also have a greater decision-making role in these international institutions. The Security Council expanded to include nonvoting representation from the Third World. However, the Great Powers still retained their veto power and effective control of this institution.

In the 1970s Third World solidarity matured under the nonaligned movement as the battle against economic inequality and the demand for economic justice (pan-proletarianism) became the basis for unity. Third World leaders were much more successful in building consensus and coordinating their policies in international institutions. Several regional and international institutions beyond the United Nations General Assembly provided venues in which these actors could build consensus and coordinate policies, including the International Labor Organization (ILO), the United Nations Economic Commission for Latin America (ECLA), the United Nations Conference on Trade and Development (UNCTAD), the United Nations Educational, Scientific, and Cultural Organization (UNESCO), and the Association of Southeast Asian Nations (ASEAN), to name a few. The Group of 77 and the Non-Aligned Movement were pivotal instruments for policy coordination. The North-South conflict and symbolic political issues were especially important to this coalition.

Side by side with the North-South conflict, Third World leaders sought to isolate the Republic of South Africa and the state of Israel. This policy focused on their violation of the human rights of blacks and Arabs, respectively. Third World diplomats sought to gain observer status for the Palestine Liberation Organization in international institutions. Third World leaders sought a similar policy of recognition by the Arab League and the Organization of African Unity (OAU) for other liberation movements. These leaders challenged Northern prerogatives in maintaining their control over the decision-making processes. The South sought to democratize the decision-making processes in other international institutions and, where possible, to adopt the "one man one vote" procedure. Third World delegations were successful in getting their concerns on the agenda of many of these international institutions and temporarily transforming some of them (ILO and UNESCO) into South forums.

In the late 1970s, the United States led the industrial democracies of the North in their fight to retain Northern control over the locus of decision making in the ILO and other international institutions. In 1977 the United States withdrew its membership from the ILO, stating that this international organization had become excessively politicized. Third World leaders used it as a forum to condemn Israel and to attempt to grant the Palestine Liberation Organization (PLO) observer status in 1975, which had nothing to do with labor standards. At this juncture, the Third World sought to change the locus of decision making by affirming the "one man, one vote" principle as the new regime for making rules in these international institutions. Third World leaders also sought to exclude the participation of both Israel and South Africa from the ILO. The ILO emerged as a major arena of contention between the North and South and the East and the West. The North-South dimension of this conflict revolved around the Third World's selective concern for human rights, especially with reference to the South's condemnation of South Africa and Israel, while exhibiting less concern for violations in the socialist bloc and in developing countries. These actors sought to reduce the influence and power of the Northwest, and to exercise a greater role in decision making, in spite of the fact that ten industrial democracies contributed approximately 75 percent of the revenue used to support the ILO and other international institutions.

The East-West dimension of this conflict revolved around what U.S. policy makers perceived as the weakening of the tripartite principle by the socialist bloc. Since its inception, the ILO has established a unique form of tripartite representation that included employer, worker, and government interests in its policy making arenas. Each member state is required to send two government delegates and one worker delegate to the annual meeting of the International Labor Organization conference, and the same tripartite distribution is found in its fifty-six-member governing body. The business community provided its own representative. U.S. policy makers felt that the tripartite representation principle was being threatened by delegations from the Soviet bloc and some other states whose employers and labor representatives were, for all practical purposes, government representatives under a different label.[96]

American policy makers argued that countries with the greatest economic and financial stake in international organizations require greater representation on a continuing basis. The United States and its allies refused to change the decision-making processes in the IMF, the World Bank, and the United Nations Security Council, thus reinforcing this argument. The United States has opposed all attempts to change the decision-making apparatus in the ILO and related international institutions.

Conflict erupted over symbolic issues that were important to the Third World's political agenda but resulted in polarized politics in international organizations along East-West and North-South lines. These issues ranged from human rights violations in South Africa, Israel, and Chile to the unfair advantage of the United States and Western Europe in the decision-making processes of these same organizations. As a result of the increasingly politicized nature of the ILO (where debate ensued to expel the Israelis and grant the PLO observer status), the United States withdrew its membership from this organization in 1977. Neither the Russian nor the Arab delegations were willing to fill the financial vacuum created by the U.S. departure. Moscow began to apply pressure on the Third World to reduce the commitment of international institutions to their policy preferences. The United States did not renew its membership in the ILO until 1980.

In the late 1970s, the United States mobilized the industrial democracies to take a more aggressive stand toward Third World efforts to utilize international institutions as forums for the North-South conflict or other aspects of their political agenda. Washington used the power of the purse by threatening to withdraw, or actually withdrawing its membership, and in some cases reducing its financial contribution to international institutions. The ILO and UNESCO stand as vivid examples of these policies. The retreats of socialism in the former Soviet Union and the demise of the Eastern bloc have done mortal damage to the alliance between the Second and Third World in international institutions. The United Nations and its agencies are becoming more hierarchical at the very time that a new wave of democratization is evolving in some sectors of the Third World.

The new world order has reinforced the subordinate position of developing countries in the world system. These actors are still outside the decision-making circle in international institutions. The growing power of such international institutions such as the IMF and the World Bank has compromised the sovereign power of these actors, as critical national economic and financial decisions are increasingly made by these international institutions rather than domestic policy makers. The forces of globalization are increasing the gap between the North and South as Third World states are losing control over their domestic economic and financial policies. The next chapter will chart the evolution of race consciousness in the North and the new era of global apartheid.

NOTES

1. See M. Ayoob, "Security in the Third World: The Worm About to Turn," *International Affairs* 60, no. 1 (1983/84): pp. 41–51; M. Ayoob, *Regional Security in the Third World* (London: Croom Helm, 1986); Edward E. Azar and Chung-in Moon, "Third World National Security: Toward a New Conceptual Framework," *International Interaction* 11, no. 2 (1984): pp. 103–135; Nicole Ball, *Security and Economy in the Third World* (Princeton, NJ: Princeton University Press, 1988); Barry Buzan, *People, States, and Fear: National Security in International Relations* (Chapel Hill NC: University of North Carolina Press, 1983); and *People, States and Fear: An Agenda for International Security in the Post-Cold war Era,* 2nd edition, (Boulder: Lynne Rienner, 1991); Alexander Johnston, "Weak States and National Security," *Review of International Studies* 17, no. 2 (1991): pp. 146–77; Edward A. Kolodziej and Robert A. Harkavy, *Security Problems of Developing Countries* (Lexington, MA: Lexington Books, 1988); and Caroline Thomas, *In Search of Security: The Third World in International Relations* (Boulder, CO: Lynne Rienner, 1987).

2. *The Insecurity Dilemma: National Security of Third World States,* ed. Brian Job (Boulder, CO: Lynne Rienner, 1992), p. 12.

3. See Charles Tilly, *The Formation of National States in Western Europe* (Princeton, NJ: Princeton University Press, 1975).

4. K. J. Holsti, *Peace and War: Armed Conflicts and International Order 1648–1989* (Cambridge: Cambridge University Press, 1991), p. 308.

5. "International regimes" refers to codes of behavior and practice that are enforced by the hegemon or Great Powers. The hegemon establishes an array of rules and regulations governing interstate relations. The United States' involvement in the Korean

War, and the Suez and Congo crises enshrined this principle into interstate relations during the Cold War.

6. See Robert Jackson and Carl Rosberg, "Sovereignty and Underdevelopment: Juridical Statehood in the African Crisis," *The Journal of Modern African Studies* 24, no. 1 (1986): 1–31.

7. Mohammed Ayoob, "The Security Predicament of Third World States: Reflection on State Making in Comparative Perspective," in *The Insecurity Dilemma,* ed. B. Job (1992), p. 70.

8. Ali A. Mazrui, "The Triple Heritage of the State in Africa," in *The State in Global Perspective,* ed. Ali Kazencigil (Aldershot, UK: Gower, 1986), p. 112.

9. K. J. Holsti, "International Theory and War in the Third World," in *The Insecurity Dilemma,* ed. B. Job, p. 55.

10. Job, *The Insecurity Dilemma,* p. 28.

11. Joel Midgal, *Strong Societies and Weak States: The State-Society Relations and State Capabilities in the Third World* (Princeton: Princeton University Press, 1988).

12. B. Job, "The Insecurity Dilemma: National Regime and State Security in the Third World," in *The Insecurity Dilemma,* ed. Job, pp. 17–18.

13. Fred Halliday, *Cold War, Third World: An Essay on Soviet-American Relations* (London: Hutchison Radius, 1989), pp. 10–11.

14. The United States' military defeat and subsequent withdrawal from Vietnam in 1974 led to enunciation of the Nixon Doctrine, which retreated from active military intervention by U.S. forces in the Third World as a matter of policy. The Nixon Doctrine declared that the United States would provide military and economic assistance "as appropriate" to a friend threatened by a neighbor, but that "we shall look to the nation directly threatened to assume the primary responsibility of providing manpower for its own defense." The Vietnam War contributed to the loss of bipartisan consensus on foreign policy and the hesitancy to confront the Soviet Union and radical Third World states in direct military campaigns. The Ford and Carter foreign policy teams continued this policy until the Afghanistan crisis of 1979.

15. Michael T. Klare, *American Arms Market* (Austin, TX: University Press, 1984), p. 30.

16. Joanna Spear and Stuart Croft, "Superpowers Arms Transfers to the Third World," in *Superpower Competition and Crisis Prevention in the Third World,* ed. R. Allison and P. Williams (Cambridge and New York: Cambridge University Press, 1990), p. 91.

17. David E. Albright, *Soviet Policy Toward Africa Revisited* (Washington, DC: The Center for Strategic and International Studies, 1987), p. 17.

18. R. Sivard, *World Military and Social Expenditures 1991* (Washington, DC: World Priorities, 1991), p. 24.

19. R. Sivard, *World Military and Social Expenditures 1991,* p. 23.

20. R. Sivard, *World Military and Social Expenditures 1991,* p. 24.

21. R. Sivard, *World Military and Social Expenditures 1991,* p. 24.

22. *The Washington Post National Weekly Edition,* 16–22 May 1994, p. 16.

23. Lahuoari Addi, "Algeria's Army, Algeria's Agony," *Foreign Affairs* 77, no. 4 (July/August 1998): 44–53.

24. R. Sivard, *World Military and Social Expenditures 1991,* p. 24.

25. On October 7, 1992, the Mozambique government and RENAMO formally reached an agreement ending Southern Africa's most brutal bush war, which lasted approximately sixteen years.

26. After lengthy negotiations, a preliminary peace agreement for the region, based

in part on the leadership of President Oscar Arias Sanchez of Costa Rica, was approved by five Central American chief executives at Guatemala City, Guatemala, on 7 August 1987.

27. Arthur Banks, *Political Handbook of the World 1991* (Binghamton, NY: CSA Publications, 1991), pp. 491–492.

28. A. W. Singham and S. Hune, *Non-Alignment in An Age of Alignment* (London: Zed Books, 1986), pp. 17–18.

29. Fred Halliday, *Cold War, Third World: An Essay on Soviet-American Relations* (London: Hutchison and Radius, 1989).

30. Data for this section is derived from *SIPRI Yearbook: World Armaments and Disarmament 1991* (New York: Oxford University Press, 1991) and Michael Braoska and Thomas Ohlson, *Arms Transfers to the Third World, 1971–85* (London: Oxford University Press, 1987). Values of arms transfers are in constant 1985 U.S. dollars.

31. Member states include Angola, Botswana, Lesotho, Malawi, Mozambique, Namibia, Swaziland, Tanzania, Zambia, and Zimbabwe.

32. Member states include Antigua and Barbuda, Dominica, Grenada, Montserrat, St. Lucia, St. Kitts-Nevis, St. Vincent and Grenadines. The British Virgin Islands is an associated member.

33. See *SIPRI Yearbook 1991: World Armaments and Disarmaments*, pp. 247–248, especially Table 7.8.

34. United Nations, *World Economic Survey 1991/92: A Reader* (New York: United Nations Publication, 1991), p. 171; also see *SIPRI Yearbook 1990: World Armaments and Disarmaments*, pp. 245–249.

35. Ian Anthony, "The Global Arms Trade," *Arms Today* (June 1991), p. 5.

36. I. Anthony, "The Global Arms Trade," p. 4.

37. I. Anthony, "The Global Arms Trade," p. 5.

38. The Gulf Cooperation Council is composed of Bahrain, Kuwait, Oman, Qatar, Saudi Arabia, and the United Arab Emirates.

39. See A. Banks, *The Political Handbook of the World 1991*, pp. 4–6.

40. The member states of ASEAN are Brunei, Indonesia, Malaysia, Philippines, and Thailand.

41. Michael T. Klare, "The Next Great Arms Race," *Foreign Affairs* 72 (Summer 1993): 3, 145–46.

42. See Peter Calvocoressi, *World Politics Since 1945* (New York: Longman, Inc., 1991), pp. 600–602; Robert M. Price, *The Apartheid State in Crisis: Political Transformation in South Africa 1975–1990* (New York and Oxford: Oxford University Press, 1991); and Sergio Vieira, et. al., *How Fast The Wind? Southern Africa 1975–2000* (Trenton, NJ: African World Press, 1992).

43. See Sue Branford and Bernard Kucinski, *The Debt Squads: The U.S., the Banks and Latin America* (London: Zed Books, 1988); and Jeffrey A. Frieden, *Debt, Development, and Democracy: Modern Political Economy and Latin America, 1965–1985* (Princeton, NJ: Princeton University Press, 1991).

44. "Russia and France Gain on U.S. Lead in Arms Sales, Study Says," *New York Times,* 4 August 1998, p. A5, International edition.

45. Ibid. p. A5.

46. Ibid. p. A5.

47. R. J. Hill, *Communist Politics Under the Knife: Surgery Or Autopsy?* (New York: Pinter Publishers,1990), p. 194.

48. R. J. Hill, *Communist Politics Under the Knife,* pp. 40–41.

49. Joseph S. Nye, Jr., *Bound to Lead: The Changing Nature of American Power* (New York: Basic Books, 1990), p. 121.

50. J. S. Nye, Jr., *Bound to Lead,* p. 122.

51. B. Russett and H. Starr, *World Politics: Menu of Choice* (New York: W. H. Freeman and Company, 1981), p. 496.

52. B. Russett and H. Starr, *World Politics,* p. 497.

53. The Lomé Convention was created as a result of French insistence that its colonies and former colonies be given associate status in the European Economic Community. The French insisted on associate status when the Treaty of Rome was being negotiated in the 1950s. In 1974 the first Lomé Convention was negotiated (replacing previous agreements such as the Yaoundé Convention) between the EEC and forty-six African, Caribbean, and Pacific states. It made provisions for nonreciprocal tariff reductions, created an aid fund of $1,600 million and a scheme for stabilizing export prices, and promised Commonwealth sugar producers access to EEC for all their sugar at prices assured by the Commonwealth Sugar Agreement. Lomé II took effect by 1979. The Europeans undertook to take exports from the ACP countries to the value of $15,000 million a year and provide annual aid rising from an initial base of $850 million, most of it designed for roads, hospitals, water, electricity, and education. Lomé III and IV followed in five-year intervals, but by 1990 aid flowing from the conventions, while certainly helpful, was equivalent to no more than half of the aggregate given by members of the Community separately and bilaterally. Recipients were angry over their growing dependence on the EEC and the increased cost and bureaucratic problems associated with this aid. By 1990 recipients numbered sixty-six, and they were worse off than when Lomé I was launched.

54. E. J. Keller and D. Rothchild, *Afro-Marxist Regimes: Ideology and Public Policy* (Boulder: Lynne Rienner, 1987), pp. 192–193.

55. G. Chaliand, *Revolutions in the Third World: Currents and Conflicts in Asia, Africa, and Latin America* (New York: Penguin Books, 1989), p. 258.

56. A. G. Frank, *Crisis in the Third World* (New York: Holmes and Meier, 1981).

57. These states included Angola, Mozambique, Nicaragua, and Vietnam.

58. P. Armstrong, A. Glyn, and J. Harrison, eds., *Capitalism Since 1945* (Oxford: Blackwell, 1991).

59. R. J. Hill, *Communist Politics Under the Knife,* p. 202.

60. R. J. Hill, *Communist Politics Under the Knife,* p. 204.

61. F. Halliday, *Cold War, Third World,* p. 124.

62. R. Kuttner, *The End of Laissez-faire: National Purpose and the Global Political Economy After the Cold War* (New York: Alfred Knopf, 1991), p. 5.

63. "Weimar on the Volga," *The Economist* (18–24 December 1993): 45.

64. Ibid.

65. "Russian Voters, Upsetting the Apple Cart," *The Washington Post,* 20–26 December 1993, p. 12, National weekly edition.

66 .George J. Neimanis, *The Collapse of the Soviet Empire: A View from Riga* (Westport, CT: Praeger Publishers, 1997), p. 140.

67. Daniel Treisman, "Why Yeltsin Won," *Foreign Affairs* 75, no. 5 (September/October 1996): 72.

68. "Cool, Calm and Collected on Russia: Growing stability there has erased nerves here, despite what happens to Yeltsin," *The Washington Post,* 7–13 August 1995, pp. 16–17, National weekly edition.

69. Samuel Huntington, *The Clash of Civilizations and the Remaking of World Order* (New

York: Simon and Schuster, 1996), p. 28.

70. John Gray, *False Dawn: The Delusion of Global Capitalism* (New York: The New Press, 1998), pp. 121–123.

71. John Gray, op. cit., p. 123.

72. *The Washington Post,* 13–19 September 1993, p. 7, National weekly edition.

73. See Michael Ignatieff, "Nationalism and the Narcissism of Minor Differences," in *Theorizing Nationalism,* ed. Ronald Beiner (Albany, NY: SUNY Press, 1999), pp. 91–102.

74. William Pfaff, "Invitation to War," *Foreign Affairs* 73, no. 3 (Summer 1993): 101.

75. Zaki Laidi, *A World Without Meaning: The Crisis of Meaning in International Politics* (London and New York: Routledge, 1998), p. 55.

76. Michael Ignatieff, op. cit., p. 92–93.

77. Michael Ignatieff, op. cit., p. 93.

78. Michael Ignatieff, op. cit., p. 94.

79. Zaki Laidi, op. cit., p. 57.

80. Michael Ignatieff, op. cit., p. 95.

81. Adam Zwass, *From Failed Communism to Underdeveloped Capitalism: Transformation of Eastern Europe, the Post-Soviet Union, and China* (Armonk, New York: M. E. Sharpe, 1995), p. 215.

82. Warren Zimmerman, "Milosevic's Final Solution," *The New York Review of Books,* 46, no. 10 (10 June 1999):. 41–43.

83. Warren Zimmerman, op. cit., p. 42.

84. Vaclav Havel, "Kosovo and the End of the Nation-State," *New York Review of Books* 46, no. 10 (10 June 1999): p. 4, excerpts from an address given by Vaclav Havel to the Canadian Senate and House of Commons in Ottawa on 29 April 1999.

85. R. C. Longworth, "A New Kind of War," *Bulletin of Atomic Scientists* 55, no. 4 (July 1999): p. 28.

86. R. C. Longworth, op. cit., p. 42.

87. Franz Fanon, "The Pitfalls of National Consciousness," in *The Wretched of the Earth,* ed. F. Fanon.

88. *The Washington Post,* 18–24 October 1993, p. 14, National weekly edition.

89. Adam Roberts, "Not a Prototype for World Government," *Times Literary Supplement,* 27 February 1998, p. 27

90. Brian Urquhart, "Looking for the Sheriff," *The New York Review of Books* 45, no. 12 (16 July 1998): 50.

91. *The Washington Post,* 18–24 October 1993, p. 15, National Weekly edition.

92. "Mandela Proclaims South Africa Free At Last," *New York Times,* 3 May 1994, p. A14, International edition.

93. "Reluctant Warriors: U.N. Member States Retreat From Peacekeeping Roles," *New York Times,* 12 December 1993, p. 22, International edition.

94. Ibid.

95. Ibid.

96. Robert E. Riggs and Jack C. Plano, *The United Nations: International Organizations and World Politics* (Belmont, CA: Wadsworth Publishing Co., 1993), p. 363.

8

Toward a New Era of Global Apartheid: The Development of Race Consciousness in the North

Starting in the 1980s, Third World solidarity became increasingly on the defensive as the global political and economic environment underwent dramatic change. At the same time, the global economic crisis of the 1980s drove a wedge between the more affluent and less affluent states. Their diversity increased the difficulty of mobilizing a united diplomatic front on North-South issues. Growing collaboration between the Northeast and the Northwest reduced the maneuverability of Third World states in the world system. The retreat of the Soviet bloc from support of antisystemic movements in the Third World also made it more difficult for Third World nations to contemplate challenging the global status quo. The former Soviet Union and its remnants and the former Warsaw Pact nations turned their backs on anti-imperialism and, in effect, on the antisystemic forces in the South. In the post-Cold War era, Third World leaders find themselves in a world system with one superpower. U.S. policy makers are committed to supporting political and economic models of society that are conducive to the promotion of democratic capitalism.

Nations in the Northeast and the Northwest are moving closer together, contributing to a polarization along racial lines, with an increasingly unified North facing a disintegrating South. With the emergence of democratic capitalism as the predominant ideology in the 1990s, divisions in the North are no longer the result of ideological and economic divergence. Parliamentary democracy and market capitalism are being introduced as the new covenants for political freedom and economic development throughout the Northeast.

As the Northeast competes for economic aid, foreign investment, and technology transfers, nations of the South may find that they cannot successfully contend for such amenities from their traditional donors in the Northwest. Donors may prefer to give foreign aid to the Northeast. Donors may also lack additional capital to assist developing nations in their quest for development.

Investors also insist that the new enthusiasm for the market in Eastern Europe as well as the existence of the required infrastructures gives the Northeast a comparative advantage over developing countries in terms of investments, political risks, and returns. Since the collapse of the Soviet Union, aid to the Commonwealth of Independent States has fundamentally altered Northwestern foreign aid regimes: Germany gave $34.88 billion; Italy, $5.85 billion; the United States, $4.08 billion; the EC, $3.88 billion; Japan, $2.72 billion; Spain, $1.36 billion; France $1.22 billion; the UK, $.07 billion; and others gave $14.01 billion to this entity. The Group of Seven has also promised aid totaling $24 billion to help the Russian Republic stabilize its currency and restructure debt. In April 1992, the U.S. announced a Special Marshall Plan totaling $150 billion to support the restructuring process in the Northeast.[1]

Third World leaders find themselves in a new dispensation in which the old rules governing interstate relations are being torn asunder. The end of the Cold War has contributed to the convergence of interest between former antagonists as geopolitics gives way to geoeconomics and the world system becomes more divided along the North-South divide. As the twentieth century has drawn to an end, the world system is moving toward a new era of global apartheid. Global apartheid is a structure of the world system that combines political economy with racial antagonism. It is a system in which a minority of whites occupy the pole of affluence, while a majority composed of other races occupies the pole of poverty; social integration of the two groups becomes very difficult due to barriers of complexion, economic position, political boundaries, and other factors; and the affluent white minority possess a disproportionately large share of the world system's political, economic, and military power. Thus, as its South African counterpart, global apartheid is a system of extreme inequality in political, social, economic, cultural, racial, military, and legal terms.[2]

Third World leaders find themselves out of the decision-making loop of the new world order, although Saudi Arabia, the Gulf states, Egypt, Syria, and South Korea have become targets for recruitment as junior partners. These states are beyond the rule-making and agenda-setting sector of the Northern coalition and are not part of the inner circle of the Group of Seven. In the past the North was divided along ideological and military lines. Nations from developing regions could count on economic and military assistance from the Northeast. Today, leaders from developing nations can no longer rely on help from either the Northeast or Northwest if they lack strategic economic and political resources. The convergence of interest between the Northeast and Northwest has created an atmosphere of benign neglect toward the Third World, especially with reference to its economic problems. In the new world order, Marxist-Leninism is dead and the Russians are neither anti-imperialist nor anti-racist in their foreign policy.

In the past, Leninism rescued Marxism from racism, ethnocentrism, and the evolving global apartheid that plagued the Third World at the beginning of this century.[3] In an earlier era, British imperialism in India was celebrated by Marx as a progressive and revolutionary force that would destroy the Hindu precapitalist formation. Similarly, Engels also articulated the same proposition with reference to French imperialism in Algeria. Engels and Marx were so Eurocentric that their paradigms legitimated racial sovereignty and racial capitalism.

V. I. Lenin, the father of the first Russian Revolution, deserves credit for dividing the white world along ideological lines by challenging the legitimacy of European imperialism. He accomplished this through his book *Imperialism: The Highest Stage of Capitalism,* which marked a watershed in the history of European Marxism as white Marxists became major protagonists in the anti-imperialist forces in the twentieth century. Since the introduction of Gorbachev's new thinking, Marxists in Eastern Europe have turned their backs on Leninism, and socialist anti-imperialism has been in decline. White socialists are far less likely to support antisystemic movements in the Third World today. By joining forces with the Northwest, the Northeast made a dramatic return to its Eurocentric past.[4]

In July 1991, Mikhail Gorbachev met with the Group of Seven, requesting financial and technical assistance to help accelerate Russia's transition from a planned to a market economy. He received assurances that financial and technical aid would be forthcoming. The Russians joined GATT and accelerated the transition to a market economy. Prior to the 1992 parley, Russia joined the IMF and GATT. In July 1992, Boris Yeltsin also attended the Group of Seven parley and requested additional economic and financial support to make the ruble a convertible currency on the world market. Moscow received promises for approximately $7 billion in financial and technical assistance. During the 1994 Group of Seven summit, Yeltsin participated as a full-fledged member, making the final transition from an antisystemic belligerent. The Russian Republic was no longer considered a special agenda item by the Group of Seven, but emerged as a full partner in the post-Cold War era. These events underscore the breakup of the communist historic bloc and its departure from support of Third World states challenging the global status quo.

THE CONVERGENCE OF RACE AND POVERTY

The political economy of North-South relations has undergone dramatic changes in the last two decades. Select Third World regions have become the new global manufacturing networks, especially South Korea, Taiwan, Hong Kong, and Malaysia in East Asia and Brazil and Mexico in Latin America. However, the majority of nations in the developing world are external to this new international division of labor. Over the last two decades, the terms of trade have continued to operate to the comparative disadvantage of sub-Saharan Africa. In 1975, a ton of African copper could purchase 115 barrels of oil, but in 1980, only 58 barrels; a ton of African cocoa could acquire 148 barrels of oil in 1975, but in 1980, only 63 barrels; a ton of African coffee could buy 148 barrels of oil in 1975, but in 1980, only 82 barrels; and most African commodities experienced the same negative slide in value during the 1970s and 1980s.[5] Several conferences sponsored by the United Nations and donor countries were convened to address this problem. Nevertheless, the solution was the same: keep producing commodities to import goods that African states were not producing for themselves. The majority of sub-Saharan countries continued their dependence on agricultural production. In the words of Ali A. Mazrui,

> The continent still produces what it does not consume, and consumes what it does not produce. Agriculturally, many African countries have evolved into dessert and beverage economies, producing what are, at best, elements of incidental consumption in the Northern hemisphere. These dessert and beverage economies produce cocoa, coffee, tea and other incidentals to the Northern dining table. In contrast, Africa imports fundamentals of its existence, basic equipment to staple foods.[6]

During the early 1990s, the weather was not favorable to the African continent, as droughts and insufficient rainfall curtailed agricultural output. These weather-related disasters became extremely critical in northern and eastern Ethiopia, northern Sudan, parts of the Sahel, central Mozambique, and parts of Southern Africa. At the same time, these regions experienced civil wars and ethnic conflict, worsening the situation. A fragile economic recovery in 1989 reached its climax during the early 1990s. Agricultural production grew only 2.8 percent in 1989 and became virtually stagnant after 1990. Since 1990, food imports have had to compete with a sharply increased oil bill for most African states.[7] These ecological deprivations retarded economic development, while the militarized civil disputes severely aggravated these natural disasters.

African and Third World states do not control the prices of primary commodities. The debt crisis that is plaguing African and Latin American states is also contributing to economic stagnation in these developing regions. Although some nations in the Northwest have made overtures to address the debt problem, this is not a major agenda item of the Group of Seven, especially during times of economic uncertainty. Nevertheless, concerted action on solving the debt crisis could go a long way in retarding the drift toward global apartheid. Poverty and economic stagnation pervades most of the Third World, replicating the racial divide in South Africa. (See Table 8.1)

In the new world order, the United States is no longer the predominant economic force in a world system that has become increasingly characterized by economic pluralism. Japan, Germany, and East Asian semiperipheral states are emerging as the new pole of affluence, although the United States remains an important economic actor. Nevertheless, U.S. policy makers have established a series of collective institutional structures that provide a mechanism for

Table 8.1

Comparison of Market Economies with South Africa, 1985

| | | Market | | | South Africa | |
	OCED	3rd World	Total	White	Non-White	Total
Life Expectancy (in years)	75	55	60	70	55	60
Infant Mortality per 1000 births	25	130	100	20	120	100
Maternal Mortality per 100,000 live births	10	600	n.a.	n.a.	n.a.	n.a.
Daily Supply of Food Calories per person	3,100	2,100	2,400	n.a.	n.a.	2,600

Source: *World Resources, 1988–89.*

addressing global economic and political concerns. U.S. policy makers have established a decision-making framework that will operate to coordinate policies within the North and to resolve conflicts. Again, Third World states are outside the decision-making equations of these international bodies, thus reaffirming their subordinate role in the new order.

In a recent study conducted by Richard Barnet and John Cavanagh, the economic and racial stratification of the world economy was highlighted. These analysts ranked the world economy into a pyramid comprising seven groupings of nations. At the very top they identified twenty-four nations located in North America, Western Europe, Japan, Australia, New Zealand, and South Africa. These economies generate about four-fifths of the world's economic activity. The next tier is comprised of eight countries – Brazil, Mexico, Argentina, South Korea, Taiwan, Singapore, Hong Kong, and India – which do large scale manufacturing. A third tier includes China, Thailand, Indonesia, and Malaysia, countries that have reached a stage of limited industrialization. Until recently, these states were developing rapidly with large influxes of western capital. The former communist states of Eastern Europe make up a fourth group. The oil-producing countries of the Middle East constitute a fifth group and their status is equivalent to Eastern Europe. The sixth group is composed of the poor nations in Asia, Latin America, the Caribbean, and Africa whose prospects for development are dim, making them vulnerable to exploitative investment and economic dependence. At the very bottom are the poorest nations, essentially all located in Africa, with the conspicuous exception of Haiti.[8]

RACIAL CHAUVINISM AND GLOBAL APARTHEID

The disintegration of the Soviet empire coincides with renewed efforts to break down the remaining barriers of subnationalism on the European continent. Europe is moving closer to achieving the supranational dream of a new continental polity. As Europe makes this giant step, it is moving toward closing the borders to people of color, especially from the Third World. The European Community is evolving into what E. Balibar has called "Fortress Europe."[9] Starting in the 1960s Western Europeans began recruiting laborers from Turkey, Greece, and other Third World areas rather than from Europe's periphery. Migrant laborers were initially perceived as temporary sojourners and the entire system of recruitment rested on the rotation of workers, which was designed to deter settlement and reduce the social cost of migrant labor in Western Europe. Policy makers in Western Europe assumed that those who decided to stay would, like previous migrants, become incorporated into European society on the host society's terms. However, many of these migrants became prisoners of the "emigrant traps" and were either unable to save enough to return to their homeland, or were unwilling to do so because of the deterioration of the homeland's political and economic milieu.[10]

Racial conflicts in Western Europe erupted as racially and ethnically mixed inner-city sectors became contested localities. These new "foreigners" or "unmeltable ethnic and racial minorities" seemed to lack any legitimate claims to rights of citizenship, including rights to welfare payments and state recognition of their social and cultural aspirations. The revival of racism in the postwar era is a continuation of 19th-century traditions of classifying people by mythological identity markers that predate the current political and economic scene. Immanuel Wallerstein asserts that it is also a claim to a solidarity that prevails over those defined along class or ideological lines. Nationalism tends to divide core and periphery intrazonally. National categorization mirrors competition between states in a hierarchically structured world system. Race and racism integrate intrazonally the core zones and peripheral zones in their battle for control of one over the other.[11] Over time the principle of *jus soli* gains favor over the principle of *jus sanguinis*. Hence, there is a movement away from inclusive to exclusive definitions of citizenship in the European Community. Thus, the binding guarantees of citizenship rights for colonial subjects that became law during the twilight of European imperialism have been abandoned or circumvented by subsequent legislation. While technological innovations in communication have transformed the operation of the world economy and the connections between Europe and the Third World in the postcolonial era, they did not transform attitudes toward racial minorities in Europe or alter significantly racial attitudes about Third World societies.[12]

In the mid-1980s, Britain experienced a number of urban riots that had a strong racial dimension. The influx of a large number of West Indian and Asian immigrants into Britain led to racial confrontations in such cities as Liverpool, Manchester, Bristol, Birmingham, and Nottingham, to name a few. The severity of a number of these race riots was comparable to their American counterparts in the 1960s.[13] Increasingly, former subjects of the British empire found their presence in Britain unwanted in the middle 1980s. Britain passed laws restricting immigration from its former colonies. African and Arab immigrants have experienced similar discriminatory practices as the French rebel against the increased flow of people from North Africa. France has had a number of racial incidents involving violence against Arab and North African immigrants. Conservative politicians in France are calling for new citizenship legislation based on the "right of blood" as a mechanism to stem the invasion by "dark-skinned immigrants." The National Front, a very conservative party, has gained a foothold in the French electorate since the late 1970s by emphasizing xenophobia, neighborhood security, and the safeguarding of the "French identity" as its major themes.[14]

Political support for ultra-right wing political parties appears to be strongest in places near large immigrant communities rather than in racially mixed communities. Support for the ultra-right is also significant in the "slow lane" of a "two-speed" economy, particularly in urban areas marked by industrial decline where the disintegration of the working class leads to the erosion of communal identities. It is in such areas that immigrants and their descendants often settle. These actors tend to join a confused and apolitical underclass, perhaps to preserve their own identity, which may result in fostering the type of racism that supports the ultra-right. Similar conservative coalitions are gaining support beyond the urban areas of Britain and Germany. It is also penetrating Copenhagen's Blaatgaard district and extending to Nice, Lyons, and Cote d'Azur where working-class supporters of right-wing French leader Le Pen resolve their identity crises by opposing immigration and scapegoating migrant workers and their descendants.[15]

The twin influences of global economic restructuring and the forces of globalization have contributed to the racialization of conflicts in Europe. In the United Kingdom, more than a million manufacturing jobs were lost between 1966 and 1976, and in Germany, new technological innovations enabled manufacturers to eliminate more than 500,000 jobs in a single 12-month period between 1992 and 1993. People of color held many of these jobs throughout Europe. Official employment and economic data from Canada, England, and the United States document that black unemployment is twice that of white unemployment.[16]

Increasingly, people of color are organizing regionally and nationally to combat what they perceive as negative racial consequences of globalization. These actors are juxtaposing their dual interest in eradicating economic and racial injustices. In 1990, the Standing Committee on Racial Equality in Europe (SCORE) was organized to address the economic, social, and racial impact of a supranational Europe on black and other ethnic minorities. In 1994, they issued their Black Manifesto for the European community. Among the demands of the manifesto were the following:

* Amend the treaty of Rome to outlaw racial discrimination;
* Adopt as a European Community Directive a legal framework for promoting racial equality in the law;

* Allow free movement of all European Union residents, whether citizens or not;
* Ban incitement to racial harassment and eradicate racial violence;
* Create an anti-racist and anti-sexist immigration policy that is open to democratic
    review, in conjunction with black, migrant, and minority communities, who are
    most affected;
* Grant independent legal status to black, migrant, and minority women and promote
    the mainstreaming of their concerns in all areas of European work; and
* Give asylum seekers easy access to the EU and proper legal representation; they
    should not be detained, nor returned to countries where they could be in danger.[17]

In addition, SCORE has outlined a racial bill of rights for the European Community. It asserts that all black, migrant, and minority residents of the EU should have the right to vote in all elections; equal rights to housing; equal rights to education, including their own language, history and culture; equal rights to health and social services; and the right to family reunion.

After the demise of the Soviet empire, anti-Semitism grew dramatically throughout Eastern Europe. As Germany made giant strides toward unification, Bonn experienced a corollary turn toward racism and xenophobia that characterized the Nazi period. In recent years, Vietnamese and black Africans have become the new targets of these attacks. Children have been maimed by bombs. Murder and riots with a racial intent became a serious problem in Italy, which had enjoyed a long history of racial tolerance before these incidents occurred.[18] Throughout the new Europe, nonwhite immigrants are encountering new levels of insecurity. Increasingly, discrimination based on skin color and religion, especially for Muslims, has become a serious problem for the emerging world order. Racial chauvinism by Europeans in the nineteenth century led to the passing of immigration laws restricting migration by nonwhites to such exotic places such as Australia, New Zealand, and even Argentina.[19] In the new Europe, laws are emerging once again to limit the immigration of nonwhite people from the Third World. Increasingly, Third World ethnic and racial minorities are being placed at the hostile end of the traditional-modernity continuum as the European Community evolves toward a new form of supranationalism. Third World unmeltable minorities do not have the option of challenging assimilation and are generally in a worse position than ethnic minorities of 19th-century Europe's age of "big nation" nationalism. At best, they are expected to accept social inferiority and follow the logic of assimilation, despite the obstacles to assimilation. At worst they are expected to return to their homeland in the Third World. This is especially true of Algerians and other Muslim minorities in France, Germany, Spain, and the Netherlands.[20] In the early 1990s France enacted the Pasque laws. These laws granted French police far-reaching power to stop, interrogate, and arrest those they perceived to be potential undocumented immigrants.

France continued its conservative course with the election of President Jacques Chirac in May 1995. During the Presidential elections, National Front candidate M. Jean Le Pen asserted that he wanted to expel three million foreigners and to cut all welfare payments to non-French residents. The French conservative political course was reinforced in recent municipal elections, as the extreme rightist National Front experienced a surge in support. The Nationalist Front targeted Third World emigrants as a growing political problem confronting contemporary French society. The Chirac government deported a planeload of undocumented Africans on July 22, 1995, moving quickly to demonstrate that it would take a tough line against illegal immigration.[21] The French also deported 43 people to Zaire. Human rights groups have criticized the new French immigration policy. However, nationwide polls in France consistently show that a majority of the French favor policies that discourage new legal immigration and fight illegal immigration, particularly from the Third World.

France and Belgium are following the recent German policy of amending its legislation on rights to political asylum. Both countries attract many French-speaking Africans, and allege that a number have abused the right of asylum to come there to join prostitution and drug smuggling rings. Europe is closing its doors to Third World immigrants as the second phase of global apartheid unwinds. The European Community is finding it difficult to adjust to its new multicultural and multiracial environment.

RACIAL CHAUVINISM IN THE U.S. AND THE LOS ANGELES REVOLT

The rising tide of racism did not occur only in the Europe. It re-emerged in the United States, dressed in the new uniform of political culture during the 1970s. Christopher Lasch asserts that "de facto racism continues to manifest itself in the United States without the ideology of white supremacy."[22] The transition from restrictive to competitive race relations produced new stereotypes: in place of the childlike, carefree, irresponsible, impulsive Negro appeared the "combative, uppity, offensive, dangerous" Black.[23] In the post-Civil Rights era, the role of reprocessed stereotypes in influencing perceptions and performing the ritual (so necessary for racism) of depersonalization is all-important. Such stereotypes become assimilated as prejudicial identifications into institutional settings, thus maintaining the racial division of labor. Handicaps once attributed to genes were now ascribed to culture.[24]

During the post-Civil Rights era, symbolic racism has emerged as a significant assertion of resistance to both racial equality and equal opportunity. The underlying premise of this new form of racism is a strong element of anti-black "effect" and negative black stereotypes. Hence, African American demands for affirmative action policies in the hiring and promotion spheres have been interpreted as "reverse discrimination," while labor market failure receives the blame for the lack of modern, salable African American skills and sufficient motivation for success.[25] Symbolic racism is grounded in the American belief system that revolves around the culture of individualism. Through the culture of individualism, Americans attribute advantages and disadvantages to individuals rather than institutions and society. The American national ethos places tremendous responsibility on the individual for personal economic liberation and tends to assign defeat to personal rather than market inadequacies. In this context, every individual has the capacity to make her/his own way by employing specialized training, skill, cleverness, and the appetite for sustained hard work. Symbolic racism also functions on the belief that there has been a level, colorblind playing field in the marketplace since 1965.[26]

The Convergence of Race and the Restructuring of the U.S. Economy

At the end of the 1960s the postwar economic boom came to an end with a decline in the general living standards and occupational mobility that had distinguished the twenty-five years since the Second World War. By the end of the 1970s the U.S. economy had endured three recessions, and price escalation that had resulted in stagflation. American multinational corporations began losing their competitive advantages at home and abroad as they failed to increase productivity and extend their profit margins. This structural crisis led to the wholesale disappearance of industrial jobs, which were exported, automation strategies, and instabilities in the financial markets. Starting in 1973, the real income of U.S. working and lower-middle-class families began to decline. The increase in female labor market participation kept it from sliding further. U.S. corporations responded to this crisis in profits and job sites' controls by cutting labor costs. The postwar social contract between labor and management lost legitimacy as production sites were constructed overseas, forcing domestic wages down, and outsourcing of products to nonunion suppliers. Traditional leaders of heavy manufacturing sector underwent dramatic restructuring and dropped a considerable portion of their industrial capacity in the process.[27]

Starting in the 1980s, Black economic progress reached its zenith and began to shrink as economic stagnation and decline became the dominant feature in the U.S. economy. The end of the economic boom was a calamity for African Americans' economic aspirations. African Americans became increasingly insecure, given their location in unstable unskilled and semiskilled jobs in the secondary sector. African American primary sector workers were clustered in declining goods-producing industries such as steel, automobiles, and rubber. The stable African American working class lost ground to plant closings, automation, and export of jobs. Manning Marable has estimated that approximately 550,000 African American workers who lost their jobs were victims of a structurally racist system.[28]

After the crisis of the late 1960s and the early 1970s, capitalist business enterprises moved with all deliberate speed to reorganize their production system to reduce the cost of labor and to roll back the power of unions. The deindustrialization that followed had a negative impact on black workers, who worked in a large number of factories in such cities as Detroit, St. Louis, Chicago, Pittsburgh, and other industrial cities. These corporations were driven by a desire for higher profits, close proximity to natural resources, access to local markets, and most critically, cheap labor. The increased proletarianization of select Third World zones accelerated the departure of large and medium-size corporations from the U.S. and Europe. In 1950 one-third of all U.S. jobs were in manufacturing. By the mid-1980s, only 20 percent of all U.S. jobs were in manufacturing, and by 1990 that had declined to between 10 and 14 percent; and it is projected that by 2005, the number will drop to between 2.5 and 5 percent.[29]

The increased hypermobility of capital, particularly that involved in textiles, apparel, electronics, footwear, etc., caused those manufacturers to refashion significant proportions of their operations into a global division of labor. Many of these firms moved the labor-intensive aspects of their operations to areas where wages are low and unions nonexistent or under repressive governmental control. These corporations continued their research, development, design, engineering, testing, and coordinating aspects of their operations in the United States. In recent years, some firms have exported some of these arenas as new ways to cut cost and increase profits.[30] Labor cost in the Third World is a small fraction of labor costs in the United States. For example, in 1982 the average hourly wage for a production worker was $11.79 in the United States, $1.97 in Mexico, $1.77 in Singapore, $1.57 in Taiwan, and $1.22 in South Korea. At this juncture, South Korea and Taiwan became the Third World production sites for U.S. multinational corporations.[31]

Increasingly African American youth found themselves caught in a structural and demographic vise. They entered urban labor markets at a time when these markets underwent dramatic restructuring from goods' production and distributive function into sophisticated information processing, financial, governmental, and business services. Industrial restructuring precluded the hiring of an entire cohort of 1970s African American youth in the core manufacturing industries. The declining smokestacks of the United States resulted in a diminishing opportunity structure for African American young people. A large sector of African American youth no longer participated in the labor market and became fodder for the developing lumpen proletariat, which later was labeled the "underclass." The grouping of African Americans constituting this category is a result of structural displacement and cumulative racism: they are essentially unemployed workers beset by automation, export of historically urban blue collar jobs, inadequate transportation and job information networks, poor education facilities, and the lack of marketable interpersonal skills.[32]

As capitalist business enterprises engaged in their ceaseless quest for cheap and tractable labor, they abandoned the traditional bipolar racial segmentation of labor, and no longer confined their quest within national boundaries. Jacqueline Jones observes that employers with mobile forms of capital sought local supplies of immobile workers; thus a particular region of the United States might offer a surplus supply of illegal aliens, or destitute sons or daughters of isolated rural folk, or inner-city blacks or Latinos, all potential employees willing to work for cheap wages. African American workers, who historically were located the lower tier of the work force, found themselves in the midst of a new competitive arena as multi-ethnic and multi-racial distressed communities proliferated throughout the country. As a direct result of their resistance to various forms of labor exploitation, black people as a group continued to bear the stigma of "troublemakers," in contrast to allegedly quiescent "Fourth Wave" immigrants from Latin America and Southeast Asia. Jones notes that in every sector of the economy, employers responded warily to blacks at all levels of the work force who were declaring, in the words of Thomas Rush, an airline sky cap, "I look at everybody at eye level. I neither look down nor up. The day of the shuffle is gone."[33]

The African American middle class experienced a decline in their growth rates around the middle 1970s. College-educated African American cohorts were finding it more difficult to translate their training into middle-class incomes. American corporations continued to have racial and promotional discrimination while the public sector that had been more open to minority labor participation stagnated as the fiscal crises of the country reduced employment opportunities at the local, state, and federal level. The convergence between black and white middle classes came to a halt as lower-middle-class black families found two incomes more fundamental to self-maintenance than their white counterparts. African Americans also experienced difficulty in maintaining their lower-middle-class status in an increasingly changing political and economic milieu.

Ronald Reagan and the Rolling Back of the State: Phase I

In the 1980s the United States entered a new era of limited abundance, where social class, professional networks, educational and political resources were integral to becoming a success. African Americans and their Latino counterparts found themselves at a decisive disadvantage. National commitment to antidiscrimination policies and intervention to balance an unfavorable market became absolutely critical to accomplish the goal of greater equality. Ronald Reagan was elected the same year and became committed to rolling back the state in this arena. The allocation of social cuts underscored this administration's racial antagonism and its continuing class objectives of making the lower classes bear the brunt of restructuring the U.S. political economy.

Racism reached new heights in American politics with the election of President Ronald Reagan. At a speech delivered in Philadelphia, Mississippi, in August 1980, the conservative Ronald Reagan made it very clear where he stood on the racial issues in America. Before a cheering white crowd, he pledged that his administration would defend the principle of states' rights. This southern town was the location of the brutal murders of three civil rights workers in 1964. The phrase, "states' rights," became a code word for white supremacy in the African American community. African Americans could no longer look to Washington, DC for relief from racial injustice. Once Reagan was in power, he sought to create a new conservative and unequal order in the United States. The Reagan administration did not tolerate any concessions to the poor, the dispossessed, racial minorities, and labor. President Reagan and his advisors launched a broad attack on the welfare state. It initiated a campaign to withdraw the Comprehensive Employment and Training Act, funded in 1981 for $1 billion, and to eliminate its 150,000 federally funded jobs; close the National Consumer Cooperative Bank, which granted loans to small economic cooperatives; reduce the federal Food Stamp Program by $2 billion by fiscal year 1983; eliminate $2 billion from the Guaranteed Student Loan Program; reduce by fiscal year 1983 $1.7 billion funding for the child nutrition program sponsored by the federal government; and close the Neighborhood Self Help Planning and Assistance program. Under the guise of the need to bolster economic growth and corporate profits, the Reagan administration reduced drastically the federal government's enforcement of affirmative action. Under the Reagan administration, worker safety was compromised under the new policies of the Occupational Health and Safety Administration as part of an overall attack on governmental regulation of business.[34] During the 1980s, the United States also experienced a rise in the number of hate groups, ranging from the Ku Klux Klan to the skin heads. These groups began to increase their violence against African Americans and other people of color.

There were several positive developments in the political arena that contributed to increased black empowerment. During the 1980s, the late Harold Washington became the first black mayor of Chicago in 1983 and he was re-elected in 1987; Chicago was one of the most segregated cities in the United States. In 1989, New York City elected its first black mayor, David Dinkins. Dinkins lost his bid for re-election in November 1993. The former confederate state of Virginia elected the first black governor in the United States, Douglas Wilder. These developments were surpassed by other events that reinforced the negative influence of race in American politics.

In Louisiana, David Duke, the former Grand Dragon of the Ku Klux Klan in that state, ran for governor of the state. Although Duke lost the governor's race, he successfully garnered political and monetary support throughout the United States. Harvey Gant, a black Democrat, led in most polls in 1988, but lost in his bid for the South Carolina Senate seat of Strom Thurmond. Thurmond attacked affirmative action hiring policies in television commercials designed to mobilize white voters through fear in order to turn back the challenger.

During the 1988 presidential campaign, George Bush also exploited white racial fears in his bid for the presidency, employing a television commercial about Willie Horton, a black convict from a Massachusetts prison, that projected an extremely negative image of African American males. Horton was a convicted murderer who committed rape while on a furlough from prison.

This television commercial was a significant factor behind Bush's victory in the presidential election of 1988.[35]

Increasingly in the early 1990s, large numbers of African Americans came to the conclusion that the Civil Rights Act of 1965 had failed to reverse the historic patterns of economic inequality that relegated large numbers of blacks to poverty and political powerlessness in the "new concrete plantations" of urban America. Similar in function to the localized plantation economy, the ghetto consisted of an enclosed residential area where educational and employment resources were sparse. During the 1970s and 1980s, African Americans made dramatic gains in terms of completing secondary school; in 1989 their dropout rate was down 15 percent from 27 percent in 1968, about the same level as whites and half the rate of Latinos. However, these gains did not pay off in increased employment opportunities in entry-level and low-skill jobs, more and more of which migrated to the suburbs. The increased commitment of African Americans to education did not lead to more job opportunities. At the same time, major retail establishments in black communities were increasingly owned and operated by other minorities, ranging from Koreans in East Los Angeles and Brooklyn, to Chaldeans in Detroit, to Arabs in Chicago. African American customers patronized entrepreneurs who plowed profits back into nonblack families and institutions. With the flight of the African American middle class from the ghettos, these communities lacked role models of entrepreneurs and business professionals who were participants in the new microelectronics and communication innovations revolutionizing the U.S. economy. Lacking also were the kinship networks that provided business training and entrepreneurial activities, which disappeared with the flight of African American middle class. These communities found it nearly impossible to attract capital. Red-lining and gentrification intensified the deterioration of these concrete plantations.[36] These black ghettos evolved into arenas where poverty, drug addiction, crime, broken homes, unemployment, and infant mortality were dominant features, and where the AIDS epidemic disproportionately afflicted those residing in these war zones of America.

The Second Reconstruction had failed in the economic arena as the first had been unsuccessful in guaranteeing political equality for African Americans. The Reagan and Bush administration policies of benign neglect toward urban areas increased the economic dependency and political alienation that these communities felt as the American dream increasingly became a nightmare for those trapped in urban America. The new American capitalist revolution of the 1980s and 1990s was bypassing the vast majority of African Americans as well as their Latino and Native American counterparts. In a global economy that depended on highly trained workers in specific technical fields, employees in the traditional service sector, as well as those in manufacturing pursuits, increasingly dominated by computers and robotics, suffered a drop in wages during the 1970s and 1980s. At this juncture, poverty became more and more a problem of gainfully employed persons; employment per se became less an issue than the kind of jobs that are available to people without formal education.[37]

Ali A. Mazrui has observed that the holocaust of the Western hemisphere continues to inflict pain and humiliation on Native Americans, the descendants of African slaves, as well as Latinos.[38] In 1990, approximately 40 percent of those on death row in the United States were African Americans. In the early 1990s, the poverty rate among African Americans was 28 percent, compared to 8.8 percent among whites. Approximately 50 percent of all African American children lived in poor households (compared with 13 percent for whites), and nearly 75 percent of these children lived in female-headed households (as opposed to 46 percent of poor white children). Approximately half of all African American families were headed by females, compared to 14.3 percent for white families. Of all poor African Americans, six out of ten lived in central cities, but only one out of three poor whites lived in these areas. These figures point out that poverty was not the exclusive domain of African Americans but did affect black people to a disproportionate degree.[39] At present there are more African American males in prison than in college.

The Howard Beach and Bensonhurst murders and the Central Park assault in the state of New York polarized citizens throughout the nation along racial lines. However, the March 1991 beating of Rodney King by four policemen in Los Angeles captured on videotape what generations of African American males had encountered from law enforcement departments around the nation. This incident of police brutality demonstrated the continued existence of two separate and unequal legal systems in the United States. The initial acquittal of the four policemen in April 1992 by an all-white jury reinforced this image of an unjust legal system.

The United States experienced its first post-Cold War urban rebellion as the African American and Latino dispossessed burned down East Central Los Angeles, looted a number of businesses, and expressed their political rage toward a society that had ignored their political and economic needs during the Reagan/Bush era and had tolerated a dual justice system since the slavery era. The Korean business community experienced the wrath of their rage as a number of these new immigrants took on the social and political power characteristics of white America. Their interactions with the African American communities where they operate their establishments resemble those in the former South where whites were in a superior position to blacks. In both situations, black customers were treated very discourteously, and were often suspected of stealing. In Los Angeles, a Korean business woman killed an African American teenager who was accused of stealing in 1990, and received a suspended sentence and community service as punishment for her crime. This incident increased tensions between Koreans and the African American community.

The Los Angeles revolt demonstrated that the African American and Latino dispossessed were no longer willing to accept their underdog status in urban America without a fight. These actors had been participants in black-on-black and Latino-on-Latino violence and conflict among rival gangs had become the norm as these groups entered a state of war with one another. The Rodney King incident galvanized some of the gangs to launch a moratorium on inter-gang violence. As the violence and destruction escalated, whites became targets for violence. The seeds for such rebellions exist in many urban communities in the United States. Unless American politicians and business elites make investments to rebuild these communities, the fire next time may be more destructive. African states are experiencing similar political crisis as ethnic and cultural communities challenge the privileging of one group over another, leading to civil wars in some cases. These events remind us of Franz Fanon's advice to pay attention to the perils of national culture when it is not inclusive of others who possess minor differences from the rest of us.[40]

The Los Angeles riot pointed to demographic changes underway in the United States, which will move this nation toward a post-Western society within a generation or so. Demographic changes suggest that there will be a near majority of Asian, African, and Latino Americans. By the year 2050, according to U.S. Census Office, Latinos will outnumber the combined total of African Americans, Asian Americans, and Native Americans, and non-Latino Whites will have declined from 73.1 per cent of the population in 1996 to 52.8 per cent. At this juncture, the United States will diverge sharply from the rest of the states in the Americas, particularly Chile and Argentina, that remain unmistakably European in their ethnic mix and cultural traditions. Why should we expect a population in which Americans of European descent are approaching a minority to accept European cultural and political traditions? Nevertheless, this does not foreordain that the allegiance of the new elites are Latino, Asian, or African. On the whole, they are becoming more indigenously American; but the American identity that they embody is no longer a construct of an early modern Europe ideology. It is an emerging post-Western nation.[41]

The rebellion in Los Angeles also demonstrated that the bipolar categorization of the U.S.'s racial mix into "black" and "white" has become obsolete. The flow of immigrants from the Third World has diversified the U.S. minority population. Increasingly, immigrants are coming from such diverse locations as Kenya, Nigeria, India, South Korea, Haiti, and most states in the Americas. The Black-White racial divide no longer reflects the emerging racial and ethnic mosaic. Competition for jobs, housing, economic and financial resources have intensified among minority groups. The Black and White divide has continued to define race relations even as the U.S. population has become more diversified.

The Republican Party's Contract with America and Rolling Back the State: Phase II

Newt Gingrich introduced the "Contract with America" as a political manifesto geared toward revolutionizing how the federal government operated in several arenas ranging from the environment, government regulations of business and commerce, and welfare policies to term limits and campaign reform. The vast majority of Republican candidates adopted the Contract as an integral part of their 1994 Congressional campaign. The 1994 U.S. election resulted in a Republican majority in both the House of Representatives and the Senate. This election marked a dramatic shift to the right as the new Republican majority sought to restructure critical social policies that governed the United States starting with the Roosevelt's New Deal and reaching its height with Johnson's Great Society programs.

During the 1994 election Governor Pete Wilson fanned the anti-immigration fires as he made his bid for governor of California. He called on President Clinton to put an end to the benefits which illegal immigrants receive, such as health care and education. Wilson also urged the federal government to deny American citizenship to children born in the U.S. of illegal immigrants. Although this action would be in violation of the U.S. constitution, Wilson urged Congress to amend this document to reflect his proposal. Pete Wilson placed this issue before California voters under the rubric of California Proposition 187. The proposition was passed with a vote of 5,039,344 voting yes, while 3,827,114 voted no. Opponents of proposition 187 filed a suit in California courts questioning the constitutionality of this measure.

Clarence Lusane makes a convincing argument that the debate revolving around proposition 187 and immigration, in general, has never been about Canadians, Russians, or Swedes coming to take American jobs. It is tied to racial notions and conceptions. Lusane also observes that contemporary conflicts over immigration are also tied to the forces of globalization. All through Latin America, and Mexico in particular, labor migration to the United States has intensified in recent years, as transnational corporations from Asia, Europe, Canada, and the United States have located their operations there to take advantage of low wages and limited labor regulations as well as governments willing to repress their workers. Lusane also observes that since the passage of the NAFTA, treaty workers in Canada, the United States, and particularly Mexico felt the impact of this new legislation. According to a watchdog group, Public Citizen, 1,850,000 jobs have been lost in Mexico since NAFTA passed. The number of Mexicans classified as extremely poor grew from 31 percent in 1993 to 50 percent in 1996. The ratio of pesos to dollars during the same period went from 3.1 to 1 to 7.8 to 1. According to Public Citizen, approximately 40 million of Mexico's 92 million population live on less than $5 a day.[42] The forces of globalization and poverty are contributing factors to the increase in immigration.

Nevertheless, the anti-immigrant campaign has become part of Republican welfare reform. Several Republicans have urged U.S. lawmakers to deny welfare and other federal benefits to legal immigrants as a way to reduce the federal budget. Most of the hostility toward immigrants has been targeted toward those coming from the Third World.

Starting in 1995, affirmative action policies and racially constructed voting districts came under attack not only from the new Republican majority but also from the Supreme Court. Since the Reagan and Bush administrations, Republicans have sought to classify civil rights and affirmative action legislation as racial quota policies. Republicans found a new ally in the conservative Supreme Court justices constituting the majority in the judiciary.

The U.S. Supreme Court ruled on June 30, 1995 that the use of race as a "predominant factor" in drawing Congressional District lines should be presumed to be unconstitutional. The five-to-four decision declared unconstitutional Georgia's 11th Congressional District, now represented by an African American Democrat, Cynthia A. McKinney, which the Georgia Legislature drew in 1992 to satisfy the Justice Department's insistence that a third majority-black district be created for the state's 11-member Congressional delegation. Writing for the majority, Justice Kennedy cited a long list of Supreme Court rulings from the era when federal courts were desegregating public facilities throughout the South. He stated: "just as the state may not, absent extraordinary justification, segregate citizens on the basis of race in its public parks, buses, golf courses, beaches and schools," the government also "may not separate its citizens into different voting districts on the basis of race."[43] The Court announced that it would hear and decide two more redistricting cases, from Texas and North Carolina, during its new term that began in October 1995. The Supreme Court failed to provide guidelines for lower courts to decide when race has been the predominant factor among others in the ethnic, geographic, and partisan stew of electoral politics. African American and Latino districts will now face additional court challenges threatening to reduce their gains in recent years. When the federal court reheard the Shaw vs. Reno case (1993) in June 1996, it did not depart from its original ruling. It let the district stand as drawn. Later in 1996, the Supreme Court ruled once again along similar lines in a Texas case. The same five justices ruled that both districts were unconstitutional for essentially the same reason as given previously.

In June 1996, a panel of Republican-appointed federal judges in Texas modified thirteen districts. They threw out the results of the primary elections and ordered new ones. In North Carolina, a panel of three judges decided that redistricting could linger for legislative action the following year. This will likely lead to future suits challenging the legality of federal affirmative action policies. The new colorblind policies of the Supreme Court will undermine the gains African Americans and Latinos have made in recent years in Congress, particularly with respect to representation.

The Supreme Court established a stricter standard for federal affirmative action policies during the 1995 session. The Court ruled, 5-4, that the federal government's affirmative action programs must be able to meet the same constitutional review to which the Court had already subjected state and local programs that classify people by race. The decision in Adarand Construction v. Pena, No. 93-1841, has reduced programs designed to impart special federal benefits to members of minority groups, but is unlikely to end such programs entirely. This decision was the result of a challenge by a white contractor to a minority-preference provision in a federal highway construction program, based on the Court's understanding of the constitutional guarantee of equal protection. Justice O'Connor noted the nation's legacy of racial discrimination and stated that the government is not disqualified from acting in response to it. She also observed that the Constitution protects "persons, and not groups."[44]

California Governor Pete Wilson introduced the affirmative action issue to the 1996 presidential campaign. The California Board of Regents voted to end thirty years' effort to include African Americans, Latinos, and Native Americans among the system's 160,000 students. California became the first state to eliminate racial preferences in college admissions and put the state at the forefront of national efforts to end affirmative action. California's change in policy took place just after a news conference in which President Clinton asserted that affirmative action had been good for America and required only minor modifications. The eighteen-member board enjoyed the political cover provided by the governor as well as a Wilson appointee, an African American, Ward Connerly. In his pursuit of the presidency, Governor Wilson drew attention to affirmative action policies as a compelling national issue. African American neoconservatives, including Justice Clarence Thomas, Shelby Steel, Walter Williams, Congressman Gary A. Franks, and Thomas Sowell, have opposed affirmative action policies, thus providing moral and political support to conservative Republicans and others united in the battle against the remnants of the Civil Rights era. Representative J. C. Watts, an African American Republican from Oklahoma, represents the moderate sector of the Republican Party. J. C. Watts has called for modest changes in affirmative action policies. He has also charged that dramatic transformation of civil rights policies will make the Republican party more unattractive to African Americans. Most Republican candidates for the presidency had called for a repeal of most affirmative action policies at the federal level.

Ward Connerly played a pivotal role in mobilizing support among California voters to support Proposition 209 – the California Civil Rights Initiative. The objectives of CCRI were very clear: the complete elimination of state affirmative action programs in all applications. The proposition prohibits any state agency from implementing affirmative action programs, ends all minority or women set-aside programs, and ends all minority- or women-designated scholarships.

Affirmative action policies have come under increasing criticism during this era of globalization. Critics, regardless of their color, complain that employment of African Americans under the rubric of affirmative action raises the specter of "unqualified" blacks getting jobs at the expense of qualified whites. These same critics offer market forces as the answer to affirmative action policies of racial and gender preferences and argue that market forces would promote pure unencumbered meritocracy. During this era of globalization, many employment opportunities, even in business and the high-technology sector of the economy, still provide a considerable amount of on-the-job training, indicating that candidates with a diversity of credentials, formal or otherwise, possess the potential to succeed in any position. African Americans in those jobs are drawn from a presumably large applicant pool of "qualified" workers of all races, rather than plucked from a pool of "unqualified" workers of all races. The dual allegations that African Americans as a group are both lackadaisical (as welfare recipients) and predatory job seekers (as beneficiaries of affirmative action policies) recapitulates the defensive and confused rhetoric of early nineteenth-century white workers.[45]

During this late-twentieth-century wave of globalization, postindustrial America is being wracked by several social and economic dislocations similar to those that shaped the antebellum North a century and a half earlier. The technological imperatives of global business enterprises are displacing whole categories of workers, and waves of immigration are contributing to the restructuring of employment opportunities. The economic forces of globalization result in massive dislocations when African Americans take their places in line for skilled and professional "white" jobs, when women compete for blue-collar "men" jobs, and when immigrants seek access to jobs traditionally reserved for the native-born poor of both races.[46]

Side by side with the attacks on affirmative action, politicians of a variety of stripes, including conservatives, liberals, and independents, have sought to end welfare, as we have known it, for approximately six decades. Welfare reform became a critical element of Bill Clinton's presidential campaign in 1992. As leader of the Democratic Leadership Committee, he seized on this issue with which Democrats could whittle away at the Republican's bread-and-butter issues against the "undeserving poor." Starting in the 1980s, President Ronald Reagan had incorporated the image of alleged "welfare queens" as the emblem of the undeserving poor who exploited the welfare system for personal and family advantage rather than making it the "old fashioned way" through hard work. He was so successful in delineating the image of African American and Latino women taking advantage of the system that it became a push-button emotional issue for Republicans, particularly during the height of the recession in the 1980s. Republicans were able to attract many whites to the party by drawing attention to the welfare system. The DLC developed a line of attack that was a replication of the Republican's. The DLC asserted that welfare had led to a "cycle of dependency;" it had shattered the motivation of individuals to seek work. It was the cause of the increase in teenage pregnancies and women were deliberately having more children in order to collect additional welfare benefits. In their book *Putting People First,* Clinton and Gore declared that it was time to honor and reward people who worked hard and played by the rules. Their primary objective was to get those who were able-bodied off of the welfare rolls and reward those with children who were willing to work. The primary difference between the Republican and Democrat approaches to ending welfare was that the Democrats wanted to spend significant amounts of money for such things as education, job training, childcare, etc.[47]

President Clinton's bill call for such funding died in Congress early in his administration. The Republican-dominated Congress passed two bills that were vetoed by Clinton. In August 1995, with the election just four months away, Republicans presented Clinton with a third bill. He signed the bill. This bill concluded over six decades of the federal government's commitment to the poor that provided assistance to mothers and their dependents since the New Deal. Instead, it provided block grants of money to states along with most of the control of welfare programs. Once these funds were expended there was no promise that they would be replenished, thus discontinuing welfare as an entitlement program. Recipients were also restricted to a two-year limit on assistance without getting a job and a five-year lifetime restriction. States are required to compel a large percentage of beneficiaries into workfare programs under the threat of losing funding. Noncitizens would no longer be eligible to receive benefits and food stamps. Future immigrants who are not citizens would not get benefits for their first five years in the country.[48] The passage of the so-called welfare reform bill in 1996 aimed to compel recipients of Aid to Families with Dependent Children (38 percent of whom were black) out of the home into the work force, thus aggravating a market already jammed with low-wage workers, without providing child sufficient care services for the mothers affected. Likewise, public and private employers alike prepared to reduce their unionized labor force through attrition in order to make way for "workfare" employees.[49]

Social Darwinism was reincarnated in the public discourse with the appearance of Richard J. Herrnstein and Charles Murray's *The Bell Curve: Intelligence and Class Structure in American Life.*[50] Herrnstein and Murray provided the theoretical and ideological fodder for policy makers and the general public alike to assert African American inferiority. These scholars measured intelligence through quantitative techniques. They believe that intelligence is partially an inherited attribute. For these analysts, numerical representation of intelligence is broadly correlated (although such correlations are weak at best) with such indicators as job performance, rates of birth, marriages, divorce, illegitimacy, as well as crime, welfare dependency, and participation in the political system. They argue that intelligence test scores tend to diverge among different ethnic and racial groups. They concluded that Asians tend to score a few points higher than whites and African Americans some 15 I.Q. points lower than whites. The authors do acknowledge that a change in environmental factors can and does increase intelligence scores, but they insist that genetic factors play a much greater role in determining intelligence. According to this perspective, ethnic and racial hierarchies in the United States are the results of genetic differences rather than race, class, and control over decision-making power.

The Bell Curve assumes that remedial education programs and other societal social engineering policies represent a poor usage of societal resources given the genetic traits of the disadvantaged. Politicians and policy makers are admonished not to devote scarce resources to the disadvantaged. Benign neglect replaces social engineering and investment in the development of human capital regardless of ethnicity or race.

The growth in racial chauvinism in Europe and the United States emerged at the same time that South Africa was abandoning its apartheid policies and moving toward a multiracial democracy. Nevertheless, South Africa did experience black-on-black violence and terrorism from white right-wing groups seeking to disrupt the movement toward democracy. Authorities in Europe and the United States are making efforts to combat racial chauvinism. These events have occurred as both sectors of the world system are coping with the forces of globalization. Transnational corporations are eliminating the borders that separate nation-states. Increasingly, states are losing their ability to control international economic and financial forces. Ethnic, racial, and religious tensions are increasing throughout the world system as the rising tide of ethnic and cultural nationalism has placed the nation-state at bay, thus sowing the seeds of a new world disorder. A new world order based on democracy and a market economy is being challenged by ethnic and racial conflicts within and between nation-states.

The New Era of Global Apartheid and the Haitian Tragedy

Racial chauvinism in the United States moved beyond the domestic arena in the 1980s, when economic degradation and political repression forced many Haitians to flee their homeland in search of political and economic refuge in the U.S. Haitian immigration, relatively small in the 1970s, had become a tidal wave by the 1980s. American policy makers sought to stem the rising tide of immigration from this island nation. Race looms large as an explanation for their change in policy. At the same time, American policy makers continued to support and encourage refugees from Castro's Cuba and Eastern Europe to seek political sanctuary in the United States. These immigrants received political asylum as political refugees fleeing communist oppression, while their Haitian counterparts who suffered at the hands of the Duvalier dictatorship were designated as economic refugees in the American political landscape.

The Haitian immigrants are part of a regional pattern of new migrants to the United States seeking political asylum and economic rejuvenation. The Caribbean islands' tourist and sugar industries have failed to provide a decent living for the inhabitants. The Cold War between the United States and the USSR spilled over into Central America, triggering new migration to the United States. Donald Johnson has observed that the United States emerged as the promised land for a large number of Caribbean migrants seeking both political and economic asylum.[51]

In the late 1980s, pressure from the Haitian pro-democracy movement,

France, and the United States were responsible for the fall of the Duvalier regime. Washington provided a safe exit for "Baby Doc" who went into exile in Paris. Following the departure of Duvalier, Haiti drifted back and forth between civilian and military regimes until Father Jean-Bertrand Aristide reached the presidency through the electoral arena in December 1990. On September 30, 1991, Father Aristide became the victim of another military coup, and mass migration of Haitians to the United States accelerated. Since September 1991, more than 37,000 Haitians have fled to the United States. The Organization of American States imposed economic sanctions on the military government in order to restore democracy.

The Bush administration responded by declaring these new immigrants economic refugees and returning them to Haiti. The Coast Guard was deployed in order to intercept refugees on the high seas and return them to Haiti. Supporters of the Haitian refugees accused the administration of employing race as a determinant of U.S. immigration policy and took the federal government to court, citing lack of due process. Temporary refugee camps were established on a U.S. military base in Cuba to interview Haitians and to differentiate between political and economic refugees. In the spring of 1992, the U.S. Supreme Court ruled that the government had the right to return Haitians to their homeland and such a return did not violate American law or due process.

Initially, presidential candidate Bill Clinton criticized the Bush administration's policy of interception and return of Haitians to their homeland. However, President Clinton continued the Bush policy. The Clinton foreign policy team sought to restore democracy in Haiti by negotiating with the military. They lobbied for the return to power of ousted President Aristide. On July 3, 1993, United Nations negotiators, the Clinton administration, and Haitian military leaders agreed on a plan to return Father Aristide to power on October 30, 1993, in exchange for lifting the oil embargo. On August 27, 1993, the Security Council suspended the oil embargo against Haiti. In September 1993, a number of Aristide supporters were gunned down while attending mass. Assassination attempts were made on Aristide supporters, Port-Au-Prince Mayor Paul and Jean-Claude Bajeux. The military refused to disarm, threatening to withdraw its promise to return to the barracks. On October 11, 1993, Haitians refused to allow 200 American troops, whose mission was to prepare for the return of Aristide to power, to land in Port-au-Prince. On October 30, 1993, the deadline for Aristide's return passed as the military refused to cooperate. The United States returned to the United Nations to intensify the economic sanctions against the military. U.S. warships were dispatched off the Haitian coast, hoping to intimidate the military, led by Lt. General Raoul Cedras, into returning to the bargaining table. The economic conflict between Aristide, the military, and business elites precipitated a crisis. These elites feared retribution by the masses and did not want to give up their power base to Aristide and his followers. Aristide represented the first real threat to the system established by

Duvalier. The conflict between Aristide, the military and business cadre was a classic struggle between the haves and have-nots.[52] These privileged few were unwilling to transfer power back to Aristide and other civilians who supported political reform. In a move to further consolidate their power, the military named eighty-one-year-old Emile Jonassaint, former head of the Supreme Court, as provisional president on May 11, 1994.[53]

Starting in April 1994, Randall Robinson, the director of TransAfrica,[54] went on a liquid-only fast, protesting the policy of repatriating Haitians seeking political asylum in the U.S. President Clinton rescinded his policy on repatriation and articulated more hostile language toward military rule in Haiti as Robinson's condition worsened. Robinson was joined in his crusade to change U.S. policy toward Haiti by the Congressional Black Caucus. The Caucus emerged as a potent force on this issue, pressing the Clinton Administration to adopt a more aggressive policy toward the military junta. At this juncture, a third country was sought as the location for processing Haitian boat people seeking political asylum in the U.S. In June 1994, Jamaica agreed to allow the U.S. to use its waterways to process Haitians immigrants. In the meantime, Haitian military leaders consolidated their power and selected a new president to replace the exiled Aristide. The Clinton administration pushed new, tougher sanctions through the United Nations in an effort to persuade Haiti's military leaders to turn over power to ousted President Aristide voluntarily. Finally, in September 1994, after a real threat of military intervention was made by President Clinton, a three-man delegation of President Jimmy Carter, former Joint Chief of Staff General Colin Powell, and Senator Sam Nunn was able to persuade the military to give up power and allow the return of President Aristide. In September 1994 foreign military presence began when 20,000 American soldiers invaded this island nation in order to expel General Raoul Cedras and his military junta. Later, United Nations troops took over and stayed until the mission finally ended in December 1997. Approximately 500 American support troops remain in Haiti.

On June 25, 1995 Haiti held its first legislative and local election since the return of President Aristide. The election was marred by many electoral and administrative irregularities. The United States has taken on the responsibility to lead an international team to help Haiti develop democratic institutions and practices where there were none. President Clinton dispatched a high-level team to Haiti to expedite electoral reform. To date, Haiti's new civilian police force and its judiciary are still very weak. The democratic transition processes are still underdeveloped. General Cedras was exiled to Panama, while death squad leader Emmanuel Constant resides in New York City. Other supporters or enforcers of the former military junta are free and still at large.

The elite financiers of the coup − the small cabal families who have held Haiti in misery for decades − remained in a position of economic power. Their economic position has been made stronger by an elite prime minister (businessman Smark replaced by businessman Michel Rosny Smarth, who resigned in June 1997) and an economic program that the World Bank and the United States required first as a condition for President Aristide's return, and later as a condition for foreign aid. The economic program, which included freezing minimum wages, dropping tariffs, eliminating government service jobs, and privatizing Haiti's state-run industries, benefitted this island nation's small number of business owners who make their fortunes importing and exporting, primarily with the United States. The cost of living continued to soar and in 1997 famine in the Northwest forced many people to eat dirt in order to quell their hunger.[55] In July 1999, Haiti's population was approximately 6,884,264 with an immigration rate of -3.26 per 1,000.[56] Justice and democracy in Haiti have become hostage to the forces of globalization.

NUCLEAR PROLIFERATION IN THE NEW ERA OF GLOBAL APARTHEID

When Saddam Hussein invaded Kuwait in August 1991, he did not realize how much the world had changed. The Iraqi leader was still living under the spell of the Cold War era, when the Soviets supported their Third World clients and employed their nuclear weapons as a mean of deterrence with respect to the U.S. and the NATO alliance system. From the Korean War and the Cuban missile crisis to the Vietnam War in the 1970s, and the anticolonial wars in Africa in the 1970s and 1980s, the former Soviet Union and the Warsaw Pact nations had demonstrated their resolve by supporting Third World states in conflict with the United States and its allies. The Persian and Arabian Gulf War marked the first major war in the new era of global apartheid.

In the postwar period, most Third World military establishments were weak in comparison to their Northern counterparts and employed the weapons of the powerless in their militarized campaigns. Starting with the People's Republic of China and culminating with the Second Indo-China War, which included American participation, guerrilla warfare was the most important strategy employed by Third World military forces. The success of China and Vietnam led to the export of "people's wars." The failure of the French in Algeria and Vietnam to counter guerrilla warfare popularized guerrilla warfare as the chosen method of the weak. The United States also engaged in counterinsurgency warfare, at first in Korea and later in Vietnam. The Americans were successful in Korea until General MacArthur crossed the 38th parallel in an attempt to defeat the North Koreans. At this juncture, the Chinese entered the war and American casualties increased. Eventually a peace accord reinforcing the Cold War divisions between North and South Korea settled this dispute. Under the Johnson administration, America's counterinsurgency war in Vietnam intensified. The Soviets and the Chinese provided arms and a nuclear deterrence policy. Washington became reluctant to expand the war to the North out of concern that escalation might lead to nuclear exchange between the superpowers. In the early 1970s, as détente between the superpowers began to develop, the Nixon administration bombed sites in North Vietnam. The American defeat led to withdrawal from Vietnam in 1974. After Vietnam, U.S. policy makers refused to actively engage American troops in Third World military disputes until the 1980s. The Nixon Doctrine called for continued support of American allies in the Third World by providing arms and military training. However, Washington refused to employ American soldiers in such conflicts. At this point, counterinsurgency policy lost favor with American policy makers until Ronald Reagan came to power in 1981.

Guerrilla warfare expanded on the African continent during the 1970s. Anticolonial wars unfolded in the former Portuguese colonies of Mozambique, Guinea-Bissau, the Cape Verde Islands, and Angola. Insurgents from Rhodesia also employed guerrilla warfare to end white minority rule. The Palestine Liberation Organization preferred terrorism and hijacking as their modus operandi for achieving statehood. Egypt and Syria became involved in interstate wars with the Israelis starting in 1948. They suffered defeat from the Jewish state. Terrorism emerged as the tactic of the weak in the 1970s. The Palestine Liberation Organization under the leadership of Yasser Arafat employed terrorism as a weapon to remind the rest of the world of the Palestinian plight. Starting in the early 1980s, with the advent of an Islamic fundamentalist regime in Iran, terrorism emerged as the preferred weapon of a number of groups associated with this new political movement. Many Westerners became victims of kidnappers and were taken hostage throughout the 1980s. Syria, Iran, and Libya provided political and economic support to a number of these groups. By the late 1980s, terrorism and kidnapping had become politically unacceptable, as a number of Middle Eastern states sought to normalize relations with the United States. Increasingly in the Middle East and elsewhere, acquiring a nuclear arsenal and more sophisticated ballistic missiles replaced government-sponsored terrorism as a military strategy for the 1990s.

At the same time as the Cold War began, terrorism emerged as the weapon of the weak and as a means of drawing attention to the political causes that failed to reach the agenda of the international community. Actors employing this weapon sought to overthrow colonialism or the capitalist system, and they drew attention to those aims in lengthy news bulletins. These antisystemic surreptitious operations were sponsored by radical governments that did not bother to hide their identities. Their desire for political legitimacy placed some limits on the level of violence deployed. Examples of groups employing terrorism included the Palestinian Liberation Organization (PLO), the African National Congress (ANC), and the Irish Republican Army (IRA).

Recent episodes of terrorism portray its confused role in the post-Cold War era. New terrorism has no particular political agenda and its participants have no realistic timetable for taking power. These actors are not influenced by questions of political legitimacy and they are not striving to influence world opinion with reference to their cause. These antisystemic actors are protesting against the West in general, and the United States in particular, fuelled by an impotent rage over the "Great Satan's cultural and geopolitical hegemony." The non-state actors involved in these bellicose activities ranged from religious zealots to so-called "patriots" who opposed the federal government and alleged that federal authorities are involved in a conspiracy with the United Nations to construct a new world order that violates U.S. sovereignty. Their objective has been to wreak the maximal measure of pain on their enemies. The recent bombings in New York World trade Center in 1993 (by Middle Easterners) and the Oklahoma City bombing (by American ultra-rightists) were outcomes of the same anarchist brand of intolerance. The collapse of the Soviet Union and its antisystemic campaign made it easier to start a terrorist movement without government support. The demise of the Soviet Union contributed to the significant increase in the availability of the Warsaw Pact arsenal to the black market. The United States and it allies nevertheless categorize seven states as sponsors of terrorism – but it concedes that several of them, including Cuba and North Korea, have become less active lately.[57]

Since 1945, a number of Third World states have come to the conclusion that guerrilla warfare and terrorism are inadequate weapons in an era when U.S. policy makers are willing to employ "total war" against the South, as for example, in Washington's invasions of Grenada in 1983 and Panama in 1990. The new counterinsurgency and low-intensity wars of the 1980s kept a number of Third World states from consolidating their socialist revolutions by overextending their commitment to defend their regimes against anti-Marxist movements. The global economic crisis also contributed to the demise of those Third World states as these regimes were unable to provide the basic economic necessities for their populations.

The Persian Gulf War of 1991 demonstrated the problem of relying on out-of-date Soviet conventional weapons. This global conflict also demonstrated to the Third World that they could no longer rely on the Soviet nuclear shield in any conflict with the United States and its allies. A number of Third World states embarked on a program to acquire more sophisticated conventional arms, nuclear weapons, and other weapons of mass destruction. Starting in the 1980s, several Third World states established collaborative schemes to build their own ballistic missile programs employing technical assistance from West Germany and Italy. These states included Argentina, Brazil, Libya, and Syria. This became known as the Condor missile program. Syria and Iran became involved in a collaborative scheme to produce their own version of the Scud missile with chemical warheads.[58] Third World states are developing their own nuclear arsenals.[59] India, Israel, and North Korea are much further along in the development of their nuclear weapons and ballistic missile program. These Third World states have invested capital in the human resources necessary to place their nations in a position to take advantage of nuclear technology. Others have launched a recruiting campaign to lure nuclear scientists from Russia and the Commonwealth of Independent States to their nations, in order to acquire nuclear weapons. The U.S. and its allies have also initiated policies to keep scientists from Russia and its remnants from emigrating to Third World states seeking to build nuclear arsenals. Several states, including Israel, China, North Korea, and India, have evolved as important sources of weapons technology.[60]

In the political sphere, Washington applied pressure to the Group of Seven, the former Soviet Union and its remnants, and the People's Republic of China to refrain from exporting chemical and nuclear weapons or sophisticated ballistic missiles to Third World regions in the wake of the Persian Gulf War. The Persian Gulf War made it very clear to any Third World state contemplating challenging the global, regional, or local status quo that the costs are very high in a unipolar world system. A new international regime is emerging to combat the proliferation of weapons of mass destruction in the South. The Coordinating Committee on Multilateral Exports Control (CoCOM) will be recycled to manage the diffusion of technology that might aid Third World states bent on joining the nuclear club and deploying ballistic missiles. During the Cold War era, the nuclear non-proliferation regime was very fluid and was not universally applied, as acquisition of nuclear technology by some states, for example, Israel and South Africa, was not frowned upon. Again, the United Nations and its agencies are being used to halt the spread of weapons from the strong to the weak. United Nations inspection of suspected nuclear facilities in Iraq in the early 1990s as an aftermath of the Gulf War is an important test case of an emerging new nuclear nonproliferation regime.

Starting in 1993, North Korea was targeted by U.S. policy makers as the new pariah state seeking to acquire a nuclear arsenal. By targeting North Korea, U.S. policy makers were also sending strong signals to other Third World states with nuclear intentions, that is, to Libya, Iraq, Iran, and other powers, that they cannot ignore the controls that the nuclear non-proliferation treaty imposes. The North Koreans' bid to join the nuclear club became increasingly antisystemic to leaders throughout the Northwest. Diplomatic pressure was applied by the Northeast and Northwest on Pyongyang to allow inspections of its nuclear facilities by the International Atomic Energy Agency (IAEA). U.S. intelligence agencies suspect that North Korea has already produced a number of low-grade nuclear weapons. South Korea and the United Nations have continued to favor negotiations over military solutions to the stalemate over this issue. In late December 1993 United Nations General Secretary Boutros Boutros-Ghali visited North Korea, lobbying their leaders to settle this dispute through diplomatic means. Diplomats in South Korea and the United Nations fear a military option would only lead to a resumption of the Korean War. U.S. policy makers have offered economic aid, trade concessions, and termination of the joint military exercise between American and South Korean armed forces in order to accommodate Pyongyang. At the end of 1993, U.S. and North Korea appeared to be moving toward a compromise that would allow IAEA inspection of some of North Korea's nuclear facilities. However, this was only a temporary reprieve, as the conflict between IAEA and North Korea worsened in June 1994, threatening to escalate into a major crisis in the post-Cold War era. The Clinton administration is seeking to use tighter economic sanctions through the Security Council as the stick to return policy makers in Pyongyang to diplomacy and acceptance of IAEA inspections. North Korea has declared that such sanctions would be the equivalent of a threat of war. Acquisition of a nuclear arsenal by Third World states has emerged as a major bone of contention in North-South relations in the new world order.

The People's Republic of China, North Korea, and Iran have emerged as new conduits of sophisticated conventional weapons to the Middle East. Strong efforts are being launched to persuade the Chinese of the dangers of nuclear proliferation and the spread of more sophisticated weapons to the Third World. The United States and its allies engaged in arms transfers in the Middle East. The arms industry in the former Soviet Union is still transferring sophisticated ballistic missiles to India and Iran. The diffusion of military technology is spreading to a number of Third World states in the Middle East and East Asia. These technology transfers are making it more difficult to create a new disarmament regime with respect to ballistic missiles and weapons of mass destruction. The North-South divide over the acquisition of a nuclear arsenal by developing countries also reinforces the assumption that the world system is entering a new era of global apartheid.

The Nuclear Nonproliferation Treaty was renewed in 1996 after intensive discussion among the signatory states. The Comprehensive Test Ban Treaty of 1996 banned any future testing of nuclear weapons and created a Preparatory Commission (PrepCom) and a Provisional Technical Secretariat (PTS) in Vienna to implement the treaty. The United Nations General Assembly voted on September 10, 1996, to adopt the Comprehensive Nuclear Test Ban Treaty (CTBT). Since September 24, 1996, the CTBT has been open to all states for signature.[61] To date, the U.S. Congress has refused to ratify the treaty. The U.S. Congress has raised doubts concerning the verification instrument of the treaty. Both India and Pakistan have refused to sign the new treaty and moved full speed ahead with their nuclear programs. North Korea has continued the development of long-range missiles as a result of the lucrative market for these weapons of war and the decline of its economy. The combination of threats and diplomatic overtures toward North Korea have lessened tensions and reduced North Korea's commitment toward nuclear proliferation. The recent meetings between the two Koreas were important steps toward resolving this outstanding Cold War conflict.

In recent years the United States and other members of the nuclear club have employed a variety of strategies to contain nuclear proliferators. These strategies include a combination of export controls, sanctions, economic incentives, and security assurances. These policy postures have successfully worked with countries such as Argentina, South Korea, and the Ukraine. However, these same policies have been less effective with reference to India and Pakistan. At this juncture, these countries are more determined and less amenable to outside influence. The conflict between India and Pakistan makes the recent nuclear tests by both countries a salient issue for the international community.

Before their partition in 1949, during the colonial and immediate post-colonial periods, India and Pakistan existed as one country. Since then, they have become major antagonists. India acquired its independence in 1947. At that time, the Indian nation was divided into Hindu-dominated India and Muslim-dominated Pakistan. The partition was followed by massive riots and population flux as Muslims and Hindus found themselves on the wrong side of the border. Approximately 500,000 people lost their lives as a result of the violence and communal riots. Casualties were higher in the Sikh-occupied Punjab, which was split in two. However, the most problematic arena emerged in predominantly Muslim Kashmir. This region was expected to become part of Pakistan. However, after weeks of rioting, the Hindu rulers of this province transferred it to India in return for military aid. Pakistan refused to accept the decision formally and the two countries have been embroiled in conflict that has at times become militarized. In 1949, India and Pakistan signed an armistice. The western third of Kashmir fell to Pakistan while the rest of it stayed under Indian direction, and the two sides agreed to hold a UN-supervised plebiscite to determine the state's future. India never fulfilled this commitment, and Kashmir became a source of conflict between these states. Conflict between these two states became militarized in 1965 and 1971.

Since the 1970s, relations between these adversaries have worsened as a result of the developing arms race. India initiated its nuclear weapon program in response to China's nuclear tests in the 1960s. In 1974, India conducted its first nuclear test, the so-called "Smiling Buddha" detonation in the Rajasthan Desert. Pakistan commenced its nuclear development program a few years later with the assistance of arms deliveries from the United States. Both countries have been engaged in developing and testing short-range and intermediate-range missiles. As a result of their continuing conflict over Kashmir, the two countries came together in December 1990, and agreed not to attack each other's nuclear facilities. At this juncture, neither country has signed the Nonproliferation Treaty or the Comprehensive Test Ban Treaty. India refused to sign the Comprehensive Test Ban Treaty in 1996, protesting that it reserved the right to exclusive possession of nuclear weapons held by a few states.

Pakistan tested its new Ghauri intermediate-range missile in April 1998. The missile was named after a 12th-century Muslim fighter who subjugated part of India. This is postulated to have provoked India's nuclear tests the following month. On May 11, 1998, India declared that it had conducted three underground tests at Pokhran in the northern state of Rajasthan. Two days later it announced another two explosions had taken place. Pakistan and the global community widely condemned India's action. On May 28, 1998, Pakistan declared that it had conducted five nuclear tests of its own in south western Baluchistan.[62] The United States and its allies imposed economic sanctions on both countries. Both countries were urged to reduce their bellicose language and slow the arms race as well as the tension in South Asia. However, India and Pakistan have continued to carry out border incursions and limited military action over the Kashmir region as the new millennium approaches. On July 23, 1998, Iran successfully tested a medium-range missile. The weapon would allow Iran to strike all of Israel, Saudi Arabia, and parts of Turkey and Russia. North Korea is believed to be the source of the missile technology.[63] The United States and its fellow members of the exclusive club of nuclear powers are slowing down nuclear proliferation but lack the capability, beyond surgical air strikes on such facilities, to prevent select Third World nations with the wherewithal from acquiring this pernicious technology.

The end of the Cold War has resulted in neither a new momentum toward nuclear disarmament nor renewed arms controls. Policy makers in the United States are seriously considering deployment of a new antiballistic missile system to protect Americans against attacks from "rogue states" such as North Korea, Iraq, Iran, and Libya. Both China and Russia view American action as a potential violation of the ABM treaty and a step toward restarting the arms race. The Pentagon executed three tests of an ABM system between 1999 and August 2000. However, these tests raised questions concerning the current state of technology, and particularly in light of the progress made in stabilizing the nuclear arms race, both the financial and diplomatic costs that such a system would incur. In addition, with the failure to destroy an incoming missile in two out of three tests, President Clinton decided to postpone deployment. He left the fate of the antiballistic missile system to the next president.

Jonathan Schell drew attention to the folly of arms control and how some nations have the capacity but lack the will to construct nuclear missile systems because of the potential lethal destruction to their adversaries, themselves, and others. He also focuses on those states that have the will but lack the scientific capacity to build a nuclear arsenal. Schell questions the logic behind the non-proliferation treaty which maintains the status quo among the nuclear club, but insists that states without a nuclear arsenal forego investment in deadly weapon systems. He sounds the alarm that technology for constructing these systems is available in a variety of nonclassified sources.[64] He concludes that arms control has become a way of avoiding the responsibility of making a fateful choice: a world of uncontrolled proliferation, or a world with no nuclear weapons at all.

At this point in the evolution of the world system, there is a profound gap between the structure of the United Nations system and the new functions it is being called upon to occupy. The current United Nations structures still reflect the post-World War II world system in which the U.S. and Russia were the dominant powers. This configuration also reflects the U.S.' predominant economic position in the world system at that juncture. Germany and Japan have emerged as key players in the global economic system, challenging the U.S. and the rest of Europe in this arena. Nevertheless, these actors lack an effective voice that is commensurate with that of the five permanent members of the UN Security Council. Likewise, there are a number of Third World economic and nuclear powers whose voices are also underrepresented in the present structure of the United Nations Security Council. These states include Brazil,

India, a post-apartheid South Africa, and Saudi Arabia, to name a few. The present United Nations system does not reflect the political and economic power structure of the post-Cold War world order.

The United Nations held a two-day Millennium Conference to outline the course for this global institution for the twenty-first century. Leaders and statesmen from 185 countries attended this affair and sought to resolve several outstanding conflicts and hammer out agreements for tackling issues, from global poverty and women's and children's rights, to disarmament and globalization. The conferees also focused on the problem of peacekeeping by the United Nations. Most leaders from the Northeast and Northwest are critical of peacekeeping exercises that often lead to mission creep, and the lack of necessary military capacity to engage adversaries in conflict resolution when no disarmament agreements are in place. Nevertheless, the United Nations' ability to confront global conflicts and problems rests firmly in the hands of the major powers. The United States is the principal actor whose policies are at odds with multilateral diplomacy that is embedded in the United Nations system. Unless these actors provide the United Nations with the tools to act in these arenas, the only thing that will come out of this gathering is more unfulfilled promises.

Conflict resolution remains a global puzzle, partially as a result of the identity politics and the politics of differences that cloud most conflagrations. Efforts to resolve the Middle East conflict through a new Camp David initiative by the United States fell apart in the summer of 2000. Neither the Israelis nor the Palestinians were able to move on the question of national sovereignty over Jerusalem. Both Arafat and Barak faced opposition and dissension within their own ranks. The outcome of Middle East conflict resolution remains in the hands of future leaders willing to compromise and overcome their differences.

THIRD WORLD SOLIDARITY IN THE NEW ERA OF GLOBAL APARTHEID

The end of the Cold War concluded one of the fundamental crises over hegemonic power and ideology to confront humanity since the end of the Second World War. The world system has become increasingly unipolar in this new dispensation of Pax Americana, under which Third World states may find themselves without protection and vulnerable to the vagaries of the Great Powers in the political and economic arenas. At this point, a number of important Third World states in the Middle East and East Asia have become integrated into supportive roles in the post-Cold War era. States ranging from Egypt, Syria, Saudi Arabia, and the Gulf States to South Korea and Taiwan have become junior partners in this new world order. A number of Third World states are falling apart as a result of civil wars and militarized disputes within their borders, as for example, Afghanistan, Cambodia, Rwanda, Somalia, the Sudan, and Sri Lanka. Still others are disintegrating as a result of their failure to create a domestic economic and political order and a social contract among diverse ethnic and religious communities – Nigeria, Burma, and Algeria.

The nation-state is no longer the primary instrument of decision-making with reference to international economic issues. State structures are collapsing in such diverse regions as sub-Saharan Africa, South Asia, and South America. Northern international institutions including the International Monetary Fund, the World Bank, and General Agreement on Tariffs and Trade are more important actors in this arena. At this time, national sovereignty in many regions of the Third World is crumbling as Northern economic and financial institutions dictate policies with consequences for the domestic political order and foreign policy preferences of states in the Southern Hemisphere. When the nation-state can no longer guarantee the safety of its citizens, and when the state loses its monopoly over violence, it ceases to carry out its historical and juridical role. Increasingly, states in the North and South no longer control their economic and fiscal policies, and the growing influence of international financial institutions plus Wall Street are also penetrating the sovereignty of states. Likewise, when the state loses control over domestic economic policies, it ceases to function as a sovereign in this arena. Third World solidarity is being fragmented from within and without.

In the 1950s the notion of a buffer zone between socialism and capitalism became a cornerstone of Third World ideology. It was no accident that first in Colombo, then in Bandung, and finally in Belgrade the leading proponents of nonalignment were determined to protect their nation's sovereignty. Leaders in the Third World were fearful of socialism and opposed the overwhelming influence of American capitalism. From the 1950s to the 1990s, Third World leaders sought domestically and internationally to find a middle passage between these two social systems and ideologies. In this new era of global apartheid, these actors will be pressured to adopt the political and economic models of democratic capitalism. In a unipolar world system, Third World nations pursuing alternative and innovative strategies beyond the capitalist model will be isolated and may face military invasions, penetration, and subversion if their experiments are conceptualized as antisystemic. The world system is moving on a dialectical course along a racial divide as the North-South conflict becomes the dominant feature in the post-Cold War era.

At the end of the Second World War, the Cold War and the anti-imperialist thrust within Marxist-Leninism challenged the North's imperialistic projects in the Third World. The East-West conflict was critical in preventing a new and more sophisticated era of global apartheid. Solidarity among Third World states has evolved from pan-pigmentationalism, solidarity based on race and geography, to pan-proletarianism, solidarity based on the development of an international class consciousness in North-South relations and fragmentation in the new era of global apartheid. Third World unity of purpose is disintegrating at the very time the Northeast and Northwest is developing a united front on a variety of issues from conflict resolution in developing areas to nuclear nonproliferation.

Third World leaders will need to adopt new strategies to address the growing global oligarchy in international institutions and to attack the diminution of their roles in the decision-making networks of the world system. In the 1990s Third World states may attempt to restructure international institutions such as the United Nations Security Council by challenging the continuation of veto power by the Great Powers and the maintenance of this institution as a "white man's club." One way to address the power imbalance is by granting select Third World states veto power and permanent membership on the Security Council. Candidates for this role may include India, the post-apartheid Republic of South Africa, Brazil, Mexico, North Korea and/or South Korea, as well as Saudi Arabia. Japan and Germany are also candidates from the Northwest. Restructuring is essential in other international institutions if they are going to reflect the diversity of interests and power in the world system.

The quest by Third World states to overcome political, economic, and racial inequality in the world system will continue well into the twenty-first century. Semiperipheral states, along with those in the South seeking nuclear power and more sophisticated conventional military arsenals, will play an important role in the Third World's quest to develop a counterbalance of power in this new era of global apartheid and one superpower. It was the Haitian Revolution that shook the very foundation of global apartheid under the regime of slavery and laid the groundwork for the final dismantling of this regressive form of capitalism. It may take the unfolding battle throughout the developing world for racial dignity and political and economic democracy to shake the foundation of the emerging regime of global apartheid and develop a new base of solidarity that focuses on the political, economic, racial, and military dimensions of global inequality. The present capitalist world system represents the interest of those actors with the prerequisite military and economic power. It is not in the interest of these actors to create a world order that addresses the interests of the South. Third World states will need to develop a counterbalance of power in the economic and military arena in order to create a new world order that addresses their needs and interests.

THE NONALIGNED MOVEMENT IN THE POST-COLD WAR ERA

If the nonaligned movement plans to emerge as a champion of the weak and powerless in the post-Cold War era, it must become an important actor in conflict resolution, especially in inter-Third World conflicts. Although the Cold War has come to an end, a number of civil wars and ethnic conflicts persist despite Washington's and Moscow's disengagement from regional Third World conflicts in such diverse locations as Rwanda, the Sudan, Somalia, Mozambique, and Sri Lanka, to name a few. In the past, the nonaligned movement, like other Third World regional organizations, has failed to resolve such conflicts and to keep them from escalating to levels warranting outside intervention. A number of civil wars, ethnic and communal conflicts, and interstate war intensified during the 1970s and 1980s, reducing dramatically the ability of Third World-oriented international and regional organizations to broker peace between combatants once these disputes became militarized.

During the era of détente, the nonaligned movement underwent another crisis of identity and purpose. Many scholars and diplomats pronounced the end of the Third World and nonalignment as a result of the growing cooperation and convergence of interest between the two superpowers. Under the leadership of Algeria, the nonaligned movement was reorganized and reinvigorated with a new and more dynamic thrust as these actors began to focus on the "poverty curtain" that separated the states located in the Southern Hemisphere from their Northern counterparts. The movement became increasingly concerned with the international class structure, global economic inequality, the continuation of colonialism and white minority rule in Southern Africa as well as the lack of self-determination and sovereignty for the Palestinians. Third World leaders began to conceptualize the North-South conflict as the most salient issue confronting this coalition of states. At least for a short while, the Third World put the Cold War on the back burner of international politics.

Détente came to an end with Ronald Reagan's presidency. U.S. policy makers initiated the Second Cold War and began to challenge the Soviets and their allies in the Third World. Unlike the Nixon, Ford, and Carter administrations which retreated from active competition for power and influence in the Third World following the Vietnam fiasco, the Reagan and Bush administrations were assertive, contesting with the Russians and their Third World allies who were engaged in antisystemic campaigns. Washington and Moscow competed for influence, allies, and power in the Third World as the Southern Hemisphere evolved into the arc of crisis between these two nuclear powers. Third World states became pawns on the chessboard of international affairs as both superpowers sought to establish their spheres of influence in the Southern Hemisphere. The raison d'être for nonalignment crumbled as Washington and Moscow shifted their ideological and military contest for hegemony from Europe to the Southern Hemisphere in the 1980s. Global economic crisis of the 1980s also dampened Third World leaders' enthusiasm for collective action as they turned to the World Bank and the IMF for debt relief and structural adjustment. Global economic restructuring led to a new international division of labor that divided the Third World along economic and ideological lines. Fragmentation replaced solidarity among this collectivity of states by the early 1990s.

The nonaligned movement met for the first time in the post-Cold War era in late August 1992 in Jakarta, Indonesia. It sought to chart a new path and to revitalize the movement by redefining its mission to become "a United Nations of the developing world," with authority to resolve inter-Third World conflicts. Foreign Minister Ali Alatas of Indonesia asserted that the movement was founded in 1961 by nations wishing to remain independent of what were then the world's two superpowers. The change from a bipolar to a unipolar world system of one superpower did not necessitate a change in the name of the movement.[65] President Suharto of Indonesia was the leader of the movement over the next three years and had the responsibility for steering it on a new course.

Over 100 large and small nations that account for more than half the world's population comprise the nonaligned movement membership. These same nations possess nearly two-third of the seats in the United Nations but represent only 10 per cent of the global economic output.[66] Small and weak states throughout the Third World will be looking to the nonaligned movement to support the cause of the powerless and lead the charge to restructure the power imbalance in international institutions.

Ethnic and religious conflicts in Yugoslavia threatened to disrupt the nonaligned gathering in Jakarta as some delegates questioned the continuation of Belgrade's membership as a result of its ethnic cleansing policy. The Muslim nations led the charge on this volatile issue. Non-Muslim members, concerned that they might face similar condemnation over the treatment of secessionist territories, resisted efforts to condemn Yugoslavia. In its final communiqué, a compromise was reached condemning the ethnic cleansing policies of the Serbs in Bosnia and Herzegovina. Even Indonesia had its ethnic problems with the Timors. Despite the focus on ethnic cleansing, the nonaligned movement failed to adopt a policy for addressing inter-Third World conflicts. If the nonaligned movement expects to continue as a viable entity in the post-Cold War era, it must address the problems of ethnic conflict and violence and emerge as an important institution for conflict resolution. The nonaligned movement will need to support and value the coexistence of ethnic, religious, and cultural differences. This Third World actor will need to become a champion of multi-ethnic, multi-religious, and multi-cultural democracy in the Third World.

TOWARD A NEW ERA OF GLOBAL APARTHEID

Former President Bush, with the assistance of Western Europe, Japan, and the new Russian republic proclaimed a new world order following the Persian Gulf War. This new world order functions on the basis of intensified collaboration between the United States and the Great Powers to manage regional conflicts in Third World regions and to demilitarize the arms race in such arenas of conflict. Leaders in the Northeast and Northwest have rediscovered the United Nations' collective security apparatus and are employing this diplomatic instrument in global conflicts. Convergence of interest between the Northeast and Northwest has become a dominant feature of the post-Cold War era. The Northeast and Northwest have ceased to interact along ideological lines as democratic capitalism replaces democratic centralism as the gospel for developing political and economic communities. The Northeast is no longer following the teachings of Karl Marx and V. I. Lenin. Marxist principles are being replaced by the entrepreneurial principles of Adam Smith. As this process of convergence proceeds in the North, a new global rift is emerging along

North-South lines that has a decisively racial character. This new era of global apartheid is also narrowing the political and economic space in which Third World leaders may experiment with alternative models of political economy.

The decision-making instruments of power for facilitating collective security are in the hands of the North. Northern states from the East and West control the United Nations Security Council, the International Monetary Fund, the World Bank, the General Agreement on Tariffs and Trade, and other relevant multilateral financial institutions. The Third World's challenge for the twenty-first century will be to democratize the decision-making processes in international institutions to make the power of Third World states comparable to the North. Without such changes the world system will carry through the transition toward a new era of global apartheid precisely when this racial order is in retreat in the Republic of South Africa.

At this juncture, we will explore the implications of globalization, democratization, and transitions in the world system for Third World solidarity and fragmentation. As we approach the 21st century, globalization has replaced the concern for a New World order. The forces of globalization and democratization are increasingly conceptualized as natural forces that all states must adopt. The epilogue will examine the implications of globalization and democratization for Third World solidarity and fragmentation.

NOTES

1. Julius O. Ihonvbere, "The Third World and the New World Order in the 1990s," in *Annual Editions: Third World 94/95* (Guilford, CT: Dushkin Publishing Group, Inc., 1994), p. 6.

2. See Gernot Kohler, *Global Apartheid: World Models Project Working Paper Number Seven* (New York: Institute for World Order, 1978). His definition does not require solidarity among Northern nations. My definition conceptualized Northern solidarity as a critical element in the new era of global apartheid.

3. See Chapter 1, pp. 21–30.

4. See Ali A. Mazrui, "Global Apartheid: Race and Religion in the New World Order" (paper presented at the 90th Anniversary Nobel Jubilee Symposium, panel on "The Changing Pattern of Global Conflict: From East-West to North-South Conflicts?" Oslo, Norway, December 1991).

5. Basil Davidson, *The Black Man's Burden: Africa and the Curse of the Nation-State* (New York: Times Books, 1992), p. 220.

6. Ali A. Mazrui, "Global Apartheid," 14.

7. United Nations, *World Economic Survey 1991/92* (New York: United Nations Publications, 1992), p. 63.

8. Richard Barnet and John Cavanagh, eds., *Global Dreams: Imperil Corporations and the New World Order* (New York: Simon & Schuster, 1994), p. 286.

9. E. Balibar, "Racism and Politics in Europe Today," *New Left Review* 186 (1991): 5–19.

10. Jim McLaughlin, "Defending the Frontiers: The Political Geography of Race and Racism in the European Community," in *The Political Geography of the New World Order,* ed.

Colin H. Williams (London: Belhaven Press, 1993), p. 28.

11. Immanuel Wallerstein, *Geopolitics and Geoculture: Essays on a Changing World-System* (Cambridge: Cambridge University Press, 1993), p. 193.

12. Jim McLaughlin, "Defending the Frontiers," p. 36.

13. See John Benyon and John Solomos, *The Roots of Urban Unrest* (Oxford and New York: Pergamon Press, 1987).

14. See Roger Kaplan, "France through Kofi's Eyes," *The Atlantic Monthly* 269, no. 4 (April 1992): 43.

15. Jim MacLaughlin, "Defending the Frontiers," p. 36.

16 . Clarence Lusane, ed., *Race in the Global Era: African Americans at the Millennium* (Boston, MA: South End Press, 1997), p.7.

17. Ibid., p. 8.

18. See Roger Kaplan, "France through Kofi's Eyes," p. 34.

19. See Paul G. Lauren, *Power and Prejudice: The Politics and Diplomacy of Discrimination* (Boulder, CO: Westview Press, 1988), especially Chapter 2.

20. Jim MacLaughlin, "Defending the Frontiers," p. 42.

21. "France Moves On Deporting Illegal Aliens," *New York Times,* 23 July 1995, p. 4, International edition.

22. Christopher Lasch, *Culture of Narcissism: American Life in the Age of Diminishing Expectations* (New York: Norton, 1978), p. 117.

23. Pierre L. Van den Berghe, *Race and Racism in Comparative Perspective* (New York: Wiley, 1967), pp. 20–35.

24. Noel Jacob Kent, "To Polarize a Nation: Racism, Labor Markets, and the State in the U.S. Political Economy, 1965–1986," in *The Rising Tide of Cultural Pluralism: The Nation-State at Bay,* ed. Crawford Young (Madison, WI: The University of Wisconsin Press, 1993), p. 62.

25. Ibid., 62.

26. Ibid., 62.

27. Ibid., 63. Also see B. Harrison and B. Bluestone, *The Great U-Turn: Corporate Restructuring and the Polarizing of America* (New York: Basic Books, 1990); and J. Kolko, *Restructuring the World Economy* (New York: Pantheon, 1988).

28. Manning Marable, *How Capitalism Underdeveloped Black America?* (Boston: South End Press, 1983).

29. Clarence Lusane, *Race in the Global Era,* p. 10.

30. Carter A. Wilson, *From Slavery to Advanced Capitalism* (Thousand Oaks: Sage Publication: 1995), p. 208–209.

31. Bennett Harrison and Barry Bluestone, *The Great U-Turn: Corporate Restructuring and the Polarizing of America* (New York: Basic Books, 1990).

32. W. J. Wilson, *The Truly Disadvantaged* (Chicago: University of Chicago Press, 1987).

33. Jacqueline Jones, *American Work: Four Centuries of Black and White Labor* (New York: W.W. Norton & Company, 1998), p. 370.

34. Manning Marable, *How Capitalism Underdeveloped Black America?* p. 181.

35. See Robert Cook, *Sweet Land of Liberty? The African-American Struggle For Civil Rights in the Twentieth Century* (London and New York: Longman, Inc., 1998), p. 279.

36. Jacquelyn Jones, *The Dispossessed: America's Underclass From the Civil War to the Present* (New York: Basic Books, 1991), pp. 276–277.

37. Ibid., p. 272.

38. Ali A. Mazrui, "Global Apartheid," p. 14.

39. Jacquelyn Jones, *The Dispossessed,* p. 270.

40. See Franz Fanon, "On National Culture," in *The Wretched of the Earth*, ed. Franz Fanon (New York: Grove Weidenfeld, 1963), pp. 206–248.

41. John Gray, *False Dawn: The Delusion of Global Capitalism* (New York: The New Press, 1998), pp. 129–130.

42. Clarence Lusane, *Race in the Global Era*, p. 46.

43. "Justices, in 5-4 Vote, Reject Districts Drawn with Race the Predominant Factor," *New York Times*, 30 June 1995, p. 1.

44. "Farewell to Old Order in the Supreme Court," *New York Times*, 2 July 1995, p. 4.

45. Jacqueline Jones, *American Work*, p. 384.

46. Jacqueline Jones, op. cit., p. 384.

47. Leslie G. Carr, *The Color-Blind Racism* (Thousand Oaks, CA: Sage Publications, 1997), p. 134.

48. Ibid., pp. 136–137.

49. Jacqueline Jones, *American Work*, p. 381.

50. Richard J. Herrnstein and Charles Murray, *The Bell Curve: Intelligence and Class Structure in American Life* (New York: The Free Press, 1994).

51. See Donald Johnson, *Factors Affecting Outward Mobility in the Virgin Islands: A Developing Caribbean Micro-State* (Ph.D. diss., University of Michigan, 1982).

52. *Washington Post*, 8–14 November 1993, p. 15, National weekly edition.

53. "Haiti's New Government Fights Potholes," *New York Times*, 5 June 1994, p. 18, International edition.

54. TransAfrica Forum is a foreign policy institution established to provide for the collection, analysis and dissemination of information about Africa and the Caribbean and about U.S. policies affecting them. Indeed, it is an African American foreign policy institution.

55. Catherine Orenstein, "Second-hand Democracy: Human Rights Workers in Haiti," *Tikkun* 13, no. 4 (July-August 1998), pp. 44–53.

56. Central Intelligence Agency, The World Factbook 2000: Haiti, web site at www.odci.gov/cia/publications/factbook/geos//ha.html#People.

57. "The New Terrorism: Coming Soon to a City Near You," *The Economist* (15–21 August 1998): pp. 17–19.

58. Clyde Haberman, "Israel Says Syria Is Testing Advanced Scud Missiles," *New York Times*, 15 August 1992, p. 3, International edition.

59. These states include India, Libya, Pakistan, North Korea, South Korea, Argentina, Brazil, Syria, Israel, and South Africa.

60. See Jane Nolan, *Trappings of Power: Ballistic Missiles in the Third World*, (Washington, DC: Brookings Institution, 1991); W. Seth Carus, *Ballistic Missiles in the Third World: Threat and Response* (New York: Praeger Publishers, 1990).

61. The Comprehensive Test Ban Treaty, http:/www.usun-vienna.usia. co.at/ctb.htm, p.1.

62. BBC News, "India Stands Firm on Nuclear Policy," 23 July 1998, http://news.bbc.co.uk/hi/english/events/a...isis/latest_news/newsid.

63. "Iran Said To Test Missile Able To Hit Israel and Saudis," *New York Times*, 23 July 1998, p. A1.

64. Jonathan Schell, "The Folly of Arms Control," *Foreign Affairs* 79, no. 5 (September/October 2000): 22–46.

65. "Non-Aligned Movement Decides It Is Still Relevant," *New York Times*, 7 September 1992, p. 4, International edition.

66. Ibid.

Epilogue:
Globalization, Democratization, and
Transitions in North-South Relations

Scholars engaged in research revolving around the relationship between Third World solidarity, changing hegemonic structures, and racial capitalism must constantly contend with the tidal wave of current events that confront many of the assertions and underlying assumptions of their inquiry. This inquiry is no exception to this general principle. Since completing this study, several international developments have erupted that shed light on the basic hypothesis of this investigation. I have organized these upheavals under the rubric of globalization, democratization, and transitions in the Third World. The end of the Cold War era has intensified the globalization of capitalism thus integrating every sector of the globe. We are crossing a new threshold as the new millennium approaches with no fundamental challenge to global capitalism except capitalism itself. What are the forces behind globalization and how does this phenomenon influence Third World solidarity and fragmentation in the post-Cold War era? To what extent do the forces of globalization reinforce the second era of global apartheid? These questions will be addressed below.

GLOBALIZATION AND RESISTANCE IN THE THIRD WORLD

Starting in the 1990s, the discourse that once centered on the specificity of the New World Order lost ground to the forces of globalization. Scholars and practitioners alike considered the processes of globalization as natural, inevitable, and beneficial to every sector of the world system, including the transitional societies that were once included the former Soviet Union. Some observers even declared that we had reached the "end of history" through the triumph of planetary capitalism and a third wave of democratization. The concept of globalization normally includes the spatial reorganization of production, the magnification of industries across borders, the dispersion of financial markets, the diffusion of identical consumer goods to distant countries, massive transfer of population within the South and the East to the West, resultant conflict between immigrant and established communities in formerly tight-knit neighborhoods, and a worldwide preference for democracy. This conception of globalization involves framing a multilevel analysis: economic, political, cultural, and ideological.[1] We have entered the age of globalization, when the world system has truly become a global village, at least with reference to the economic, financial, and technological reach of transnational corporations. The current global predominance of transnational corporations has incorporated a variety of frantic nations, peoples, and cultures. The world system is being shaped and defined by the digital-information era. As a worldwide phenomenon, globalization is a coalescence of varied transnational processes and domestic structures, allowing the economy, politics, culture, and ideology of one country to penetrate another. The globalization processes ranged from the spatial reorganization of production to international trade, and the integration of financial markets. Driven by changing modes of competition, globalization compresses the time and space aspects of social relations. In a word, globalization is a market-induced, not a policy-induced process.[2] Rapid innovations in microelectronics, material science, and biotechnology led to what some have labeled a new "technological revolution" or the "creative destruction" phase of capitalism. Research and development in these arenas involve complex and expensive laboratory facilities, and in some cases, increased use of proprietary research. The latter, of course, increases the barrier of entry as has the velocity of technological impulse. At the same time, microelectronics has made possible the transition from mass production to flexible specialization, producing smaller batches of differentiated goods.[3] Lester Thurow has observed: "for the first time in human history, anything can be made anywhere and sold everywhere.[4]

In this study, I compared and contrasted conflicting Third World zones with reference to their ability to carve out a niche for themselves in the new international division of labor. The result of this analysis suggested that states in the East and Southeast Asian zone performed much better than did their counterparts in the rest of the Third World. Several states in Latin America and their counterparts in Europe (Portugal and Turkey) were exceptions to this trend. The comparison revolved around what Gary Geriffi refers to as "producer-driven networks" and "buyer-driven networks." Producer-driven networks are centralized, vertically integrated production chains, found in capital-intensive sectors such as autos, computers, and aircraft. Subcontracting involves manufacturing of parts in various countries around the world for later assembly in appropriate locations. Buyer-driven networks are decentralized, design-intensive industries such as clothing and footwear. Subcontractors produce finished goods according to specification for retail outlets in advanced market countries. Barbara Stallings draws attention to the fact that the new premium placed on technological expansion has made it difficult for Third World nations to break into high valued-added production, and at the same time, the cost of not doing so has also risen.[5] This new international context of development reinforces our notion of global apartheid. While there are certain niches for specialization in low value-added goods, countries that rely exclusively on these products run the risk of falling further behind. These same actors face the traditional problems of low-income elasticity's demand for basic food items, textiles, and low-grade steel, as well as the spillover in terms of training and technology that are lost. Those countries that continue to concentrate their exports on commodities and raw materials are an even greater disadvantage because the new technologies minimize the use of such commodities.[6]

Third World states have taken divergent approaches toward trade and industrialization, allowing select states to take advantage of the huge gaps in production and international marketing. As a result some Third World states have become key investors (East Asia), while the majority cannot sell without requiring high levels of protectionism (Africa, South Asia, and some parts of Latin America). As the forces of globalization accelerate, the future for this latter group becomes more precarious.

In this new age of capitalism – postindustrial, post-Cold War, transitional, informational, and high-technology-driven, global capitalism has the capacity to produce and distribute any commodity on a global scale. This new capacity of global capital has transformed the existing fragile bargaining power between the North and South. This new phase of capitalism is undermining the ability of Third World states, both individually and collectively, to negotiate their interests: that is, better prices for the products they produce, improved working conditions, environmentally sustainable industrial policies, and increased employment opportunities for their citizens.

Side by side with changes taking place in the real sector of the world economy has been the imminent development of a globally integrated market for capital. The connection between these markets – the financial markets and the market for goods and non-financial services – are increasingly complex. Transactions in this arena are partially dependent on innovations in telecommunication technology that make possible immediate transmittal of money and information across the globe. International bank lending by countries increased from 1.9 trillion dollars to 6.2 trillion dollars in 1991. As Sassen Saskia has observed, substantial attention has revolved around the new technologies' capability for instantaneous transmission while very little has been devoted to the location of financial centers in particular cities in highly developed countries.[7] These centers are located in such diverse countries as the United States, the United Kingdom, Japan, Switzerland, France, Germany, and Luxembourg. At the same time, stock markets worldwide have also been integrated. Deregulation of the all-important stock market intensified in most of Europe and North America throughout the 1980s. During the early 1990s, the pace of deregulation quickened in such diverse markets as Buenos Aires, São Paulo, Bangkok, Taipei, etc. Nevertheless, deregulation also reflects the declining significance of the state in this arena. The concentration of global capital markets at this juncture epitomizes the consolidation of power beyond the nation-state.

Increasingly the market exercises the accountability function normally associated with the state. These markets now perform the contractual functions normally associated with citizenship: they can vote for or veto government economic policies; they can force governments to adopt particular policy preferences and not others. In addition, private investors vote with their feet, moving quickly in and out of countries, often with massive amounts of money. The global capital market makes it possible for money to flow anywhere, regardless of national origins or boundaries, although some countries, such as Iraq and Libya, are excluded. The financial market has created innovative new methods that allow foreign investors to reap huge profits. These instruments now include derivatives, i.e., futures, swaps, and options. Foreign investors threw money into Mexico even though its current account deficit was growing at an alarming rate, reaching 8 percent of GDP in 1994. Wall Street analysts and traders were still urging investment in Mexico toward the end of 1994. It was not until February 1995 that investors began their fierce abandonment of this market. The growing power and influence of global capital markets were apparent in the 1994 Mexican peso crisis. This resulted in a panic and large outflow of capital from Mexico.[8] The global capital market lost confidence in the Mexican economy and the leadership's ability to manage the crisis. The United States intervened and defined the crisis along security lines, with important modifications. In the past, the State Department and the National Security bureaucracy participated in the formulation and implementation of policy. In this crisis, the Treasury Department played a critical role in the development of the United States' response. Security issues in the age of globalization now encompass international economic and financial issues.

Global capital has incorporated the neoliberal regimes as a critical element of its arsenal in order to influence the developmental and financial or fiscal policies and outcomes of states. International financial institutions have emerged as key sites for the formulation and implementation of neoliberal regimes during this era of globalization. Operating under a variety of names ranging from neoliberalism, neoconservatism to neoorthodoxy, the new international consensus on international finance features three main elements: macroeconomic stability (especially smaller fiscal deficits), a reduced government role in the economy (deregulation and privatization), and greater openness to the outside (reduced barriers to trade and a more receptive approach toward capital).[9]

Starting in the early 1990s, most advocates of free-market ideology were very optimistic that the benefits of unfettered financial markets outweigh the potential problems. The proponents asserted that freeing up trade is good; why not also let capital move freely across borders? These same proponents assumed that free capital mobility among all nations was exactly like free trade in goods and services, a mutual-gain phenomenon. Hence, restricted capital movement, just like protectionism, was seen as harmful to economic performance in each country, whether rich or poor.[10]Capital mobility has not lived up to its high expectations, particularly with the repeated crisis that have wreaked havoc on emerging markets.

The Asian economic crisis of the late 1990's has settled down and slowly returned to business as usual. One cannot detach the Asian quandary from excessive borrowing of foreign short-term capital as Asian economies relaxed their capital account controls and allowed their banks and firms to borrow from abroad. In 1996, the total private capital inflows to Indonesia, Malaysia, South Korea, Thailand, and the Philippines were $93 billion, up from $41 billion in 1994. In 1997, that suddenly changed to an outflow of $12 billion. Capital mobility crisis tends to follow a standard pattern regardless of the nation or region involved. The debt crisis of the 1980s cost Latin America a decade of growth. The Mexicans, who were vastly overexposed through short-term inflows, were devastated in 1994. This financial disturbance increases immigration flows to the United States.

The Asian economies of Thailand, Indonesia, and South Korea, all heavily burdened with short-term debt, went into a tailspin in 1997, drastically lowering their growth rates. The countries experiencing the crisis are required to follow certain policies in order to restore foreign-capital confidence in their economies. This usually involves raising interest rates, as the IMF required in Indonesia. This policy posture has wreaked havoc on firms across Asia that have large amounts of debt. Capital mobility dilemmas necessitate selling of domestic assets, which are greatly undervalued as a result of the credit crunch. Consequently, countries such as Thailand and South Korea have been required to further open their markets, even though the short-term capital flows played an important role in fostering the problems in the first place.[11]

Accompanying their economic reversals, these countries also lose their sovereign right to implement economic and financial policies as they and their domestic constituencies see fit. Capital-mobility calamity has provided the IMF, the World Bank, and increasingly, U.S. policy makers the tools to penetrate domestic policy-making processes on matters of social policy. The Frank Sanders Amendment of 1994, which sought to attach labor standards to any increased bailout funds, is a small example of this process. Jagdish Bhagwati notes that any nation leaning toward the embrace of free capital mobility must calculate these costs and also consider the prospect of running into a crisis.[12] He contends that the Wall Street-Treasury Complex, following the tradition of its predecessor, that is, the military-industrial complex, strongly influences the Western response to capital mobility crises. He observes that the IMF is also influenced by this network in that its solutions to problems tend to reinforce the Wall Street mantra. What is good for Wall Street is also good for the global community, particularly with reference to capital flows.

The multiplying aftereffects of the Asian crisis and the diffusion of economic and financial calamity to the Russian Republic in August 1998, demonstrates the increasing complexity as well as the dilemma of conceptualizing international financial regimes along the same lines as notions of free trade. Latin American states as diverse as Brazil and Chile are bracing their societies for the advancing currency and financial catastrophe. Once again, the IMF, reacting to concerns on Wall Street, brokered a bailout package for Brazil to be implemented following the fall 1998 presidential election. The IMF rescue plan has been tailored to the needs of foreign capital.

The recent flood of bad economic and financial news from such diverse sectors of the world economy as East and Southeast Asia, the Russian Republic, and the unfolding calamity in Brazil, cracked the Northern consensus on international financial issues. This became quite apparent at the IMF meeting in Washington D.C. during the week of October 3, 1998. At the conference a wide range of proposals were offered to confront the capital mobility dilemma. Tony Blair, Britain's Prime Minister, called for a new Bretton Woods for the next millennium, while Gerhard Schroder, Germany's newly elected chancellor, called for "target zones" for the world's principal currencies. The French proposed to endow international financial institutions with "genuine political legitimacy," while the Japanese called for a special fund to rescue Southeast Asian countries and a new regime to discipline capital flows. President Clinton articulated a six-point plan to resolve the global financial calamity. The conferees agreed to disagree. They failed to develop any consensus to resolve or manage this situation. Nevertheless, the Wall Street-Treasury Complex may have suffered a major setback as a result of the flood of problems associated with capital mobility. The U.S. Congress finally approved the $18 billion that the Clinton administration had requested since early 1998 in order to replenish the funds of IMF. The Republican members of Congress have also insisted on some basic reforms of the IMF.

Most of the states that suffered economic and financial setbacks during the Asian financial crisis have rebounded with the exception of Indonesia. Indonesia is caught up in a wave of political instability that threatens to break up this multiethnic and multicultural society. Former President Suharto and his family face legal problems over the $500 million in wealth that they accumulated over thirty years. Citizens are demanding accountability for the money and for crimes committed against the citizenry. Conflict between Muslims and non-Muslims threatens the very fabric of the state.

Fernand Braudel observed that capitalism is not just a means to organize the economy. Capitalism, in each of its divergent historical formations, has also been a particular system of values, pattern of consumption, social structure, and form of state. Each configuration or form has also projected a conception of world order. The new capitalism with its global vocation incorporates all of these things. At the same time, the divergent models of accumulation found in the Anglo-American, German, and Japanese formations, as well as alternative models of economic organization in East Asia, are being exported as paradigms to the developing world.[13] The third wave of democratization that has swept the world system is an example of how values are embedded in the global restructuring of capitalism.

DEMOCRATIC TRANSITION IN THE THIRD WORLD

The end of the Cold War conflict unleashed a new tidal wave of democratization throughout the world system. The transitional states of the former Soviet Union also were penetrated by the so-called third wave of democratization, resulting in a variety of transition processes in the Soviet Empire. Leaders of the North emerged as principal supporters of democratic transition throughout the world system. They conceptualize democracy as the twin engine of market democracy. At this point the traditional Cold War justification for tolerating and supporting authoritarian regimes in the Third World no longer operated in the new post-Cold War milieu. The collapse of the Berlin Wall accelerated this process as authoritarian leaders and dictators of diverse stripes lost power. Examples abound, such as the overthrow of Mobuto Sese Seko before his death as well as the arrest of former Chilean leader General Augosto Pinochet by the British authorities after a warrant was released by Spanish authorities for his incarceration. Under the umbrella of globalization human rights advocates are creating new international regimes that may end heads of states' ability to escape punishment for human rights violations committed during their tour of duty.

Robert W. Cox and Stephen Gill maintain that most of the contemporary scholarship on globalization and the so-called third wave of democratization lacks a historical perspective. Both of these neo-Gramscian scholars draw attention to Karl Polanyi's *The Great Transformation* as an example of scholarship that examines how values are embedded in global restructuring of capitalism.[14] Polanyi analyzed what he labeled "substantive economics," that is, economic processes firmly established in particular historical societies – how societies constitute themselves to satisfy their material wants. He differentiated this study from formal economics, which is based on an analytical detachment of economic conduct from other human activities and is based on definite presumed human characteristics assumed to be universal – the classic concept of economic or rational man. Accordingly, substantive economics directs thoughts in the historical diachronic dimension, while formal economics, in its quest for universally authoritative regulation, follows synchronic logic.[15]

In *Great Transformation's* interrogation of the evolution of capitalism from the industrial revolution through the first half of the twentieth century, Polanyi identified what he referred to as a double movement. During the first stage, the state was eliminated from meaningful participation in the economy, but retreated to the role of enforcer of the rules of the market. The market was assumed to be self-regulating, and its automatic function through the instrumentality of an invisible hand was postulated by the theory to advance the general will.

The second stage of Polanyi's double movement was society's response to the socially insidious aftereffect, unforeseen in theory, of the self-regulating market – the response to what Robert W. Cox refers to as the Dickensian picture of society torn asunder by greed and competition. This rejoinder reincorporated the state as regulator of the economy and guarantor of a degree of social equity. Conservative politicians, ranging from Bismarck to Disraeli, who understood that the state required a strong social base, initiated this second stage; and it continued through the action of labor and antisystemic movements, culminating in the creation of the welfare state and the idea of social democracy. Contemporary neoconservatives deride politics and fail to appreciate the significance of a supportive political base to the stability of society.

As we know, Polanyi did not live to see the full fruition of this second stage. Scholars operating in the world system and neo-Gramscian analytical frameworks traced it to the late 1960s and the early 1970s, when the pattern of regulation built up through the second phase of his double movement appeared to have reached its limits in stagflation and crisis.

In the post-Cold War era the state has been reconfigured to perform certain tasks that are meaningful and significant for the processes associated with globalization. They include deregulation, privatization, and dismantling of the protection for vulnerable sectors of societies in both the North and the South. The mantra of free trade and unregulated market is loud and clear. Correspondingly, the magic of market forces to resolve all outstanding societal and global problems has become the most important incantation for the post-Cold War era. Neoliberalism is ushering in a new wave of democratization celebrating the triumph of democratic capitalism, or more precisely, market democracy. As Steve Gill has observed, the democracy that is being celebrated and exported adheres to the philosophical traditions of John Locke and Joseph Schumpeter.[16] Hence, it is more elitist and less representative, particularly with reference to the humble and increasingly dispossessed masses in the North and the South.

The once-celebrated third wave of democracy has come under question in recent years as a result of the resurgence of traditional political authority on the African continent as well as the various negotiated pacts, particularly in Latin America, that restrict political participation to select groups. These same pacts make it impossible for some societies to confront historical atrocities committed by military regimes in the past.

The role of the North in supporting low-intensity democracy was very clear in Nigeria and Indonesia in the 1990s. The North's international financial institutions and multinational corporations were content to tolerate the arrest of Chief Moshood Abiola, the apparent victor in the June 1993 Presidential elections in Nigeria. They were also content to continue business as usual, notwithstanding the increase in human rights violations and corruption, including the hanging of writer and political activist Ken Saro-Wiwa in 1995 along with eight other Ogoni activists, that accompanied the General Sani Abacha era. As long as the oil continued to flow, the nature of the regime was less important than the interest of the North. U.S. policy makers even sought to persuade a reluctant Chief Abiola to renounce any desire to assume the presidency in exchange for release from prison. Chief Abiola paid a high price for the democratic forces in Nigeria, suffering a deadly heart attack in 1997. Subsequently, a heart attack also took the life of General Abacha in the summer of 1998. Since then, Nigeria has been making critical steps toward democratic transition. The continuing struggle in Nigeria will have ramifications for the African continent.

In the latter part of 1998, people throughout the Nigerian delta region staged protests against continuing corruption and collusion between the central government and the oil multinationals. Citizens in this area are alarmed at the environmental degradation that is taking place in the oil region. Oil companies have not demonstrated any concern for the environment in their exploitation of petroleum resources in Nigeria. Their behavior in Nigeria mirrors the action of other transnational corporations in other areas of the South where environmental racism is rampant. The same scenario as in Nigeria is also taking place in minority communities in the United States, where environmental racism is also problematic. The Nigerians are challenging and resisting critical components of globalization that do not take into account local political, economic, and environmental concerns.

Indonesia played a critical role in the evolution of Third World solidarity in the 1950s and the 1960s. Sukarno seized power in 1966 through a military coup, bringing to an end a very important radical regime in the Third World. Since the mid-1960s Bandung evolved as a critical component of the North's foreign policy goals to support more conservative and less antisystemic Third World regimes. During the 1980s, Indonesia emerged as one of the darlings of Wall Street and the international financial community. As the Asian crisis swept the region in 1998, Indonesia, once considered a bulwark of stability, began to experience rampant political disorder. The ongoing struggle in Indonesia has serious ramifications for globalization and democratization in the Developing World.

In Indonesia, democratic forces led by students and their supporters played a critical role in persuading Sukarno to step down. Riots and violence against the Chinese community in Indonesia accompanied the confrontation between the students and military forces. Chinese merchants have played a critical role in sustaining economic growth and development in Indonesia. The democratic movement in Indonesia was not satisfied with Sukarno's departure from power and the return to the status quo. They are waging a massive campaign to persuade Indonesia's new President B. J. Habibie to call early elections in June 1999 and to investigate the Sukarno family business enterprises in order to ascertain what state assets were appropriated during Sukarno's reign in power. These democratic forces are seeking to return to the former relationship between the state and economy and provide a safety net for the dispossessed, as in the past. Their struggle represents a new form of resistance to democratic capitalism or market democracy.

At the very twilight of Yeltsin's reign he selected Vladimir Putin as his new prime minister, and in 1999 Putin was elected overwhelmingly as the new president of the Russian Republic. Putin's national security background has led to questions concerning his commitment to democratic processes. Likewise, his scorched-earth and total war approach toward the conflict in the Caucasus has also raised serious questions along these lines. Although Putin has sought to reassure the West and foreign capital that he is committed to reforming the state and ending corruption and criminality associated with the Russian brand of capitalism, foreign capital has not been willing to invest in Russia. Despite Putin's assurances, democracy remains unrealized in Russia.

So far, capitalism is the most successful wealth-generating economic system the world has ever known; Joseph Schumpeter asserts that no other system makes available so many benefits to the "common people." According to Schumpeter, capitalism produces affluence and material goods through endlessly developing to ever-advanced levels of productivity and technological complexity; this process necessitates that the "mature" be destroyed before the "contemporary" can take over.[17] Technological progress, the fundamental source of power of global capitalism, requires the continuing elimination of obsolescent factories, economic zones, and even human skills. Global capitalism rewards the adaptable and efficient; it punishes the redundant and less productive.

It is through the process of "creative destruction" that global capitalism produces many winners but also many losers, at least in the short term, and poses a serious threat to traditional social values, beliefs, and institutions. In addition, periodic recessions and downturns that can foster pandemonium in people's lives come with the advance of global capitalism. Although capitalism in the long run distributes affluence and material goods more equally than any other known system, it does have a propensity to reward the most efficient and productive, and it tends to concentrate wealth, power, and economic activities.

The survival of global capitalism is tied to vigorous and prudent leadership which must promote international cooperation to establish and enforce rules regulating trade, foreign investment, and international monetary affairs. Robert Gilpin notes that it is equally crucial that leadership ensures at least minimal safeguards for the inevitable losers from market forces and from the process of creative destruction; those who lose must at least believe that the system functions fairly.[18] Continuation of the market or capitalist system remains in danger unless attention to efficiency is counterbalanced with social protection for the economically weak and with training and education of those workers left behind by rapid economic and technological change. Insurgencies in the international system against divergent waves of globalization characterized by open markets, unrestricted capital flows and activities of transnational corporations appear repeatedly in the guise of trade protection, closed economic blocs, and various kinds of cheating. The association of globalization with corporate greed on the part of transnational corporations and international financial institutions ranging from the World Bank, the World Trade Organization, and the International Monetary Fund has spawned new waves of resistance by workers and students alike. These actors have taken up the cause of the workers and nations who have not benefitted from the promise of globalization.

Since 1998, protests and movements against globalization have taken on a new life, beginning with the anti-World Trade Organization protest which included the participation of a well-organized anarchist group. Since November, 1999, college and university students in the United States have demonstrated against corporate greed and working conditions in sweatshops that produce, among other items, Nike shoes and college athletic apparel. Anti-sweatshop protests took place at the universities of Michigan, Wisconsin, Oregon, Iowa, and Kentucky, as well as at SUNY-Albany, Tulane, Purdue, and Macalester. Students have also organized anti-globalization workshops on their campuses and increased their recruitment of new protesters against corporate greed. Since the WTO protest in Seattle, global economic leaders have had a difficult time holding business meetings that are free from protest and negative publicity. In April, 2000, protest politics and demonstrations against globalization also marred the IMF/World Bank annual meeting. The recent meeting of Latin American economic ministers in Windsor, Canada, and Detroit, Michigan, also was accompanied by protests from students, the Teamster Union, and the United Auto Workers Union. A hodgepodge global coalition stretching across several constituencies – labor unions, students, and workers – make up the new movement against globalization.

Like the Civil Rights Movement of the 1960s, it was difficult at that time to assess its impact and global reach. When the Berlin Wall came tumbling down in 1989, European participants in the Democratic Movement were singing "We Shall Overcome," a song revived by the 1960s civil rights workers. The late Dr. Martin L. King, Jr., Rosa Parks, and Andrew Young, along with countless nameless participants in the Civil Rights Movement, were unaware at the time that their efforts would inspire similar movements for social change across the globe. Similarly, it was difficult to fathom the impact that the Black Power Movement might have in the Caribbean and later on the Black Consciousness Movement in South Africa. The late writer and political activist Ken Saro-Wiwa, along with eight other Ogoni activists in Nigeria, who were hanged in 1995, also realized the global scope of their efforts against corporate globalization and corporate greed. Like their Indonesian counterpart, they have inspired a new generation of resistance to globalization. This recalls the Frederick Douglass' 1857 statement concerning the necessity of struggles:

> The whole history of progress of human liberty shows that all concessions yet made to her august claims, have been born of earnest struggle. This struggle may be a moral one, or it may be a physical one, and it may be both moral and physical, but it must be a struggle. Power concedes nothing without a demand. It never did and it never will.[19]

Global capitalism has consistently created resistance and struggles against the barbarism that accompanies globalization.

TRANSITIONS IN THE NORTH-SOUTH CONFLICT: THE WORLD IS A GHETTO

The end of the Cold War conflict has transformed the way scholars look at the world system. The concept "Third World" no longer has significance in the post-Cold War era. At the same time, the New World order does not quite capture the continuities and discontinuities that are operating. Instead of Third World zones or regions which have fixed geographical representation, we are witnessing the evolution of a Third World or a peripheral capitalist sector within the Northeast and the Northwest. Hence, our theme "the world is a ghetto," where a large segment of the population is excluded from the benefits of globalization, or more accurately, market democracy. There are islands of wealth located throughout the globe, surrounded by a vast sea of poverty. Increasingly, large numbers of Europeans of a variety of stripes are joining this sea of poverty. However, they are combating their impoverishment by drawing attention to citizenship and rights based on blood ties and, increasingly, skin color. The state has established an array of immigration laws and welfare reform packages that limit economic and financial benefits to a restricted number of people, particularly people of color and their European counterparts who are not from the core sectors of the Northwest. Affirmative action and equal rights policies are in retreat throughout the globe as neoconservatism and the politics of indifference prevails in the political arena.

This new situation has propelled many Third World people to exit via immigration to the Northwest, pursuing both political and economic asylum. The unfolding evolution toward a "twenty/eighty" society at the local and global levels is propelling mass migration from the South to the North. In Europe, a large number of people are fleeing ethnic and political violence in its periphery, seeking a better life. The new era of Global Apartheid is evolving as a permanent feature of the global system. Globalization and low-intensity democracy is accelerating this process. As we approach the new millennium, Third World solidarity is in withdrawal as the forces of globalization stifle efforts to build collective global communities. The struggles against globalization and low-intensity democratization in Indonesia, Nigeria, and in the ghettos of the Northwest may plant the seeds for a new framework of solidarity in the new millennium.

NOTES

1. J. H. Mittelman, *Globalization: Critical Reflections* (Boulder, CO: Lynne Rienner, 1996), p. 3.

2. Ibid., p. 3.

3. Barbara Stallings, ed., *Global Change, Regional Response: The New International Context of Development* (Cambridge: Cambridge University Press, 1995), p. 114.

4. Lester Thurow, *The Future of Capitalism: How Today's Economic Forces Shape Tomorrow's World* (New York: William Morrow and Company, 1996), p. 114.

5. Barbara Stallings, op. cit., p. 9.

6. Ibid., p. 9.

7. Saskia Sassen, *Losing Control: Sovereignty in the Age of Globalization* (New York: Columbia University Press, 1996), pp. 11–12.

8. Ibid., p. 47.

9. Barbara Stallings, *Global Change: Regional Response,* p. 12.

10. Jagdish Bhagwati, "The Capital Myth: The Difference between Free Trade in Widgets and Dollars," *Foreign Affairs* 77, no. 3 (May/June 1998): 7–12.

11. Ibid., pp. 7-8.

12. Ibid., p. 10.

13. Robert W. Cox, "Globalization, Multilateralism, and Democracy," in *Approaches to World Order,* ed. Robert W. Cox and Timothy J. Sinclair (Cambridge: Cambridge University Press, 1996), p. 527.

14. See Stephen Gill, "Globalization, Democratization, and the Politics of Indifference," in *Globalization: Critical Reflections,* ed. James H. Mittelman (Boulder, CO: Lynne Rienner, 1996), pp. 205–228; Robert W. Cox, "Globalization, Multilateralism, and Democracy," in *Approaches to World Order,* ed. Robert W. Cox and Timothy Sinclair (Cambridge: Cambridge University Press, 1996), pp. 524–534.

15. Robert W. Cox, op. cit., p. 527.

16. Stephen Gill, op. cit., pp. 213–214.

17. J. A Schumpeter, *Capitalism, Socialism and Democracy,* Fifth edition (London: George Allen and Unwin, 1976.

18. R. Gilpin, *The Challenge of Global Capitalism: The World Economy in the 21st Century* (Princeton, NJ: Princeton University Press, 2000), pp. 2–3.

19. Frederick Douglass, quoted in Lewis R. Gordon, ed, *Existentia Africana: Understanding Africana Existential Thought* (New York and London: Routledge Press, 2000), p. 8.

Select Bibliography

Abdulguni, R. *The Bandung Spirit: Moving on the Tide of History*. Singapore: Gunbing Agungy, 1981.

Abe, E. *The Shattered Bloc: Behind the Upheaval in Eastern Europe*. Boston: Houghton Mifflin Company, 1990.

Acharya, A. *US Military Strategy in the Gulf: Origins and Evolution Under Carter and Reagan Administrations*. London: Routledge, 1989.

———. *A Survey of Military Cooperation Among the ASEAN States: Bilateralism or Alliance*. Toronto: Centre for Strategic and International Studies, York University, 1990.

———. "Afghan Militia Reinforces Kabul to Halt Fighting." *The New York Times International,* June 7, 1991: 21.

Agyman, O. "The Osagyefo, The Malima, and Pan-Africanism: Study and Growth of a Dynamic Concept." *Journal of Modern African Studies* 13, no. 4 (1975): 663–675.

Ajami, F. "The Fate of the Non-Aligned." *Foreign Affairs* 59, no. 2 (Winter 1981/82): 366–358.

Ake, C. *Revolutionary Pressures in Africa*. London: Zed Press, 1978.

———. *A Political Economy of Africa*. New York: Longman, Inc., 1981.

Akpan, M. *African Goals and Diplomatic Strategies in the United Nations: An In-depth Analysis of African Diplomacy*. North Quincy, MA: Christopher Publising House, 1976.

Albright, D. *Soviet Policy Toward Africa Revisited*. Washington, DC: The Center for Strategic and International Studies, 1987.

Allison, R., and P. Williams, eds. *Superpower Crisis and Competition in the Third World*. New York: Cambridge University Press, 1990.

Alvarez, F. C. *New Horizons for the Third World*. Washington, DC: Public Affairs Press, 1976.

Ameri, H. *Afro-Asian Tactics and Voting in the General Assembly 1955–1962*. Bonn, 1970.

Amin, S. *Accumulation on a World Scale*. 2 vols. New York: Monthly Review Press, 1974.

———. *Unequal Development*. New York: Monthly Review Press, 1979.

———. "Accumulation and World Development: A Theoretical Model." *Review of African Political Economy* 1 (August-November, 1974): 9–26.

———. "Toward a Structural Crisis of World Capitalism," *Socialist Revolution* 5 (11 April 1975): 7–44.

————. "New International Economic Order and Strategy for the Use of Financial Surpluses of Developing Countries." *Alternatives* 4, no. 4 (March 1975): 477–485.

————. "Collective Self-Reliance or National Liberation." In *Dialogue for a New Order,* edited by K. Haq. New York: Pergamon Press, 1980, 153–169.

Amuzegar, J. "Requiem for the North-South Conference," *Foreign Affairs* 56, no. 1 (October 1977): 136–159.

Anabtani, S. N. "Neutralists and Neutralism." *Journal of Politics* 27, no. 2 (May 1965): 351–361.

Anell, L., and B. Nygren. *The Developing Countries and the World Economic Order.* New York: St. Martin's Press, 1980.

Anthony, I. "The Global Arms Trade." *Arms Today* (June 1991).

Apter, D. E. *Rethinking Development: Modernization, Dependency and Postmodern Politics.* Beverly Hills: Sage Publications, 1987.

Aptheker, H. *American Negro Slave Revolts.* New York: International Publishers, 1969.

Arnold, G. *Wars in the Third World Since 1945.* New York and London: Cassell Publishers Ltd., 1991.

Arrighi. G. "Custom and Innovation: Long Waves and Stages of Capitalist Development" Paper presented at the International Workshop, "Technological and Social Factors in Long Term Fluctuation," Certosa di Pontignamo, Siena, Italy, December 15–17, 1986.

Armstrong, P. et al. *Capitalism Since 1945.* Oxford: Basil Blackwell, 1991.

Ayoob, M. "Security in the Third World: The Worm about to Turn." *International Affairs* (London) 60, no. 1 (1983–84): 41–51.

————. "Perspectives from the Gulf: Regime Security or Regional Security." In *Asian Perspective on International Security,* edited by D. H. McMillen. London: Macmillan, 1984, 92–116.

————. *Regional Security in the Third World.* London, Croom Helm, 1986.

————. "The Third World in the System of States: Acute Schizophrenia or Growing Pains." *International Studies Quarterly* 33, no. 1 (1989): 67–79.

————. "The Security Problematic of the Third World." *World Politics* 43, no. 2 (1991): 257–283.

————. "The Security Predicament of Third World States: Reflections on State Making in Comparative Perspective." In *The Insecurity Dilemma of Third World States: National Security of Third World States,* edited by Brian L. Job. Boulder, CO: Lynne Rienner, 1992, 63–81.

Ayoob, M., and Chai-Anan Samudavanija, eds. *Leadership Perceptions and National Security: The Southeast Asian Experience.* Singapore: Institute of Southeast Asian Studies, 1989.

Azar, E., and Chung-in Moon. "Third World National Security: Toward a New Conceptual Framework." *International Interaction* 11, no. 2 (1984): 103–135.

Baek, K. et al. *The Dilemma of Third World Defense Industries.* Boulder, CO: Westview Press, 1989.

Bajpai, U. S. *Non-Alignment: Perspectives and Prospects.* New York: Humanities Press, 1983.

Balassi, B. *The Newly Industrializing Countries in the World Economy.* New York: Pergamon Press, 1981.

Balibar, E. "Racism and Politics in Europe Today." *New Left Review* 186 (1994): 5–19.

Ball, N. *Security and Economy in the Third World.* Princeton, NJ: Princeton University Press, 1988.

Bandyopadhyaya, J. "Non-Aligned Movement and International Relations." *India Quarterly* 33, no. 2 (April-June 1977): 137–164.

————. "Racism and International Relations." *Alternatives* 3, no. 1 (August 1977): 19–48.

Banks, A., ed. *The Political Handbook of the World 1991*. Binghamton NY: State University of New York at Binghamton, CSA Publications, 1992.

Barnet, R. J. *The Rocket's Red Glare: When America Goes to War/The President and the People*. New York: Simon and Schuster, 1990.

————. *The Alliance: America, Europe and Japan: Makers of the Postwar World*. New York: Simon and Schuster, 1983.

————. *The Giants: Russia and America*. New York: Simon and Schuster, 1977.

Barnet, R. J. and J. Cavanagh. *Global Dreams: Imperial Corporations and the New World Order*. New York: Simon & Schuster, 1994.

Bates, R. *The Political Economy of Rural Africa*. Berkeley, CA: University of California Press, 1987.

Becker, D. G., et al. *Postimperialism: Internationalism in the Late Twentieth Century*. Boulder and London: Lynne Rienner Publishers, 1987.

Bedjanni, M. *Toward a New International Economic Order*. New York: Holmes and Meier Publishers, 1979.

Bellegarde-Smith, P. *Haiti: The Breached Citadel*. Denver: Westview Press, 1990.

————. *In the Shadow of the Powers: Dantes Bellegarde in Haitian Social Thought*. Atlantic Highlands, NJ: Humanities Press International, Inc., 1985.

Bender, P. *East Europe in Search of Security*. Baltimore and London: Chatto and Windus/International Institute for Strategic Studies, 1972.

Ben-Dor, G., *State and Conflict in the Middle East: Emergence of the Post-Colonial State*. New York: Praeger Publishers, 1983.

Bennett, L. A. *International Organizations*. 2nd ed. Englewood-Cliffs, NJ: Prentice-Hall, 1980.

Bergesen, A. and R. Schoenberg. "Long Waves of Colonial Expansion and Contraction, 1415–1969." In *Studies of Modern World System*, A. Bergesen, ed. New York: Academic Press, 1980.

Bergsten, C. F., and B. Krause. *World Politics and International Economics*. Washington, DC: Brookings Institute, 1975.

————, et. al. "Threat from the Third World." *Foreign Policy* 11 (Summer 1973): 102–124.

Bettelheim, C. *Economic Calculation and Forms of Property*. New York: Monthly Review Press, 1975.

Beud, M. *A History of Capitalism, 1500–1980*. New York: Monthly Review Press, 1983.

Bhagwati, J. N. *The New International Economic Order in North-South Debate*. Cambridge MA. MIT Press, 1977.

————. "The Capital Myth: The Difference between Trade in Widgets and Dollars" *Foreign Affairs* 77, no. 3 (May/June): 1–12.

Bhagwati, J. N., and J. G. Ruggie, eds. *Power, Passions and Purpose: Prospects for North-South Negotiations*. Cambridge, MA: MIT Press, 1985.

Blaister, C., *The Hovering Giant: US Response to Revolutionary Change in Latin America*. Pittsburgh, PA: Pittsburgh University Press, 1976.

Blake, D. H., and R. S. Walters. *The Politics of Global Economic Relations*. 3rd ed. Englewood Cliffs, NJ: Prentice-Hall, 1987.

Bluestone, B., and B. Harrison, eds. *The Great U-Turn: Corporate Restructuring and Polarizing America*. New York: Basic Books, 1988.

Bornschier B., and C. Chase-Dunn. *Transnational Corporations and Underdevelopment*. New York: Praeger Publishers, 1985.

Branford, S., and Bernard Kucinski, eds. *The Debt Squads: The US, The Banks and Latin America.* London: Zed Books, 1988.

Brandt, W. *North-South: A Program of Survival.* Cambridge, MA: MIT Press, 1980.

Brecher, M. *India and World Politics: The Krishna Menon View of the World.* New York: Praeger Publishers, 1968.

———. *Nehru: A Political Biography.* Boston: Beacon Press, 1962.

Bretton, H. *International Relations in the Nuclear Age: One World, Difficult to Manage.* Albany, NY: SUNY Press, 1986.

Browett, J. *Industrialization in the Global Periphery: Significance of Newly Industrializing Countries.* Adelaide: Flinders University of South Australia School of Social Science, 1986.

Brown, M. B. *Models of Political Economy: A Guide to Arguments.* Boulder, CO: Lynne Rienner Press, 1984.

Brown, S. *New Forces in World Politics.* Washington DC: Brookings Institute, 1974.

———. *The Faces of Power.* New York: Columbia University Press, 1974.

Brundenius, C. *Revolutionary Cuba: The Challenge of Economic Growth with Equity.* Boulder, CO: Westview Press, 1984.

Brzoska, M., and Thomas Ohlson, eds. *Arms Transfers to the Third World, 1971–1985.* Oxford: Oxford University Press, 1987.

———. *Arms Production in the Third World.* London: Taylor and Francis, 1986.

Buchan, A. *The End of the Postwar Era: A New Balance of World Power.* London: Weidenfeld, 1974.

Burton, J. W., ed. *Non-Alignment.* London: Andre Deutsch, 1966.

Bukharin, N. *Imperialism and the World Economy.* New York, Monthly Review Press, 1975.

Buzan, B. *People, States and Fear: National Security in International Relations.* Chapel Hill: University of North Carolina Press, 1983.

———. *People, States, and Fear: An Agenda for International Security Studies in the Post-Cold War Era.* Boulder, CO: Lynne Rienner, 1991.

Cafruny, A. W. "A Gramscian Concept of Declining Hegemony: Stages of US Power and the Evolution of International Economic Relations." In *World Leadership and Hegemony,* edited by David P. Rapkin, 97–118. Boulder, CO: Lynne Rienner, 1990.

Callaghy, T. R. "Vision and Politics in the Transformation of the Global Political Economy: Lessons from the Second and Third Worlds." In *Global Transformation and the Third World,* edited by Robert O. Slater et al., 161–258. Boulder, CO: Lynne Rienner, 1993.

Calleo, D. P. *Beyond American Hegemony: The Future of the Western Alliance.* Bloomington: Indiana University Press, 1973.

———. *The Imperious Economy.* Cambridge, MA: Harvard University Press, 1982.

Calvocoressi, P. *World Politics Since 1945.* 6th ed. New York: Longman, Inc., 1991.

Campbell, J. C. *Tito's Separate Road.* New York: The Council for Foreign Relations. Harper and Row Publishers, 1967.

Campbell, H. *Rasta and Resistance: From Marcus Garvey to Walter Rodney.* Trenton, NJ: African World Press, 1987.

———. *Pan-Africanism: Struggle Against Neo-Colonialism and Imperialism.* Toronto: Afro-Carib Publications, 1975.

Camps, M. *The Management of Interdependence: A Preliminary View.* New York: The Council on Foreign Relations, 1974.

Cantori, L. J., and Steven L. Spiegel, eds. *The International Politics of Regions: A Comparative Approach.* Englewood Cliffs, NJ: Prentice-Hall, 1970.

Cardoso, F., and E. Faletto. *Dependency and Development in Latin America.* Berkeley: University of California Press, 1979.

Castells, M., and L. D. Tyson. "High Technology and the Changing International Division of Production." In *The Newly Industrializing Countries in the World Economy: Challenges for US Policy,* edited by Randall B. Purcell, 1–13. Boulder, CO: Lynne Rienner, 1987:

Castro, F. *The Economic and Social Crisis.* London: Zed Books, 1984.

Catrina, C. *Arms Transfers and Dependence.* Philadelphia, PA: Taylor and Francis, 1988.

Chaliand, G. *Revolution in the Third World: Currents and Conflicts in Asia, Africa and Latin America.* New York: Penguin Books, 1989.

Chan, S. *Exporting Apartheid: Foreign Policies in Southern Africa 1978–1988.* New York: MacMillan Publishers, 1990.

Chen, E. K. Y. *High Growth Rates in Asia Economies: A Comparative Study of Hong Kong, Japan, South Korea, Singapore, and Taiwan.* London: Macmillan, 1979.

Chilcote, R. *Theories of Development and Underdevelopment.* Boulder, CO: Westview Press, 1984.

Choucri, N., and Robert North, eds. *Nations in Conflict.* San Francisco, CA: W. H. Freeman and Company, 1975.

Chrisman, R., and N. Hare, eds. *Pan-Africanism.* Indianapolis: The Bobbs-Merrill Company, 1974.

Clapham, C. *Third World Politics: An Introduction.* London: Croom Helm, 1985.

Clark, C., and J. Lemco. *State and Development.* New York: E. J. Brill, 1988.

Clarke, J. H. *Notes for an African World Revolution: Africans at the Crossroads.* Trenton, NJ: Africa World Press, 1991.

Cline, W. R. *Trade Policy in the 1980s.* Washington, DC: Institute for International Economics, 1983.

Clough, M. *Free at Last? US Policy toward Africa and the End of the Cold War.* New York: Council on Foreign Relations Press, 1992.

Cohen, B. *The Question of Imperialism: The Political Economy of Dominance and Dependence.* New York: Basic Books, 1973.

Cooper, R. N. *A Reordered World: Emerging International Economic Problems.* Washington, DC: Potomac Association/Basic Books, 1973.

———. "Trade Policy in Foreign Policy" *Foreign Policy* 5 (Winter 1972-73): 18–36.

Coulson, A. *African Socialism in Practice: The Tanzanian Experience.* Nottinghouse: Spokesman, 1979.

Cox, O. C. *Caste, Class and Race: A Study in Social Dynamism.* New York: Modern Readers Paperback, 1970.

———. *Capitalism as a System.* New York: Monthly Review Press, 1964.

Cox, R. W. "Gramsci, Hegemony and International Relations: An Essay on Method." In *Gramsci, Historical Materialism and International Relations,* edited by Stephen Gill. Cambridge: Cambridge University Press, 1993.

———. "Structural Issues of Global Governance: Implications for Europe." In *Gramsci, Historical Materialism and International Relations,* edited by Stephen Gill, 259–289. Cambridge: Cambridge University Press, 1993.

———. *Production, Power, and World Order: Social Forces in the Making of History.* New York: Columbia University Press, 1987.

———. "Gramsci, Hegemony and International Relations: An Essay in Method." *Millennium: Journal of International Studies* 12, no. 2 (1983): 162–75.

———. "Social Forces, States and World Order: Beyond International Relations Theory" *Millennium: Journal of International Studies* 10, no. 2 (1981): 126–55.

————. "Globalization, Multilateralism, and Democracy," In *Approaches to World Order,* edited by Robert W. Cox and Timothy J. Sinclair. Cambridge: Cambridge University Press, 1996

Crabb, C. *The Elephant and the Grass: A Study of Non-Alignment.* New York: Praeger Publishers, 1964.

Crane, G. T., and A. Amawi. *The Theoretical Evolution of Political Economy: A Reader.* New York: Oxford University Press, 1991.

Cummings, B. "The Origins and Development of the Northeast Asian Political Economy: Industrial Sectors, Product Cycles, and Political Consequence." *International Organization* 38 (1984): 1–40.

Dallmeyer, D. G. *Joining Together, Standing Apart: National Identities after NAFTA.* The Hague, London, Boston: The Kluwer International Law, 1997

David, S. R. *Choosing Sides: Alignment And Realignment in the Third World.* Baltimore and London: Johns Hopkins University Press, 1991.

Davidson, Basil. *The Black Man's Burden: Africa and the Curse of the Nation-State.* New York: Times Books, 1992.

Dawisha, A. *Islam in Foreign Policy.* Cambridge: Cambridge University Press, 1983.

Deere, C. D., et al. *In the Shadow of the Sun: Caribbean Development Alternatives and US Policy.* Boulder, CO: Westview Press, 1990.

Deger, S. *Military Expenditures in Third World Countries.* London: Routledge and Kegan Paul, 1986.

Deger, S. and Robert West, eds. *Defense, Security And Development.* New York: St. Martin's Press, 1987.

————. "Democracy in Africa" *The Economist* (22–28 February 1992).

Denoon, D. B. *The New International Economic Order: The US Response.* New York: New York University Press, 1979.

De Rivero, B. *The New Economic Order and International Development Law.* New York: Pergamon Press, 1980.

Dhanapala, J. *China and the Third World.* New Delhi: Vikas Publishing House, 1985.

Diamond, L. et al., eds. *Democracy in Developing Countries.* 4 vols. Boulder, CO: Lynne Rienner Publishers, 1988–90.

Douglass, Frederick. In *Extistentia Africana: Understanding Africana Existential Thought,* edited by Lewis R. Gordon. New York and London: Routledge Press, 2000.

DuBois, W. E. B. *Black Reconstruction in America, 1860–1880.* New York: Meridian Books, 1964.

————. *Dusk to Dawn.* New York: Harcourt Brace, 1940.

Duncan, W. R. *Soviet Policy in the Third World.* New York: Pergamon Press, 1980.

Eckstein, H. *Regarding Politics: Essays on Political Theory, Stability, and Change.* Berkeley, CA: University of California Press, 1992.

Emmanuel, A. *Unequal Exchange: A Study in the Imperialism of Trade.* New York: Monthly Review Press, 1978.

Emerson, R. *From Empire to Nation.* Cambridge, MA: Harvard University Press, 1960.

Essien-Udom, E. U. "Marcus Garvey and His Movement." In *America's Black Past: A Reader In Afro-American History,* edited by Eric Foner. New York: Harper & Row, 1970.

Evans, P. *Dependent Development: The Alliance of Multinational Corporations, State and Local Capital in Brazil.* Princeton, NJ: Princeton University Press, 1979.

Evans, P. et. al., eds. *Bringing the State Back In.* New York: Cambridge University Press, 1985.

Fagg, J. E. *Pan-Americanism.* Malabar, FL: Robert E. Krieger Publishing Company, 1982.

Fain, H. *Normative Politics and the Community of Nations*. Philadelphia, PA: Temple University Press, 1987.

Faison, S. "Mandela Asks the UN to Help End the Township Violence." *New York Times*, 16 July 1992.

Fann, K. T., and D. C. Hodges. *Readings in US Imperialism*. Boston: Porter and Sargent Publishers, 1971.

Farrell, R. H. *American Diplomacy: The Twentieth Century*. New York: W. W. Norton and Company, 1988.

Fishlow, A. et al., eds. *Rich and Poor Nations in the World Economy*. New York: McGraw-Hill Books, 1978.

Frank, A. G. *Capitalism and Underdevelopment in Latin America*. New York: Monthly Review Press, 1969.

———. *Latin American Underdevelopment and Revolution*. New York: Monthly Review Press, 1969.

———. *Lumpenbourgeoisie and Lumpen Development: Dependency, Class and Politics*. New York: Monthly Review Press, 1972.

———. *World Accumulation 1492–1789*. London and New York: Macmillan and Monthly Review Press, 1978.

———. *Dependent Accumulation and Underdevelopment*. New York: Monthly Review Press, 1979.

———. *Crisis in the Third World*. New York: Holmes and Meier, 1981.

———. *Crisis in the World Economy*. New York: Monthly Review Press, 1981.

Freiden, J. A. *Debt, Development and Democracy: Modern Political Economy and Latin America, 1965–1985*. Princeton, N.J.: Princeton University Press, 1991.

Frieden, J. A., and D. A. Lake. *International Political Economy: Perspectives on Global Power and Wealth*. New York: St. Martin's Press, 1991.

Frey, B. S. "The Public Choice View of International Political Economy" In *Theoretical Evolution of International Political Economy: A Reader*, edited by George T. Crane and Abla Amawi. New York: Oxford University Press, 1991.

Frobe, F. "The Current Development of the World-Economy: Reproduction of Labor and the Accumulation of Capital on a World Scale" *Review* 8 (Spring 1982): 507–543.

Gaddis, J. L. *The Long Peace: Inquiries into the History of the Cold War*. New York: Oxford University Press, 1987.

———. *Russia, the Soviet Union and the United States: An Interpretative History*. 2nd ed. New York: McGraw-Hill, 1990.

Galtung, J. *True Worlds: A Transnational Experience*. New York: Free Press, 1980.

Gann, L. H., and P. Duigan. *Africa South of the Sahara: The Challenge of Western Security*. Stanford, CA: Hoover Institution Press, 1981.

George, A., and R. Smoke. *Deterrence in American Foreign Policy: Theory and Practice*. New York: Columbia University Press, 1974.

Germani, G. et al., eds. *Modernization, Exploitation and Dependency in Latin America*. New Brunswick, NJ: Transaction Books, 1976.

Gidden, A. *The Nation-State and Violence*. Berkeley and Los Angeles: University of California Press, 1987.

Gill, S. *American Hegemony and the Trilateral Commission*. Cambridge: Cambridge University Press, 1990.

———. *Gramsci, Historical Materialism and International Relations*. New York and Melbourne: Cambridge University Press, 1993.

————. "Globalization, Democratization, and the Politics of Indifference." In *Globalization: Critical Reflection*, edited by J. H. Mittelman. Boulder, CO: Lynne Rienner, 1996

Gilpin, R. *The Political Economy of International Relations*. Princeton: Princeton University Press, 1987.

————. *War and Change in World Politics*. Cambridge: Cambridge University Press, 1981.

————. *US Power and Multinational Corporations*. New York: Basic Books, 1975.

Girling, J. L. S. *America and the Third World*. London: Routledge and Kegan Paul, 1980.

Goldfrank, W. L. *World System, Capitalism of Capitalism: Past and Present*. Beverly Hills: Sage Publications, 1979.

Goldstein, J. S. *Long Cycles: Prosperity and War in the Modern Age*. New Haven: Yale University Press, 1988.

Goonatilake, S. *Crippled Minds: An Exploration into Colonial Culture*. New Delhi: Vikas Publishing House, 1982.

————. *Aborted Discovery: Science and Creativity in the Third World*. London: Zed Press, 1984.

Griffiths, J. C. *Afghanistan: Key to the Continent*. Boulder, CO: Westview Press, 1981.

Haggard, S. "The Newly Industrializing Countries in the International System." *World Politics* 38 (1986): 343–370.

Halle, L. *The Cold War As History*. London: Chatto and Windus, 1967.

Halliday, F. *Cold War, Third World: An Essay on Soviet-US Relations*. London: Hutchison and Radius, 1989.

————. *The Making of the Second Cold War*. London: Verso New Left Books, 1983.

Handel, M. *Weak States in the International System*. London: Frank Cass and Company, 1981.

Hanson, R. D. *Beyond the North-South Stalemate*. New York: McGraw-Hill, 1979.

Haq, M. T. *The Poverty Curtain: Choice for the Third World*. New York: Columbia University Press, 1976.

Harkavy, R. E., and Stephanie Neuman, eds. *Lessons of Recent Wars in the Third World: Comparative Dimensions*. Lexington, MA: D. C. Heath, 1987.

Harris, N. *The End of the Third World: Newly Industrializing Countries and the Decline of Ideology*. New York: Penguin Books, 1986.

Harrison B., and B. Bluestone. *The Great U-Turn: Corporate Restructuring and the Polarizing of America*. New York: Basic Books, 1990.

Harrison, S. S. "Nixon Journey Spurs Japan to Recast Policy" *Washington Post,* 2 March 1971.

Hassan, M. *Nationalism and Communal Politics in India, 1916–1928*. Delhi: Manohar, 1979.

Hill, R. J. *Communism under the Knife: Surgery or Autopsy*. New York: Pinter Publishers, 1990.

Hobsbaun, E. *Industry and Empire*. London: Penguin Books, 1969.

Hoffmann, S. *Gulliver's Troubles: On Setting American Foreign Policy*. New York: McGraw-Hill, 1978.

————. *Primacy or World Order: American Foreign Policy since the Cold War*. New York: McGraw-Hill, 1978.

Holsti, K. J. ed. *Peace and War: Armed Contests and International Order, 1648–1989*. Cambridge, MA: Cambridge University Press, 1991.

————. "International Theory and War in the Third World." In *The Insecurity Dilemma*, edited by Brian Job, 37–60. Boulder, CO: Lynne Rienner, 1992.

Homer, J. *The Afro-Asian People's Solidarity Organization: A Critique*. Chicago: University of Chicago, 1958.

Hopkins, T. K., and I. Wallerstein, eds. *Processes of the World System.* Beverly Hills: Sage Publications, 1980.

Housouna, A. K. *First Afro-Asian Conference in Bandung.* Cairo: League of Arab States, 1955.

Hovet, T. *Bloc Politics in the United Nations.* Cambridge, MA: Harvard University Press, 1960.

Howard, M. *War in European History.* Oxford: Oxford University Press, 1976.

Hudson, M. *Global Fracture: The New International Economic Order.* New York: Harper & Row, 1977.

———. *Arab Politics: The Search for Legitimacy.* New Haven, CT: Yale University Press, 1977.

Hutchison, A. *China's African Revolution.* London: Hutchison, 1975.

Ihonvbere, J. O. "The Third World and the New World Order in the 1990s." In *Annual Editions: Third World 94/95,* 6–16. Guilford, CT: Dushkin Publishing Goup, Inc., 1994.

Iriye, A. *The Cold War in Asia: A Historical Introduction.* Englewood Cliffs, New Jersey: Prentice-Hall, 1974.

Jackson, H. *From the Congo to Soweto.* New York: William Morrow, 1982.

Jackson, R., and Carl Rosberg. "Sovereignty and Underdevelopment: Juridical Statehood in the African Crisis." *Journal of Modern African Studies* 24, no. 1 (1986): 1–31.

Jackson, R. L. *The Non-Aligned, The United Nations and the Superpowers.* New York: Praeger Publishers, 1983.

Jacobson, H. *Networks of Interdependence: International Organizations and the Global Political System.* New York: Alfred A. Knopf, 1979.

Jaipal, R. *Non-Alignment: Origins, Growth and Potential for Peace.* New Delhi: Allied Publishers, 1983.

James, C. L. R. *The Black Jacobins.* Revised edition. London: Allison & Busby, 1980.

Jankowitsch, O. and K. P. Sauvant. *The Third World Without Superpowers: The Collected Documents of the Non-Aligned Countries.* 4 vols. New York: Oceana Publication, Inc., 1978.

Jansen, G. H. *Afro-Asia and Non-Alignment.* New York: Praeger Publishers, 1966.

Jenkins, R. *Exploitation: The World Power Structure and the Inequality of Nations.* London: McGibbon and Kee, 1970.

Jervis, R. *The Meaning of the Nuclear Revolution.* Ithaca: Cornell University Press, 1989.

———. *Illogic of American Nuclear Strategy.* Ithaca: Cornell University Press, 1984.

Job, Brian L. "The Insecurity Dilemma: National Regime and State Security in the Third World." In *The Insecurity Dilemma: National Security of Third World States,* edited by Brian L. Job. Boulder, CO: Lynne Rienner, 1992.

Johnson, D. *Factors Affecting Outward Mobility in the Virgin Islands: A Developing Caribbean Micro-State.* Ph.D. diss. Ann Arbor, MI: University of Michigan Microfilm, 1982.

Johnston, A. "Weak States and National Security." *Review of International Studies* 17, no. 2 (1991): 146–177.

Jones, Jacquelyn. *The Dispossessed: America's Underclass from the Civil War to the Present.* New York: Basic Books, 1991.

———. *American Work: Four Centuries of Black and White Labor.* New York: W. W. Norton & Company, 1998.

Jones, R. W., and S. A. Hildreth, eds. *Emerging Powers: Defense and Security in the Third World.* New York: Praeger Publishers, 1986.

Kahin, G. M. *The Afro-Asian Conference. Bandung, Indonesia.* Ithaca, NY: Cornell University Press, 1956.

Kaiser, R. G. "US-Soviet Relations: Good-bye Détente." *Foreign Affairs* 59, no. 3 (1981): 500–21.

Kaldor, M., and E. Asbjorn, eds. *The World Military Order: The Impact of Military Technology on The Third World.* New York: Macmillan, 1979.

Kanet, R. *The Soviet Union and Developing Nations.* Baltimore: Johns Hopkins University Press, 1974.

Kaplan, M. *System and Process in International Relations.* New York: John Wiley, 1967.

Kaplan, R. "France through Kofi's Eyes." *Atlantic Monthly* 269, no. 4 (April 1992): 43.

Katsikas, S. J. *The Arc of Socialist Revolutions: Angola to Afghanistan.* Cambridge, MA: Schenkman Publishing Company, 1982.

Katz, J. *Arms Production in Developing Countries.* Lexington, MA: Lexington Books, 1984.

———. *The Implications of Third World Military Industrialization: Sowing the Serpent's Teeth.* Lexington, MA: Lexington Books, 1986.

Kay, D. *The New Nations in the United Nations.* New York: Columbia University Press, 1970.

Kegley, C. *The Long Postwar Peace: Contending Explanations and Projections.* New York: Harper Collins, 1991.

Kegley, C., and E. R. Wittkopf. *American Foreign Policy: Patterns and Process.* New York: St. Martin's Press, 1979.

Keller, E. J., and D. Rothchild, eds. *Afro-Marxist Regimes: Ideology and Public Policy.* Boulder, CO: Lynne Rienner, 1987.

Kennan, G. F. *The Fateful Alliance: France, Russia and the Coming of the First World War.* New York: Pantheon, 1984.

———. *The Nuclear Delusion: Soviet-American Relations in the Atomic Age.* New York: Pantheon, 1982.

Kennedy, M. A. *Asian Nationalism in the Twentieth Century.* New York: Macmillan, 1968.

Kennedy, P. *The Rise and Fall of Great Powers: Economic Change and Military Conflict from 1500 to 2000.* New York: Random House, 1987.

Kent, N. J. "To Polarize a Nation: Racism, Labor Markets, and the State in the US Political Economy." In *The Rising Tide of Cultural Pluralism: The Nation-state at Bay,* edited by C. Young, 55–72. Madison, WI: University of Wisconsin Press, 1993.

Keohane, R. O. *International Institutions and State Power: Essays in International Relations Theory.* Boulder, CO: Westview Press, 1989.

———. *Neorealism and Its Critics.* New York: Columbia University Press, 1986.

———. *After Hegemony: Cooperation and Discord in the World Political Economy.* Princeton, NJ: Princeton University Press, 1984.

Keohane, R. O., and J. S. Nye. *Power and Interdependence.* 2nd ed. Glenview, IL: Scott, Foresman and Little, Brown, 1989.

———. *Transnational Relations in World Politics.* Cambridge, MA: Harvard University Press, 1972.

Keylor, W. R. *The Twentieth Century: An International History.* Oxford: Oxford University Press, 1984.

Kimche, D. *The Afro-Asian Movement: Ideology and Foreign Policy in the Third World.* Jerusalem: Israeli University Press, 1973.

Klare, M., and C. Aronson, eds. *Supplying Repression: US Support for Authoritarian Regimes Abroad.* Washington, DC: Institute for Policy Studies, 1981.

Kohler, G. *Global Apartheid: World Models Project Working Paper Number Seven.* New York: Institute for World Order, 1978.

Kolodziej, E. A. *Making and Marketing Arms: The French Experience and Its Implications for International Relations.* Princeton, NJ: Princeton University Press, 1987.

Kolodziej, E. A., and Robert Harkavy, eds. *Security Policies of Developing Countries.* Lexington, MA: Lexington Books, 1982.

Korany, B. *Social Change, Charisma and International Behavior: Toward a Theory of Foreign Policy in the Third World*. Geneva: Institute Universitaire des Haute Etudes Internationales, 1976.

Krasner, S. D. *Structural Conflict: The Third World Against Global Liberalism*. Berkeley, CA: University of California Press, 1985

———. *International Regimes*. Ithaca: Cornell University Press, 1983.

Kraus, J. "Debt, Structural Adjustment, and Private Investment." In *Privatization and Investment in Sub-Saharan Africa,* edited by R. A. Ahene and B. A. Katz. New York: Praeger, 1992.

Krause, K. *Arms and the State: Patterns of Military Production and Trade in Historical Perspective*. Cambridge, MA: Cambridge University Press, 1992.

Kryznek, M. J. *US-Latin American Relations*. New York: Praeger Special Studies, 1985.

Kuttner, R. *The End of Laissez-Faire: National Purpose and the Global Economy after the Cold War*. New York: Alfred Knopf, 1991.

Kydd, J. "Zambia in the 1980s: The Political Economy of Adjustment." In *Structural Adjustment and Agriculture: Theory and Practice in Africa and Latin America,* edited by Simon Commander, 127–144. London: Overseas Development Institute, 1989.

LaFeber, W. *The American Age: At Home and Abroad since 1750*. New York: W. W. Norton, 1989.

———. *Inevitable Revolutions: The United States in Central America*. New York: W. W. Norton, 1983.

Lahuoari, A. "Algeria's Army, Algeria's Agony." *Foreign Affairs* 77, no. 4 (July/August 1998): 44–53.

Langley, L. D. *America and the Americas: The United States in the Western Hemisphere*. Athens, GA: University of Georgia Press, 1989.

Larkins, B. *China and Africa*. Berkeley: University of California Press, 1971.

Lasch, C. *Culture of Narcissism: American Life in the Age of Diminishing Expectations*. New York: W. W. Norton, 1993.

Lassassi, A. *Non-Alignment and Algerian Foreign Policy*. Avebury, VT: Brookfield, 1988.

Lauren, P. L. *Power and Prejudice: The Politics and Diplomacy of Racial Discrimination*. Boulder, CO: Westview Press, 1988.

Lazlo, E., and J. Kurtzman. *Western Europe and the New International Economic Order: Representative Samples of the European Perspectives*. New York: Pergamon Press, 1980.

———. *Eastern Europe and the New International Economic Order: Representative Samples of the Socialist Perspectives*. New York: Pergamon Press, 1980.

Leaming, H. P. *Hidden Americans: Maroons of Virginia and the Carolinas*. New York: Garland Press, 1993.

Legum, C. *Pan-Africanism: A Short Political Guide*. New York: Praeger, 1965.

Lenin, V. I. *Imperialism: The Highest Stage of Capitalism*. Peking: Foreign Language Press, 1970.

Lens, S. *The Forging of an American Empire: From Revolution to Vietnam*. New York: Crowell, 1971.

Lester, J. *The Seventh Son: The Thoughts and Writings of W. E. B. Dubois*. 2 vols. New York: Random House, 1971.

Levy, J. "War and the Great Powers." In *Contending Approaches to World System,* edited by W. R. Thompson, Jr., 183–202. Beverly Hills: Sage Publications, 1983.

Liska, G. *Alliances and the Third World*. Baltimore: Johns Hopkins University Press, 1968.

———. *Nations in Alliance*. Baltimore: Johns Hopkins University Press, 1962.

Litwak, R. S., and Samuel F. Wells, eds. *Superpower Competition and Security in the Third World*. Cambridge, MA: Ballinger, 1988.

Lodge, T. *Black Politics in South Africa since 1945*. London and New York: Longman, Inc., 1983.

Looney, R. *Third World Military Expenditures and Arms Production*. London: Macmillan, 1988.

Lozoya, J. A. *Asia and the New International Economic Order*. New York: Pergamon Press, 1981.

Lozoya, J. A., and H. Chadra. *Africa, the Middle East and the New International Economic Order*. New York: Pergamon Press, 1980.

Luck, P. *The New International Economic Order and Armaments*. New York: Pergamon Press, 1980.

Lusane, Clarence. *Race in the Global Era: African Americans at the Millennium*. Boston: South End Press, 1997

Lyon, P. *Neutralism*. Leicester: Leicester University Press, 1963.

MacFarlene, S. Neil. *Superpower Rivalry and Third World Radicalism: The Idea of National Liberation*. Baltimore: Johns Hopkins University Press, 1985.

Magubane, B. M. *Ties That Bind: African-American Consciousness of Africa*. Trenton, NJ: Africa World Press, Inc. 1987.

Makhijani, A. *From Global Capitalism to Economic Justice*. New York: Apex Press, 1992.

Mallik, D. *The Development of Non-Alignment in India's Foreign Policy*. Allahabad,India: Chaitanya Publishing House, 1967.

Maoz, Z. *Paths to Conflict: International Disputes Initiation, 1816–1976*. Boulder, CO: Westview Press, 1982

Marable, M. *Black American Politics: From Marches on Washington to Jesse Jackson*. London: Zed Press, 1985.

———. *African and Caribbean Politics: From Kwame Nkrumah to Maurice Bishop*. London: Verso New Left Books, 1987.

Markovitz, I. L. *Power and Class in Africa*. Englewood Cliffs, NJ: Prentice-Hall, 1977.

Martin, L. W. *Neutralism and Non-Alignment: The New States in World Affairs*. New York: Praeger Publishers, 1962.

Mates, L. *Non-Alignment: Theory and Current Policy*. Belgrade and Dobbs Ferry, NY: Institute of International Politics and Economics and Oceana Publications Inc., 1972.

Matthews, H. *Fidel Castro*. New York: Simon and Schuster, 1969.

Mazrui, A. A. *Towards a Pax Africana: A Study in Ideology and Ambition*. Chicago: University of Chicago Press, 1967.

———. "The New Interdependence." In *Beyond Dependency: The Developing World Speaks Out*, edited by G. Urb and V. Kallab, 38–56. Washington, DC: Overseas Development Council, 1975.

———. *A World Federation of Cultures: An African Perspective*. New York: Institute for World Order Inc., 1976.

———. *The Africans: A Triple Heritage*. Boston: Little, Brown, 1986.

———. "The Triple Heritage of the State in Africa" In *The State in Global Perspective*, edited by Ali Kazancigil, 107–118. Aldershot, UK: Gower, 1986.

———. *Cultural Forces in World Politics*. London and Kenya: Heinemann, 1990.

McLaughlin, J. "Defending the Frontiers: Political Geography of Race and Racism in the European Community." In *The Political Geography of the New World Order*, edited by C. Williams, 20–45. London: Belhaven Press, 1993.

Mecham, J. L. *A Survey of US-Latin American Relations*. Boston: Houghton Mifflin Company, 1965.

Menon, B. P. *Global Dialogue: The New International Economic Order.* Oxford: Pergamon Press, 1979.

Menon, R. *Soviet Power and The Third World.* New Haven and London: Yale University Press, 1986.

Migdal, J. S. *Strong Societies and Weak States: State-Society Relations and State Capabilities in the Third World.* Princeton, NJ: Princeton University Press, 1988.

Misra, K. P., ed. *Non-Alignment: Frontiers and Dynamics.* New Delhi: Vikas, 1982.

Mittelman, J. H. *Globalization: Critical Reflections.* Boulder, CO: Lynne Rienner, 1996.

Modelski, G. *Exploring Long Cycles.* Boulder, CO: Lynne Rienner, 1987.

———. "The Long Cycles of World Politics and the Nation-State." *Comparative Studies in Society and History* 20 (April 1978): 214–238.

Molineau, H. *US Foreign Policy toward Latin America: From Regionalism to Globalism.* Boulder, CO: Westview Press, 1986.

Moodie, M. *Sovereignty, Security and Arms.* Beverly Hills, CA: Sage Publications, 1979.

Moran, T. H. *Multinationals: The Political Economy of Foreign Direct Investment.* Lexington, MA: Lexington Books, 1985.

Moran, T. H. "Multinational Corporations and Developing Countries: An Analytical Overview." In *Multinational Corporations: The Political Economy of Foreign Direct Investment,* edited by T. H. Moran, 3–24. Lexington, MA: Lexington Books, 1985.

Morgenthau, H. *Politics Among Nations.* New York: Alfred Knopf, 1979.

Morrow, L. "Africa: The Scramble for Existence." *Time* (September 7, 1992).

Mortimer, R. A. *The Third World Coalition in International Politics.* New York: Praeger Publishers, 1980.

Moss, A. C., and H. N. M. Winston. *A New International Economic Order: Selected Documents 1945–1975.* 4 vols. New York: UNITAR, 1976.

Munck, R. *Politics and Dependency in the Third World: The Latin American Perspective.* London: Zed Books, 1974.

Nathan, J. A., and J. K. Oliver. *United States Foreign Policy and World Order.* Boston: Little, Brown and Company, 1985.

Neimanis, G. J. *The Collapse of the Soviet Empire: A View From Riga.* Westport, CT: Praeger Publishers, 1997.

Neuhauser, C. *Third World Politics: China and the Afro-Asian Solidarity Organization.* Cambridge: Harvard University Press, 1968.

———. Editorial. *New York Times,* 31 August 1995. *American Online* August 31, 1995, p.1.

———. "Justice in 5-4 Vote Reject Districts Drawn with Race the Predominant Factor." *New York Times,* 30 June 1995.

———. "Farewell to the Old Order in the Supreme Court." *New York Times,* 2 July 1995,. p. 4.

———. "Haiti's New Government Fights Potholes." *New York Times,* 5 June 1994.

———. "Israel Says Syria Is Testing Advanced Scud Missiles." *New York Times,* 15 August 1992.

———. "Mandela Proclaims South Africa Free at Last." *New York Times,* 3 May 1994.

———. "Non-Aligned Movement Decides It Is Still Relevant.." *New York Times,* 7 September 1992.

———. "Reluctant Warriors: UN Member States Retreat From Peacekeeping Roles." *New York Times,* 12 December 1993.

———. "Third World Embracing Economic Reform." *New York Times,* 8 July 1991.

———. "U.N. Observers Delay Visit to Somalia." *New York Times,* 12 July 1992.

———. "Russia and France Gain on U.S. Lead in Arms Sales, Study Says." *New York Times,* 4 August 1998.

Nkrumah, K. *Africa Must Unite.* London: Heinemann, 1963.

Nolan, J. E. *Trappings of Power: Ballistic Missiles in the Third World.* Washington, DC: Brookings Institute, 1991.

Nord, L. *Non-Alignment and Socialism: Yugoslavia Foreign Policy in Theory and Practice.* Stockholm: Raben and Sjogren, 1974.

Norman, D. *Nehru: The First Sixty Years.* 2vols. New York: The John Jay Company, 1965.

Nye, Joseph S., Jr. *Peace in Parts: Integration and Conflict in Regional Organizations.* Boston, MA: Little, Brown, 1971.

———. *Bound to Lead: The Changing Nature of American Power.* New York: Basic Books, 1990.

Nyerere, J. *Address by the President of the Republic of Tanzania to the 4th Ministerial Meeting of the Group of 77, 12-16 February 1979.* In *The Group of 77: Evolution, Structure and Organization,* edited by Karl P. Sauvant. New York: Oceana Publication, Inc., 1981.

Oberdofer, D. "Japan-China Pact: Gains for both, Risk for US." *Washington Post,* 30 September 1972.

O'Connor, J. "The Meaning of Economic Imperialism." In *Readings in U.S. Imperialism,* edited by K. T. Fann and D. C. Hodges. Boston: Porter and Sargent Publishers, 1971.

Ogunsanwo, C. *China's Policy in Africa.* New York: Cambridge University Press, 1974.

Olhson, T., ed. *Arms Transfer Limitations and Third World Security.* Oxford: Oxford University Press, 1988.

Olson, M. *The Logic of Collective Action: Public Goods and the Theory of Groups.* Cambridge, MA: Harvard University Press, 1975.

Olson, R. *US Foreign Policy and The New International Economic Order.* Boulder, CO: Westview Press, 1981.

Organski, A. F. K., and J. Kugler. *The War Ledger.* Chicago: University of Chicago Press, 1980.

Packenham, R. A. *Liberal America and the Third World.* Princeton: Princeton University Press, 1973.

Padmore, G. *Pan-Africanism or Communism.* Garden City, NY: Anchor Books, 1971.

Page, D. *Prelude to Partition: The Indian Muslims and the System of Control, 1920–1932.* Delhi: Oxford University Press, 1982.

Pandey, B. N. *Nehru: A Biography.* New York: Stein and Day, 1976.

Petras, J. *Critical Perspectives on Imperialism and Social Class in the Third World.* New York: Monthly Review Press, 1978.

Pfaff, W. "Invitation to War." *Foreign Affairs* 73, no. 3 (Summer 1993): 97–109.

Pinkney, A. R. *Black and Green: Black Nationalism in America.* New York: Cambridge University Press, 1976.

Pirages, D. *The New Context of International Relations: Global Ecopolitics.* N. Scituate, MA: Duxbury Press, 1978.

Porter, K. W. *The Black Seminoles: History of a Freedom-Seeking People.* Gainesville, FL: University of Florida Press, 1996.

Poulantzas, N. *Classes in Contemporary Capitalism.* London: New Left Books, 1975.

Price, R. M. *The Apartheid State in Crisis: Political Transformation in South Africa, 1975–1990.* New York and Oxford: Oxford University Press, 1991.

Puchala, D. J., and R. A. Coate, eds. *The Challenge of Relevance: The United Nations in a Changing World Environment.* New York: Academic Council of the United Nations, 1989.

Purcell, Randell B. *The Newly Industrializing Countries in the World Economy: Challenges for the US Policy.* Boulder, CO and London: Lynne Rienner, 1989.

Radelet, S., and J. Sachs. "Asia's Resurgence." *Foreign Affairs* 76, no. 6 (November/December 1997): 44–58.

Rana, A. P. *The Imperative of Non-Aligned Movement.* Delhi: The MacMillan Co. of India, 1976.

Riker, W. H. *The Theory of Political Coalitions.* New Haven: Yale University Press, 1968.

Ritter, A. R. M., et. al. *Latin America to the Year 2000: Reactivating Growth, Improving Equity, Sustaining Democracy.* New York: Praeger Publishers, 1992.

Roberts, T. "Not a Prototype for World Government." *Times Literary Supplement,* 28 February 1998): 27.

Robertson, C. L. *International Politics Since World War II: A Short History.* 2nd ed. New York: John Wiley and Sons, Inc., 1975.

Robinson, C. *Black Marxism: The Making of the Black Radical Traditions.* 2nd ed.. Zed Press, 1991.

Rodney, W. *How Europe Underdeveloped Africa.* Washington, DC: Howard University Press, 1974.

Romelo, C. P. *The Meaning of Bandung.* Chapel Hill, NC: University of North Carolina Press, 1956.

Rose, L. A. *Roots of a Tragedy: The United States and the Struggle for Asia, 1945–1953.* Westport, CT: Greenwood Press, 1976.

Rosecrance, Richard. *The Rise of Trading States.* New York: Basic Books, 1986.

Rothstein, R. *Global Bargaining: UNCTAD and the Quest for a New International Economic Order.* Princeton, NJ: Princeton University Press, 1979.

———. *The Third World and US Foreign Policy: Cooperation and Conflict in the 1980s.* Boulder, CO: Westview Press, 1981.

Rubinstein, A. W. *Soviet Foreign Policy since World War II: Imperial and Global.* Cambridge, MA: Winthrop Publishers, Inc., 1981.

———. *Yugoslavia and the Non-Aligned World.* Princeton, NJ: Princeton University Press, 1970.

Ruggie, J. R. *The Antinomies of Interdependence: National Welfare and the International Division of Labor.* New York: Columbia University Press, 1983.

Russett, B., and H. Starr. *World Politics: A Menu of Choice.* New York: W. H. Freeman, 1981.

Sayegh, F. *The Dynamics of Neutralism in the Arab World.* San Francisco: Chandler Publishing Company, 1964.

Sauvant, K. P., and H. Hasenpflug. *The New International Economic Order: Confrontation and Cooperation between the North and South.* Boulder, CO: Westview Press, 1977.

———. *The Changing Priorities on International Agenda: The New International Economic Order.* New York: Pergamon Press, 1981.

———. *The Group of 77: Evolution, Structure, Organization.* New York: Oceana Publications, 1981.

Sassen, S. *Losing Control: Sovereignty in the Age of Globalization.* New York: Columbia University Press, 1996.

———. *Globalization and Its Discontents.* New York: New Press, 1998.

Schaffer, M. "Capturing the Mineral Multinationals: Advantage or Disadvantage?" In *Multinational Corporations: The Political Economy of Foreign Direct Investment,* edited by Theodore Moran, 25–54. Lexington, MA: Lexington Books, D. C. Heath and Company, 1985.

Schell, Jonathan. "The Folly of Arms Control." *Foreign Affairs* 79, no. 5 (September/October 2000): 22–46.

Schumpeter, J. A. *Business Cycles: A Theoretical and Historical Analysis of the Capitalist Process.* London: McGraw-Hill, 1939.

Seidman, A., and F. Anang, eds. *Towards a New Vision of Self-Sustainable Development.* Trenton, NJ: Africa World Press, 1992.

Seidman, A., and N. S. Makgetla. *Outpost of Capitalism: Southern Africa in a Changing World Economy.* Westport, CT: Lawrence Hill and Company, 1980.

Sharma, D. N. *The Afro-Asian Group in the United Nations.* Allahabad, India: Chaitanya Publishing House, 1969.

Sigmund, P. E. *Ideologies in Developing Countries.* 2nd ed. New York: Praeger Publishers, 1972.

———. *Multinationals in Latin America: The Politics of Nationalization.* Madison: University of Wisconsin Press, 1981.

Singer, M. *Weak States in a World of Powers: Dynamics of International Relations.* New York: Free Press, 1972.

Singh, J. *A New International Economic Order: Toward a Fair Redistribution of World Resources.* New York: Praeger Publishers, 1977.

Singham, A. W. *The Non-Aligned in World Politics.* Westport, CT: Lawrence Hill and Company, 1977.

Singham, A. W., and T.V. Dinh. *From Bandung to Colombo: Conferences of the Non-Aligned Countries 1955–1975.* New York: Third Press Review, 1976.

Singham, A. W., and S. Hune. "From Third World Non-Alignment to European Dealignment to Global Realignment." In *Dealignment: A New Foreign Policy Perspective,* edited by Mary Kaldor et al., 185–205. New York: Basil Blackwell, 1987.

Sithole, N. *African Nationalism.* 2nd ed. New York: Oxford University Press, 1969.

Sivard, R. *World Military and Social Expenditures 1991.* Washington D. C.: World Priorities, 1991.

Smets, P. P. *The Afro-Asian People's Solidarity Conference, Conakry, Guinea 11–15 April, 1960.* Cairo: Permanent Secretariat of Afro-Asian People's Solidarity Organization, 1960.

Smith, M. P., and J. R. Feagan. *The Capitalist City: Global Restructuring and Community Politics.* New York: Basil Blackwell, 1987.

Smith, T. *The End of Empire: Decolonization after World War II.* Lexington, MA: D. C. Heath and Company, 1975.

South Commission. *The Challenge of the South.* New York: Oxford University Press, 1990.

Spanier, J. *Games Nations Play: Analyzing International Politics.* New York: Holt, Rhinehart and Winston, 1981.

Spear, J., and Stuart Croft. "Superpowers Arms Transfers to the Third World." In *Superpowers Competition and Crisis Prevention in the Third World,* edited by Allison and Williams, 246–285. Cambridge, England and New York, NY: Cambridge University Press, 1990.

Spero, J. E. *The Politics of International Economic Relations.* New York: St. Martin's Press, 1981.

Stallings, B. *Global Change, Regional Response: The New International Context of Development.* Cambridge: Cambridge University Press, 1995.

Stavrianos, L. S. *The Global Rift: The Third World Comes of Age.* New York: William Morrow and Company, 1981.

Stevens, C. *The Soviet Union and Black Africa.* New York: Holmes and Meier Publishers, 1976.

Stockholm International Peace Research Institute. *World Armaments and Disarmament: SIPRI Yearbook 1991.* New York: Oxford University Press, 1991.

Stoessinger, J. *The Might of Nations: World Politics in Our Times*. New York: Random House, 1979.

———. *The United Nations and the Superpowers: China, Russia and America*. New York: Random House, 1977.

Stohl, M., and George L. Lopez. *Government Violence and Repression: An Agenda for Research*. Westport, CT: Greenwood Press, 1986.

Takaki, R. *Iron Cages: Race and Culture in 19th Century America*. New York: Oxford University Press, 1990.

Thomas, C. *In Search of Security: The Third World in International Relations*. Boulder, CO: Lynne Rienner, 1987.

Thomas, C., and Paikiasothy Saravanamutta, eds. *The State and Instability in the South*. New York: St. Martin's Press, 1989.

Thomas, C. Y. *The Poor and Powerless: Economic Policy and Change in the Caribbean*. New York: Monthly Review Press, 1988.

Thomas, D. C. "Evolving Patterns in Third World Solidarity." *Transafrica Forum* 4, no. 4 (September 1987): 73–92.

———. "The Impact of the Sino-Soviet Conflict on the Afro-Asian People's Solidarity Organization: Afro-Asianism vs. Non-Alignment." *Journal of Asian and African Affairs* 3, no. 2 (Spring 1992): 167–191.

Thomas, D. C., and William G. Martin. "South Africa's Economic Trajectory: South Africa's Crisis or World Economic Crisis?" In *How Fast The Wind? Southern Africa, 1975–2000,* edited by S. Vieira et al., 165–196. Trenton, NJ: Africa World Press, 1992.

Thomas, D. C., and Ali A. Mazrui. "Africa's Post-Cold War Demilitarization: Domestic and Global Causes." *Journal of International Affairs* 46, no. 1 (Summer 1992): 157–174.

Thompson, V. B. *Africa and Unity: The Evolution of Pan-Africanism*. New York and London: Longman, Inc., 1969.

———. *The Making of the African Diaspora in the Americas 1441–1900*. London: Longman, Inc., 1987.

Thompson, W. R., ed. *Global War*. Columbia, SC: University of South Carolina Press, 1988.

———. *Contending Approaches to World System Analysis*. Beverly Hills: Sage Publications, 1983.

———. "Cycles, Capabilities and War: An Ecumenical View." In *Contending Approaches to World System Analysis,* edited by W. R. Thompson. Beverly Hills: Sage Publications, 1983.

———. "Succession Crises in the Global Political System: A Test of the Transition Model." In *Crises in the World System,* edited by Albert Bergesen. Beverly Hills: Sage Publications, 1983.

———. "Uneven Economic Growth, Systemic Challenges, and Global War." *International Studies Quarterly* 27 (September 1983): 341–55.

Thurow, L. *The Future of Capitalism: How Today's Economic Forces Shape Tomorrow's World*. New York: William Morrow and Company, 1996.

Tilly, C., ed. *The Formation of National States in Western Europe*. Princeton, NJ: Princeton University Press, 1975.

Timberlake, C. E. *Détente: A Documentary Record*. New York: Praeger Publishers, 1978.

Tinbergen, J. *Reshaping the International Order*. Geneva: Institute for International Studies, 1976.

Todaro, M. P. *Economic Development in the Third World*. New York: Longman, 1985.

Treisman, D. "Why Yeltsin Won?" *Foreign Affairs* 75, no. 5 (September/October 1976).

Truman, D. *The Governmental Process: Political Interest and Public Opinion*. New York: Alfred A. Knopf, 1951.

Tucker, R. L. *The Marxist-Engels Reader*. New York: W. W. Norton and Company, 1978.

Tucker, R. W. *The Inequality of Nations*. New York: Basic Books, 1977.

United Nations. *Africa Debt: The Case for Debt Relief*. New York: African Recovery Unit/CPMD, Department of Public Information, United Nations, 1992.

United Nations. *Handbook of International Trade and Development Statistics, 1983*. New York: United Nations, 1983.

United Nations. *Statistical Yearbook 1983/84, 1986*. New York: United Nations, 1983/84, 1986.

United Nations. *World Economic Survey 1991/92: A Reader*. New York: United Nations Publications, 1991.

Urquhart, B. "Looking for the Sheriff." *New York Review of Books* 45, no. 12 (16 July 1998).

Van den Berghe, P. L. *Race and Racism in Comparative Perspective*. New York: Wiley, 1967.

———. *State Violence and Ethnicity*. Niwot, CO: University of Colorado Press, 1990.

Vieira, Sergio et al. *How Fast the Wind? Southern Africa, 1975–2000*. Trenton, NJ: Africa World Press, Inc., 1992.

Vasquez, J. A. *The Power of Power Politics: A Critique*. New Brunswick, NJ: Rutgers University Press, 1983.

Wallerstein, Immanuel. "The Colonial Era in Africa: Changes in Social Structure." In *Colonialism in Africa*, edited by L. Gann and P. Duigan. Cambridge: Cambridge University Press, 1970.

———. *The Modern World System I: Capitalist Agriculture and the Origins of the European World-Economy in the Sixteenth Century*. New York: Academic Press, 1974.

———. "The Rise and Future Demise of the World Capitalist System: Concepts for Comparative Analysis." *Comparative Studies in Society and History* 16, no. 4 (1979): 387–415.

———. *The Capitalist World-Economy*. Cambridge: Cambridge University Press, 1979.

———. *The Modern World System II: Mercantilism and Consolidation of the European World-Economy, 1600–1750*. New York: Academic Press, 1980.

———. *The Politics of the World-Economy*. Cambridge: Cambridge University Press, 1984.

———. *The Modern World System III: The Second Era of Great Expansion of the Capitalist World-Economy, 1730–1840*. New York: Academic Press, 1991.

———. "The Three Instances of Hegemony in the History of the Capitalist System" In *The Evolution of International Political Economy: A Reader*, edited by George T. Crane and A. Amawi. New York: Oxford University Press, 1991.

———. *Geopolitics and Geoculture: Essays on a Changing World System*. Cambridge: Cambridge University Press, 1991.

Waltz, K. N. *Theory of International Politics*. Reading, MA: Addison-Wesley, 1979.

Whitaker, A. P. *The Western Hemispheric Idea: Its Rise and Decline*. Ithaca: Cornell University Press, 1954.

White, J. Black. *Leadership in America: From Booker T. Washington to Jesse Jackson*. 2nd ed. London: Longman, 1990.

Wilber, C. K., and K. P. Jameson. *The Political Economy of Development and Underdevelopment*. 5th ed. New York: McGraw-Hill Book Company, 1992.

Willetts, P. *The Non-Aligned Movement: The Origins of a Third World Movement*. London: Francis Pinter, Ltd., 1978.

————. *The Non-Aligned in Havana*. New York: St. Martin's Press, 1981.

Wilson, Carter A. *Racism: From Slavery to Advanced Capitalism*. Thousand Oaks, CA: Sage Publications, n.d.

Wolf, E. *Europe and the People without History*. Berkeley: University of California Press, 1982.

Wolpin, M., ed. *Militarization, Internal Repression and Social Welfare in the Third World*. New York: St. Martin's Press, 1986.

World Bank. *Sub-Saharan Africa: From Crisis to Sustainable Growth*. Washington, DC: International Bank of Reconstruction and Development, 1989.

World Bank. *World Debt Tables, 1987/88, 1989*. Washington, DC: World Bank, 1987.

World Bank. *World Development Report, 1982, 1988, and 1989*. New York: Oxford University Press, 1990.

World Bank. *World Tables, 1955, 1960, 1970, and 1976*. First Edition. Baltimore, MD: Johns Hopkins University Press, 1976.

World Bank. *World Tables, 1980*. 2nd ed. Baltimore, MD: Johns Hopkins University Press, 1980.

World Bank. *World Tables, 1988–89*. Baltimore, MD: Johns Hopkins University Press, 1989.

World Bank. *World Debt Tables: External Debt of Developing Countries 1991–1992*. Washington, DC: World Bank, 1992.

Worsley, P. *The Third World: A Vital Force in International Affairs*. London: Weidenfield and Nicholson, 1964.

————. *The Three Worlds: Culture and World Development*. London: Weidenfield and Nicholson, 1984.

Wriggins, W. H., and G. Adler-Karlsson. *Reducing Global Inequalities*. New York: McGraw-Hill Book Company, 1978.

Wright, Q. "The Study of War." *International Encyclopedia of Social Science,* vol. 16. New York: MacMillan, 1968.

Wright, R. *The Color Curtain*. Cleveland: World Pub. Corp., 1956.

Zartman, W. *International Relations of the New States of Africa*. Englewood Cliffs, NJ: Prentice-Hall, 1964.

————. *Ripe Resolution: Conflict and Intervention in Africa*. New York: Oxford University Press, 1989.

Zimmerman, W. *Soviet Perspective on International Relations 1956–1967*. Princeton, NJ: Princeton University Press, 1969.

Zwass, A. *From Failed Communism to Underdeveloped Capitalism: Transformation of Eastern Europe, the Post-Soviet Union, and China*. Armonk, New York: M. E. Sharpe, 1995.

DOCUMENTS

Addresses Delivered at the Sixth Conference of Heads of State of Governments of the Non-Aligned Countries. Havana: Editorial de Ciencias Sociales, 1980.

The Afro-Asian People's Solidarity Organization. Cooperation between the AAPSO and the United Nations Organization. Permanent Secretariat of AAPSO, Cairo, 1975.

The Afro-Asian People's Solidarity Organization. *International Conference in Solidarity with Mozambique, Guinea-Bissua, Cape Verde, Sao Tome and Principe, Lourencos Marques*. Cairo: Permanent Secretariat of AAPSO, 1975.

The Afro-Asian People's Solidarity Organization. International Seminar on the Problem of Development and the Struggle for NIEO. Baghdad, 1976. Permanent Secretariat of the Afro-Asian People's Solidarity Organization, Cairo, 1976.

Asian Development Bank. *Key Indicators of Developing Countries.* Makati, Philippines: Economic Office, ADB, 1986, 1987, and 1989.

Colombo Summit. *Documents and Selected Speeches of the Fifth Conference of Heads of State or Government of the Non-Aligned Countries.* New Delhi: People's Publishing House, 1976.

Conference of the Foreign Ministers of the Non-Aligned Countries, New Delhi, February 9–13, 1981, Proceedings. New Delhi: Ministry of External Affairs, 1981.

The Fifth Afro-Asian People's Solidarity Conference. Preparatory Document of the Fifth Conference, January 10–13, 1972. Cairo, Egypt: Permanent Secretariat of the Afro-Asian People's Solidarity Organization, 1972.

First Afro-Asian People's Solidarity Conference. Cairo, Egypt 1958. Principal Report, 1958. Cairo, Egypt: Permanent Secretariat of Afro-Asian Peoples Solidarity Organization, 1958.

The Fourth Afro-Asian People's Solidarity Conference. Winneba, Ghana. May 1965. Cairo, Egypt: Permanent Secretariat of the Afro-Asian People's Solidarity Organization, 1965.

Fourth Conference of Heads of State or Government of Non-Aligned Countries, Algiers. Speeches (1973). *Review of International Affairs* 24 (5 October 1973): 564.

Permanent Organization for AAPSO Presidium. People's Republic of Benin, 1977. Cairo: Permanent Secretariat of the Afro-Asian People's Solidarity Organization, 1977.

The Second Afro-Asian People's Solidarity Conference. Conakry, Guinea, 1960. Cairo, Egypt: Permanent Secretariat of the Afro-Asian People's Solidarity Organization, 1960.

South African Institute of Race Relations, Survey, 1975, 1987/89. Johannesburg: SAIRR, 1975, 1987/8.

The Third Afro-Asian People's Solidarity Conference. Moshi, Tanganyika. February 4–11, 1963. Cairo, Egypt: The Permanent Secretariat of the Afro-Asian People's Solidarity Organization, 1963.

Index

Accra riots, 54
Adarand Construction v. Pena, 258
Advanced Developing Countries
    (ADCs), 145, 174
adversary partnership, 94
affirmative action, 249, 253, 258, 259,
    260
Afghan mujahideen rebels, 189
Afghanistan, 7, 77, 101, 122, 185–189,
    191, 194, 195, 197, 198, 207, 209,
    210, 230
Africa
    debt, 145, 147, 148
    nationalism, 38–40, 46, 48–52
    personality, 40
    slave trade, 44
    slaves, 29, 44, 255
African American, 24, 28, 29, 45, 46, 48,
    49, 51, 249–256, 258, 259–261
    middle class, 250, 252
    working class, 250, 252
African National Congress (ANC), 78,
    212, 227, 237, 248
Afro-Asian People's Solidarity Organiza-
    tion (AAPSO), 56
Agrarian Party, 216, 217
Algeria, 35, 57, 76–78, 94, 123–27, 146,
    156, 162, 163, 166, 167, 174, 176,
    190, 192, 193, 243, 248, 265, 273,
    275

alignment, 9, 57, 64, 75, 92
America's counterinsurgency war, 265
anticolonial struggles, 44, 190
anticolonialism, 72, 77, 80, 110
antiracialism, 29, 111
ANZUS Treaty, 69
Arab League, The, 54, 55, 70, 123, 124,
    175, 193, 233
Arafat, Yassir, 229, 272
arc of crisis, 188
arms control, 271
arms exports, 189, 195
Arrighi, Giovanni, 14
Asian Federation, 42
Assembly of Greater East Asiatic
    Nations, The, 43
Association for a Greater Asia, The, 42
Association of Southeast Asian Nations
    (ASEAN), 123, 176, 193, 201, 202,
    233
Ayoob, Mohammed, 185

Baghdad Pact, The, 70
Baltic states, 215
Bandung Conference, 38, 54, 56, 57, 70,
    71, 73, 88, 124, 173
basic need approach, 130
Bengalis, 186
benign neglect, 117, 242, 254, 262
Bensonhurst, 255

Berlin Agreement, 90, 98
Berlin Wall, 208, 214
bipolar approach, 130
bipolar system, 6, 64, 105
bipolarity, 3, 5, 85
    loose, 3
bipolycentric, 105, 122
Bishop, Maurice, 195
    New Jewel Movement, 195
black, 22–26, 28, 37, 39, 40, 42,
        44–51, 78, 228, 229, 233,
        247–50, 252–56, 258, 259,
        261, 262, 264, 266
black consciousness, 50
Black Cross Nurses, 49
Black Dragon Secret Society, 42
Black Flying Eagles, 49
black ghettos, 254
black slaves, 23
Black Star Line, 49
Blyden, Edward, 45
Bolivar, Simon, 37
Bolshevism, 215
Boumedienne, 75, 125, 127, 128
bourgeoisie, 39, 40, 47, 52, 65
    Asian, 39, 40, 47
Brandt, Willy, 95
Brazil, 27, 31, 38, 156, 157, 160, 162–72,
        176, 177, 193, 195, 196, 212, 230,
        243, 245, 267, 271, 274, 279, 286
Bretton Woods, 9, 115–17, 138, 154, 175
Brezhnev, 94, 96, 98–100, 102, 209
Brown, Seyom, 69
buffer zone, 74, 272
Bush, George, 5, 171, 182, 198, 205, 208,
        219, 225, 226, 227, 253, 254, 258,
        263, 275, 276
Buzan, Barry, 8, 235

Cabinda, 212
Cafruny, Alan W., 20, 21, 120, 138
Cairo Pact, 55
California Board of Regents, 259
Camdessus, Michael, 154
Cancun Summit, 129, 131
capital accumulation, 4, 5, 11, 13, 15, 37,
        46, 79, 113, 142, 143, 146, 158
    models of, 3, 4, 11, 13, 15, 37, 79, 113,
        142, 143

capitalism
    business enterprises, 4, 6, 10, 14, 142,
        143, 156, 158
    democratic, 5, 25, 154, 175, 184, 205,
        208, 209, 213, 215, 241, 273, 276
Carter Doctrine, 183, 193, 195
Carter, Jimmy, 78, 130, 193, 264
    administration, 130, 132, 274
Castro, Fidel, 175
Cedras, Raoul, 263
Central America, 24, 76, 82, 151, 153,
        154, 157, 189, 191, 193–96, 198,
        205, 207, 208, 262
Central Treaty Organization (CENTO),
        70, 71
Cesaire, Aimé, 41, 58
Chamorro, Violeta, 193
Charter of Economic Rights and Duties
        of States, the, 128
Chile, 38, 111, 144, 146, 156, 160–70,
        193, 234, 256
Chin, 186
Chirac, Jacques, 248
Churchill, Winston, 65
Civil Rights Act, 254
civil society, 18, 25, 205, 219, 227
civil war, 54, 76, 102, 114, 132, 145, 149,
        156, 175, 230, 244, 256, 272, 274
civilizations, 16
Clark, Cal, 17
classical dependency, 15, 79
Clinton Administration, 223, 226, 232,
        263, 264, 269, 286
Clinton, Bill, 217, 226, 227, 257, 259, 260,
        261, 263, 264, 271, 286
CMEA, 66, 89
Cold War, 3, 5, 8, 9, 16, 19, 20, 21, 29, 30,
        37, 38, 55–57, 63–74, 76, 81, 85–88,
        91–95, 100, 101, 105, 115, 123, 130,
        132, 149, 153, 183–85, 187, 188,
        190, 194, 196, 198, 201, 205–208,
        214, 219–22, 225–28, 230, 231,
        241–43, 255, 262, 265, 266, 268,
        269, 272–76, 281, 283, 287, 288, 292
coalitions, 3, 9, 37, 56, 64–68, 85, 86, 88,
        93, 105, 122, 124, 139, 140, 142,
        194, 208, 220, 247
collective action, 138, 140, 145
    theory of, 139

collective goods, 139, 140
colonial economy, 40
colonial state, 78, 185
colonization, 4, 6, 10, 19, 22, 26, 37, 45,
    46, 49, 54, 56, 80, 143
  selected, 49
Comintern, 51
Common Agricultural Policy (CAP), 119,
    120
commonwealth
  socialist, 85, 89
Commonwealth of Independent States,
    216, 242, 267
communal groups, 8, 156, 186
Communist Party, 24, 51, 89–92, 96,
    208, 214, 215, 216, 217, 220
comparative advantage, 157, 242
competitive depreciation, 118
complex interdependence, 6, 10, 121,
    122, 124, 176
Comprehensive Employment and Train-
    ing Act, 253
Condor missile program, 267
Conference on International Economic
    Cooperation (CIEC), 129
Confucianism, 16
Congressional Black Caucus, 264
Connerly, Ward, 259
containment philosophy, 65
containment policy, 66, 68–71
Contras, 193, 195
cooperative black capitalism, 49
core, 4, 13–16, 19, 56, 114, 133, 142,
    167, 188, 246, 251
corporations
  multinational, 4, 6, 10, 17, 63, 110,
    114, 124, 160, 211, 250, 251
correlation of forces, 101
Council for Mutual Economic Assistance
    (COMECON), 66, 86, 90
Cox, Robert W., 18, 19
creative destruction, 14
Crummell, Alexander, 45
Cuban missile crisis, 86, 87, 96, 122, 187,
    265
Cuffe, Paul, 45

Dar es Salaam Preparatory Conference,
    123

de Gaulle, Charles, 85, 91, 94
de Klerk, F. W., 228, 229,
de Tocqueville, Alexis, 64
Declaration and Programme of Action,
    127
decolonization, 4, 6, 8, 10, 27-28, 37, 54,
    55, 56, 63, 68, 75, 77, 79, 80, 82, 86,
    111, 143, 175, 215
  economic, 79, 111
Delany, Martin, 45
democracy, 25, 28, 37, 52, 55, 65, 78,
    154, 176, 183, 184, 193, 205, 215,
    218–21, 223, 226–29, 231, 241,
    262, 263, 265, 274, 276, 282,
    287–90, 292
  multiparty, 154
dependency, 6, 13, 15, 16, 17, 19, 21, 72,
    76, 79, 92, 174, 188, 211, 254, 260,
    261
dependent relationships, 158
destructive engagement, 78, 195
détente, 9, 10, 86, 87, 88, 90, 92, 93, 94,
    95, 96, 97, 98, 99, 100, 101, 102,
    104, 209, 265, 275
  gradual, 94, 96
development
  dependent, 3, 16, 17
developmentalist states, 17
dilemma
  insecurity, 8, 132, 154, 184, 185, 186,
    188, 192, 220
Dinkins, David, 253
discrimination
  reverse, 249
divergent spatial dimension, 3, 31
division of labor
  global, 10, 15, 19, 31, 111, 112, 129,
    138, 142, 151, 153, 156, 157, 174
  international, 3-5, 12, 16-18, 31, 113,
    123, 142, 143, 161, 163, 170, 172,
    175, 177, 243, 282
dominant powers, 12, 271
Douglass, Frederick, 291
Dubcek government, 90
Duke, David, 253
Duvalier regime, 262

Eastern Caribbean Community, the, 175
economic aid, 55, 69, 70, 154, 189, 213,

241, 268
economic crisis, 20, 81, 114, 131, 132,
    149, 212
    global, 81, 114, 131, 132, 138, 141,
    144, 145, 147, 149, 153, 164, 166,
    171, 175, 177, 205, 210, 211, 212,
    213, 241, 267, 275
Egypt, 9, 23, 41, 55, 57, 70, 71, 77, 78,
    84, 88, 102, 103, 123, 134, 157, 174,
    192, 195, 197, 207, 230, 242, 266,
    272
emerging markets, 171–172
energy crisis, 93, 103, 121, 174
ethnocentrism, 242
Eurocentrism, 40, 63, 64, 243
European Economic Community (EEC),
    92, 119, 120, 128
export promotion, 160, 216

failed societies, 219, 226, 227
Fanon, Franz, 41
Farah Aideed, Mohamed, 226, 227
Federal Republic of Germany (FRG), 95
fixed exchange rates, 117
Food Stamp Program, 253
Fortress Europe, 246
Frank, Andre Gunder, 16
Franks, Gary A., 259
Friedman, Milton, 216

Gant, Harvey, 253
Garvey, Marcus, 28, 39, 45, 46, 47, 48,
    49, 50, 58
General Agreement on Tariffs and Trade
    (GATT), 90, 115, 129, 131, 137,
    141, 144, 175, 189, 233, 243, 273,
    277
Geneva Conference, 87
gentrification, 254
geoeconomics, 242
geopolitics, 28, 242
German revanchism, 90
Ghana, 9, 50, 54, 56–57, 59, 74, 77, 145
Gilpin, Robert, 12, 120, 290
global apartheid, 5, 16, 17, 26–30, 44, 46,
    51, 74, 75, 77, 111, 112, 176, 184,
    235, 242, 244, 245, 249, 262, 265,
    269, 272, 273, 274, 276, 277, 281,
    283, 292

global bargaining, 117, 140–141
global capitalism, 281, 283, 290, 291
globalization, 20, 21, 114, 173, 184, 218,
    222, 224, 225, 235, 247, 257, 259,
    260, 262, 265, 276, 281–84, 287–92
global reach, 10, 11, 190
global restructuring, 3, 4, 18, 19, 24, 46,
    113, 132, 142, 153, 156, 157,
    170–171, 177, 209, 211, 214–15, 216
good government, 154
Gorbachev, Mikhail, 5, 194, 196, 208–10,
    214–15, 243,
Great Britain, 14–15, 63, 87, 104, 112,
    117, 120, 195
Great Powers, 5–7, 14, 18, 19, 56, 58, 64,
    76, 77, 79, 82, 120, 128, 134, 183,
    208, 222, 228, 230, 232, 233, 235,
    272, 274, 276
Great Society, 257
Greek civilization, 23
Grenada, 77, 134, 189, 194, 222, 228,
    237, 267,
Gromulko, Wladyslaw, 90
Gromyko, Andrei, 94
Group of 77, 122–124, 126, 127, 131,
    144, 146, 173, 174, 175, 178, 233
Group of Seven, 131, 134, 141, 148, 176,
    189, 209, 218, 242, 243, 268
Guaranteed Student Loan Program, 253
Guerrilla warfare, 265–267
Gulf Cooperation Council (GCC), 198
Gulf Oil of the United States, 212

Haiti, 37, 38, 46, 79, 219, 245, 256, 262,
    263, 264, 265, 274
Hapsburg, 12
Harlem, 47, 48
hegemonic power, 3, 5, 11, 15, 18, 20,
    114, 141, 143, 272
hegemony, 8, 12–14, 16, 18, 19–21, 26,
    29, 39, 40, 43, 45, 52, 68, 79, 86,
    91, 93, 95, 100, 120, 121, 131, 186,
    220, 223, 267, 275
    American, 12, 19, 29, 93
    declining, 20, 120
    integral, 20, 120
    minimal, 20, 21, 120
    Northern, 13, 26
    Soviet, 68, 86, 91, 95

Hernstein, Richard J., 261
Hiroshima, 65
historic bloc, 19, 25, 243
historical materialism, 19, 20, 120
Ho Chi Minh, 41
Hoffmann, Stanley, 122
holocaust, 55, 96, 104, 255
Hopkins, T. K., 14
Horton, Willie, 253
Howard Beach, 255
Howe, Jonathan, 226
human rights violations, 224, 234
Hune, Shirley, 194
Huntington, Samuel P., 16
Hurd, Douglas, 231
Hussein, Saddam, 264

ICBMs, 99
immigration
   Haitian, 262
imperial overstretch, 120
imperialism, 14, 16, 23, 25, 26, 29, 37,
   38, 41, 42, 44, 75, 241, 243, 246
   cultural, 40, 75
   Japanese, 44
import substitution, 153, 158, 160
incorporation, 4, 5, 13, 15, 17, 18–19, 25,
   27, 46, 63, 80, 211, 223
Indian National Congress, 42
Indonesia, 9, 41, 57, 69, 71, 88, 123, 230,
   237, 245, 285
industrial policies, 4, 153, 160
inflation
   worldwide, 118
interdependence, 6, 10, 85, 113, 114,
   115, 120, 121, 122, 124, 127, 176
interenterprise system, 14
interest groups, 138–141
International Atomic Energy Agency
   (IAEA), 268
International Labor Organization (ILO),
   78, 132, 137, 233, 234
International Monetary Fund (IMF),
   115, 129, 131, 137, 141, 143,
   144, 145, 148, 149, 151, 153,
   154, 155, 156, 170, 171, 172,
   175, 178, 189, 212, 214, 218,
   232, 234, 235, 243, 275, 285,
   286, 290, 291

Islam, 16, 23

James, C. L. R., 41
Japan, 5, 9, 16, 19, 38, 42, 43, 44, 56,
   69, 81, 158, 177, 184, 196, 202, 216,
   242, 244, 245, 269, 271, 274, 276
   283, 286
Johnson, Donald, 262
Johnson, Wallace, 51
Jonassaint, Emile, 264
Jose de San Martin, 37

Kaplan, Morton A., 64
Karens, 186
Kashmiris, 186
Kennan, George, 64
Kennedy, John F., 86
Kennedy, Paul 12, 118
Kenyatta, Jomo, 41, 50, 51, 59
Keohane, Robert, 32, 124, 138
Khan, Aga, 42
Khrushchev, Nikita, 68, 71, 87, 89, 90,
   94, 213
killing field, 191, 192
King, Rodney, 255, 256
Kissinger, Henry, 86, 93, 96, 97, 98, 99,
   100, 101, 102, 103, 107, 126, 128
Klare, Michael, 189
Kohler, Gernot, 26, 110, 112
Korean Crisis, 68, 69
Korean War, 70, 190, 220, 236, 265, 268
Krasner, Stephen, 141
Ku Klux Klan (KKK), 253
Kurds, 192
Kuwait, 77, 79, 102, 134, 174, 183, 185,
   193, 207, 222, 228, 237, 265

Laissez faire, 216
Lasch, Christopher, 249
Laski, Harold, 41
Lauren, Paul G., 22, 26
Le Pen, Jean, 247, 248
legitimacy, 7, 19, 22, 46, 53, 77, 78, 86,
   95, 105, 113, 116, 132, 141, 175,
   185, 186, 208, 215, 221, 223, 232,
   243, 250, 266, 286
Lemco, Jonathan, 17
Lenin, V. I., 41. 276
Leninism, 5, 18, 28, 29, 187, 209, 214,

242, 243, 273, see also Marxist-
   Leninism
Liberal Democratic Party, 216, 217
Liberal Party, 216
limited nationalization schemes, 146
linkage, 40, 80, 81, 99, 100, 116, 159
Lomè Convention, 212, 258
lost decade, 205
low politics, 9

Machel, Samora, 212
Magubane, Bernard M., 23, 45
Malaysia, 134, 145, 156–58, 161–70, 172,
   173, 176, 237, 243, 245, 285
Manchester Congress, 52, 59
Mandela, Nelson, 78, 228–29
Manifest Destiny, 29, 56
manufacturing, 3, 153, 156–63, 166–67,
   170–71, 176–77, 179, 198, 243, 245,
   247, 250, 251, 254, 282
Marable, Manning, 250
Marshall Plan, 66, 79, 242
Marshall, George, 66
Marx, Karl, 22, 25, 41, 243, 276
Marxism, 25, 51, 242, 243
Marxist-Leninism, 186, 207, 210, 211,
   214, 242, 272
Marxist, 5, 19, 23, 24, 28, 80, 88, 103,
   104, 187, 243, 266, 276
Mau Mau movement, 78
Mazrui, Ali A, 15, 16, 186, 244, 255
McKinney, Cynthia A., 258
Mexico, 58, 129, 131, 134, 156, 158,
   160–72, 174, 176, 192, 193, 230,
   242, 245, 251, 257, 274, 284
microstates, 157
middle class, 41, 54, 151, 229, 252, 254
military industrial complex, 203, 215
military power, 28, 43, 65, 73, 102, 104,
   105, 112, 114, 198, 233, 242
Milllennium Conference, 271
minorities, 172, 246, 248, 252, 256, 259
   ethnic, 247, 248
   unmeltable, 246, 248
   white, 242, 246, 266, 275
modernization, 210
Morgenthau, Hans, 6
Moscow Conference, the, 55
Movement for the Popular Liberation of

Angola (MPLA), 101
Mozambique National Resistance (REN-
   AMO), 212
mujahideen rebels, 189, 195, 198
multilateral policies, 129, 142
Murray, Charles, 261

Nagasaki, 42, 65
National Front, 247–49
national liberation, 6, 18, 76, 77, 87,
   187–192
National Opposition Union (UNO), 193
national security, 6, 8, 65, 66, 97, 208,
   215, 226, 235, 270, 284
National Union for the Total Independence of Angola (UNITA), 103,
   195, 210
nationalism, 28, 38–40, 42–44, 47–54,
   72, 89–91, 114, 146, 176, 209, 215,
   217, 220–222, 245, 246, 248, 262
   cultural, 39
nationalists, 40–44, 50, 51, 77, 146, 173,
   216
nationalization, 110, 127, 128, 146, 210
nationalization policies, 110
negritude, 39, 58
Negro, 23, 25, 28, 47–50, 249
Negro Improvement Association, 48, 50,
   58
Nehru, Jawaharlal, 41, 56, 72, 74, 75
neoliberalism, 132
Neorealism, 11
neutrality, 62, 24, 73, 74
New Deal, 257
new immigration policy, 249
new international economic order
   (NIEO), 13, 27, 80, 86, 112, 121,
   123–125, 127, 129, 130, 132, 137,
   138, 141, 144, 146, 170, 173–75
new racial order, 23
new world order, 5, 19, 28, 131, 138,
   141, 183, 184, 198, 208, 210, 219,
   230, 231, 235, 242, 244, 262, 267,
   269, 272, 274, 276, 277, 281, 292
newly industrializing countries (NICs), 3,
   4, 9, 17-19, 31, 72, 114, 129–31, 134,
   137, 138, 151, 156, 158, 159, 161,
   174, 202
Nicaragua, 19, 27, 77, 134, 177, 187, 189,

191, 193, 194, 195, 209

Nixon, Richard, 87, 92, 94, 96, 97, 99, 100, 102, 103, 116, 117, 118, 132, 236, 266, 275

Nkomati Accord, 212

Nkrumah, Kwame, 41, 50, 56, 59, 74, 75, 111

noncapitalist path to development, 184, 213

nonmilitary issues, 3, 10, 86, 91, 92, 94, 105, 121

nonstate actors, 6, 7, 10

nonwhite immigrants, 248

North American Free Trade Area, 177

North American Free Trade Association (NAFTA), 171

North Atlantic Treaty Organization (NATO), 37, 67, 85, 87, 90, 92, 93, 94, 102, 217, 222–25, 265

North Korea, 68, 70, 197, 201, 202, 207, 214, 265, 267–269, 271, 274, 279

Northeast, 5, 15, 16, 19, 29, 58, 112, 141, 184, 188, 208, 210, 213, 214, 219, 230, 231, 241, 242, 243, 268, 272, 273, 276, 292

Northwest, 5, 15, 16, 19, 29, 31, 56, 81, 112, 120, 121, 130, 131, 132, 141, 158, 175, 183, 184, 188, 190, 208, 210, 214, 219, 230, 231, 234, 276, 292

Northwest coalition, 183

Nubia, 23

nuclear weapons, 8, 65, 68, 88, 91, 94, 104, 112, 122, 265, 267–69, 270, 271

Nunn, Sam, 264

Nye, Joseph S., 12

Nyerere, Julius, 76, 212

Oakley, Robert, 226

Occidental Petroleum Company, 98

Occupational Health and Safety Administration, 253

OECD, 115, 131, 156, 175, 202

oil crises, 146

oil power, 10, 121, 124, 127, 174

Olson, Mancur, 138–40, 142

OPEC, 9, 72, 103, 117, 124, 125, 128, 130, 134, 137, 138, 153, 173, 174, 160, 202

Organization of African Unity (OAU), 122, 185, 193, 233

Organization of Arab Oil-Exporting Countries (OAPEC), 103, 123, 124, 127, 134

Organization of East Caribbean States (OECS), 195

Ortega, Daniel, 193

Ostopolitik, 95

outsourcing, 250

Padmore, George, 51, 52

Palestinian Liberation Organization (PLO), 229, 233, 234

Palestinians, 75, 78, 102, 126, 184, 229, 230, 272, 275

Party of Russian Unity, 216

Pax Americana, 10–12, 15, 16, 21, 29, 63, 65, 79, 111, 120, 121, 185, 272

Pax Britannica, 11, 12, 15, 51, 63, 79

Pax Nipponica, 16

peculiar institution, 22, 27

People's Republic of China (PRC), 18, 56, 57, 67, 69, 70, 75, 85, 87, 88, 96, 190, 193, 211, 213, 214, 245, 265, 268, 269, 270, 271

people's wars, 265

periphery, 3, 19, 26, 29, 82, 128, 130, 133, 142, 151–53, 157, 167, 170, 171, 246

Persian Gulf War, 79, 183, 267, 268, 276

Peru, 27, 59, 156, 160–70, 191, 230

Pfaff, William, 220

pioneering states, 9, 64, 167

Pol Pot, 191, 219
    regime, 191

pole of attraction, 125

police force of last resort, 184

political economy, 16, 17, 20, 21, 26, 30, 90, 120, 121, 130, 242, 243, 252, 277

political instability, 184, 216, 286

polycentrism, 85, 88, 91

Pompidou, Georges, 95

Portugal, 12, 92, 103, 124, 179, 161–66, 168–170, 187, 188, 190, 212, 282

Powell, Colin, 264

power cycles, 11

preferential price, 174

Programme of Action, 127
proletarian nations, 123, 137
proletariat, 29, 42
  lumpen, 251
proposition 140, 230, 243, 257, 259
protectionism, 146, 158, 173, 283, 284
public choice, 140
  analysts, 140
Putin, Vladimir, 289, 290

Rabin, Yitzhak, 229
racial capitalism, 21, 22, 24, 29, 243, 281
racial chauvinism, 245, 248, 249, 262
racial ideology, 22
racial minorities, 246, 248
racial order, 21, 22, 23, 27, 28, 72, 277
racial sovereignty, 37, 52, 56, 243
racial subordination, 22
racialism, 23
racism, 16, 62, 64, 74, 78, 289
rapidly industrializing nations, 163
rational actor, 140
Reagan, Ronald, 118, 131, 187, 188, 252,
    253, 254, 260, 266, 274
  administration, 118, 130–32, 209, 253,
    255, 258
Reaganomics, 131
realist paradigm, 6–9
Realpolitik, 100
regime analysis, 140
regimes
  international, 3, 4, 9–13, 15, 79, 112,
    113, 120, 123, 141, 142, 143, 183,
    184, 185, 231, 268, 287
revisionism, 68, 86, 89, 90
Rhodesia, 103, 104, 266
right of blood, 247
Rio Pact (1947), 9
Robinson, Randall, 264
Rodney, Walter, 44
Rome, 23, 24, 120
Rothstein, Robert, 140, 141
ruble, 214, 218, 243
Ruggie, John G., 18
rural bourgeoisie, 39
Russia's Choice, 216
Russian Republic, 5, 207, 215–18, 242,
    243, 276, 285, 286, 290
Russian Revolution, 25, 41

Russian Soviet Federated Socialist Repub-
    lic (RSFSR), 215

Salvadoran Democratic Front, 189
Sandinistas, 193, 195
Scali, John, 128
Schell, Jonathan, 271
Schumpeter, J. A., 14, 288, 290
Second Cold War, 132, 184, 187, 188,
    194, 275
Second Gulf War, 230
Second Reconstruction, 29, 254
security, 5–10, 37, 38, 46, 55, 64–67, 69,
    70, 72, 78, 82, 85, 86, 90–94, 97, 98,
    100, 115, 121, 122, 126, 127, 171,
    174, 183, 184, 186, 198, 208, 215,
    219, 226, 231, 247, 269, 276, 277,
    284, 290
security dilemma, 7, 8, 184, 185, 207
security state, 211
semiperipheral countries, 4
semiperiphery, 3, 16, 19, 130, 133, 142,
    151, 152, 156–59, 161, 163, 166,
    167, 170, 172, 177, 179, 216
Senghor, Leopold, 41, 58
Serbian nationalist, 220
Seventh Special Session, 129
Shans, 186
Shining Path, 191
Siad, Mohamed, 225
Sikhs, 186
silent partners, 157, 171, 177
Singham, Archie, 194
Sixth Special Session of the United
    Nations General Assembly, 123, 127
skin heads, 253
slave trade, 22–24, 44, 46, 59
slavery, 13, 15, 22–24, 26–28, 37, 45, 59,
    255, 274
Smith, Adam, 5, 276
Smithsonian accord, 117
Social Darwinism, 46, 261
social forces, 15, 18
socialism, 18, 25, 38, 48, 55, 66, 74, 89,
    175, 184, 209–15, 235, 273
Solidarity, 55, 56, 57, 64, 68, 70, 72–74,
    86, 89–92, 111, 112, 115, 121–25,
    130, 176, 177, 184, 192, 233, 241,
    246, 272–75, 277, 281, 289, 292

South Africa, 26, 41, 60, 78, 102, 104, 124, 134, 161–166, 168–70, 179, 184, 187, 192, 195, 196, 209, 210, 212, 228–30, 232–34, 245, 279, 291

South Korea, 31, 69, 71, 134, 161–66, 168–70, 187, 207, 216, 285

Southern African Development Coordination Council (SADCC), 195

Southern Hemisphere, 38, 57, 75, 86, 131, 132, 137, 143, 197, 273, 275

sovereignty, 7, 37, 46, 52, 55, 56, 64, 74–77, 79–81, 86, 111, 127, 128, 183, 187, 208, 214, 224, 231, 232, 243, 267, 272, 273, 275

Soviet empire, 5, 19, 91, 105, 214, 215, 217, 220, 245, 248, 287

Soviet Jews, 98

Soviet Union (USSR), 5, 8, 9, 18, 19, 24, 25, 29, 38, 55–57, 64–72, 85–91, 94–102, 104, 175, 183–185, 187–189, 194, 195, 197, 198, 208–213, 215, 219, 220, 235, 236, 265, 267–269, 281, 287

Spain, 12, 120, 133, 188, 242, 248

sphere of influence, 9, 11, 65, 71, 122, 175

stagflation, 117, 118, 146, 250, 288

Stalinist growth model, 210

state Duma, 217

Steel, Shelby, 259

Strategic Arms Limitation Talks (SALT), 96, 98, 99

superpowers, 3, 8–10, 29, 37, 38, 55, 63–68, 73, 75, 81, 87, 93, 96–102, 104, 105, 114, 121, 122, 130, 132, 175, 185, 187–94, 198, 203, 208, 209, 219, 265, 275

supranational organizations, 64

Switzerland, 64, 82

Syria, 41, 55, 70, 71, 88, 102, 192, 195, 197, 266, 267

Taiwan, 31, 98, 134, 152, 156–58, 161–70, 172, 176, 201, 207, 243, 245, 251, 272

Tamils, 184, 192

technological development, 104, 114, 151

technological revolution, 149, 151, 211, 214

terrorism, 193, 262, 266, 267

Thatcher, Margaret, 216

The Bell Curve, 261

Third World
  ADCs, 174
  debt, 127
  fragmentation, 130, 174, 273, 274, 277, 281
  ideology, 126, 273
  incorporation, 4, 5, 13, 15, 17, 18, 25, 27
  insecurity dilemmas, 8, 132, 184, 186, 188
  NICs, 4, 9, 17, 174
  semiperipheral states, 3, 4, 9, 10, 14, 29
  solidarity, 3, 4, 18, 27, 29, 30, 37, 55, 56, 57, 64, 68, 72, 73, 114, 121, 122, 123, 124, 125, 130, 170, 176, 184, 192, 233, 241, 272, 273, 277, 283, 289, 292

Thomas, Clarence, 259

Thompson, T. J., 45

Thucydides, 6

Thurmond, Strom, 253

tight bipolar nuclear system, 122

trade unions, 95, 127, 142, 148, 149

TransAfrica, 273

transnational politics, 6, 10, 11

transnational relations, 6

Trilateral Commission, 20

Truman, David, 142-143, 192

Truman Doctrine, 68, 119

Truman, Harry, 68, 119, 142-144, 192

Turkey, 68-69, 72, 79, 162, 169-173, 175, 177-179, 18-185, 197, 238, 260

Tuskegee Institute, 50

Twentieth Party Congress, 74

U.S. Supreme Court, 258, 263

ujaama movement, 211

unequal exchange, 160

UNIA, 48–50

unipolar, 5, 105, 268, 272, 273, 275

unipolar moment, 5, 105

unitary state, 8, 185, 228

United Nations
  General Assembly, 69, 73, 82, 98, 123,

127–129, 137, 175, 232, 233, 269
Security Council, 5, 67, 69, 73, 82, 98,
    183, 195, 226, 227, 230–34, 263,
    269, 271, 274 277
United Nations Educational and Cultural
    Organization (UNESCO), 78, 132,
    141, 233, 235
United Nations Industrial Development
    Organization (UNIDO), 129, 175
United Province, 14
United States Conference on Trade and
    Development (UNCTAD), 123,
    129, 131, 137, 141, 146, 173, 233
urban proletariat, 39
U.S., 16, 20, 21, 57, 65–68, 70, 71, 77, 79,
    83, 86, 87, 91–94, 96, 99–103, 105,
    111, 115–21, 124, 126, 128, 130–34,
    138, 151, 171, 174, 184, 185, 189,
    190, 194–97, 205, 207, 208, 219,
    222, 225–28, 231–34, 236, 241,
    242, 244, 245, 249–52, 254,
    256–58, 262–69, 271, 275, 285, 286,
    288
    containment policy, 66, 78–71

Vance, Cyrus, 130
Vietnam, 9, 30, 69, 70, 76, 77, 88, 93, 96,
    97, 99, 116, 118, 122, 126, 132, 186,
    187, 190, 191, 208, 209, 214, 219,
    222, 236, 238, 265, 266, 275
    Provisional Revolutionary Govern-
    ment, 131

Wallerstein, Immanuel, 13, 14, 246
Warsaw Pact, 5, 9, 29, 30, 70, 89, 90, 93,
    183, 184, 197, 216, 217, 241, 265,
    267
Warsaw Pact nations, 5, 30, 59, 191, 192,
    230, 232, 255, 274
Washington, Booker T., 28, 47
Washington, Harold, 266
Watts, J. C., 259
wave of colonization, 46
welfare state, 5, 253, 288
Western Europe, 5, 9, 19, 66, 85, 88, 89,
    91, 92, 95, 113–16, 119, 205, 234,
    246
Western Hemisphere, 44, 45, 255
Wilder, Douglas, 253

Williams, Sylvester, 45
Williams, Walter, 259
Wilson, Pete, 257, 259
Women of Russia, 216
World Bank, 82, 115, 129, 131, 137, 141,
    143–145, 147–49, 153–55, 175, 176,
    189, 232, 234, 235, 263, 273, 275,
    277, 285, 290, 291
world leadership, 11,–13
long cycle, 11
world orders, 18
world system, 3–22, 24, 26, 27, 29, 30,
    37, 38, 43, 46, 51, 56, 63, 64, 66–68,
    73, 75, 79, 81, 82, 85, 93, 101, 104,
    105, 111–14, 121, 122, 124, 125,
    130–32, 134, 138–47, 151, 155, 156,
    171, 176, 177, 181, 185, 187, 188,
    207, 208, 214, 218, 219, 222, 230,
    235, 277, 281, 282, 286–88, 292
world system theory, 141

Yabloko, 216, 217
Yeltsin, Boris, 5, 184, 215–218
Yom Kippur War, 101, 102, 104, 127
Young, Andrew, 130, 291

Zedong, Mao, 54
Zhirinovsky, Vladimir, 216
Zimbabwe, 39, 53, 77, 78, 104, 134, 156,
    157, 161–70, 187, 188, 212, 228, 237
Zinni, Tony, 266
zone of peace, 71
Zwass, Adam, 222

ABOUT THE AUTHOR

DARRYL C. THOMAS is an Associate Professor of Africana Studies and Political Science at Binghamton University. He has also taught at the University of Illinois at Springfield (formerly known as Sangamon State University, in Springfield, Illinois).

Dr. Thomas holds a B. A. from Florida A. and M. University in Afro-American Studies and American History, as well as an M.A. and a Ph.D. in Political Science from the University of Michigan. His research and publications have focused on International Relations of the Third World, Comparative Political Economy, Comparative Politics, and Africana Studies.